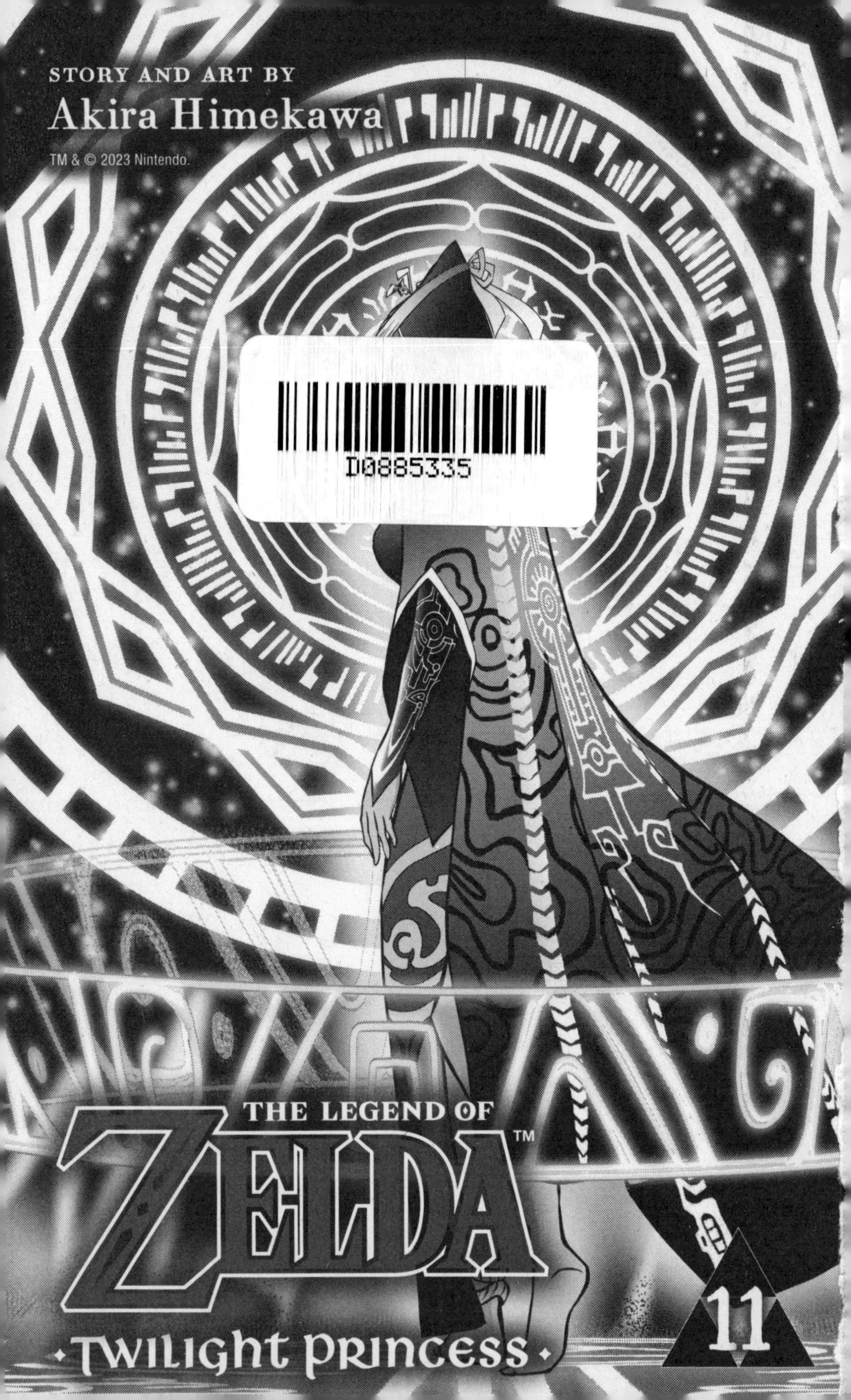
STORY AND ART BY
Akira Himekawa
TM & © 2023 Nintendo.
D0885335
THE LEGEND OF
ZELDA™
Twilight Princess
11

THE LEGEND OF ZELDA
·TWILIGHT PRINCESS·

11

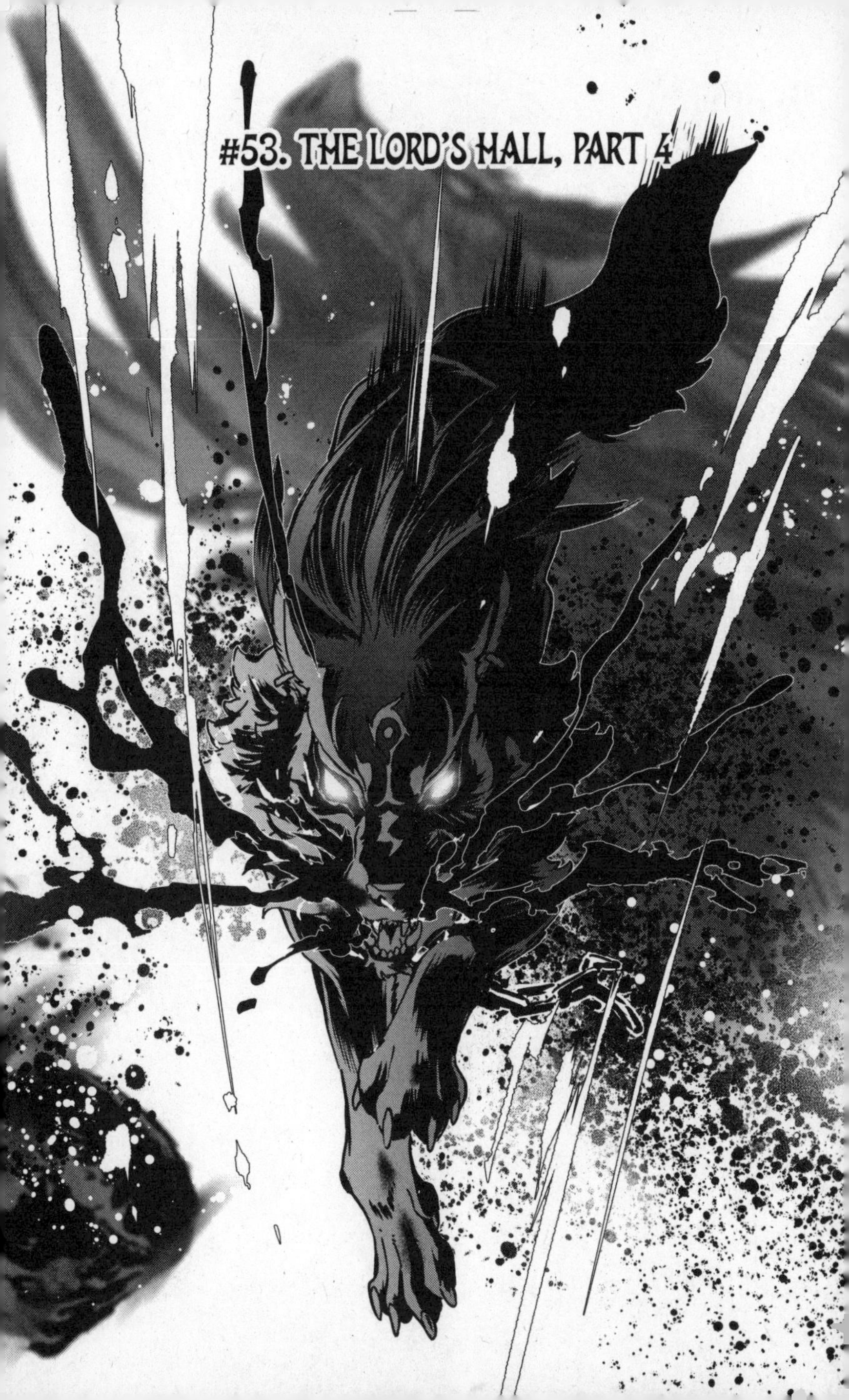
#53. THE LORD'S HALL, PART 4

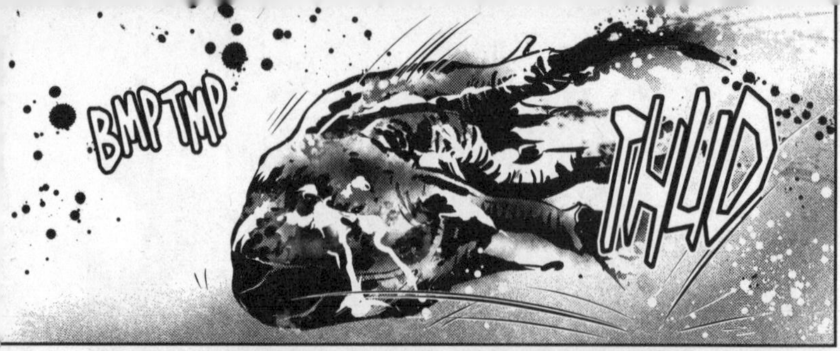
THUD
BMPTMP
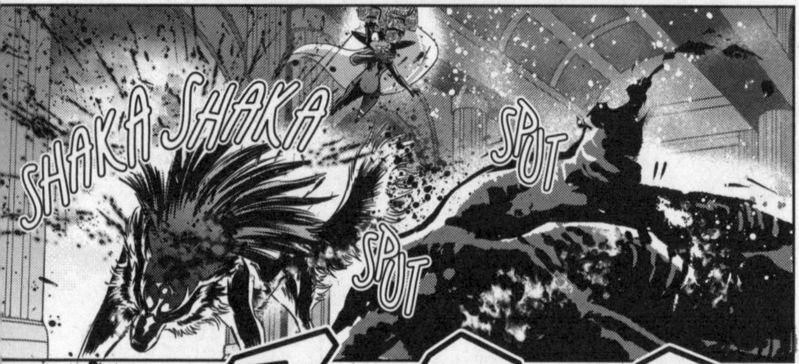
SPUT
SHAKA SHAKA
SPUT
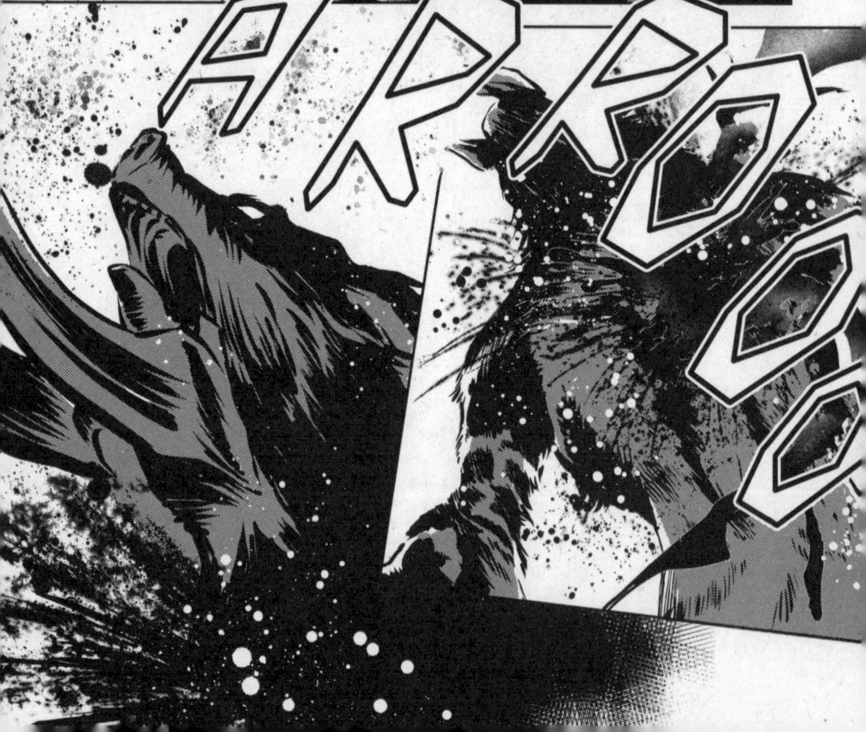
ARROOO

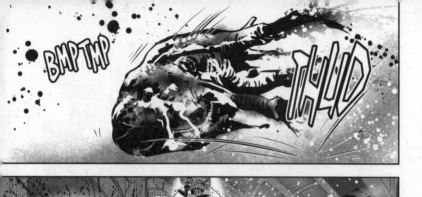

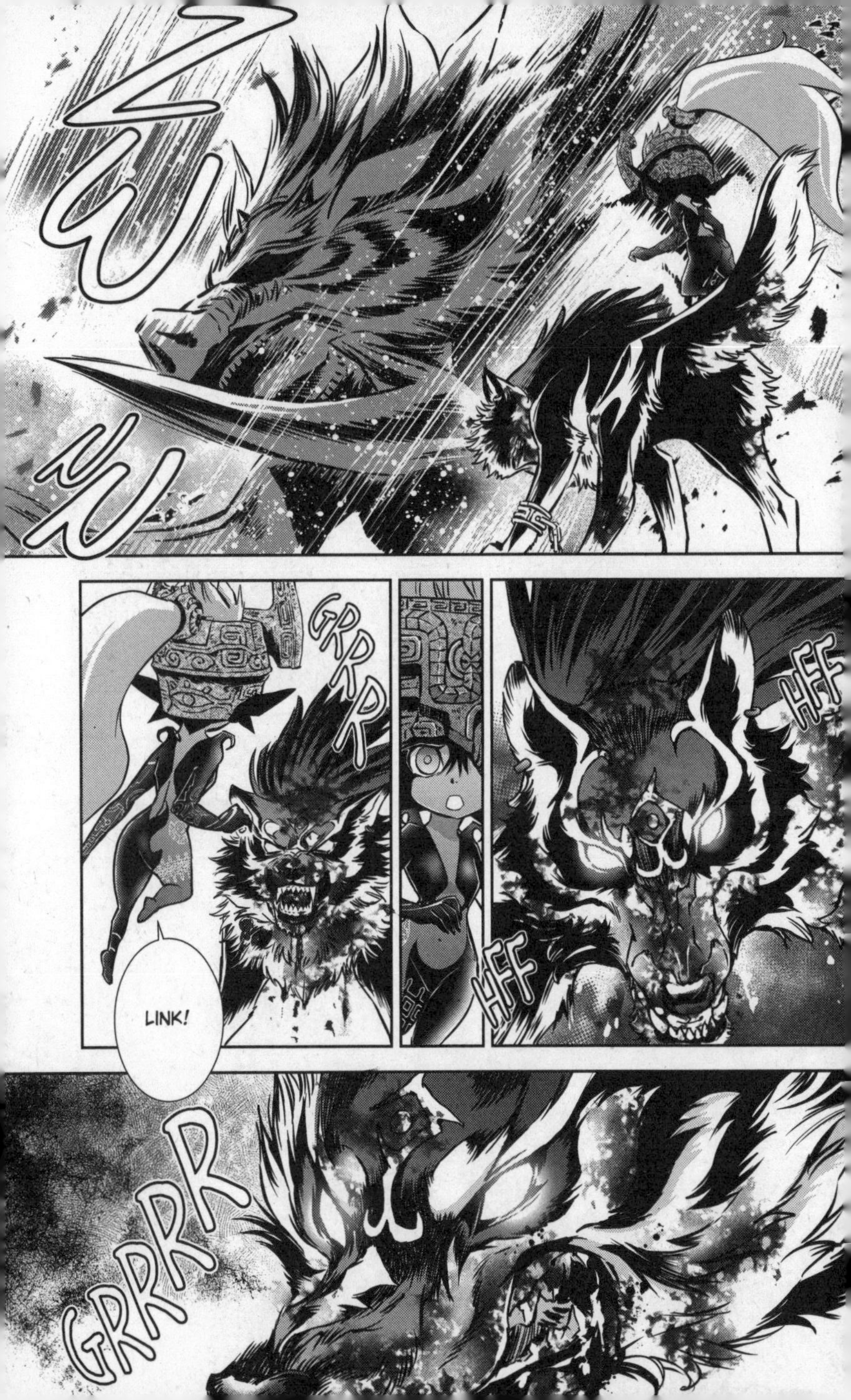
HFF
HFF
GRRR
LINK!
GRRR

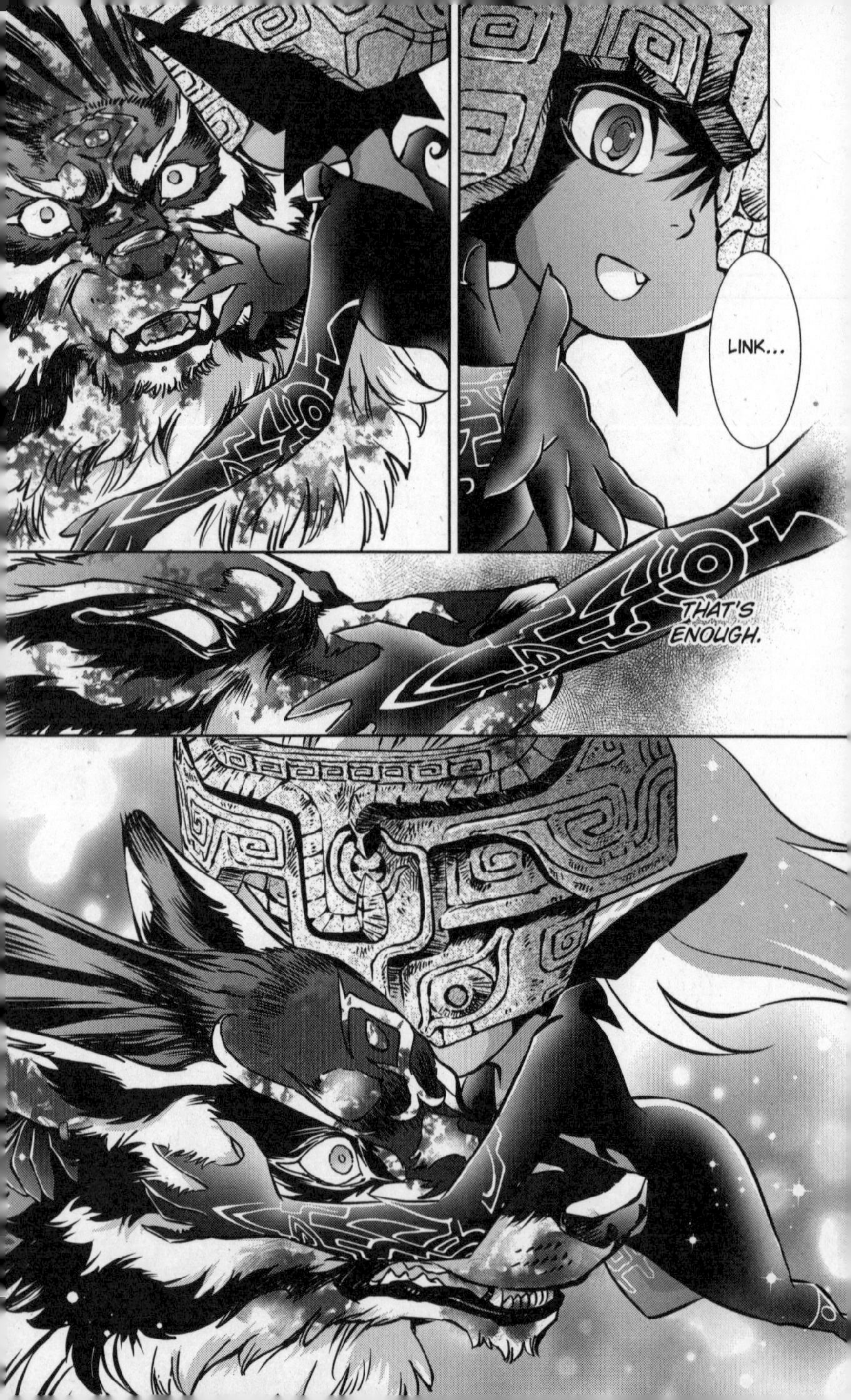
LINK...
THAT'S ENOUGH.

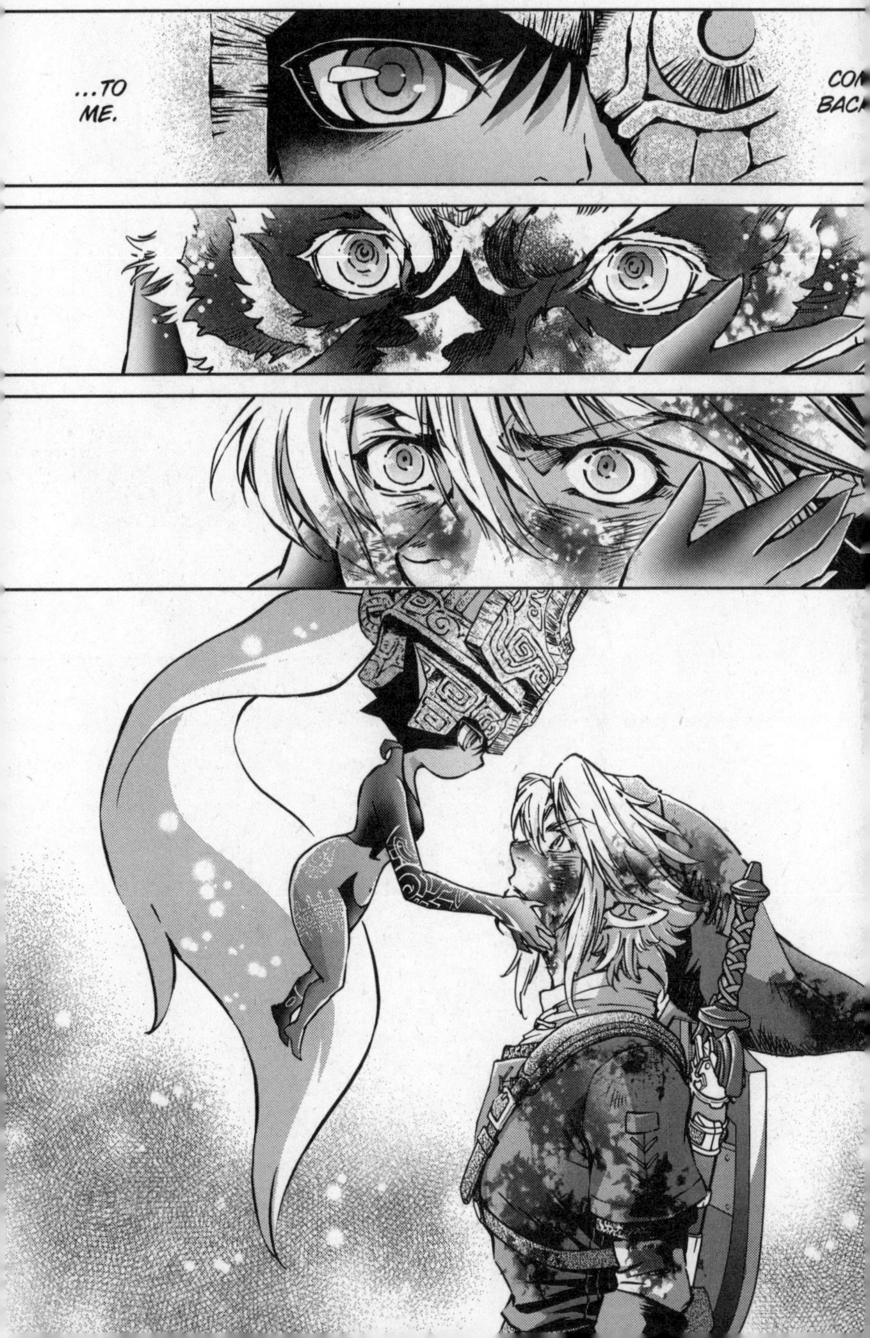
CO
BAC
...TO ME.

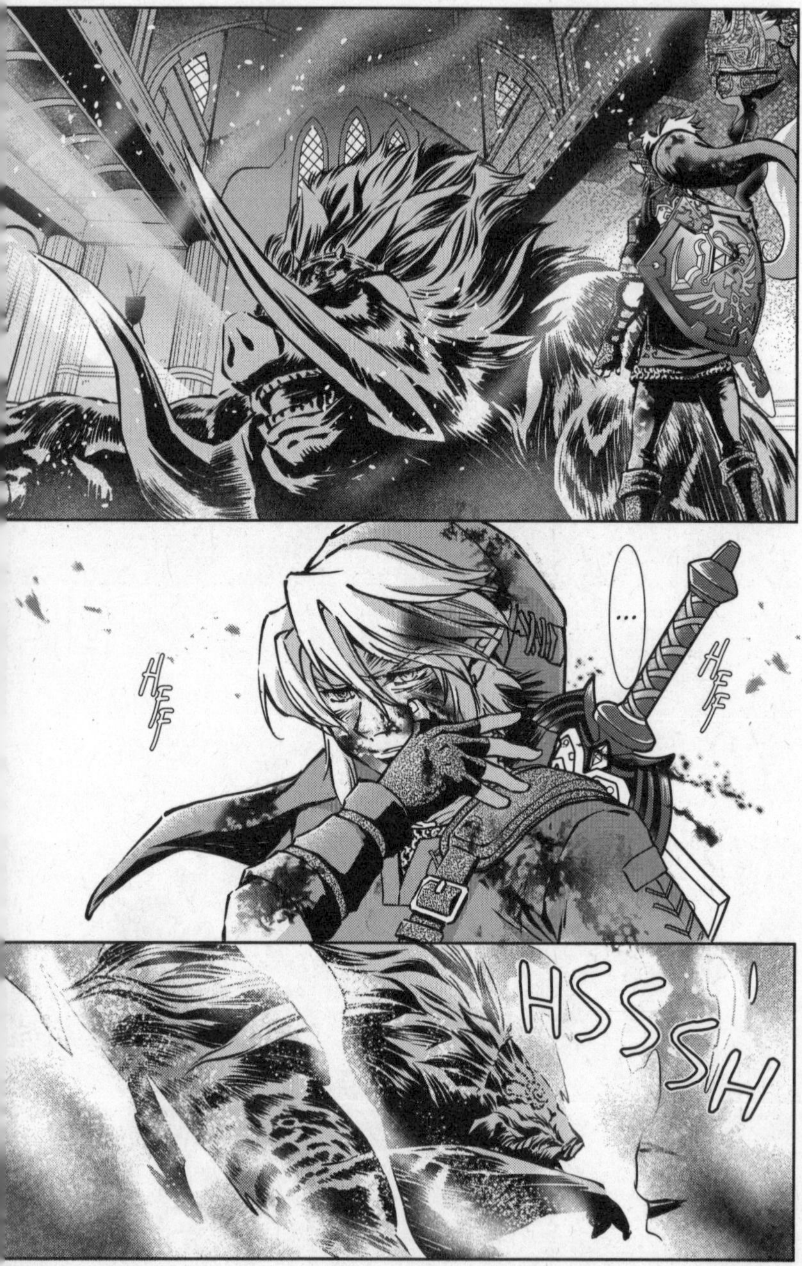
...
HFF
HFF
HSSSH

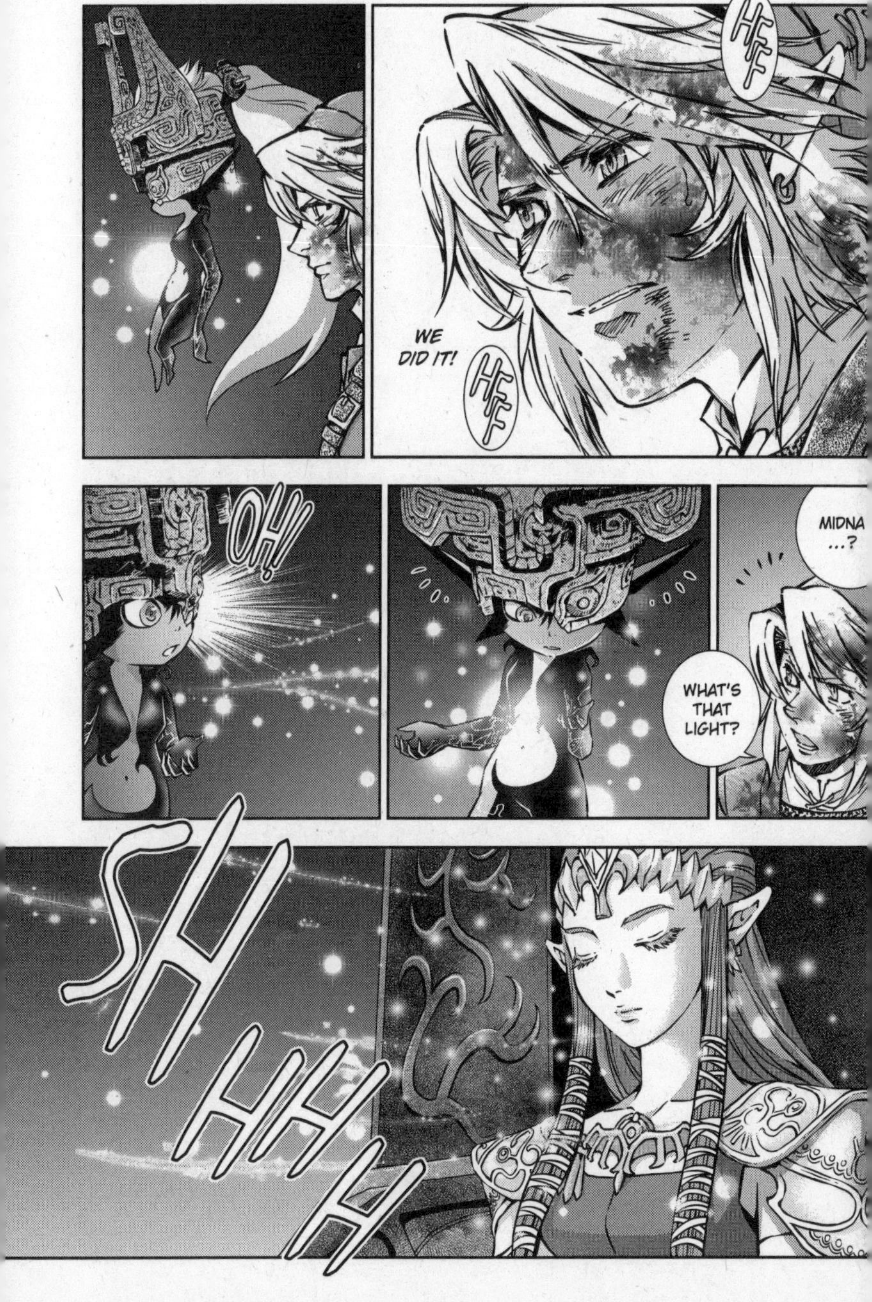
HFF
WE DID IT!
HFF
MIDNA ...?
WHAT'S THAT LIGHT?
OH!
SHHHH

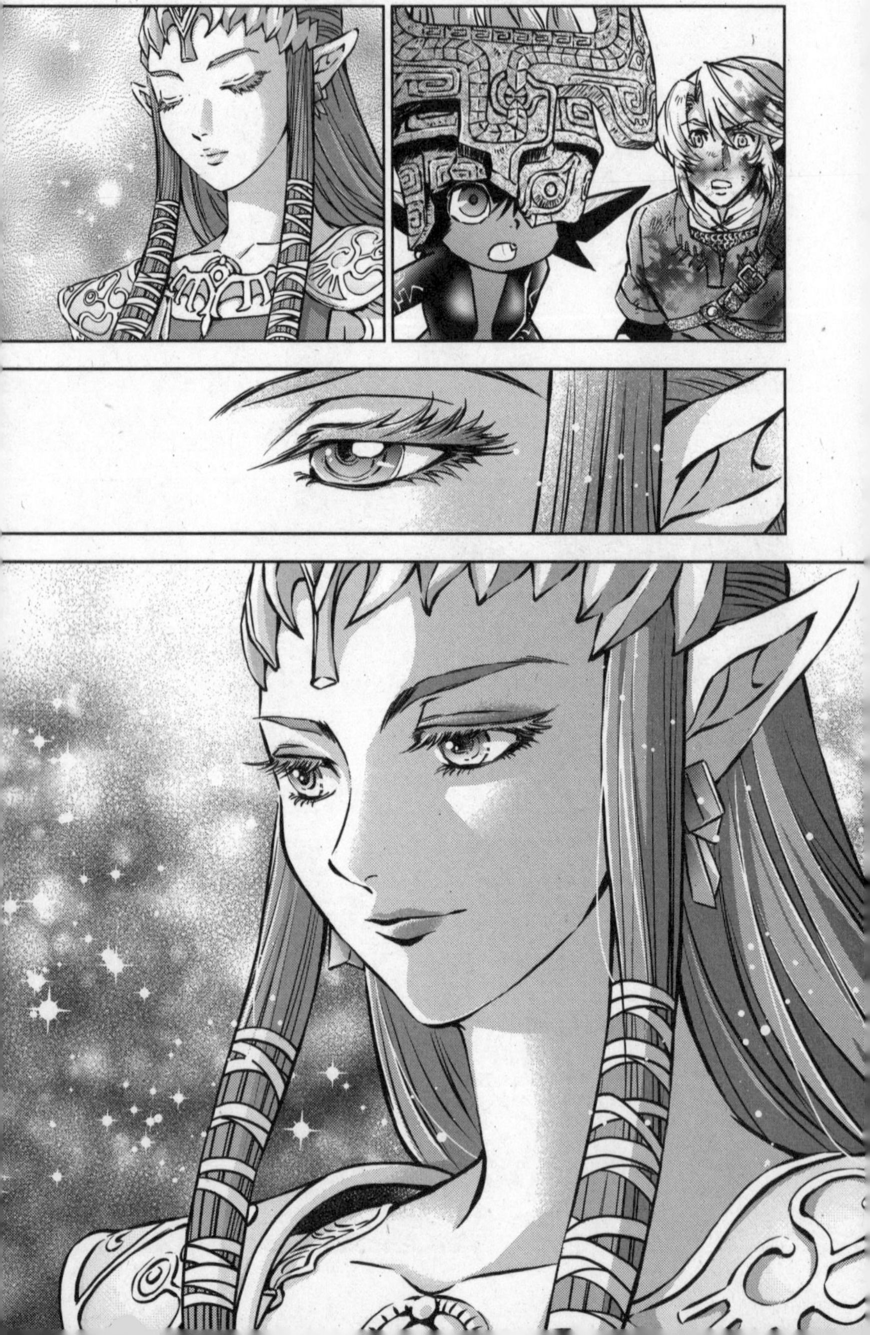

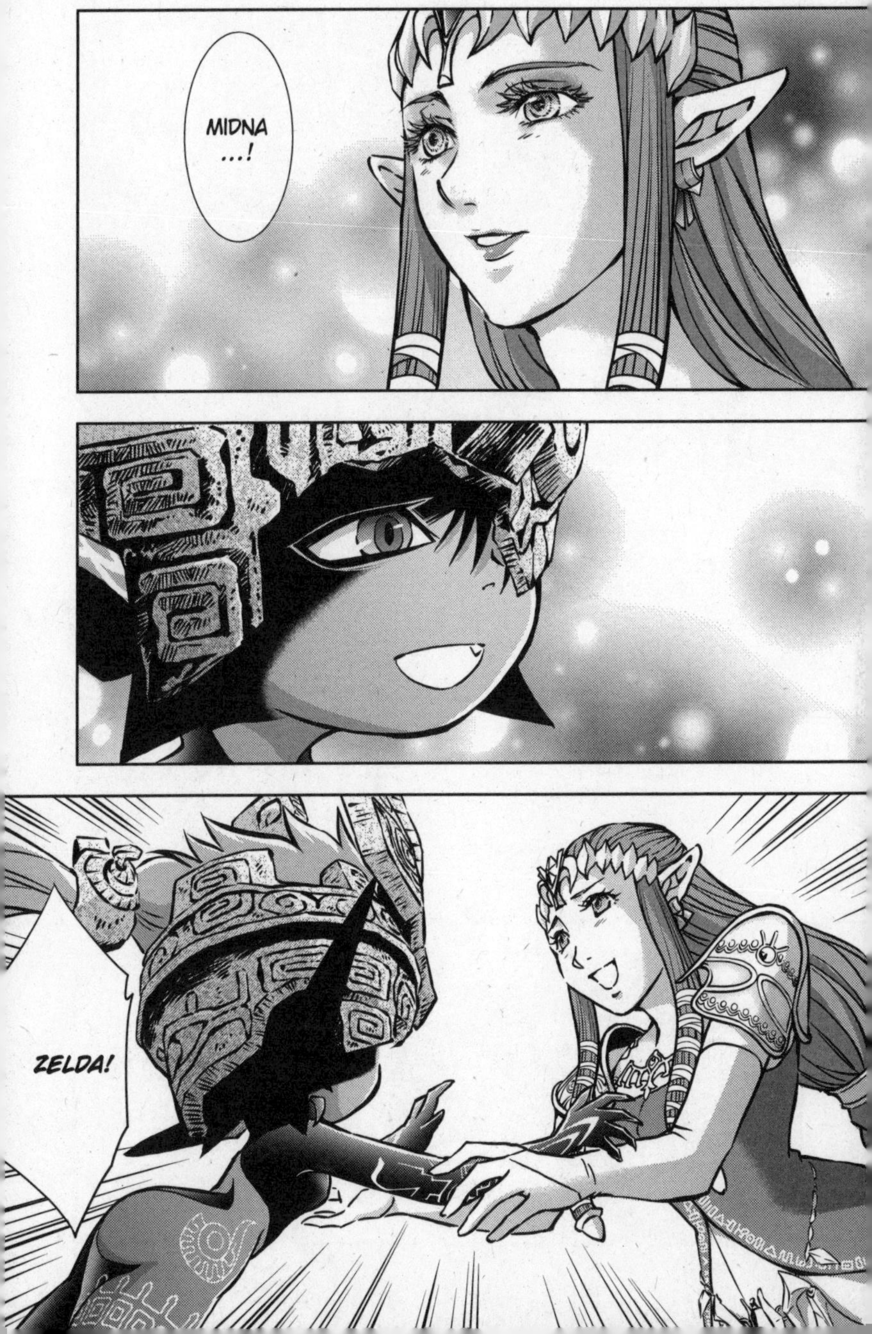
MIDNA ...!
ZELDA!

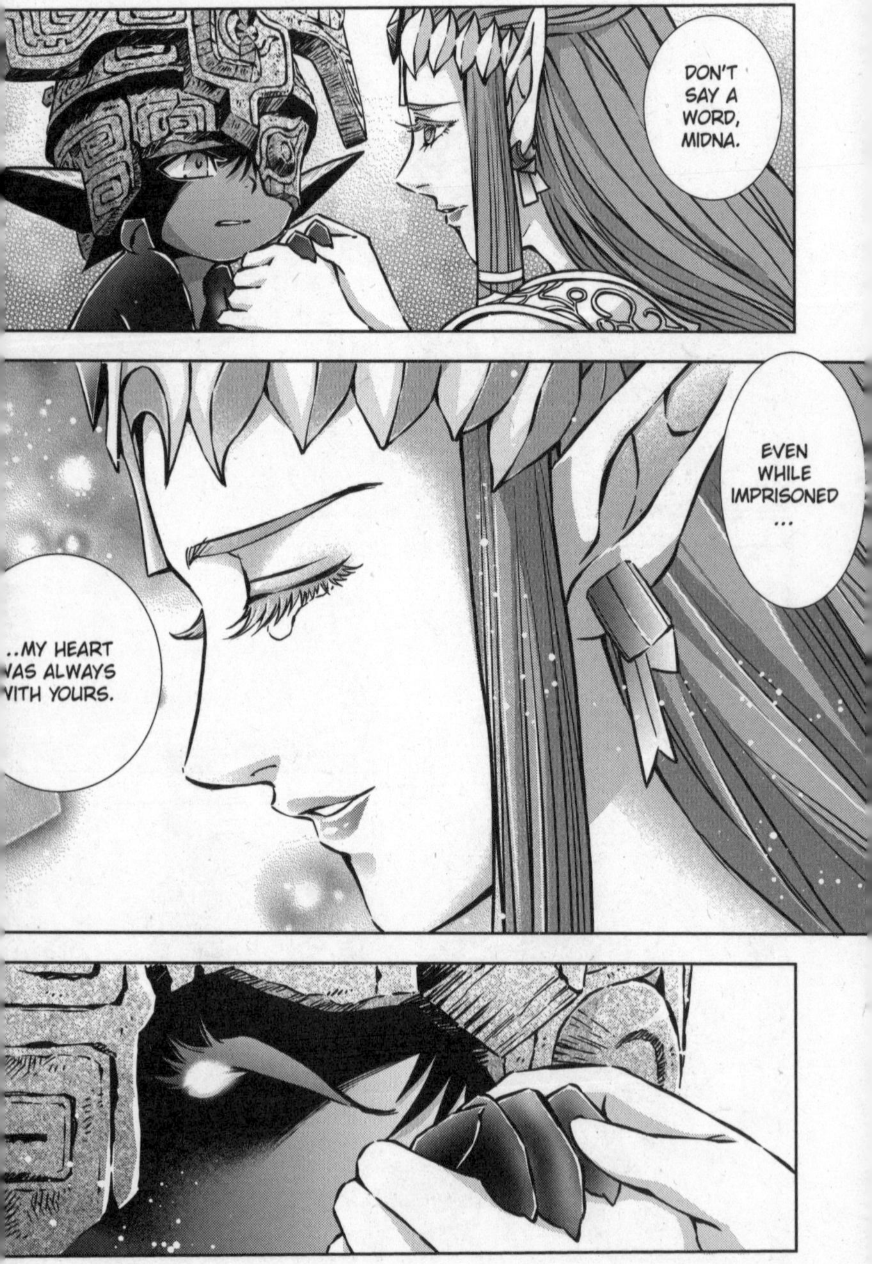
DON'T SAY A WORD, MIDNA.
EVEN WHILE IMPRISONED ...
..MY HEART WAS ALWAYS WITH YOURS.

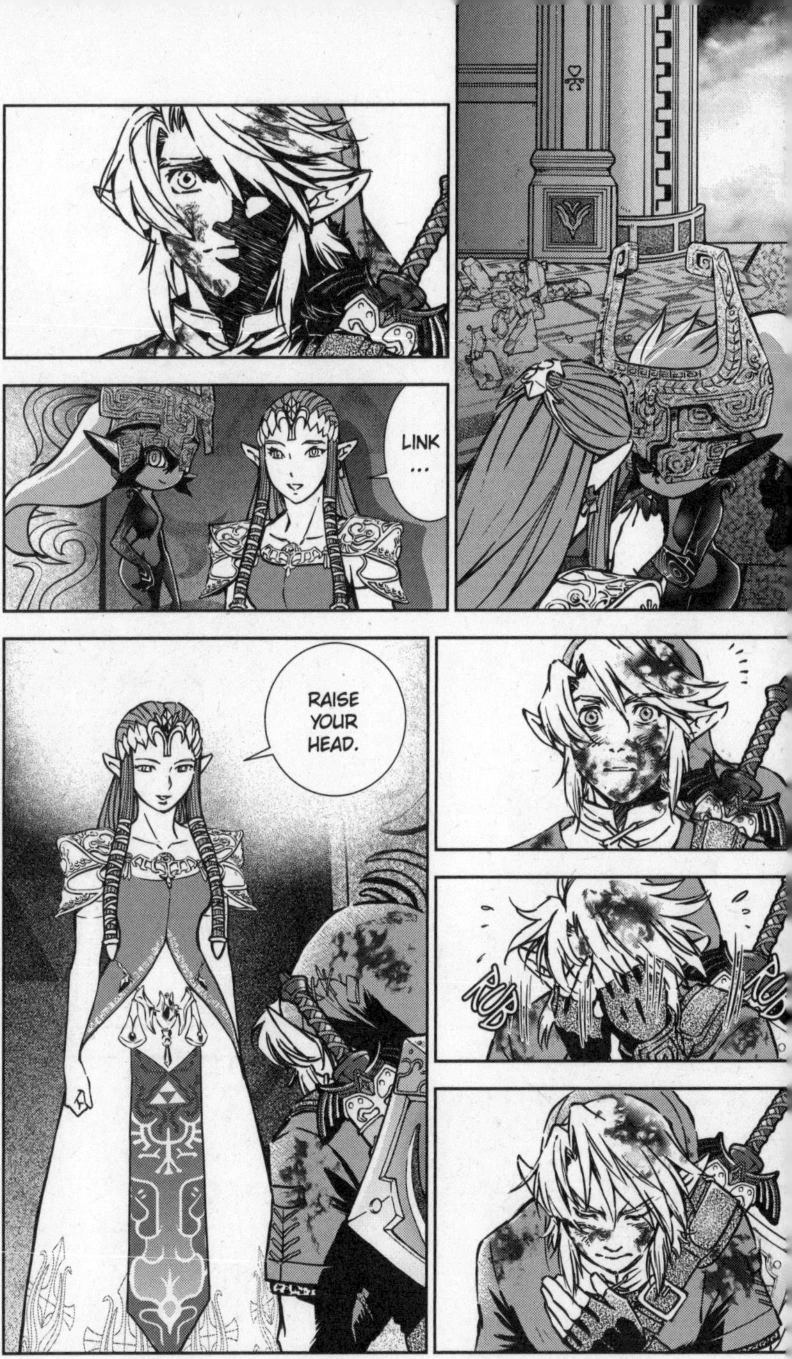
LINK ...
RAISE YOUR HEAD.
RUB
RUB

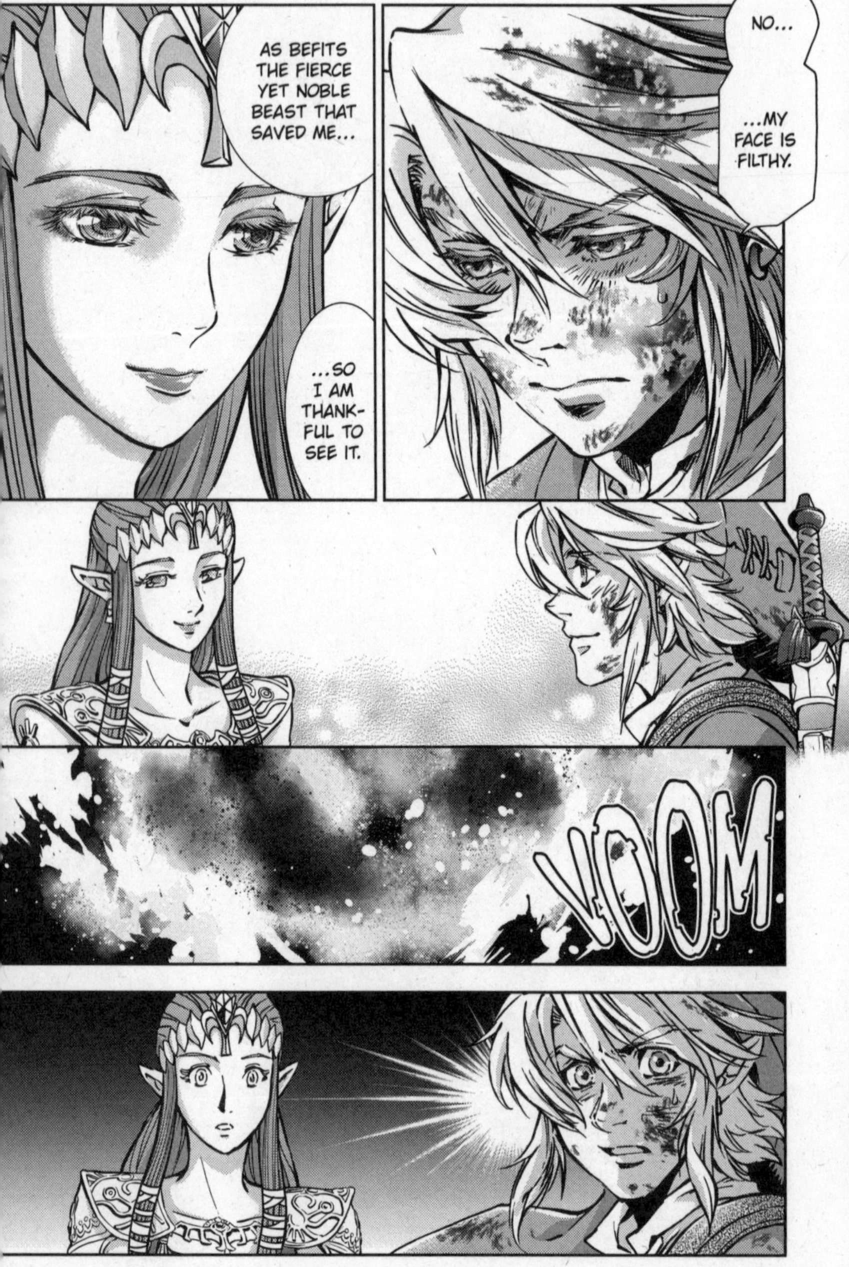
NO...
...MY FACE IS FILTHY.
AS BEFITS THE FIERCE YET NOBLE BEAST THAT SAVED ME...
...SO I AM THANKFUL TO SEE IT.
VOOM

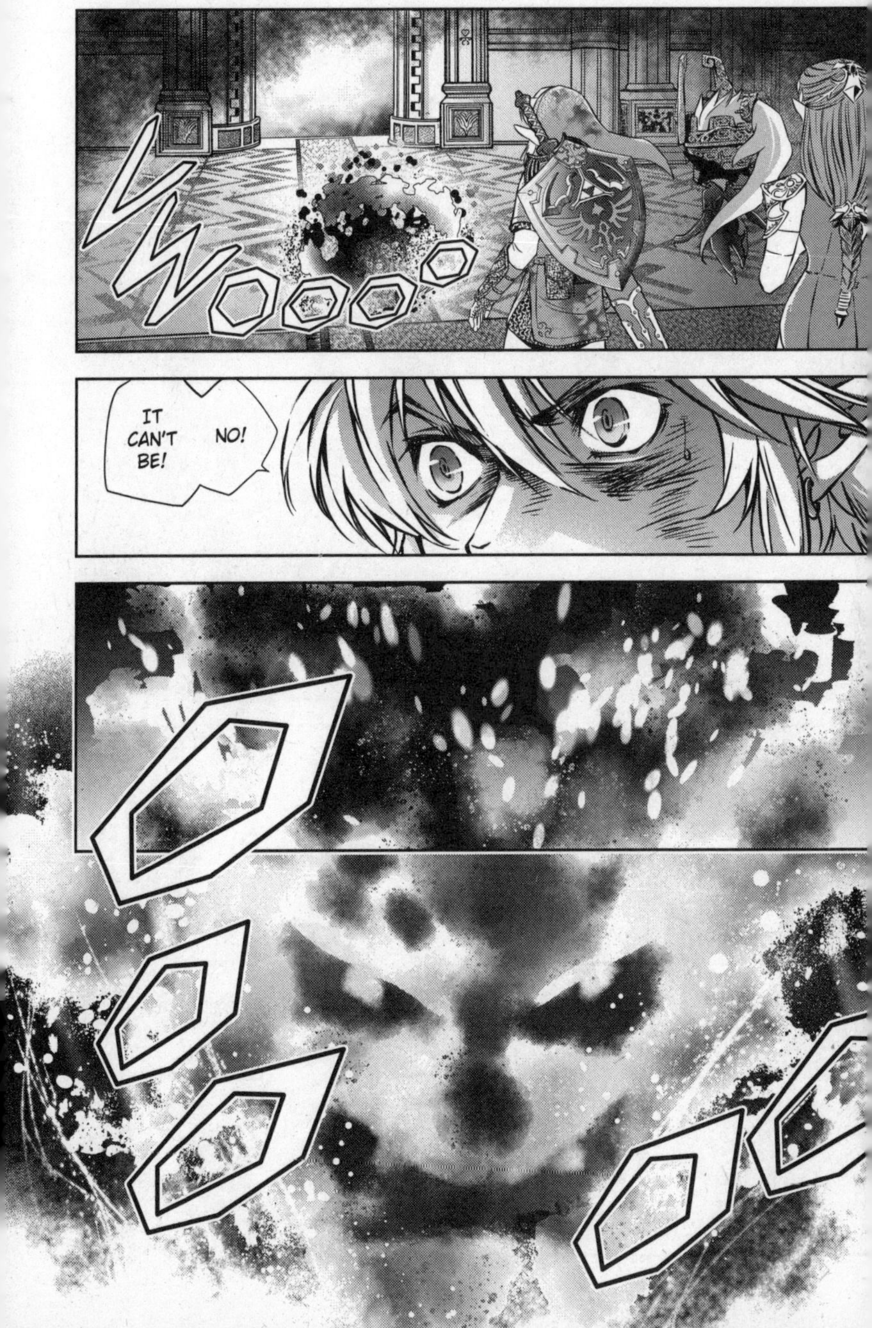
VWOOOO
NO!
IT CAN'T BE!

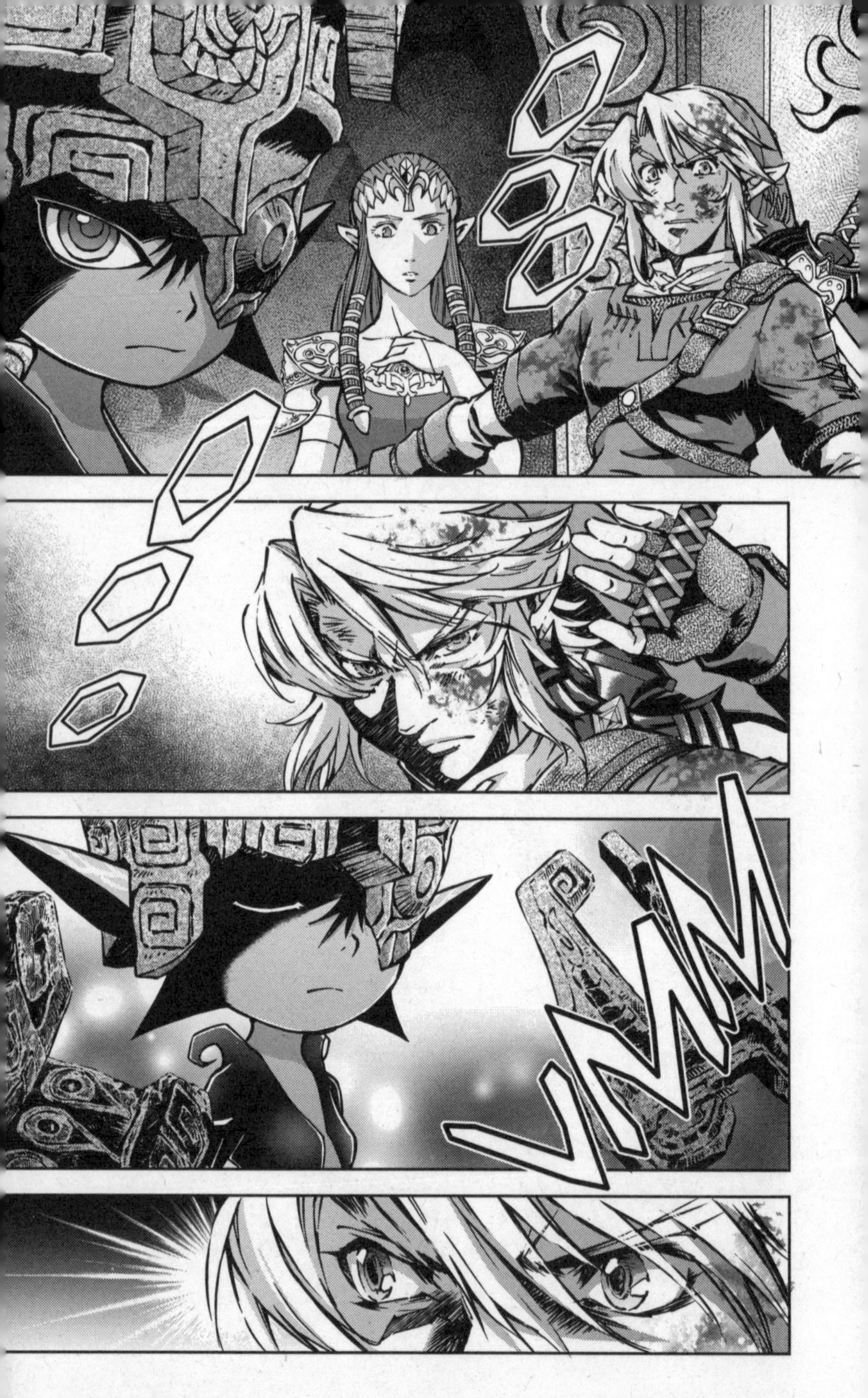

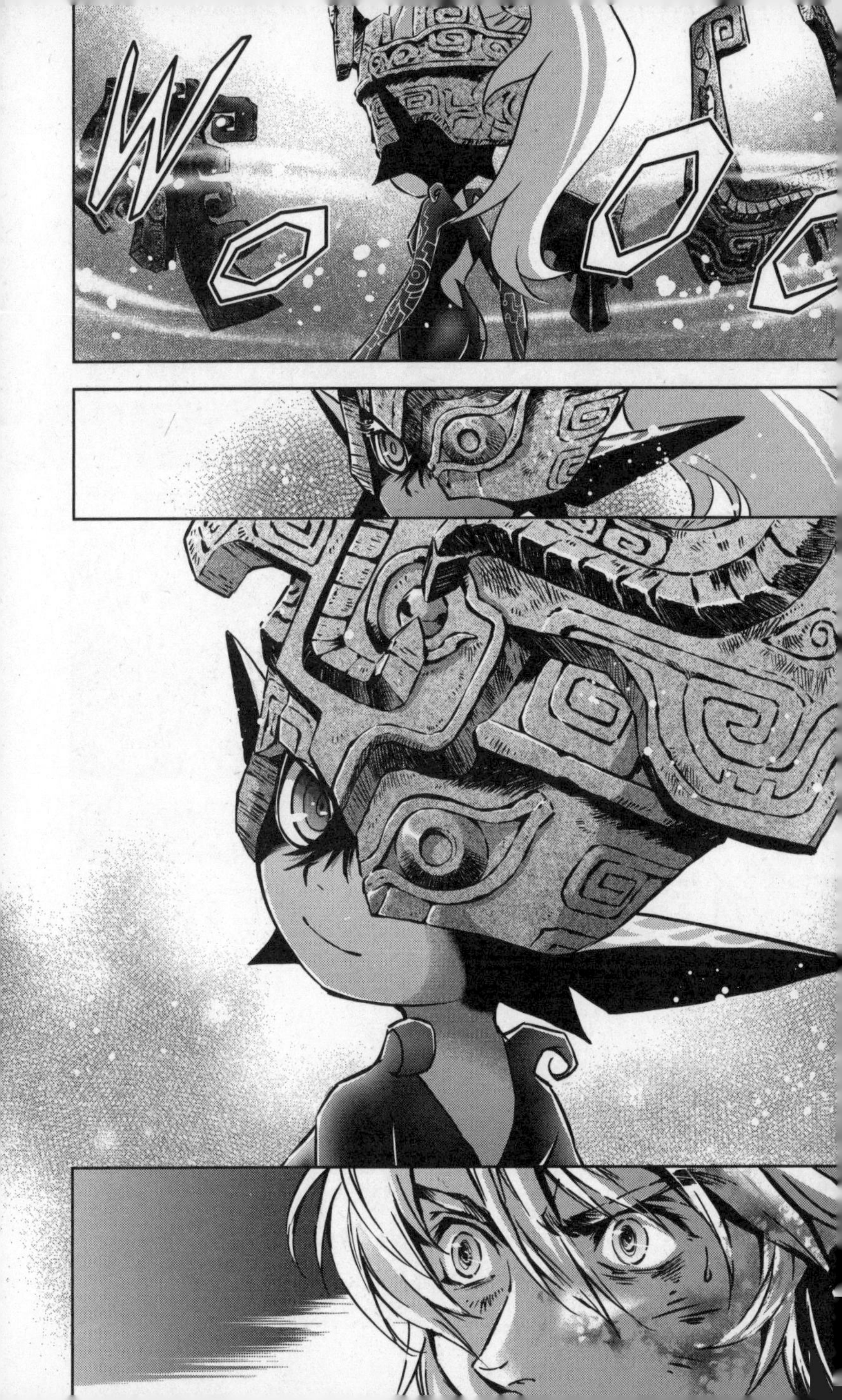
Wooo

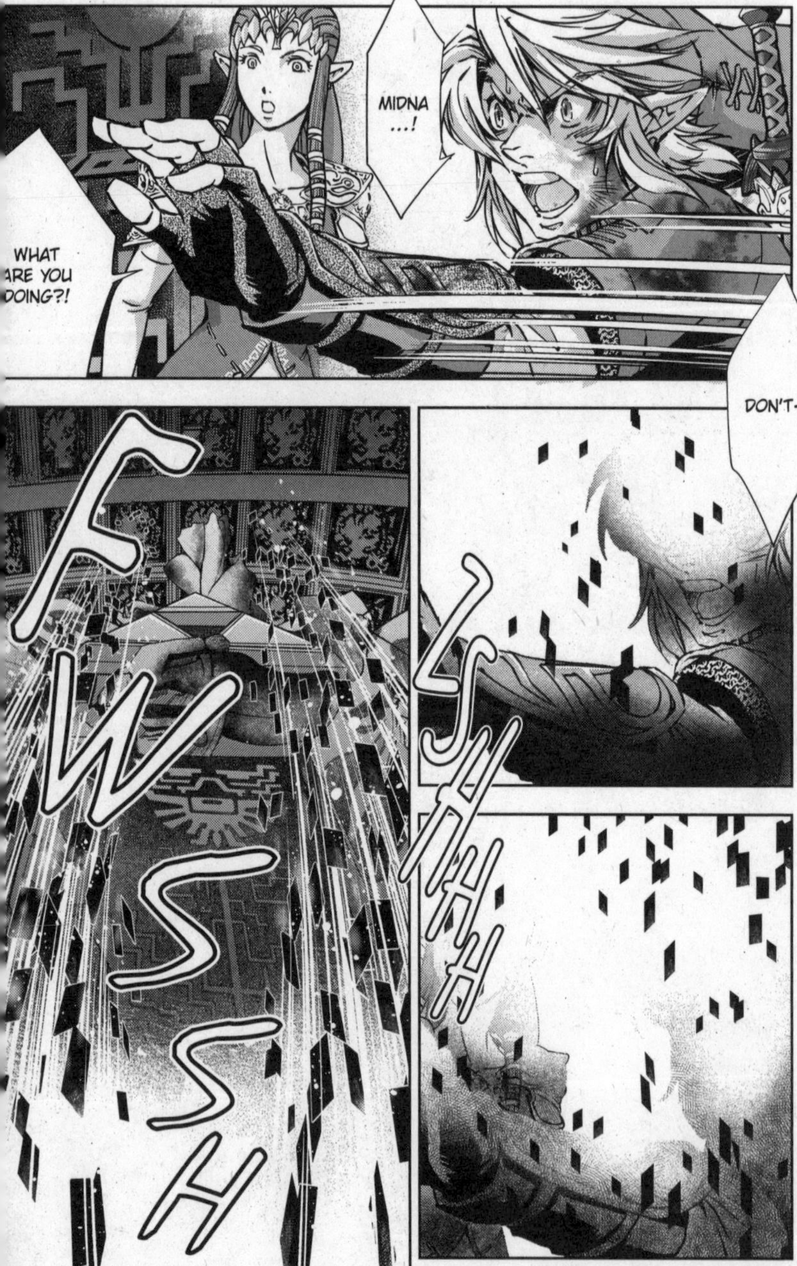
MIDNA ...!
WHAT ARE YOU DOING?!
DON'T-
SHHHH
FWSSH

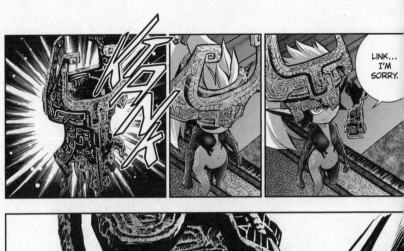

LINK...
I'M
SORRY.

NOW YOU
FACE YOUR
TRUE
OPPONENT-
ME!

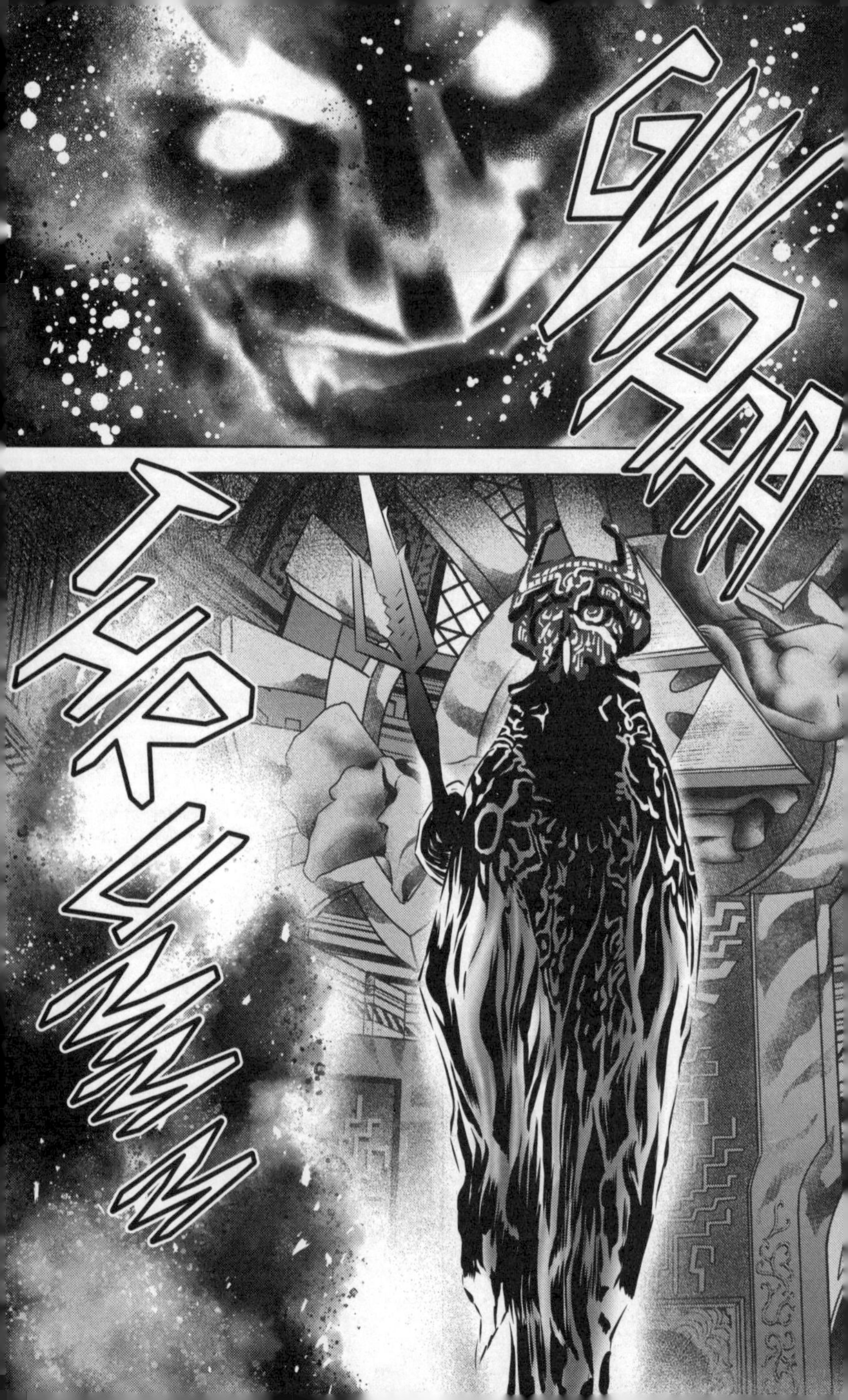
GWAAA
THRUMMMM

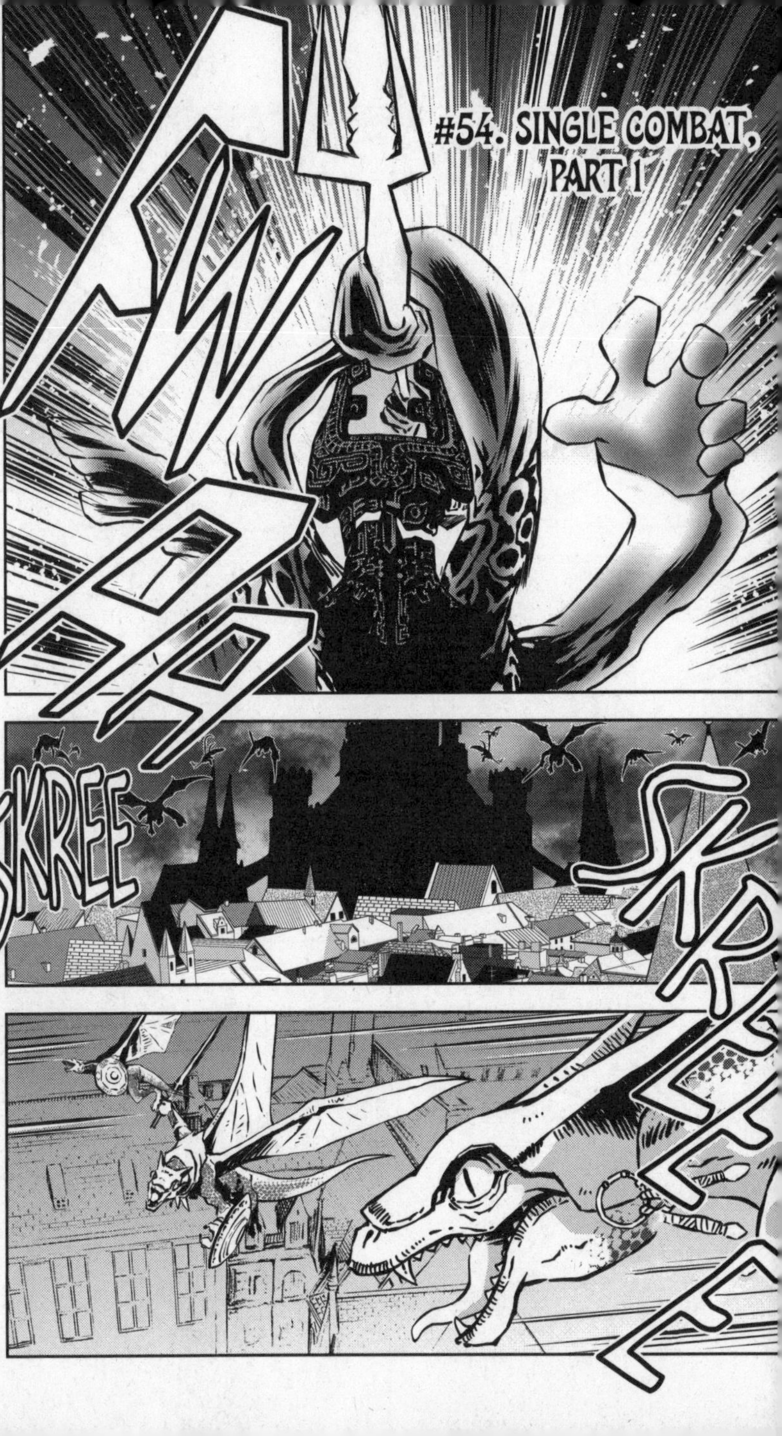
#54. SINGLE COMBAT, PART 1
SKREE

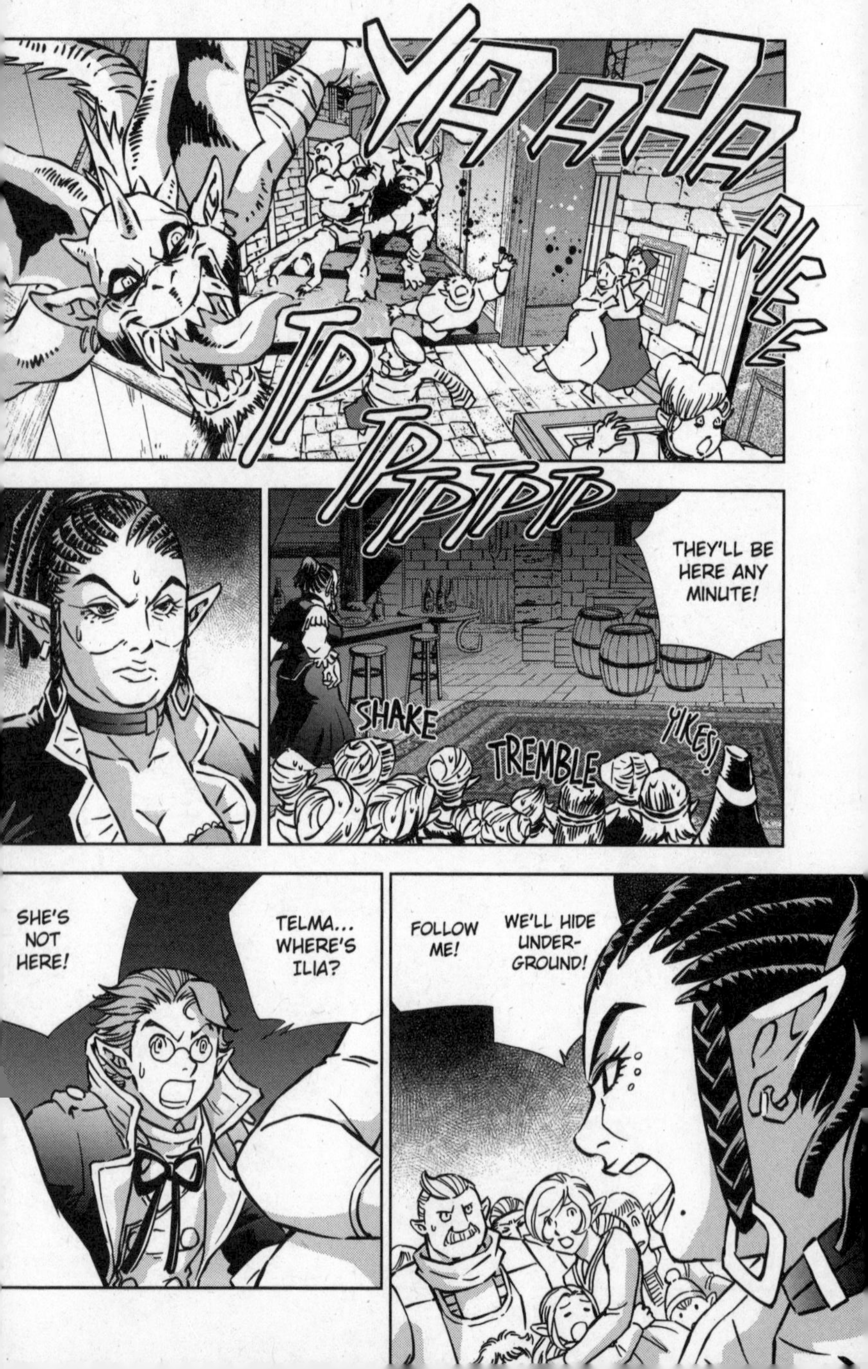
YAAAAAIEEE
TPTPTPTPTP
THEY'LL BE HERE ANY MINUTE!
SHAKE
TREMBLE
YIKES!
WE'LL HIDE UNDER-GROUND!
FOLLOW ME!
TELMA... WHERE'S ILIA?
SHE'S NOT HERE!

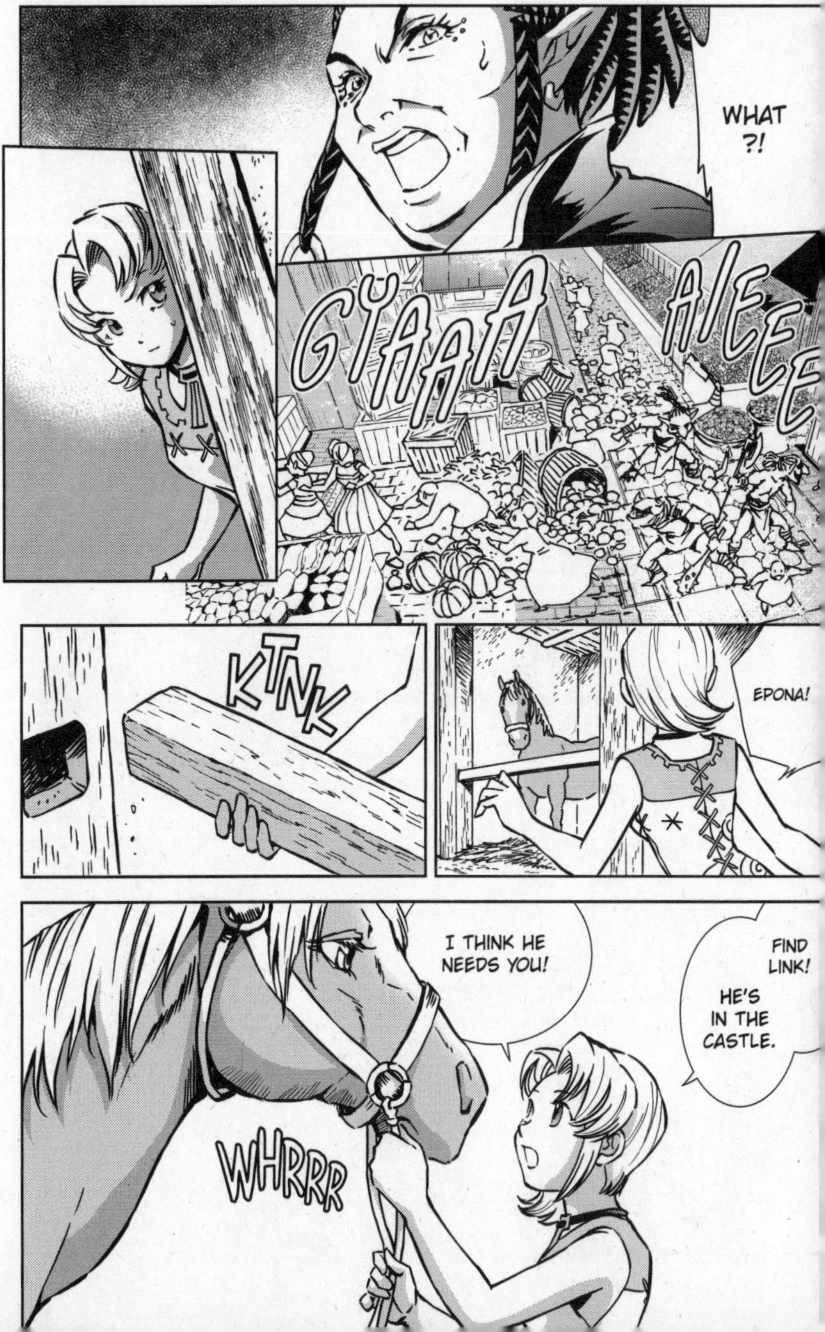
WHAT ?!
GYAAA
AIEEEE
KTNK
EPONA!
FIND LINK!
HE'S IN THE CASTLE.
I THINK HE NEEDS YOU!
WHRRR

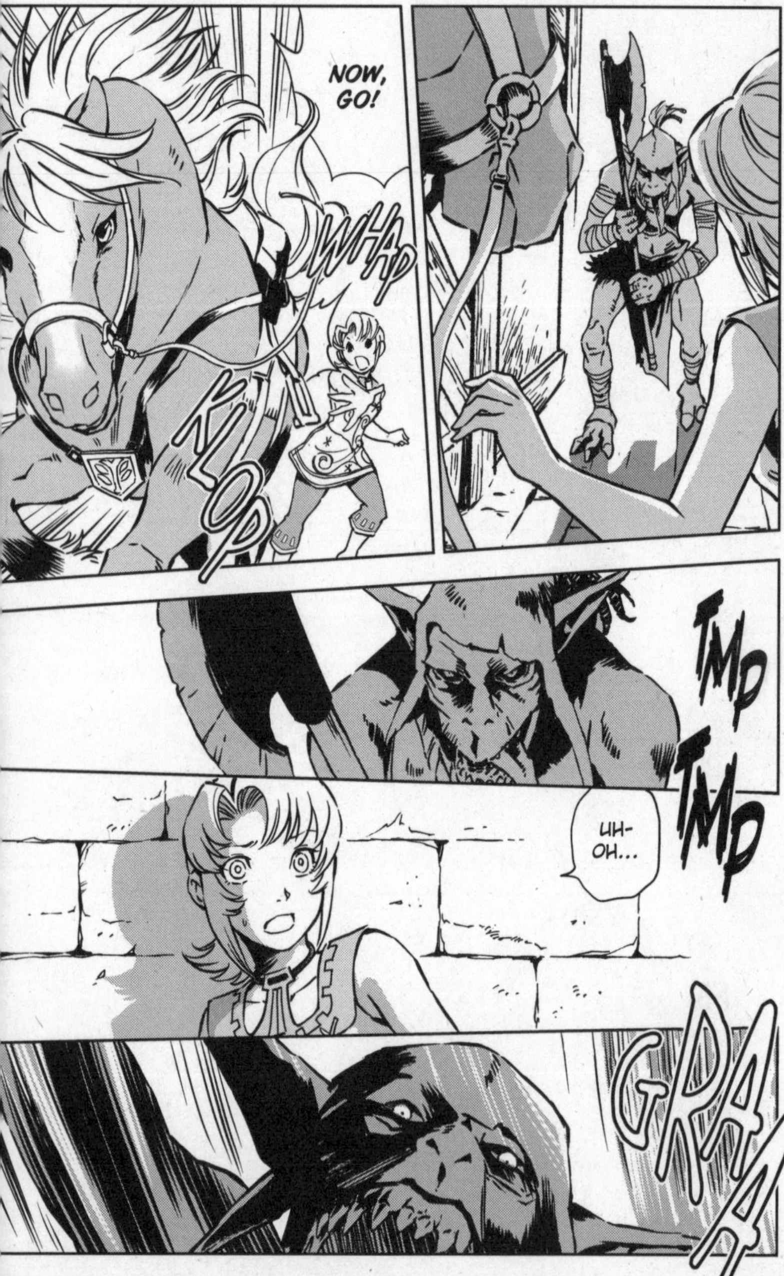
NOW, GO!
WHAP
KLOP
TMP
TMP
UH-OH...
GRAAA

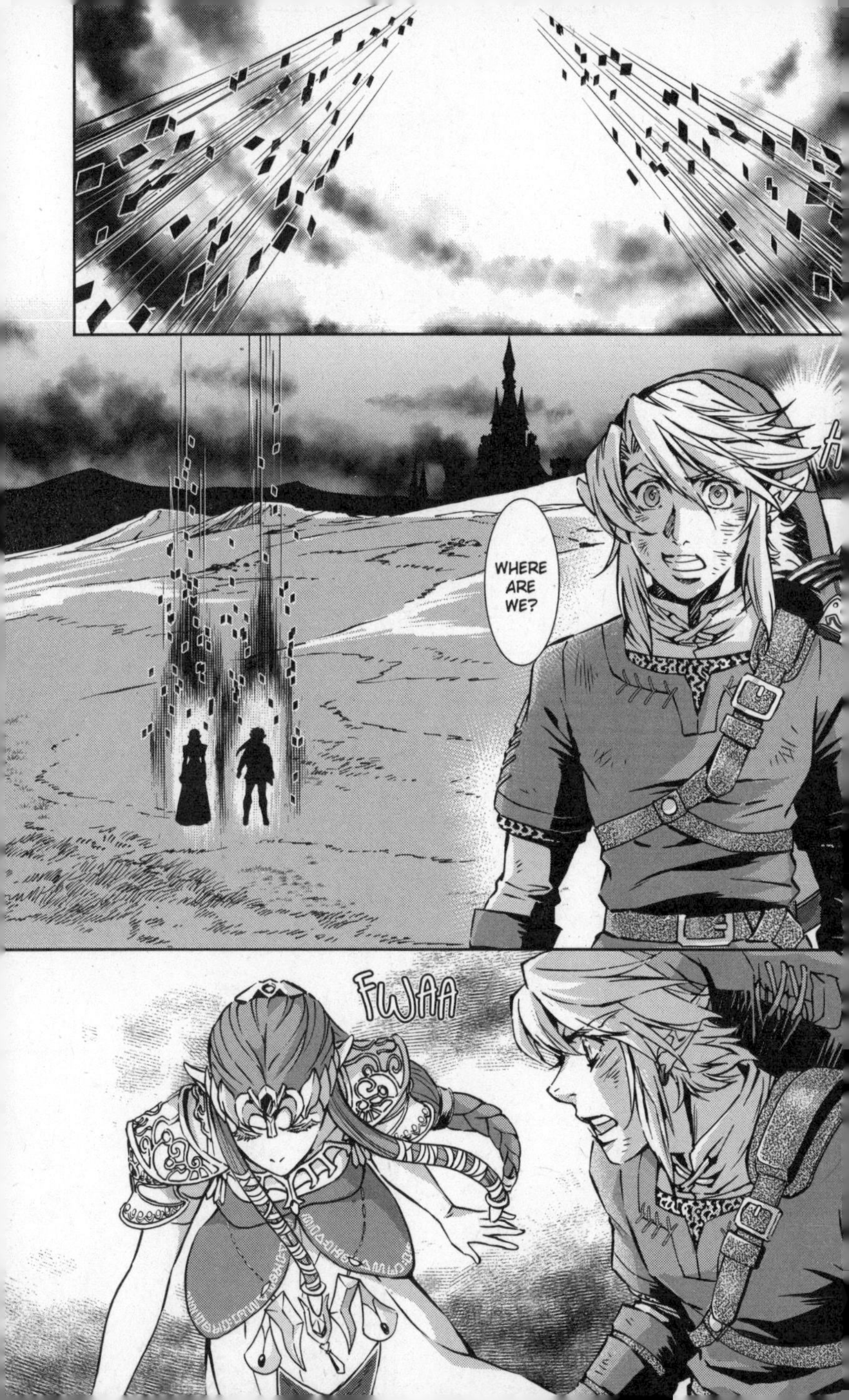
WHERE ARE WE?
FWAA

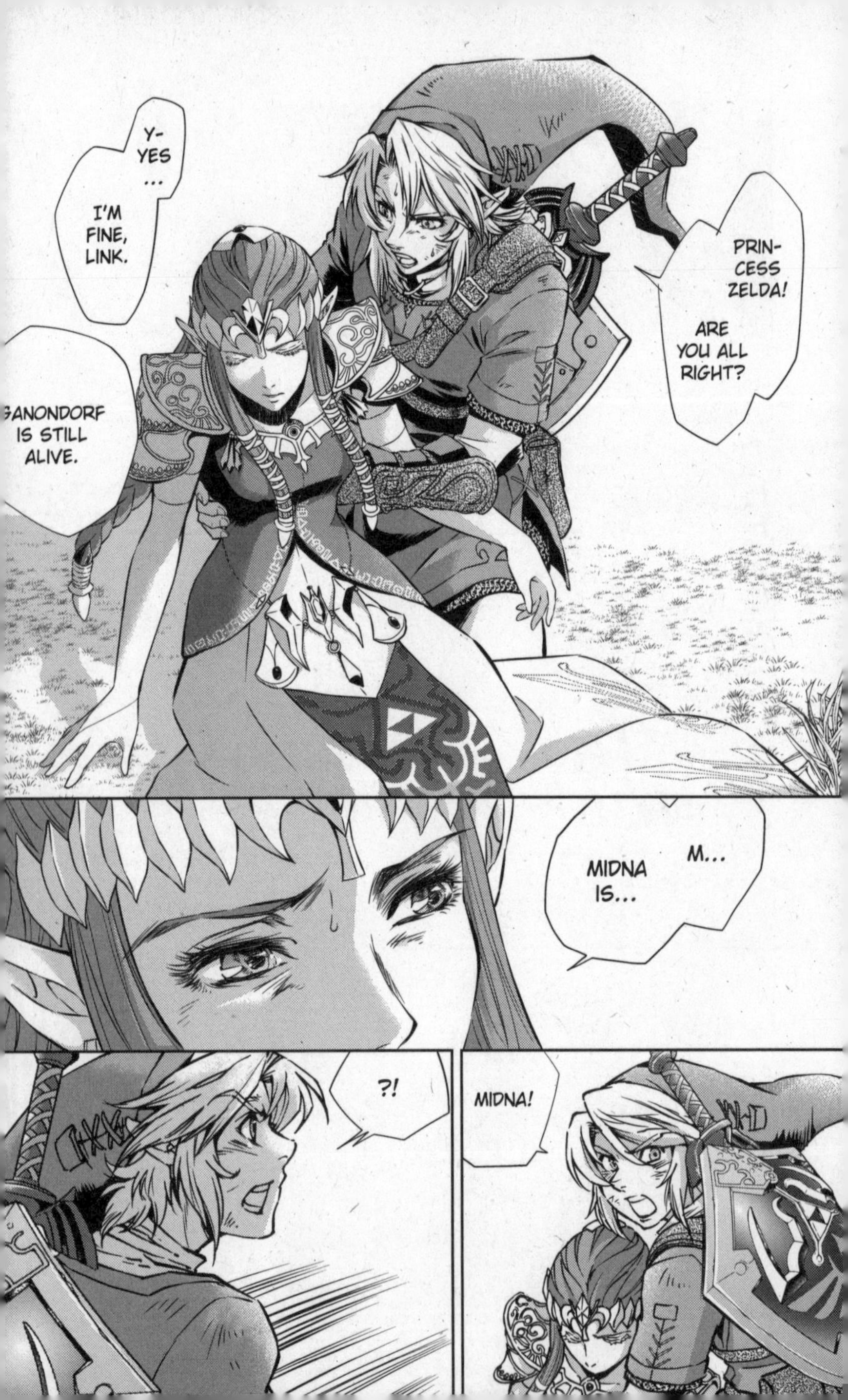
PRIN-CESS ZELDA!
ARE YOU ALL RIGHT?
Y-YES ... I'M FINE, LINK.
GANONDORF IS STILL ALIVE.
M...
MIDNA IS...
MIDNA!
?!

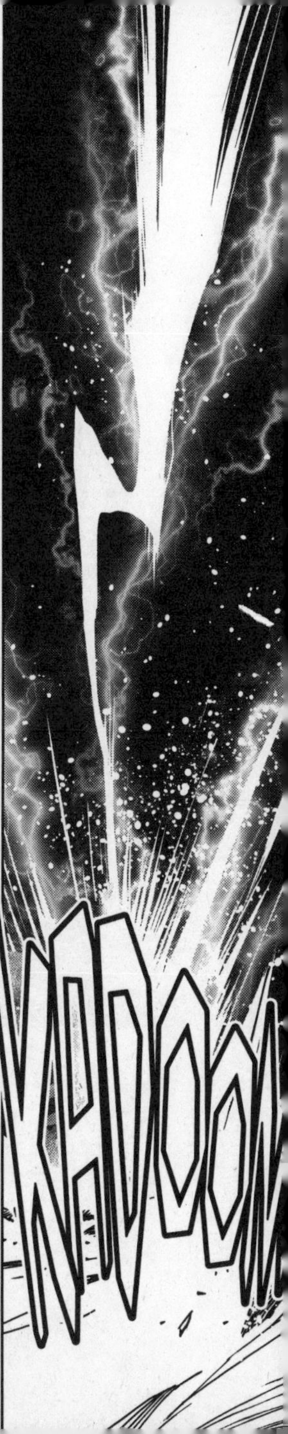
KADOOM
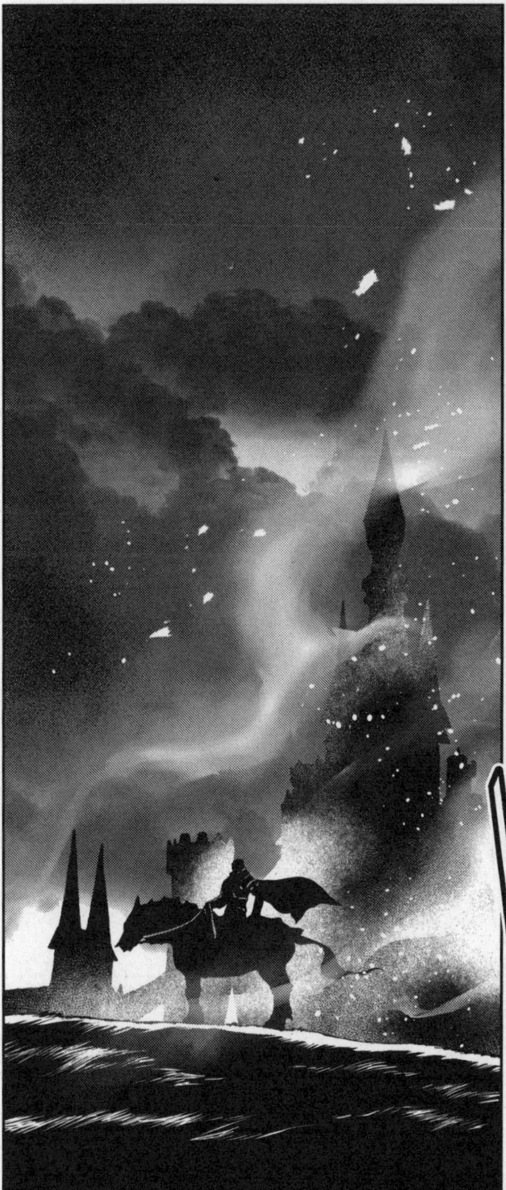

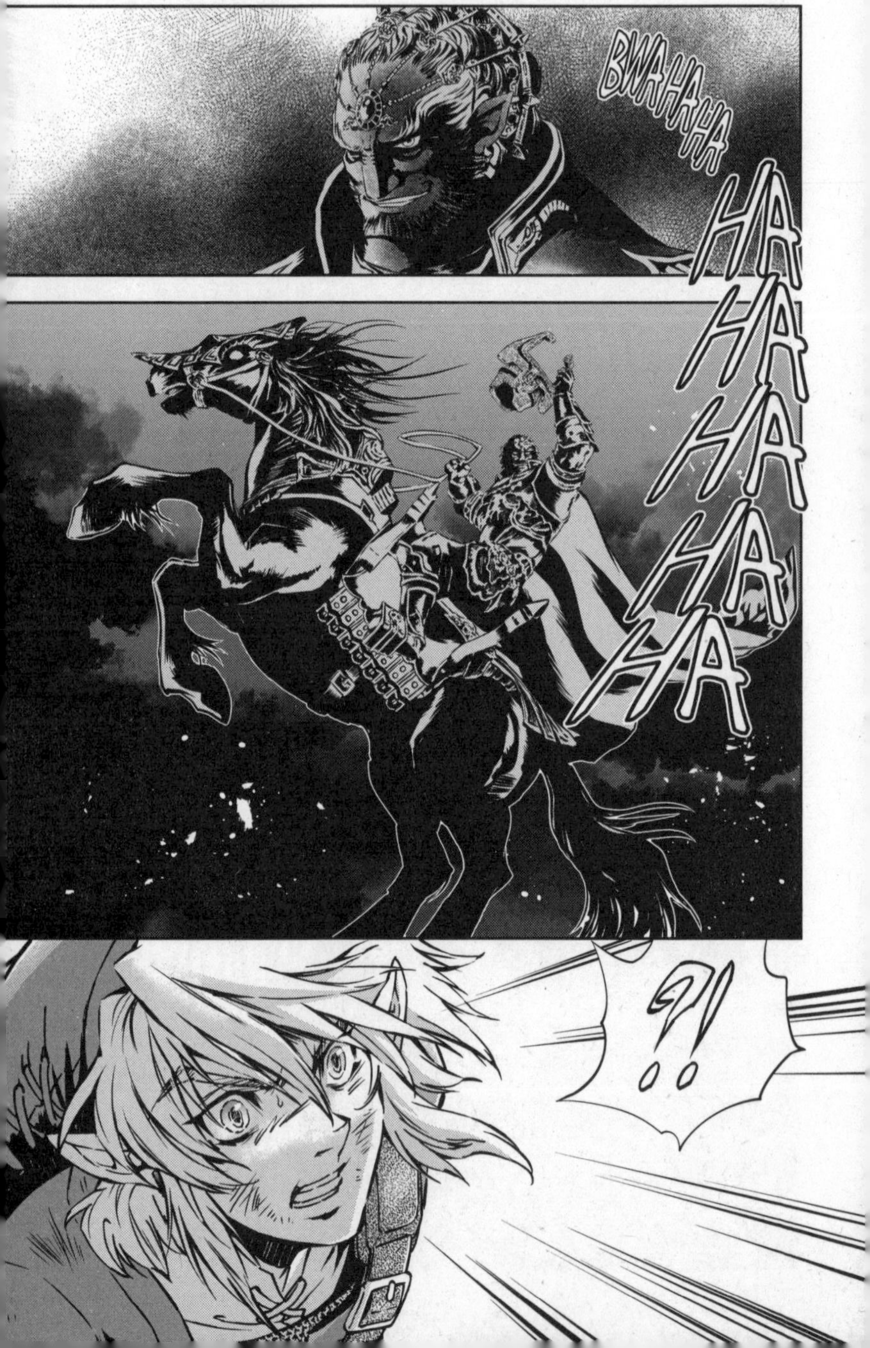
BWAHAHAHA
HA HA HA HA HA HA HA
?!

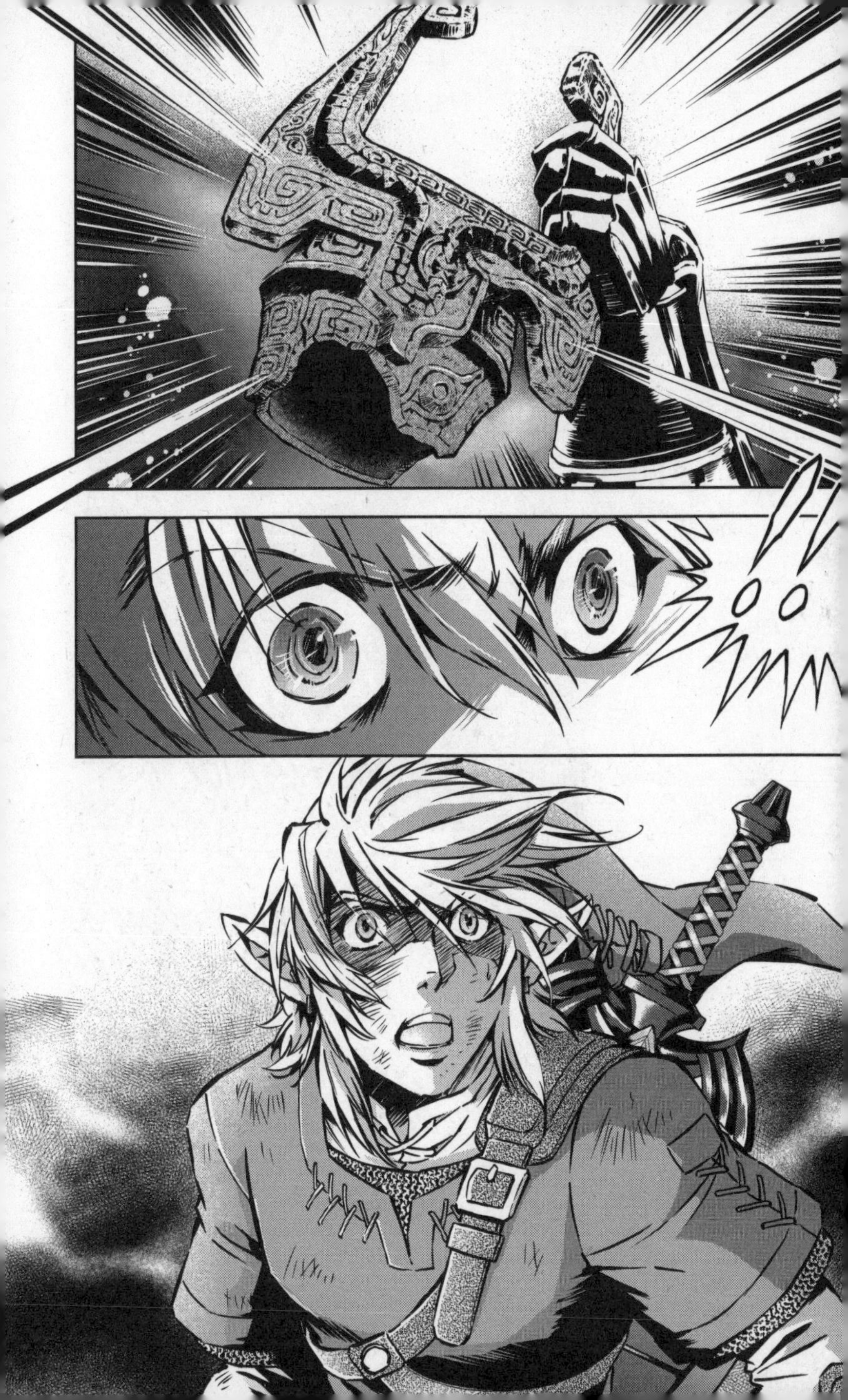
!!

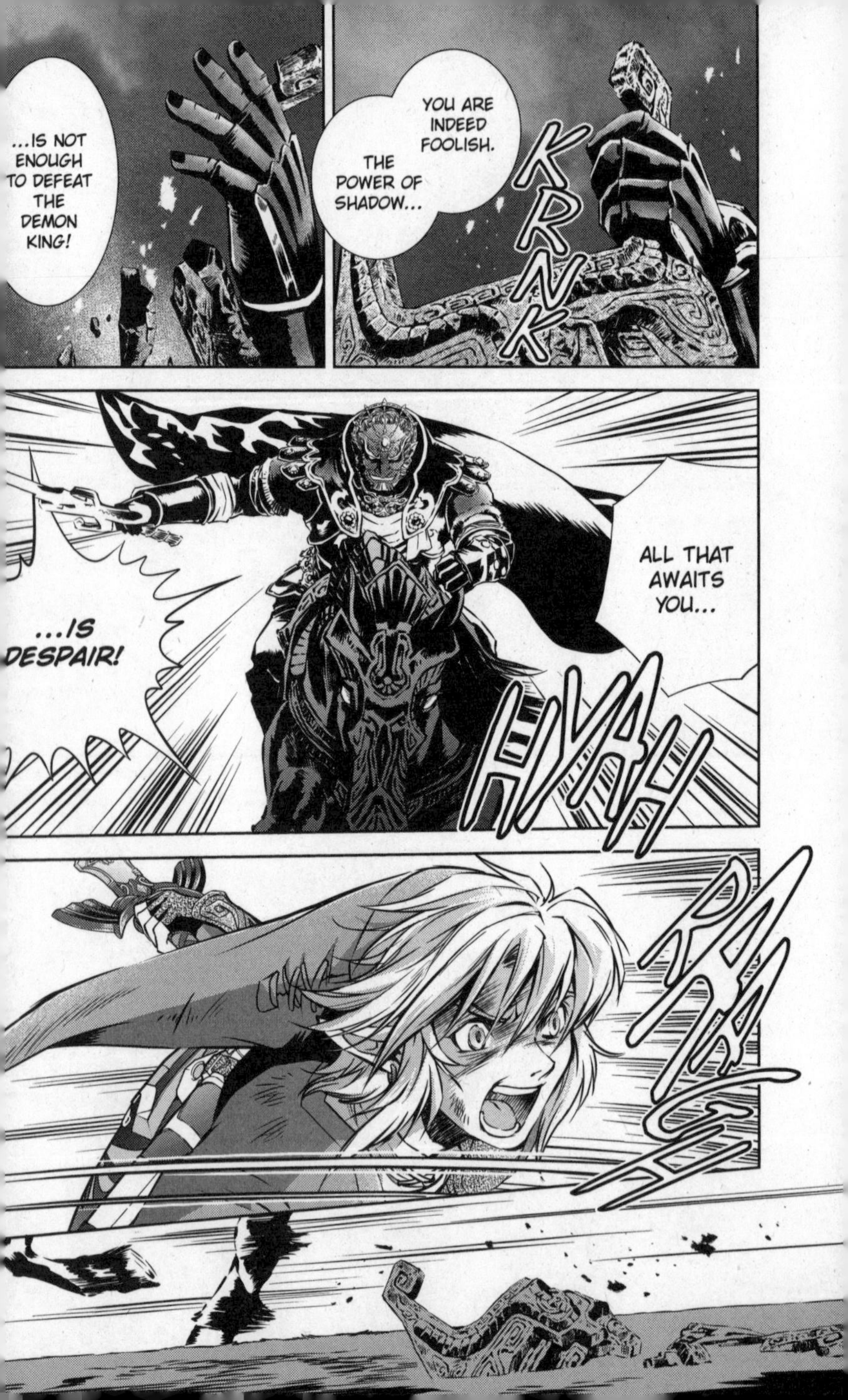
YOU ARE INDEED FOOLISH.
THE POWER OF SHADOW...
KRNK
...IS NOT ENOUGH TO DEFEAT THE DEMON KING!
ALL THAT AWAITS YOU...
...IS DESPAIR!
HYAAH
RAAAGH

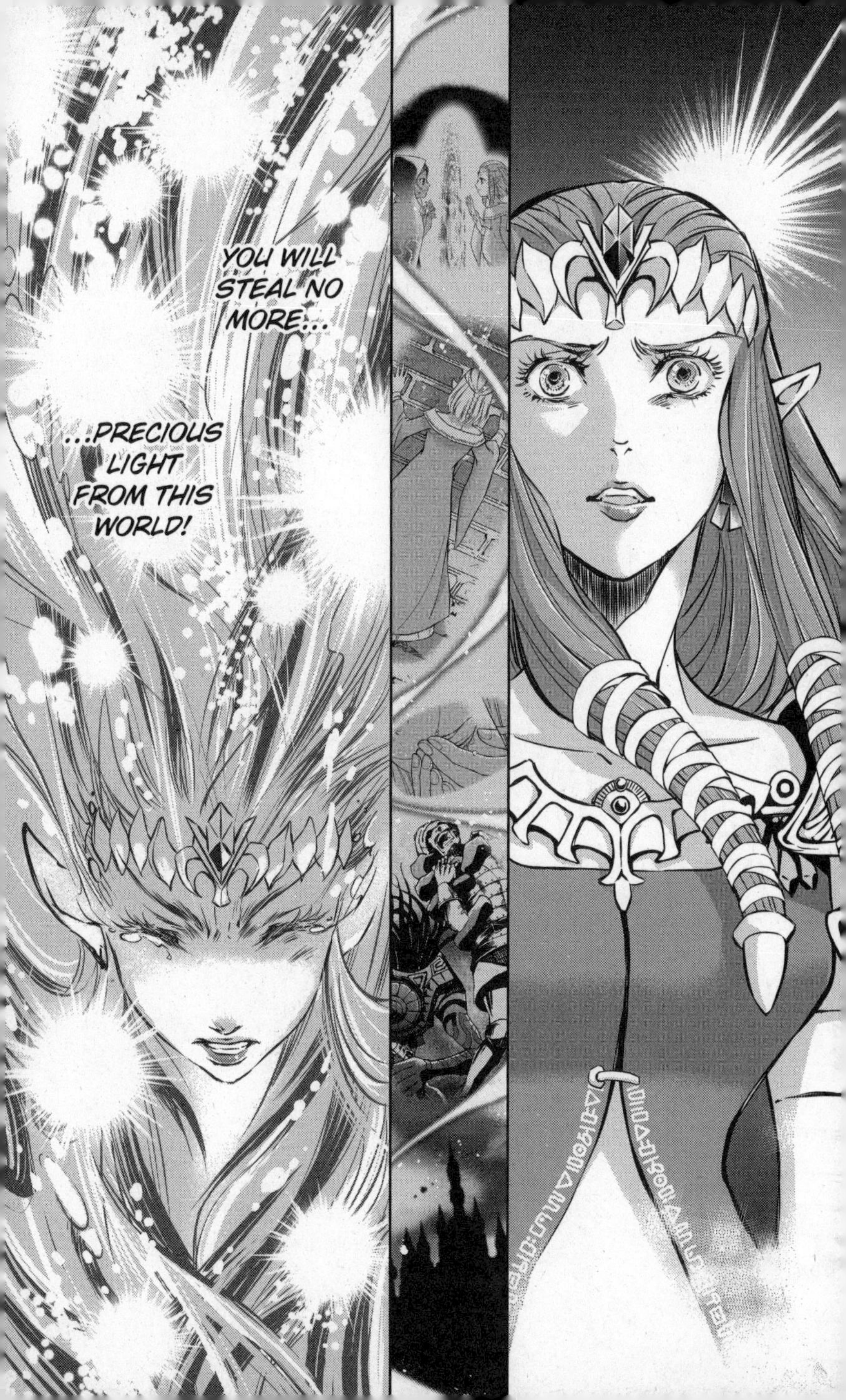
YOU WILL STEAL NO MORE...
...PRECIOUS LIGHT FROM THIS WORLD!

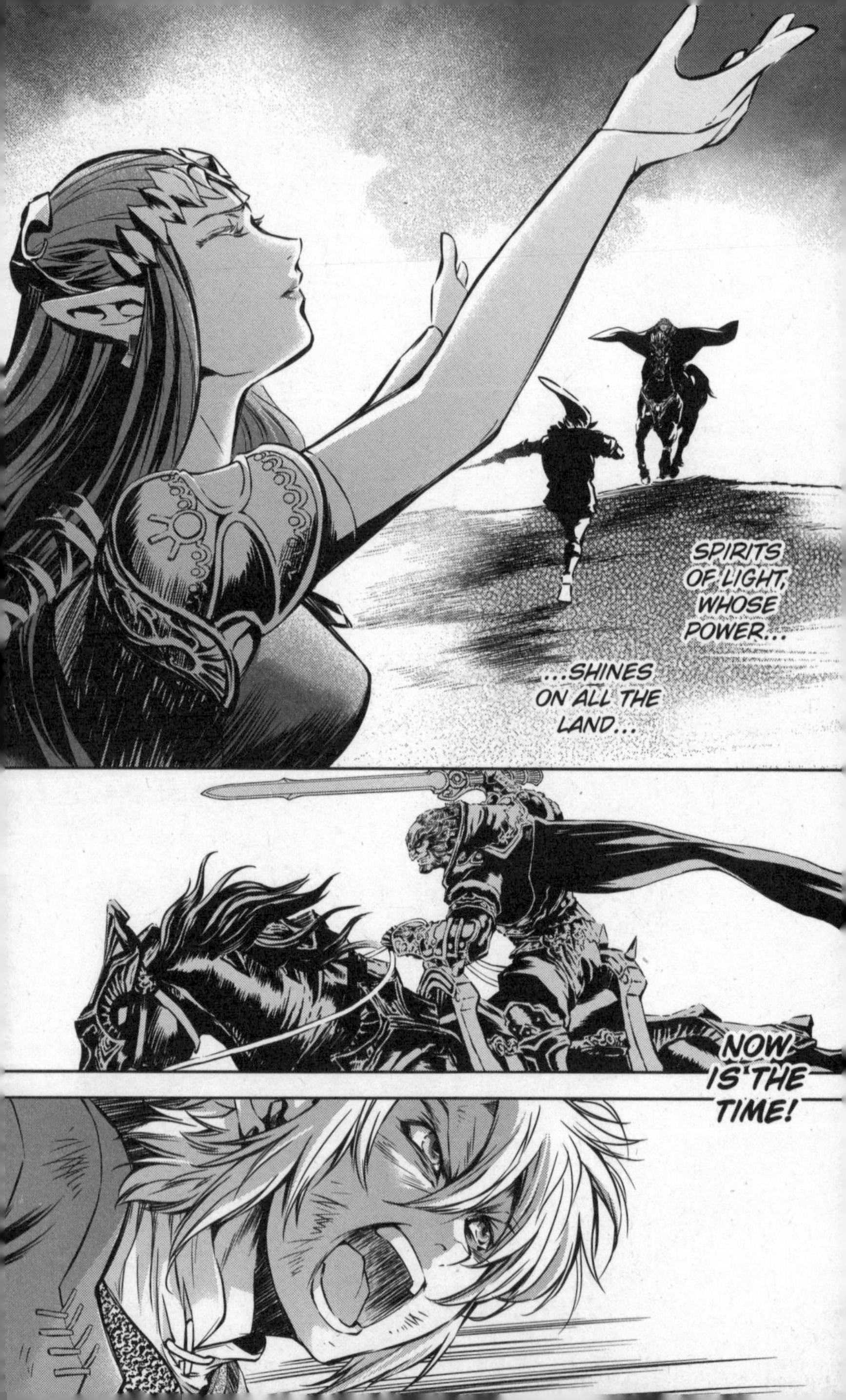
SPIRITS OF LIGHT, WHOSE POWER...
...SHINES ON ALL THE LAND...
NOW IS THE TIME!

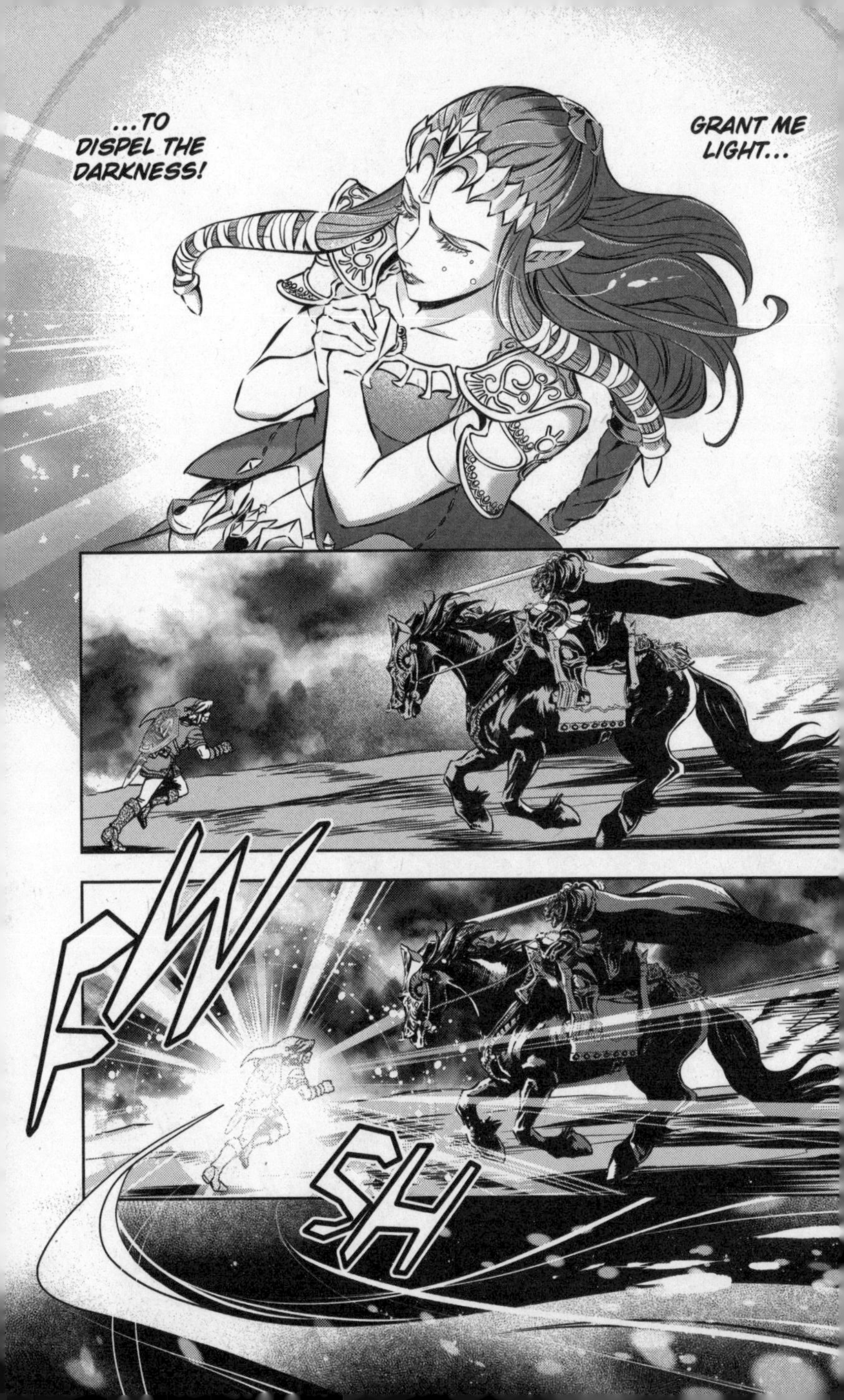
GRANT ME LIGHT...
...TO DISPEL THE DARKNESS!
FW
SH

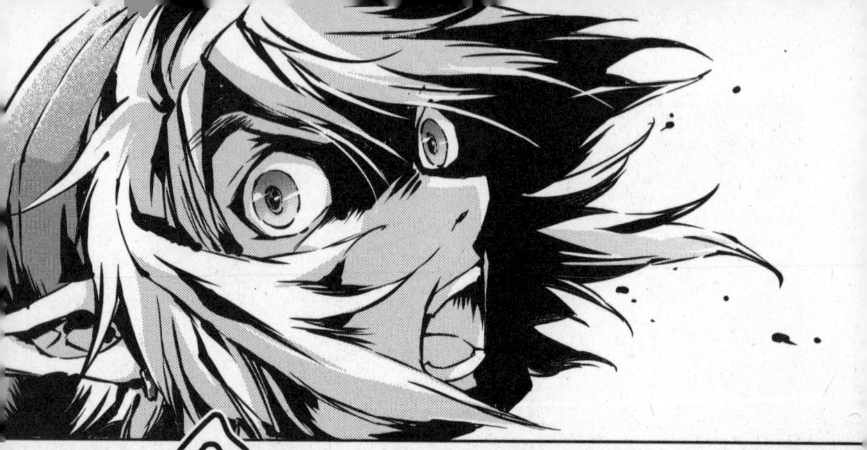

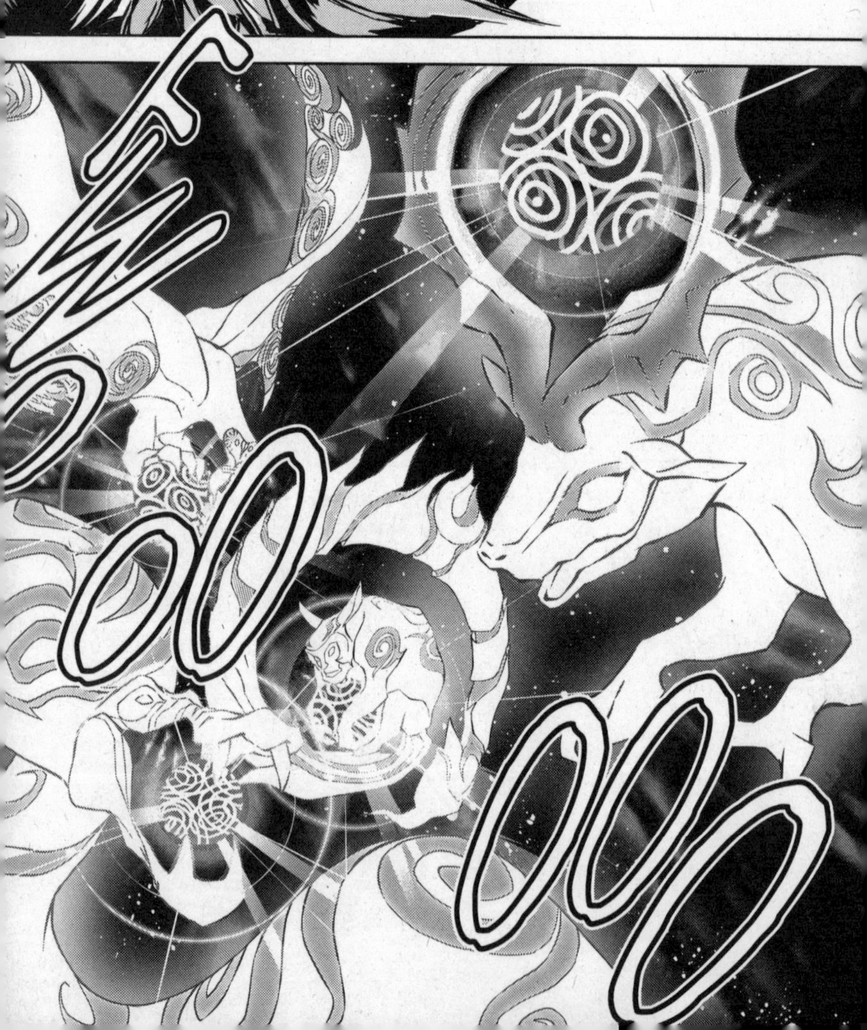
FWOOOOOO

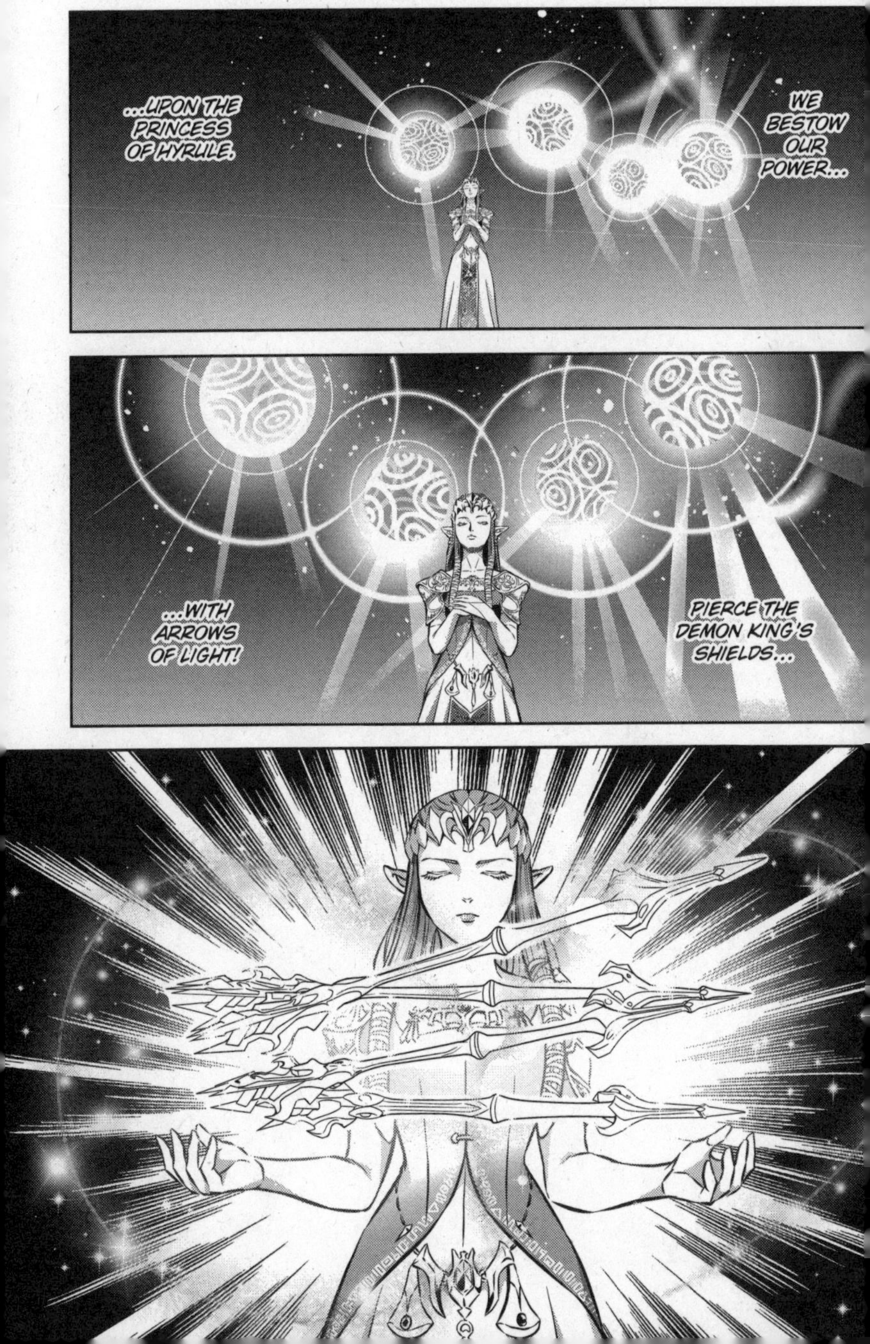
WE BESTOW OUR POWER...
...UPON THE PRINCESS OF HYRULE.
PIERCE THE DEMON KING'S SHIELDS...
...WITH ARROWS OF LIGHT!

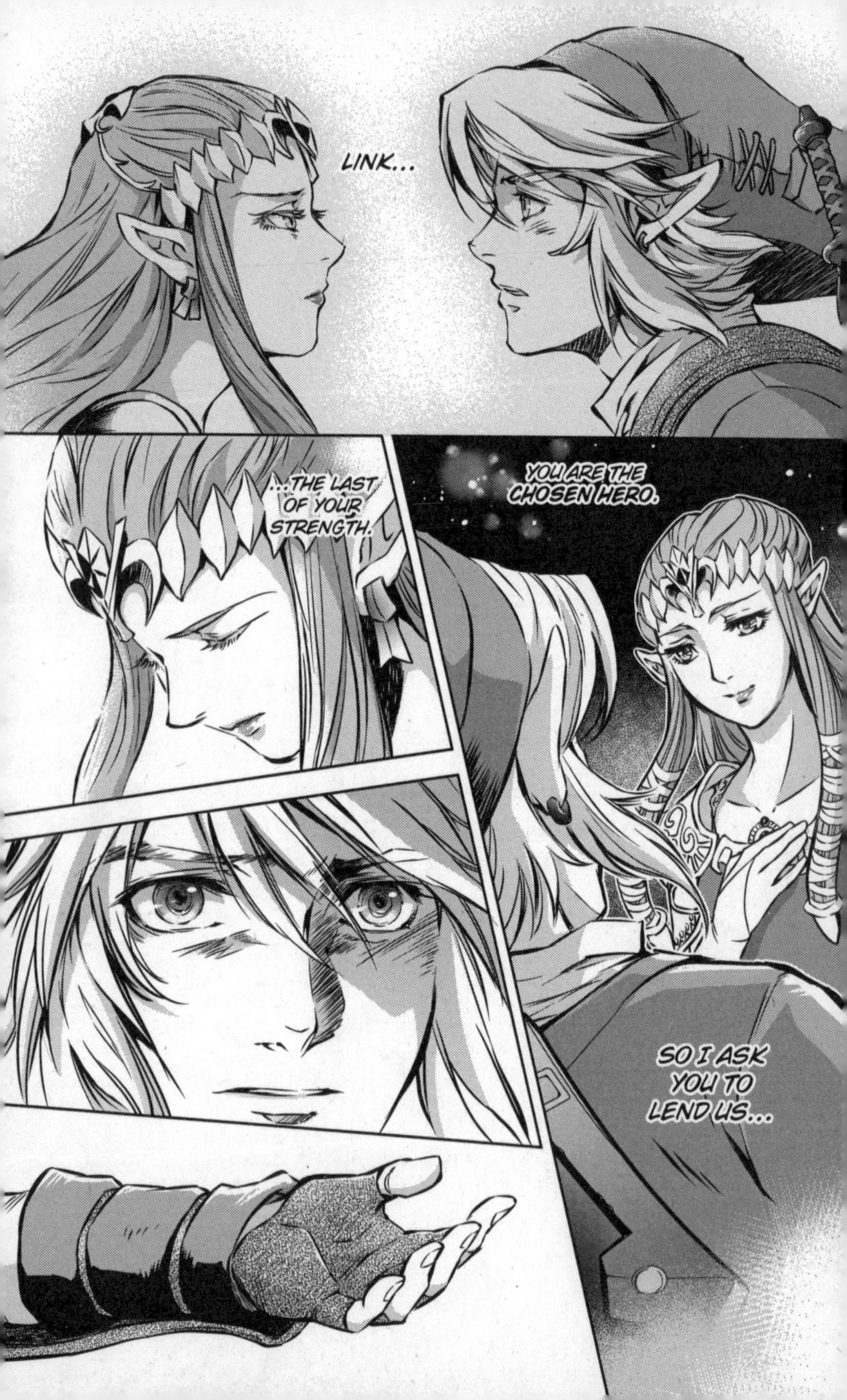
LINK...
YOU ARE THE CHOSEN HERO.
SO I ASK YOU TO LEND US...
...THE LAST OF YOUR STRENGTH.

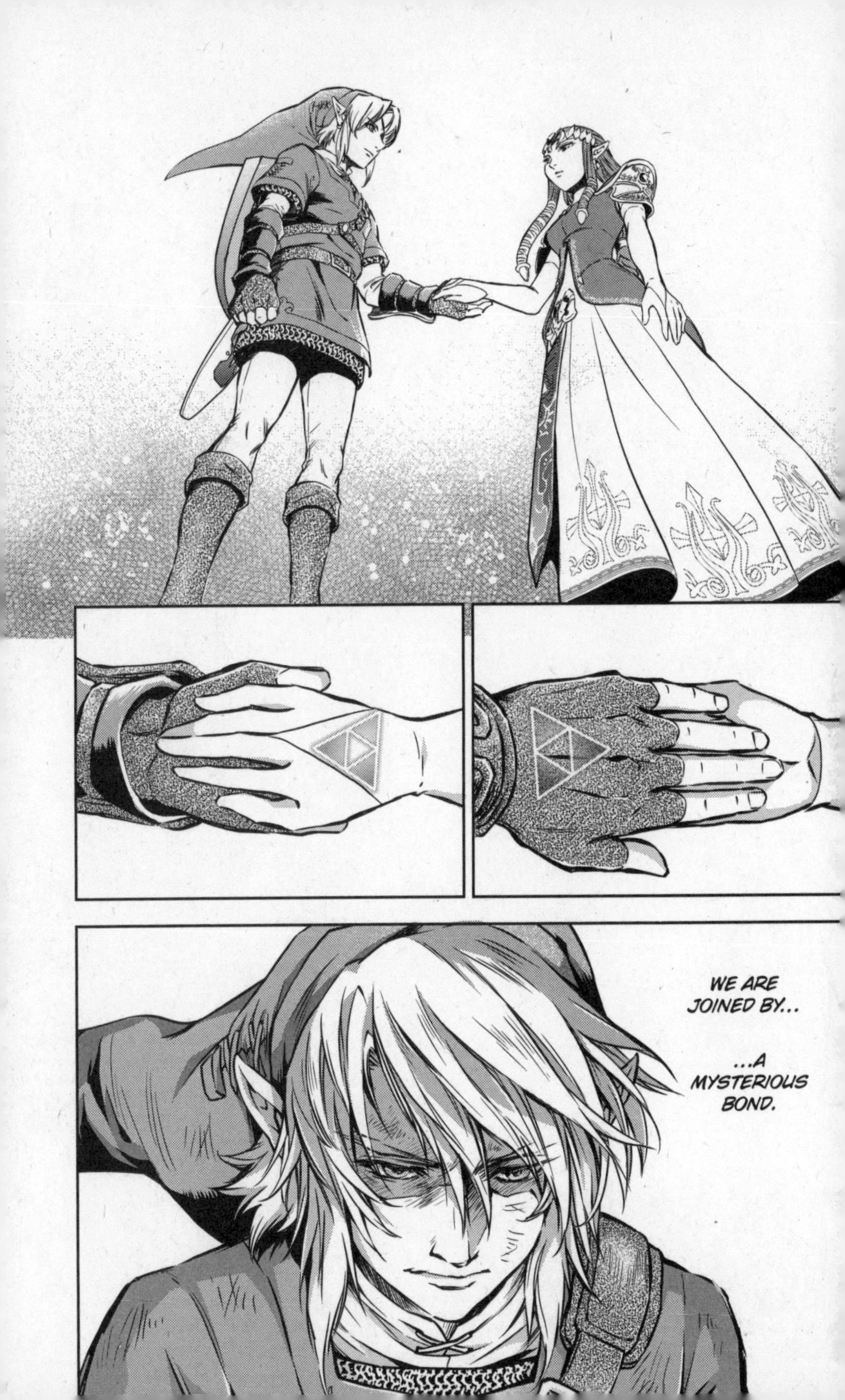
WE ARE JOINED BY...
...A MYSTERIOUS BOND.

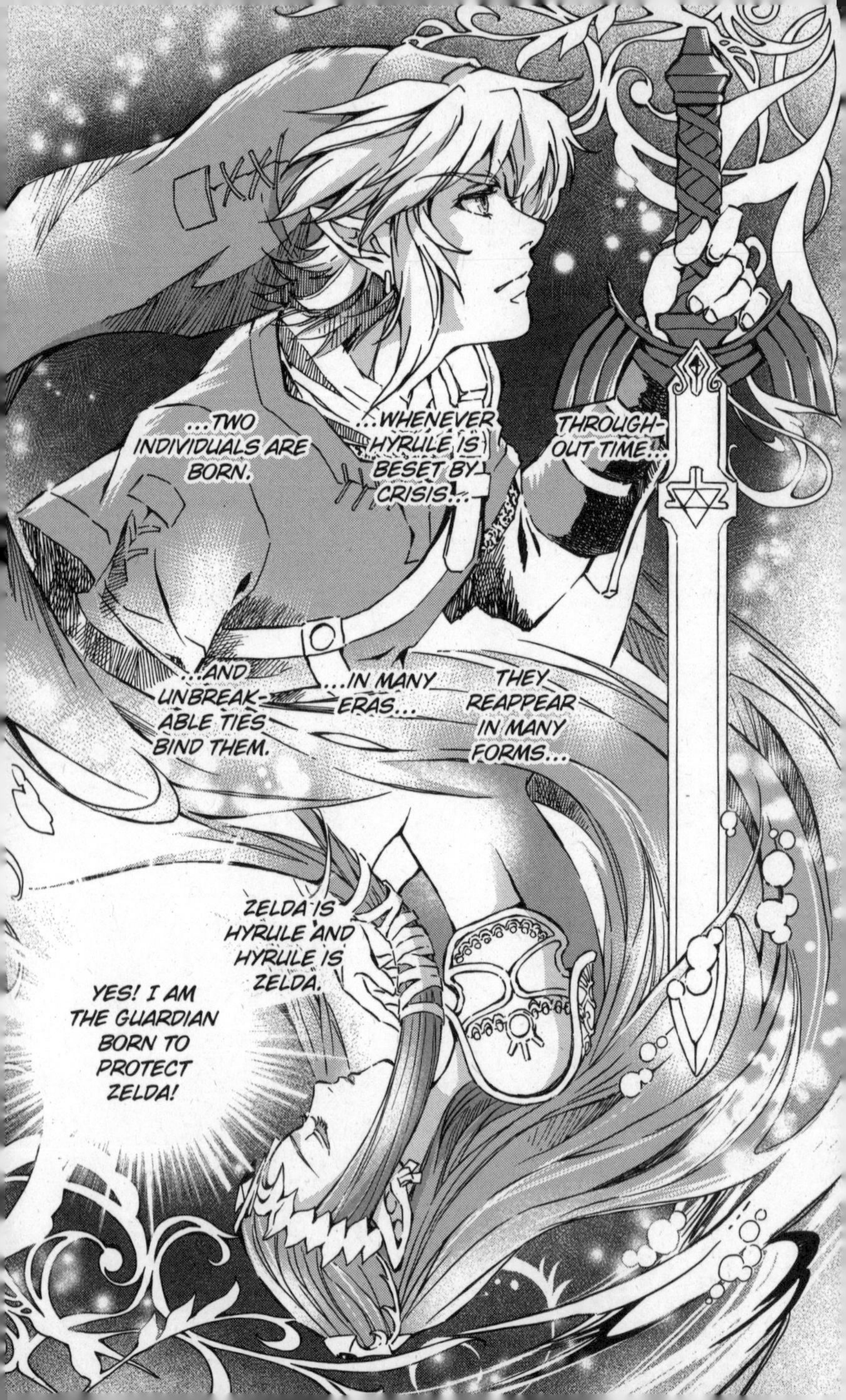
THROUGHOUT TIME...
...WHENEVER HYRULE IS BESET BY CRISIS...
...TWO INDIVIDUALS ARE BORN.
THEY REAPPEAR IN MANY FORMS...
...IN MANY ERAS...
...AND UNBREAKABLE TIES BIND THEM.
ZELDA IS HYRULE AND HYRULE IS ZELDA.
YES! I AM THE GUARDIAN BORN TO PROTECT ZELDA!

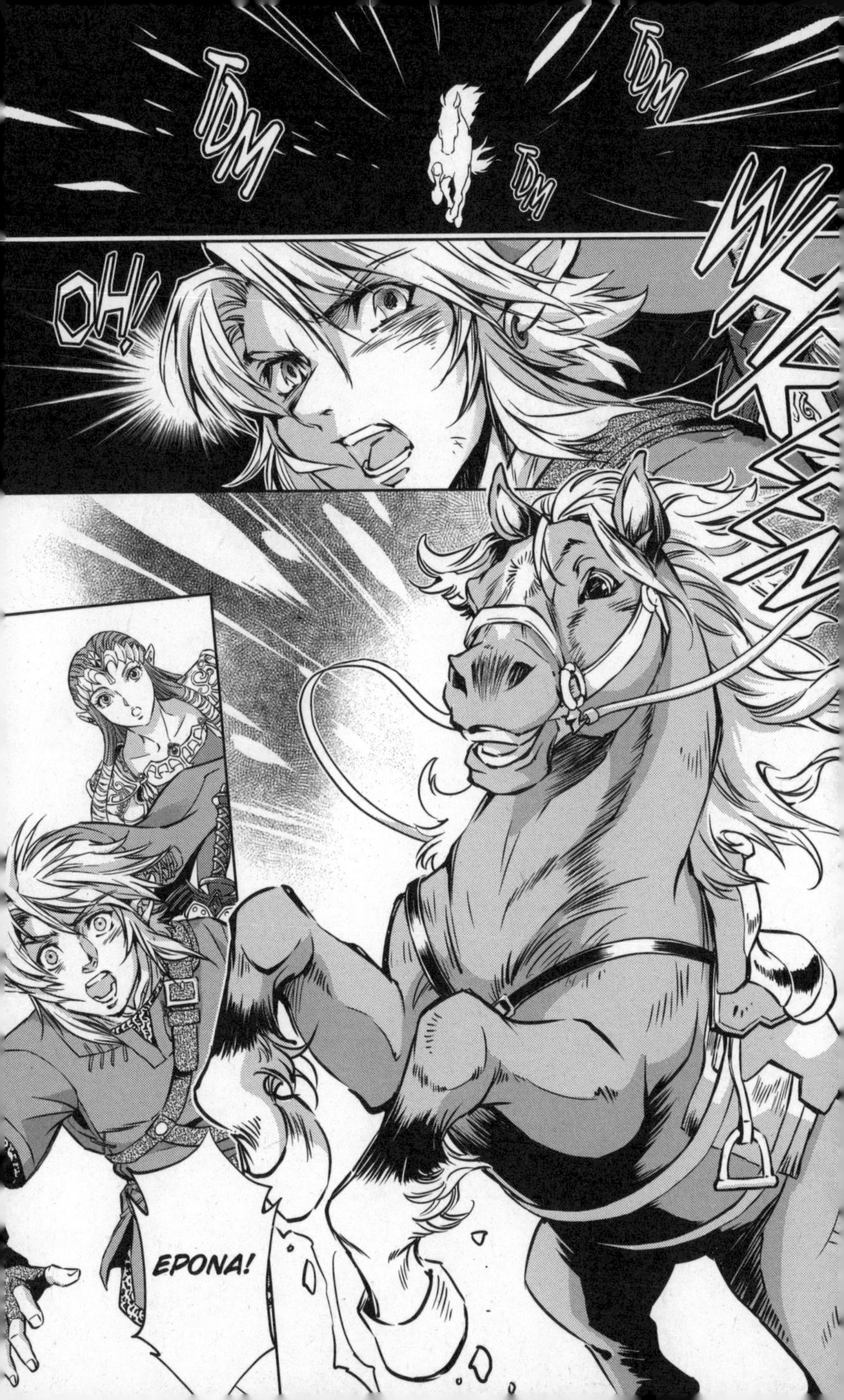
TDM
TDM
TDM
OH!
WHEEEE
EPONA!

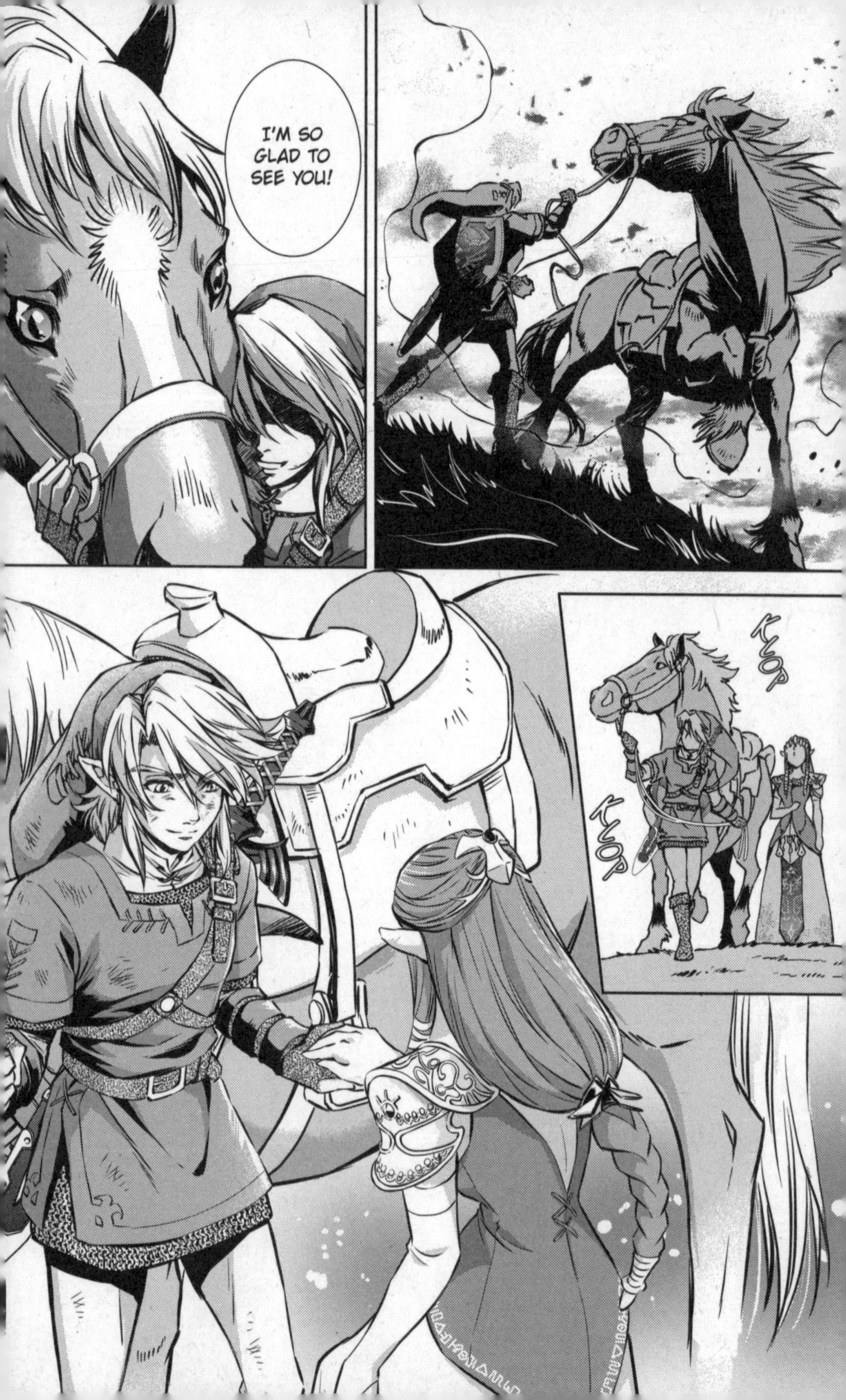
I'M SO GLAD TO SEE YOU!
KLOP
KLOP

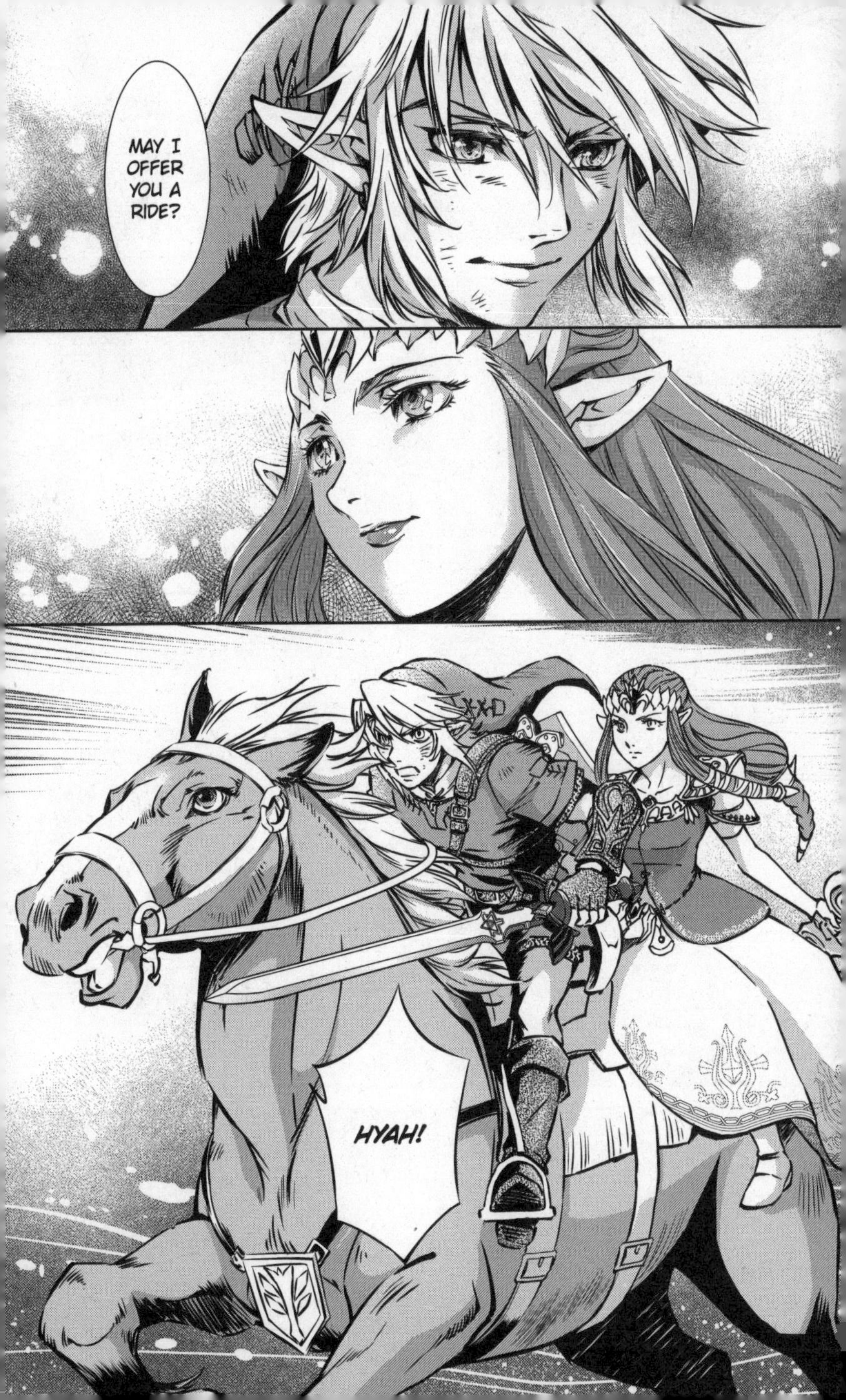
MAY I OFFER YOU A RIDE?
HYAH!

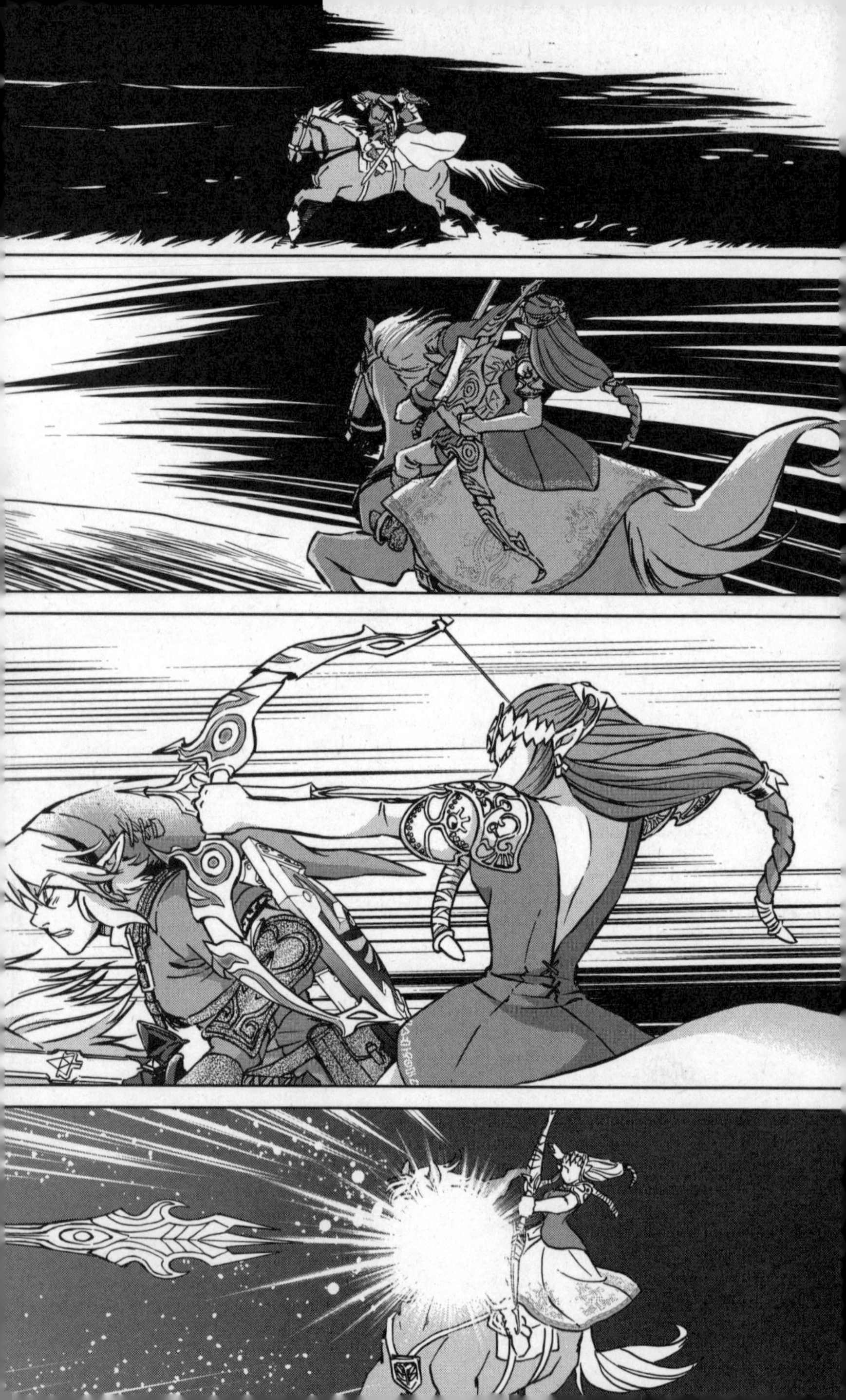

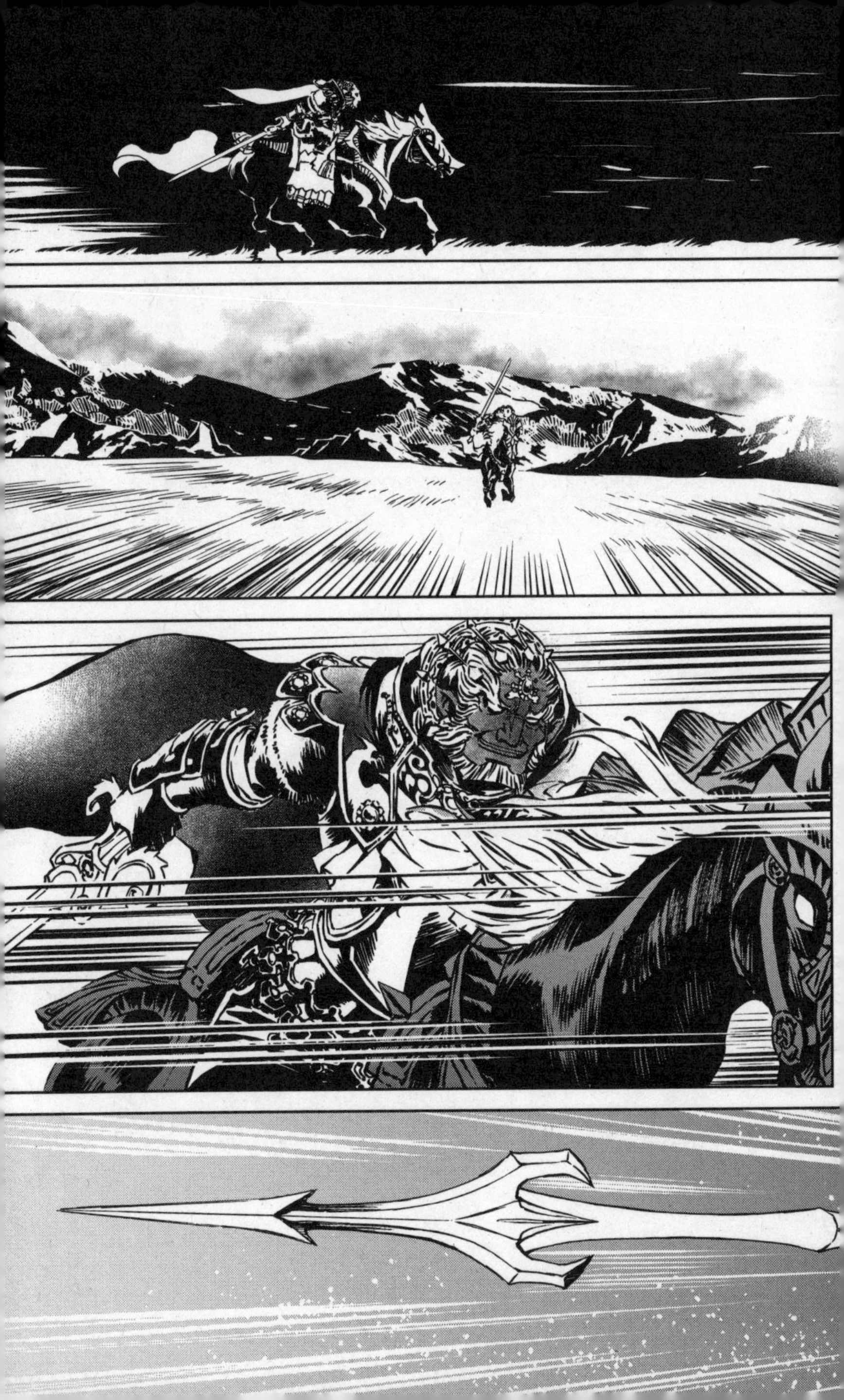

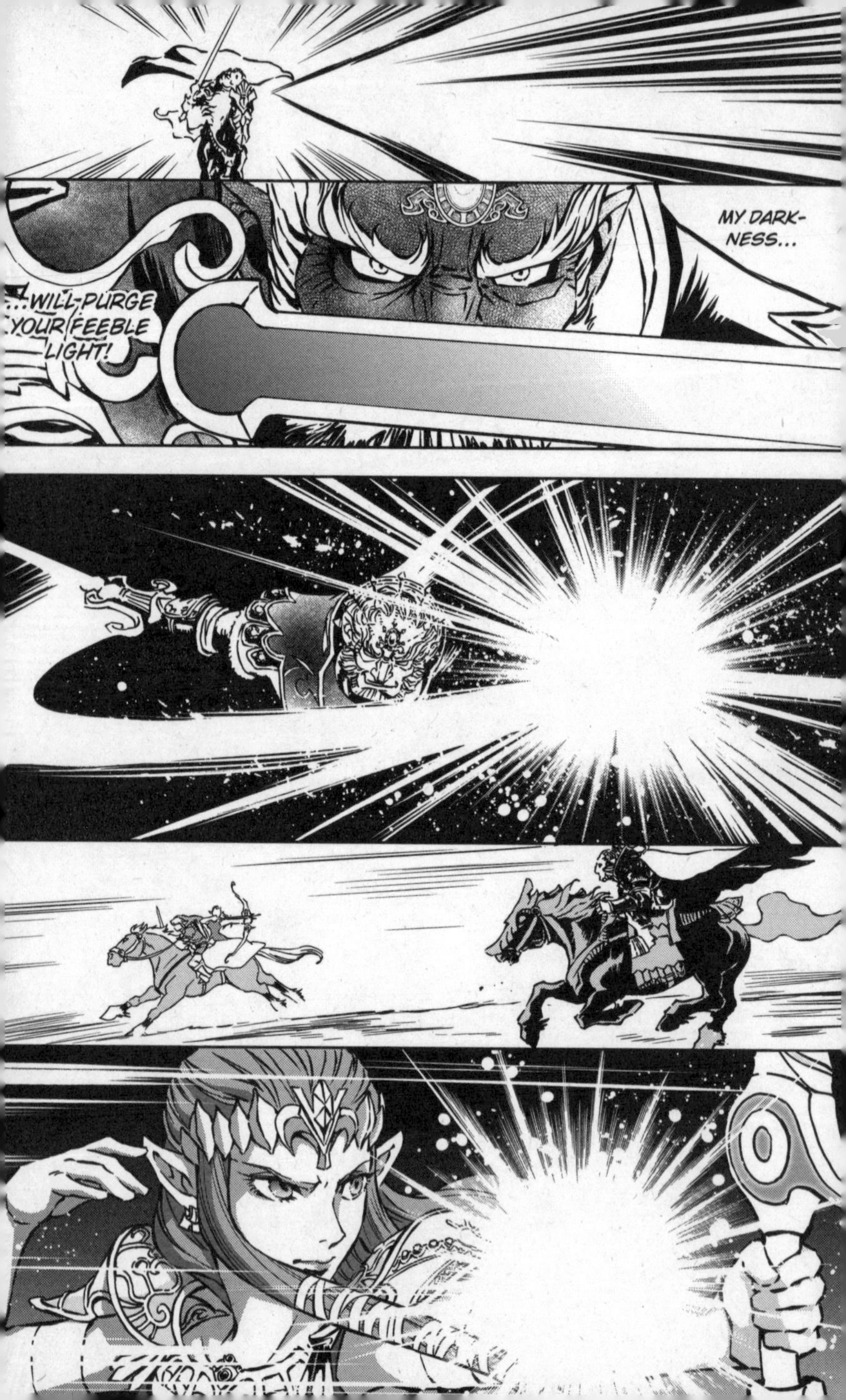
MY DARK-
NESS...
...WILL PURGE YOUR FEEBLE LIGHT!

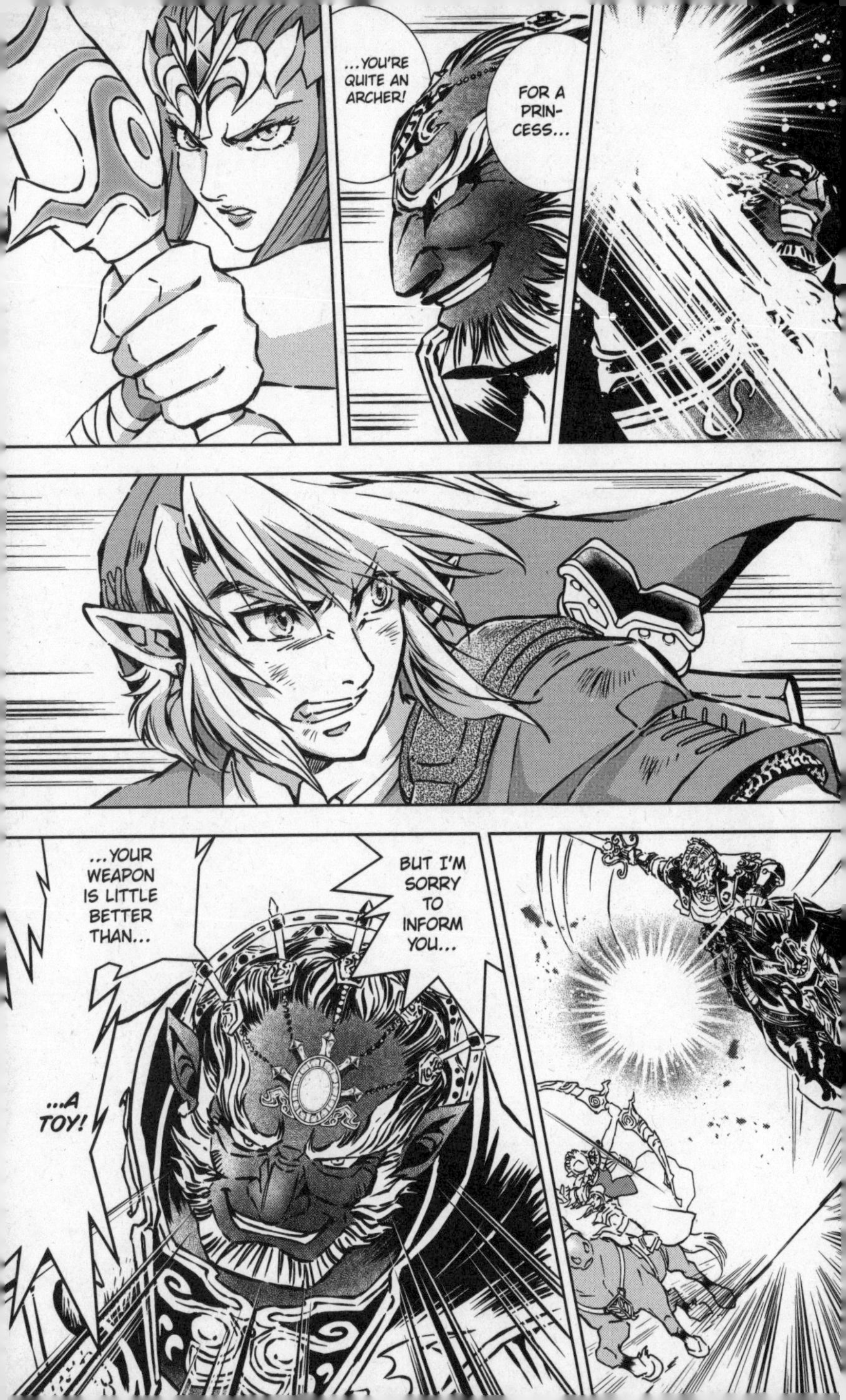
FOR A PRINCESS...
...YOU'RE QUITE AN ARCHER!
BUT I'M SORRY TO INFORM YOU...
...YOUR WEAPON IS LITTLE BETTER THAN...
...A TOY!

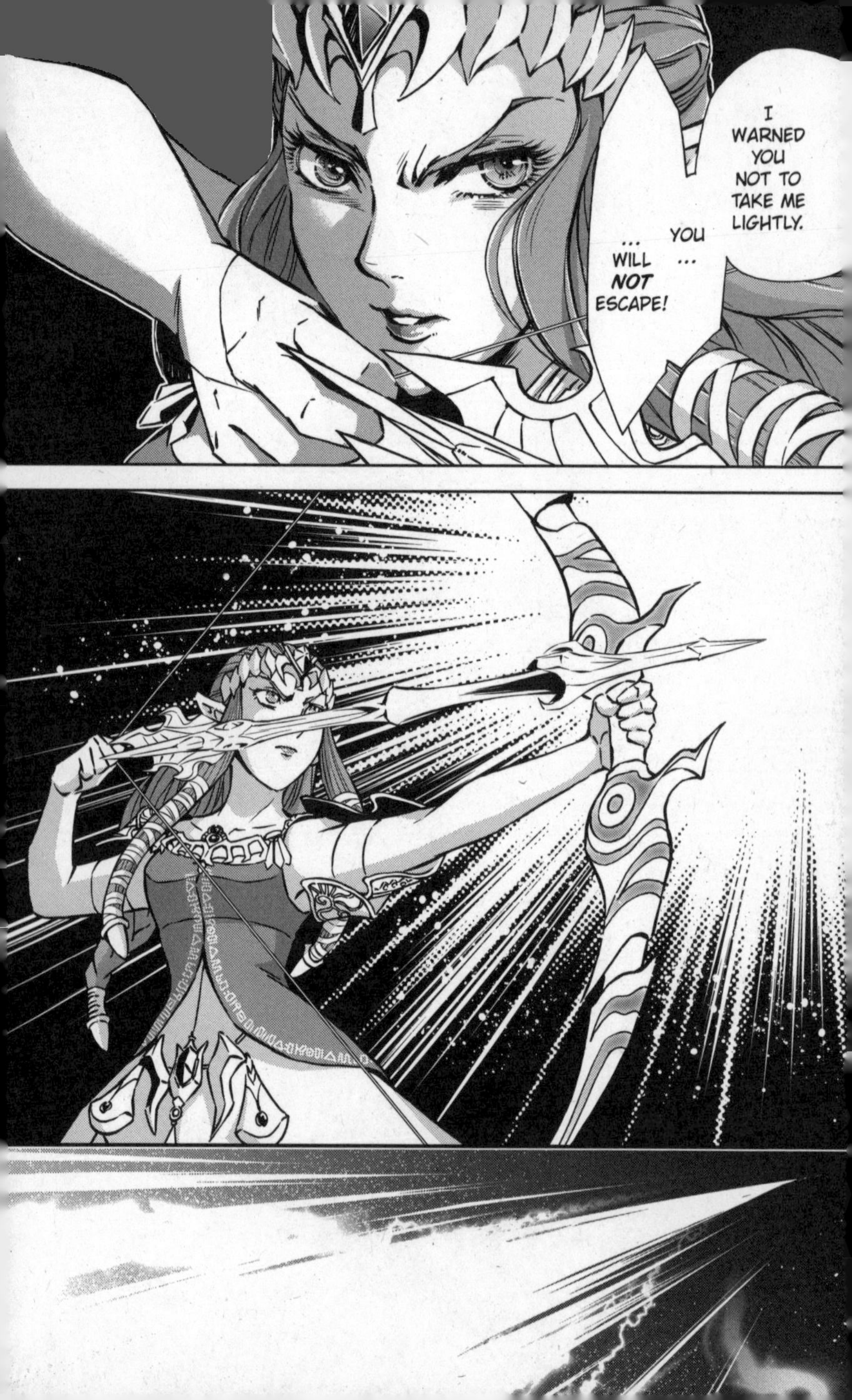
I WARNED YOU NOT TO TAKE ME LIGHTLY.
YOU ...
... WILL **NOT** ESCAPE!

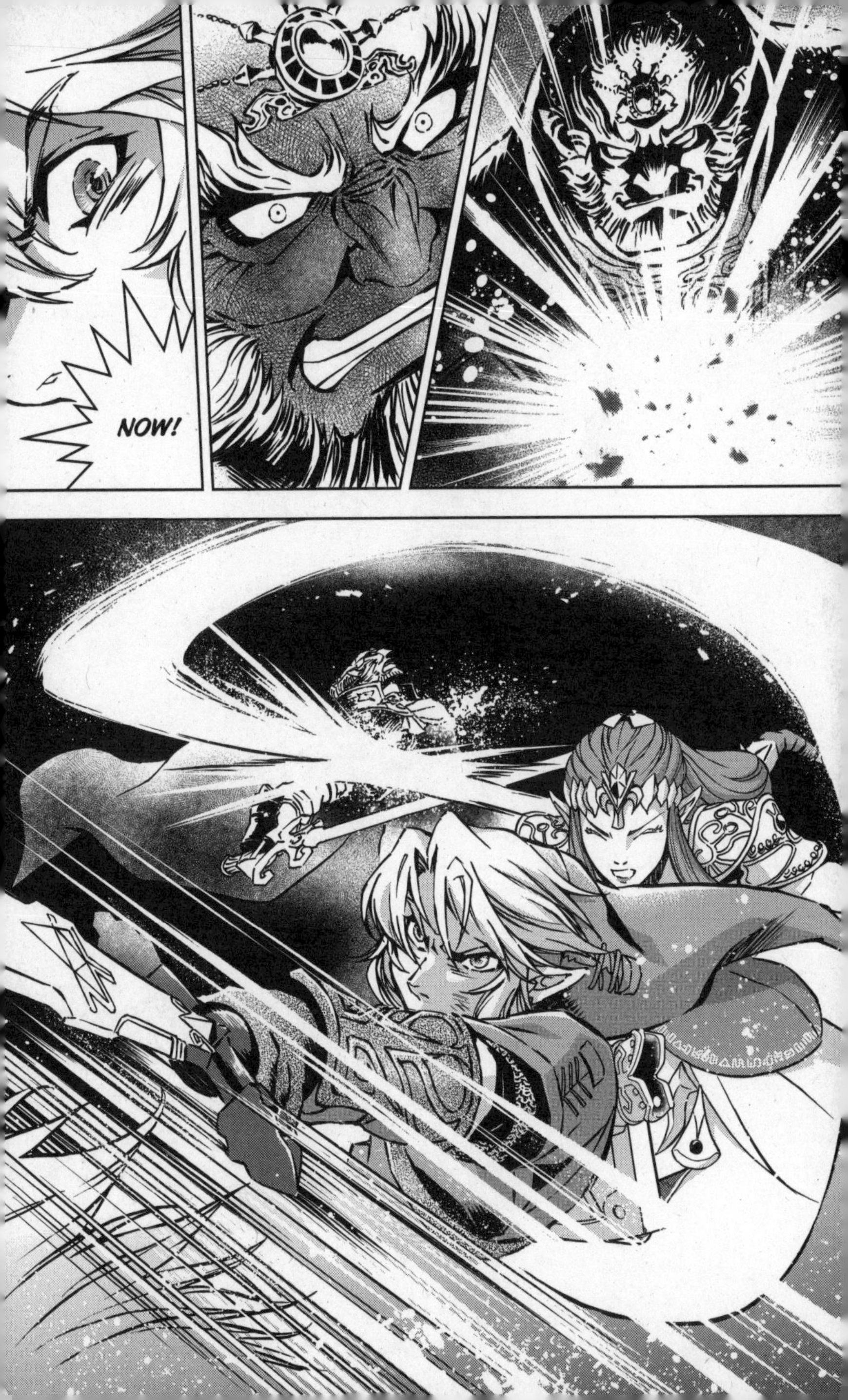
NOW!

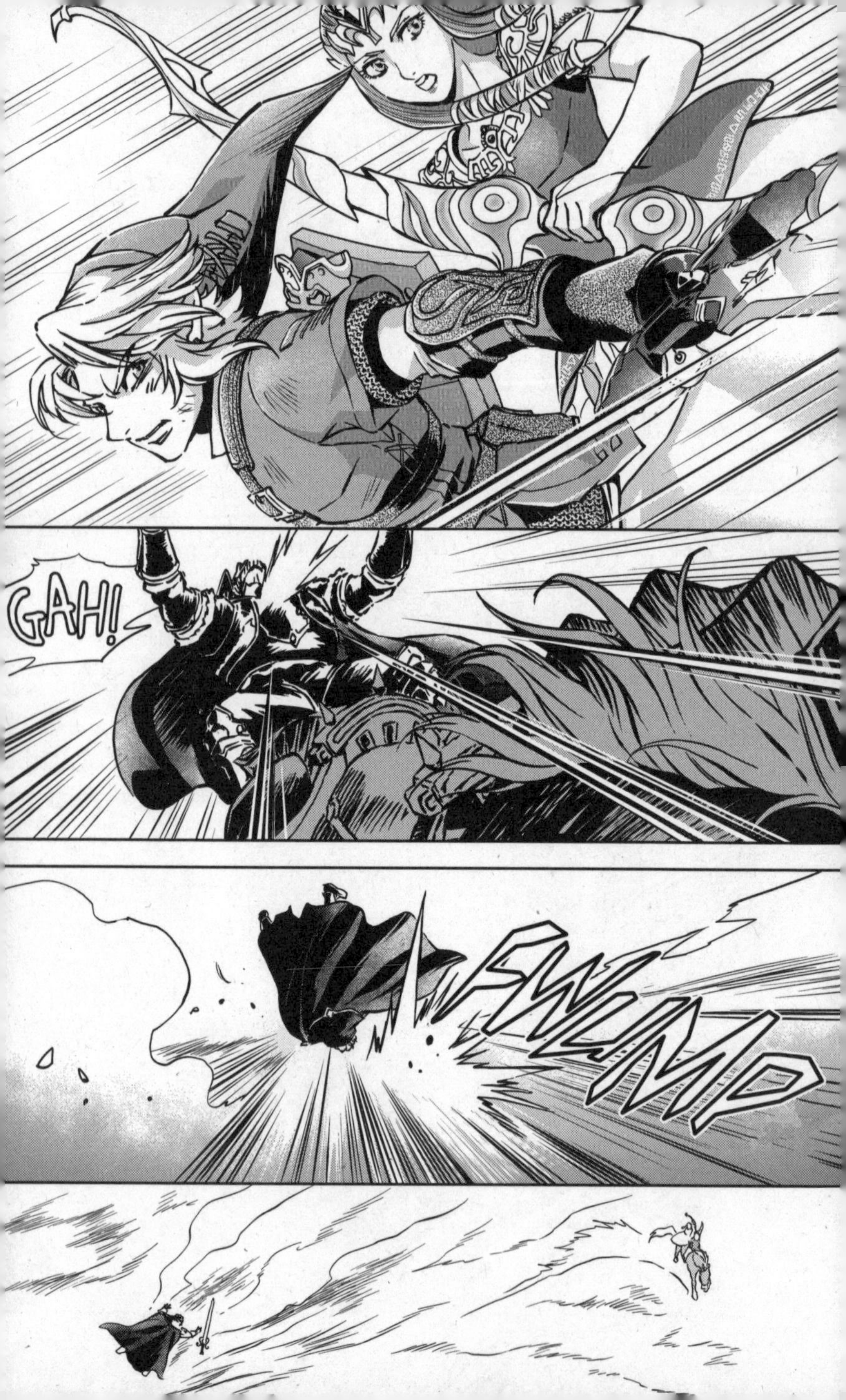
GAH!
FWUMP

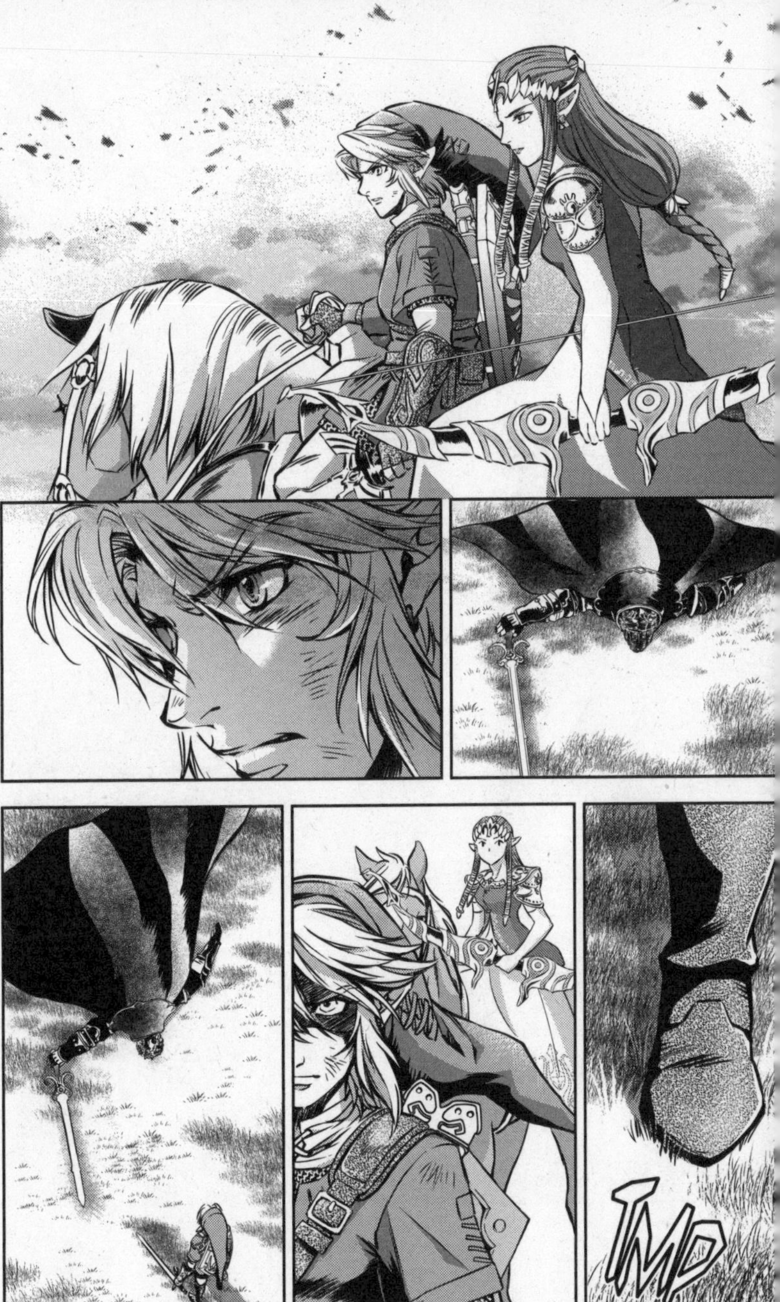
TMP

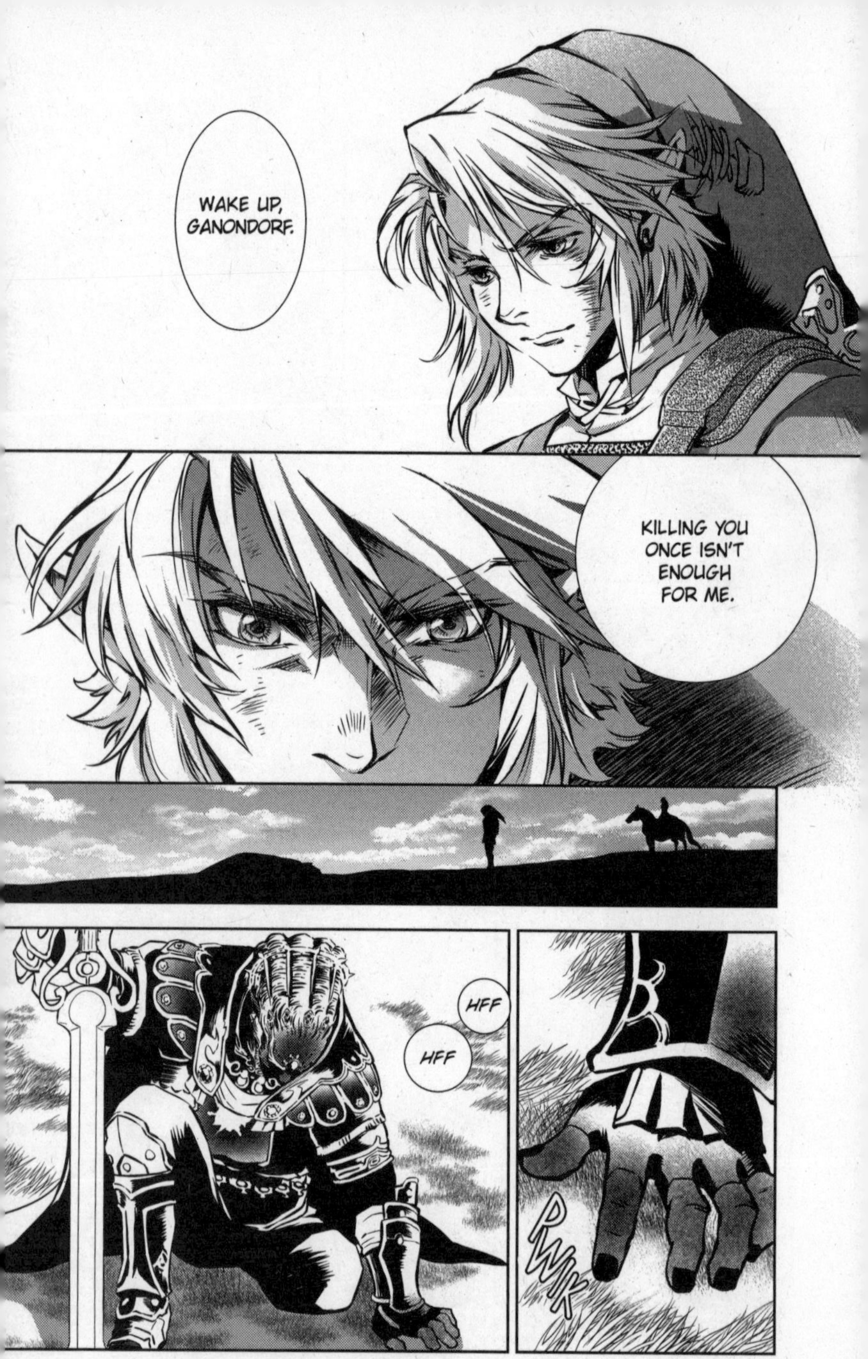
WAKE UP, GANONDORF.
KILLING YOU ONCE ISN'T ENOUGH FOR ME.
PWIK
HFF
HFF

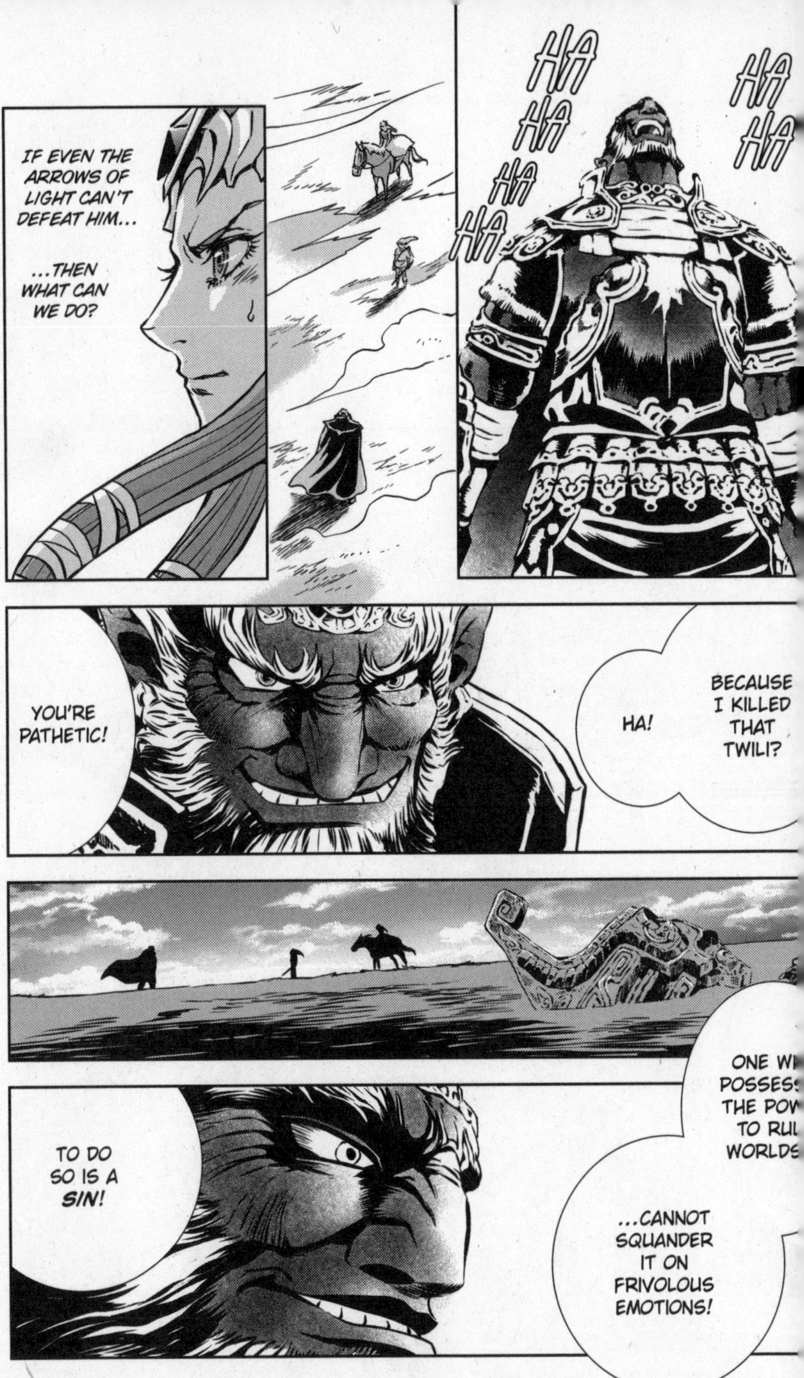
HA HA HA HA
HA HA
IF EVEN THE ARROWS OF LIGHT CAN'T DEFEAT HIM...
...THEN WHAT CAN WE DO?
BECAUSE I KILLED THAT TWILI?
HA!
YOU'RE PATHETIC!
ONE W POSSES THE POW TO RUL WORLDS
...CANNOT SQUANDER IT ON FRIVOLOUS EMOTIONS!
TO DO SO IS A SIN!

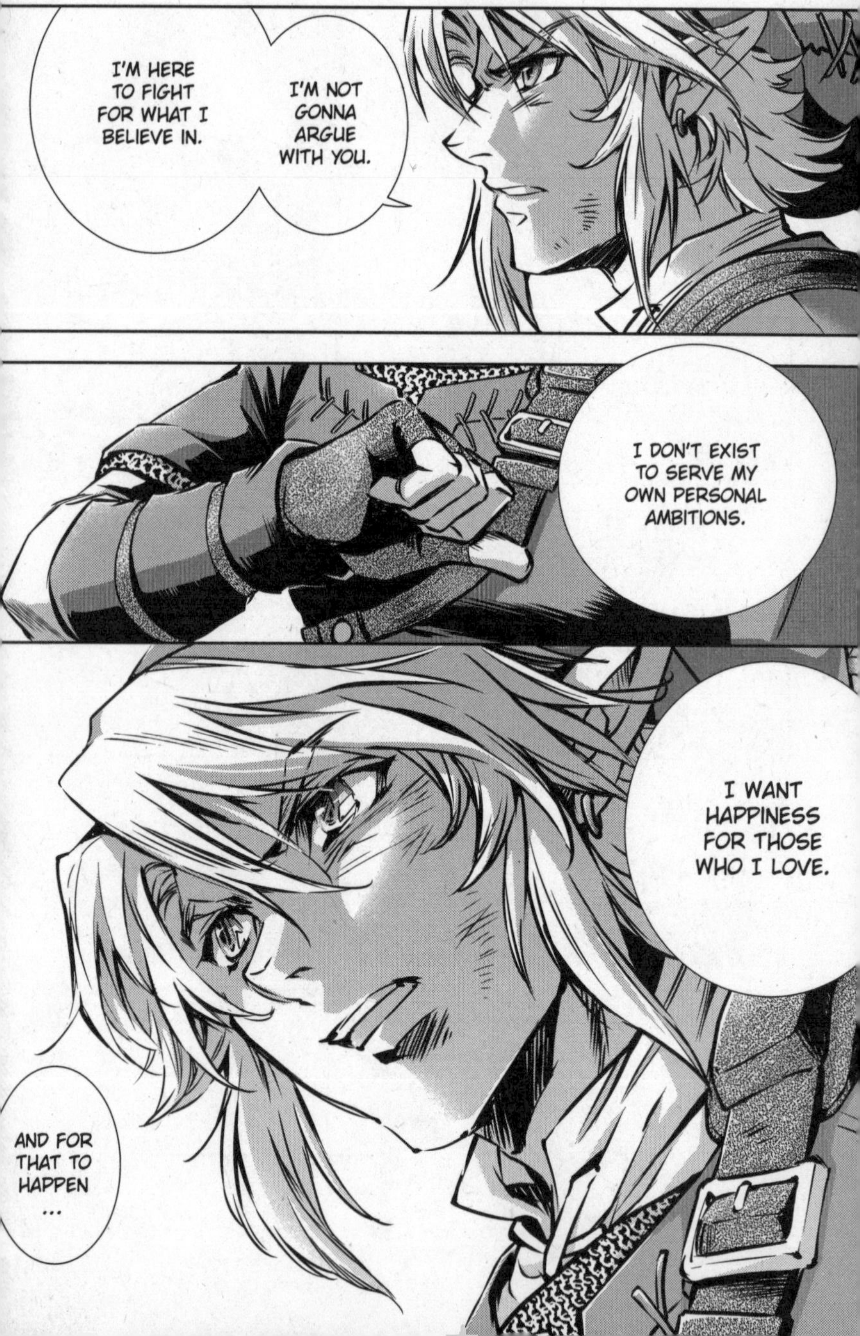
I'M NOT GONNA ARGUE WITH YOU.
I'M HERE TO FIGHT FOR WHAT I BELIEVE IN.
I DON'T EXIST TO SERVE MY OWN PERSONAL AMBITIONS.
I WANT HAPPINESS FOR THOSE WHO I LOVE.
AND FOR THAT TO HAPPEN ...

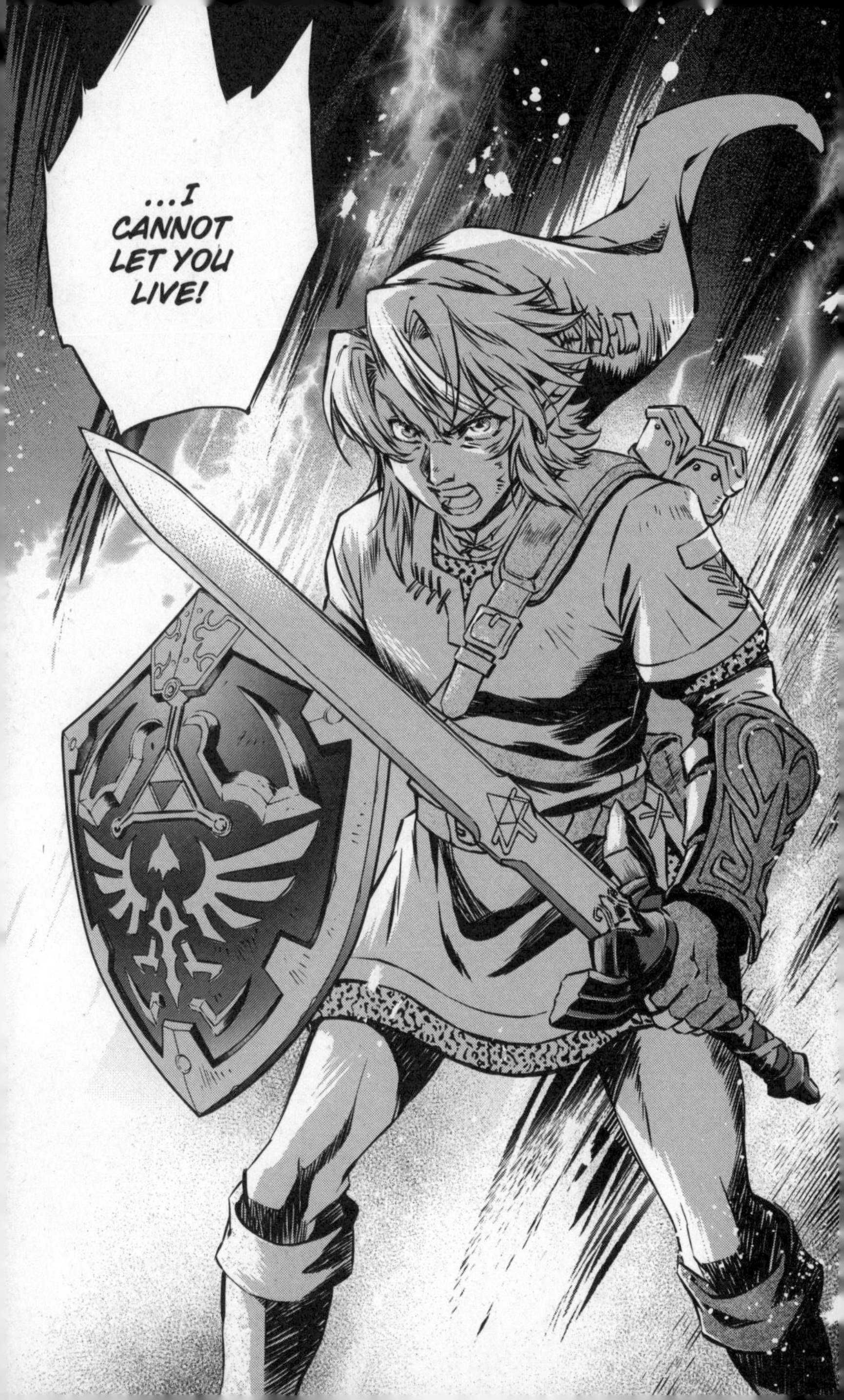
...I CANNOT LET YOU LIVE!

#55. SINGLE COMBAT, PART 2
THAT'S THE SPIRIT.
HATE ME *MORE*.
ONLY THEN WILL THIS FIGHT BE WORTHWHILE!

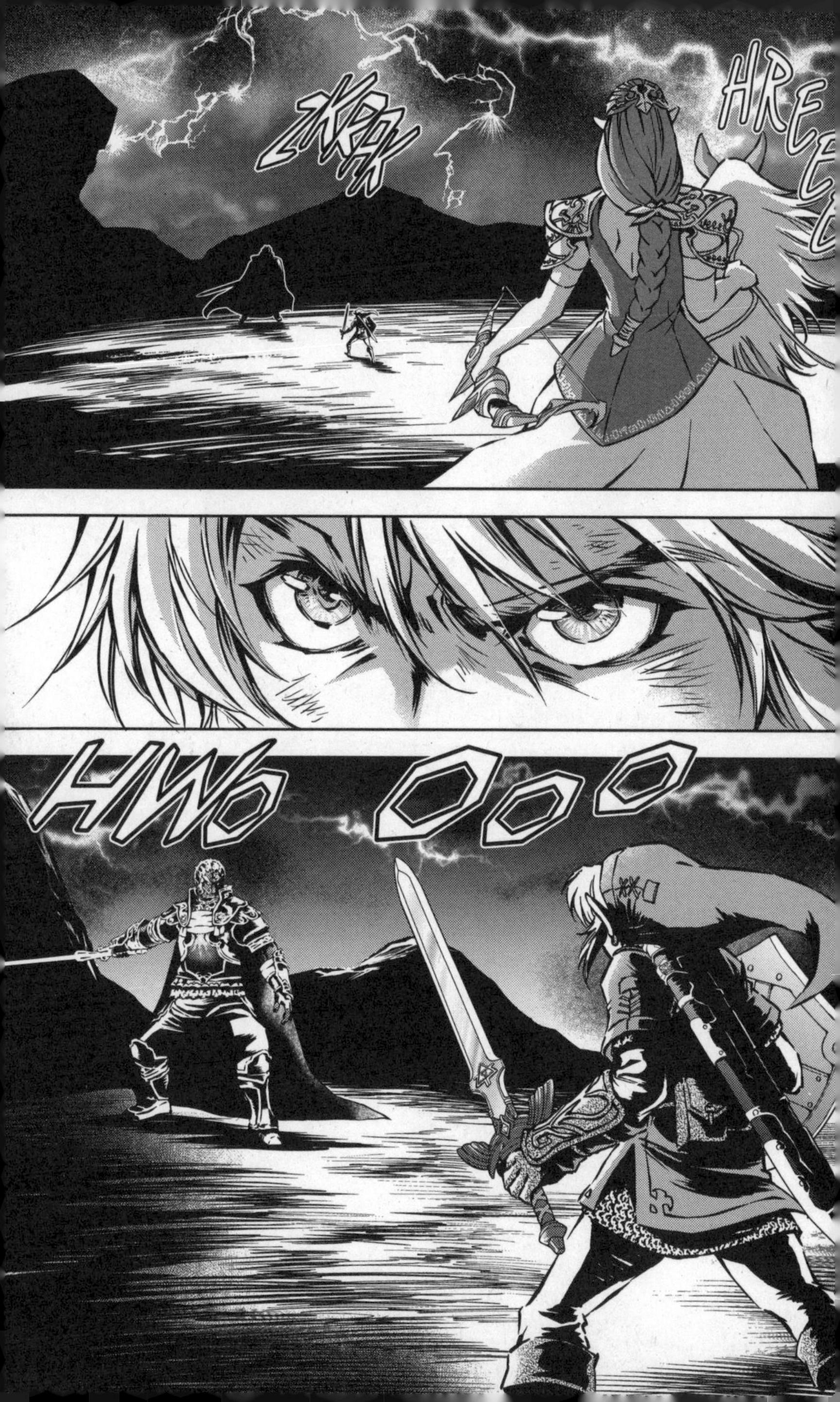
HREEE
KRAK
HWOOOO

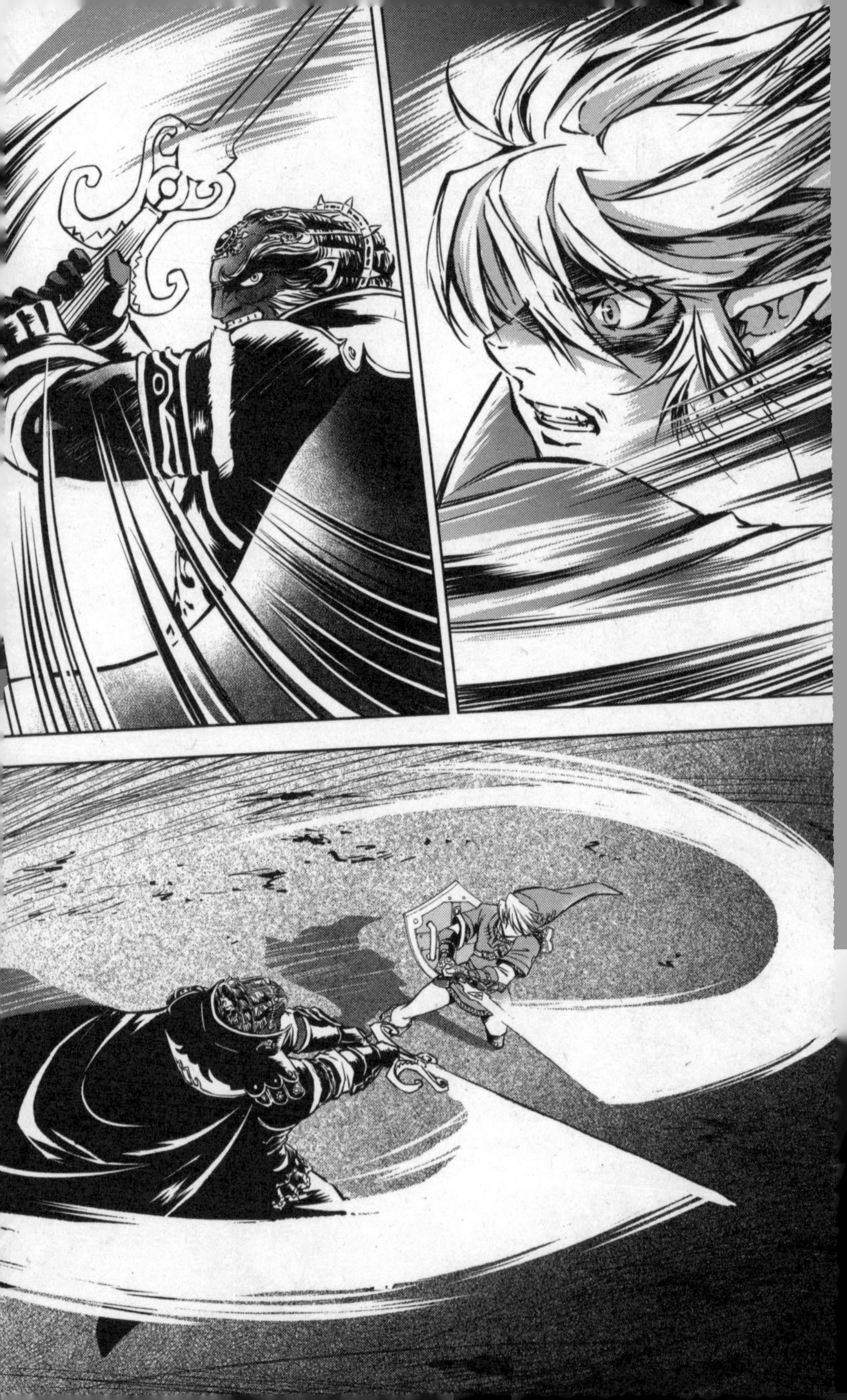

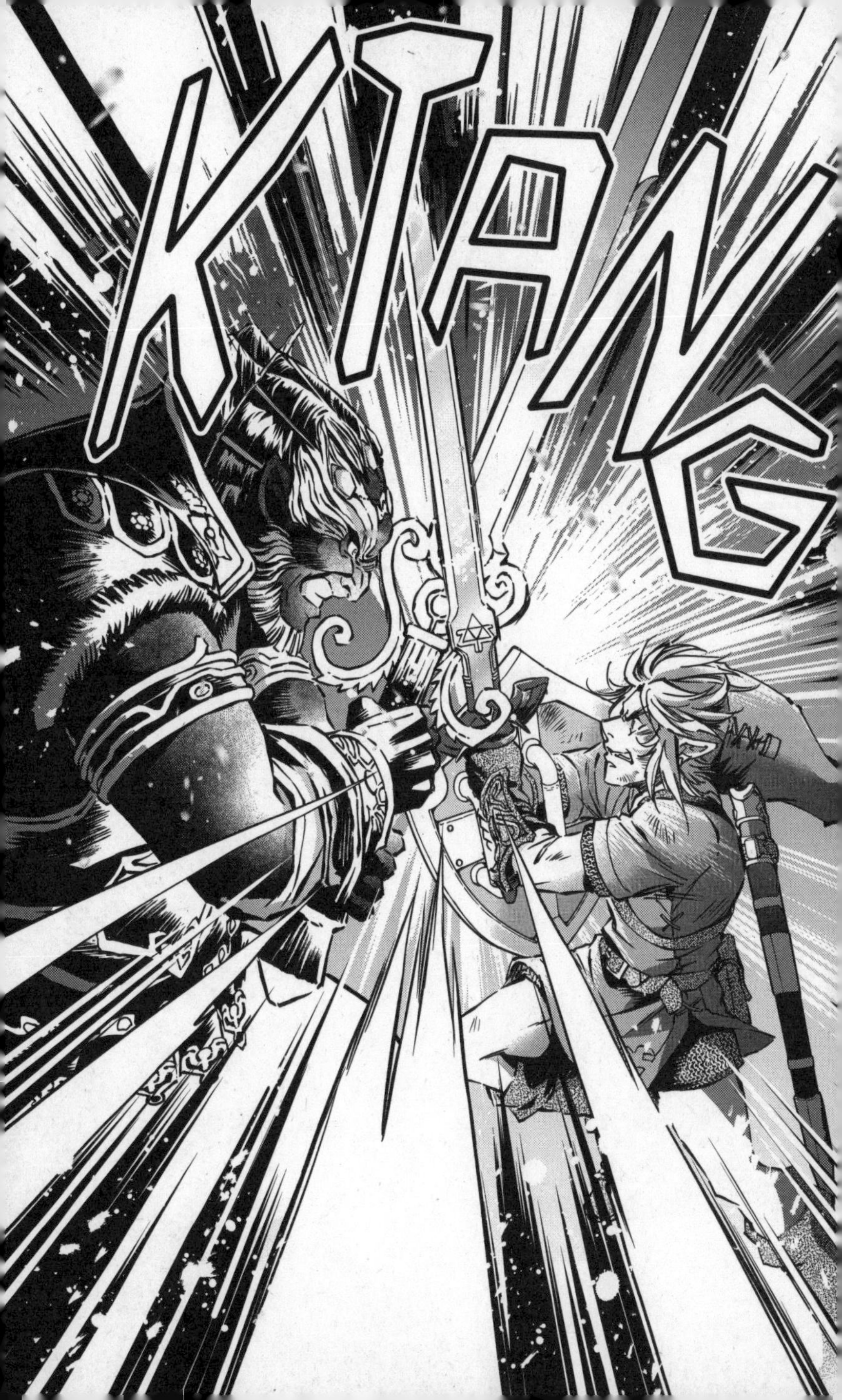
KLANG

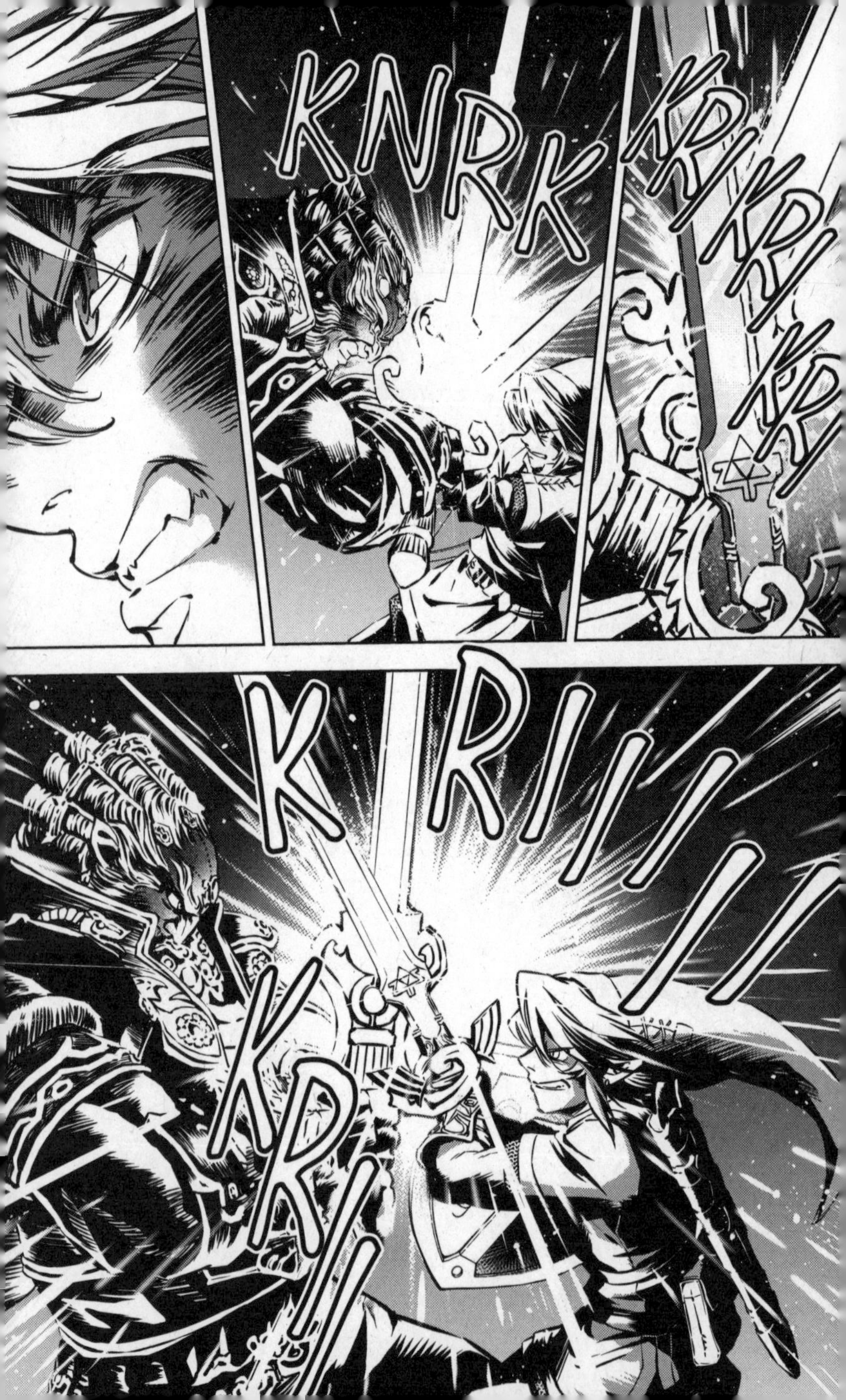
KRI KRI KRI
KNRK
KRIIIIII
KKRII

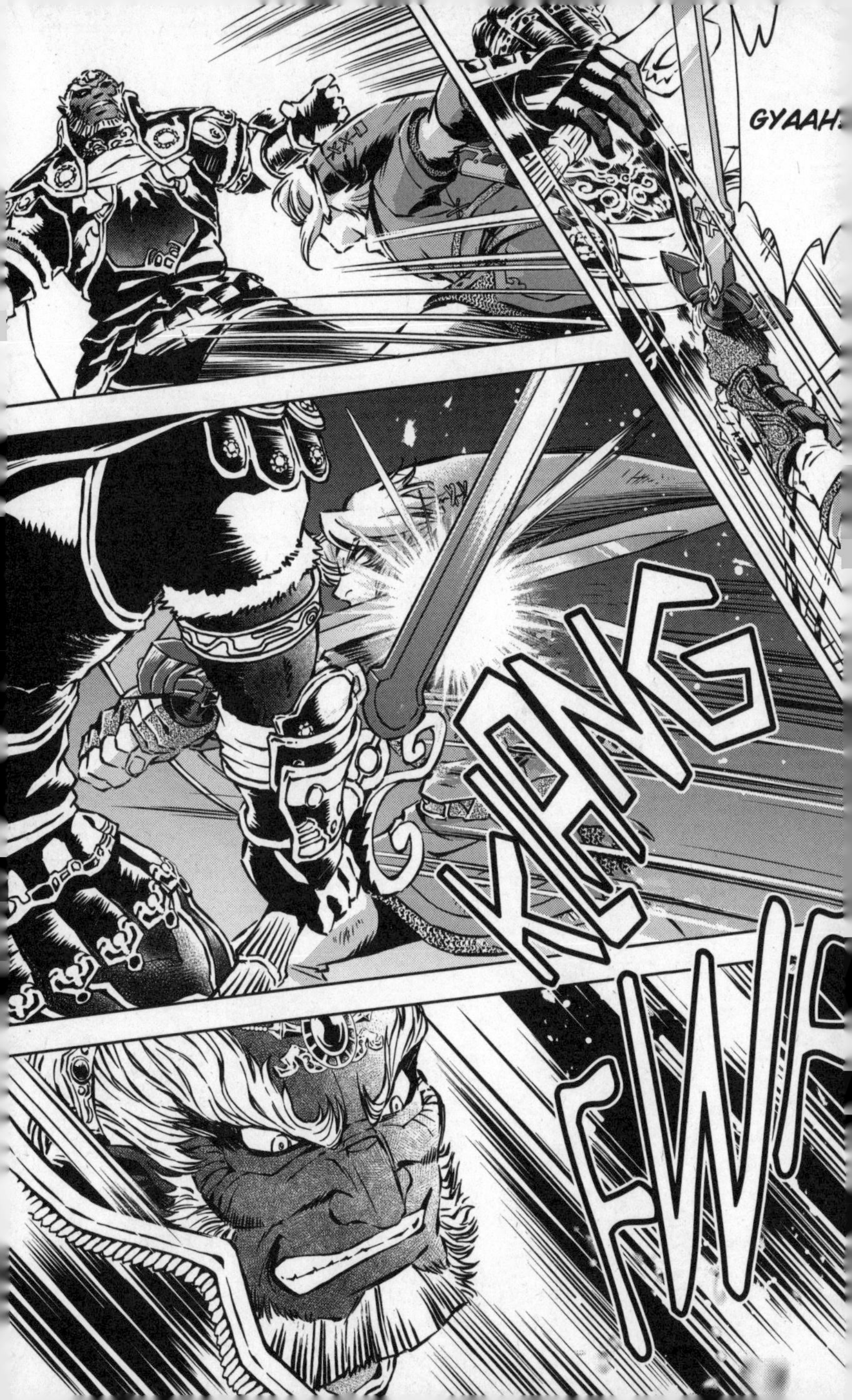
GYAAH!
KLANG

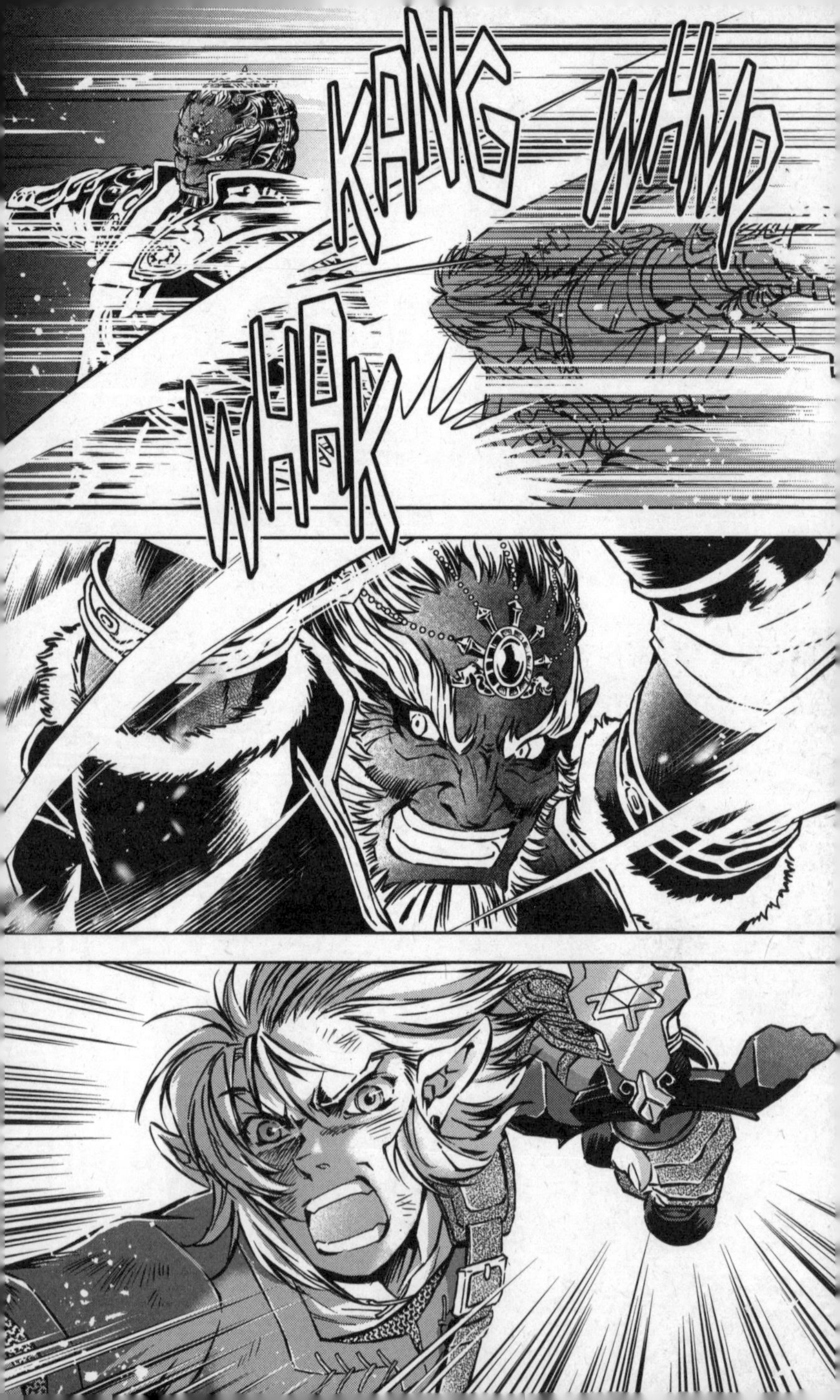
WHMP
KANG
WHAK

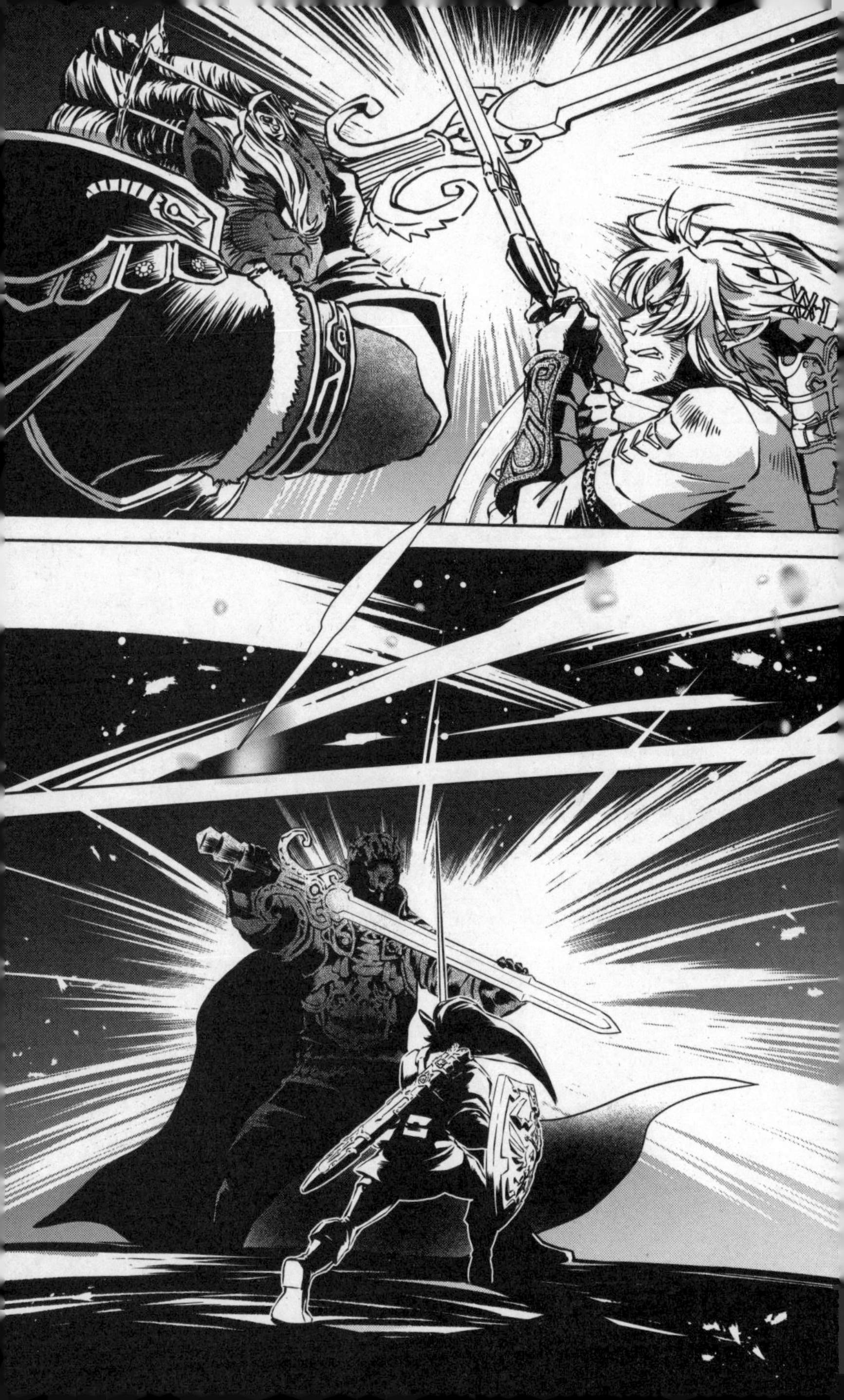

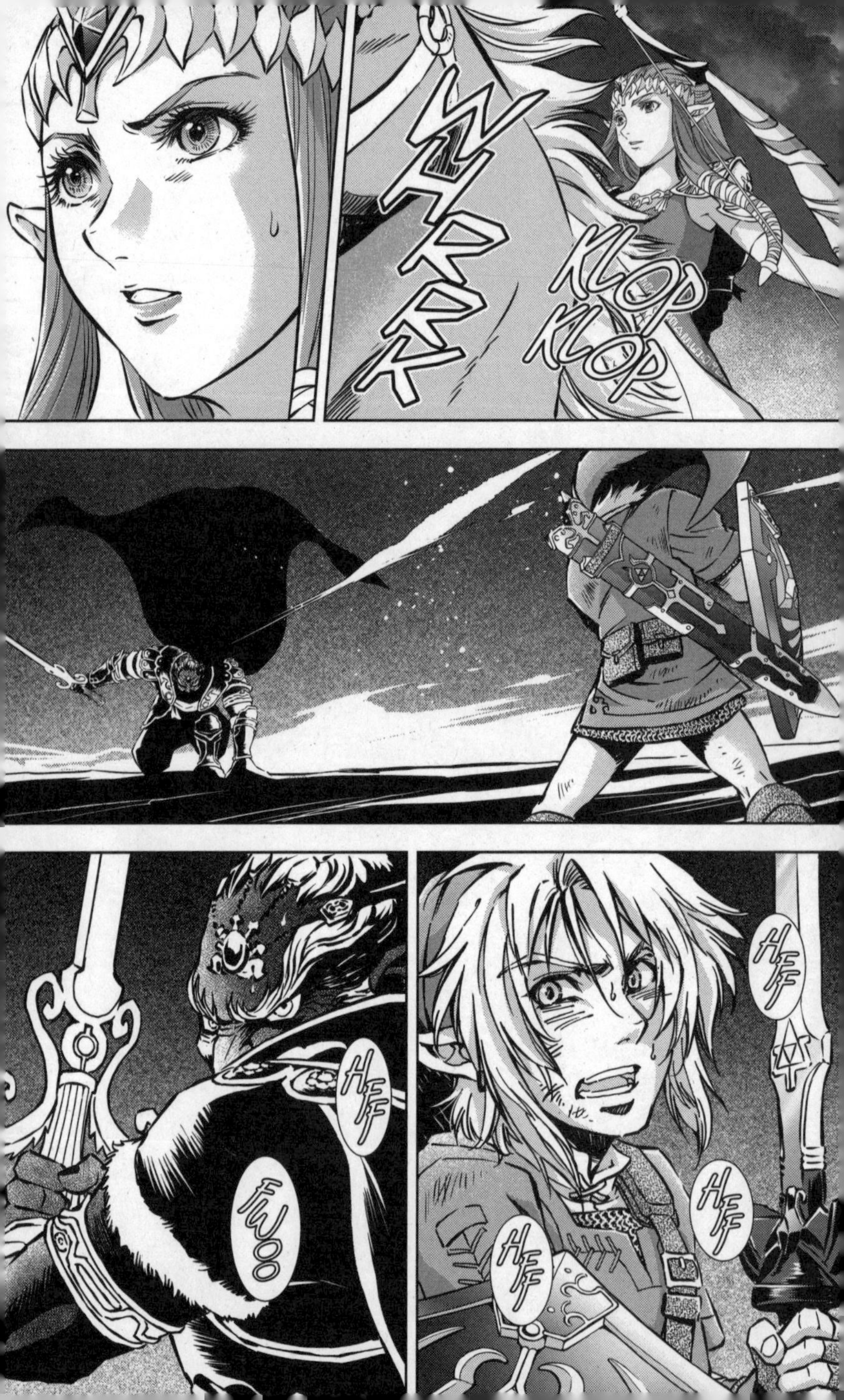

KLOP KLOP
WHRRK
HFF
HFF
HFF
HFF
FWOO

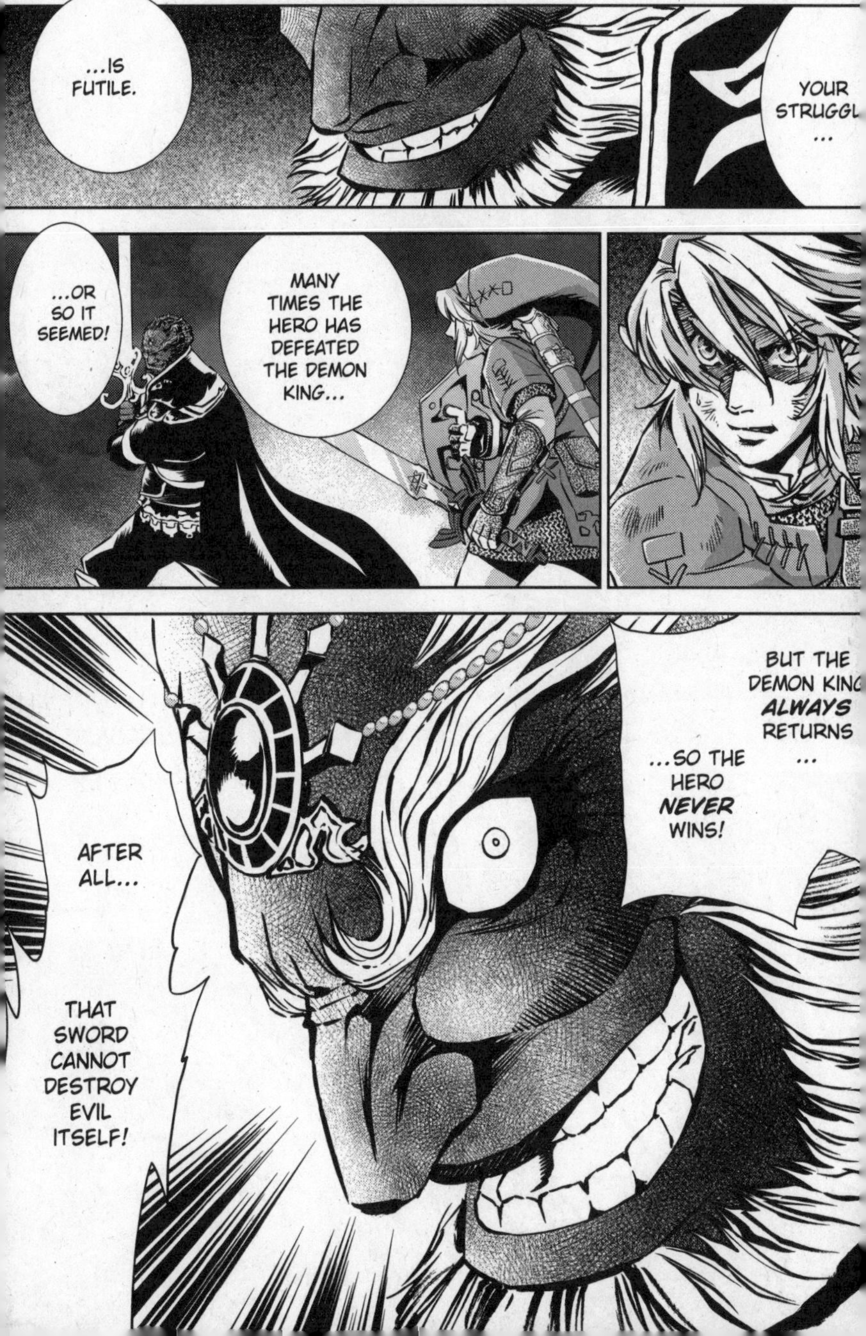
YOUR STRUGGL ...
...IS FUTILE.
MANY TIMES THE HERO HAS DEFEATED THE DEMON KING...
...OR SO IT SEEMED!
BUT THE DEMON KING *ALWAYS* RETURNS ...
...SO THE HERO *NEVER* WINS!
AFTER ALL...
THAT SWORD CANNOT DESTROY EVIL ITSELF!

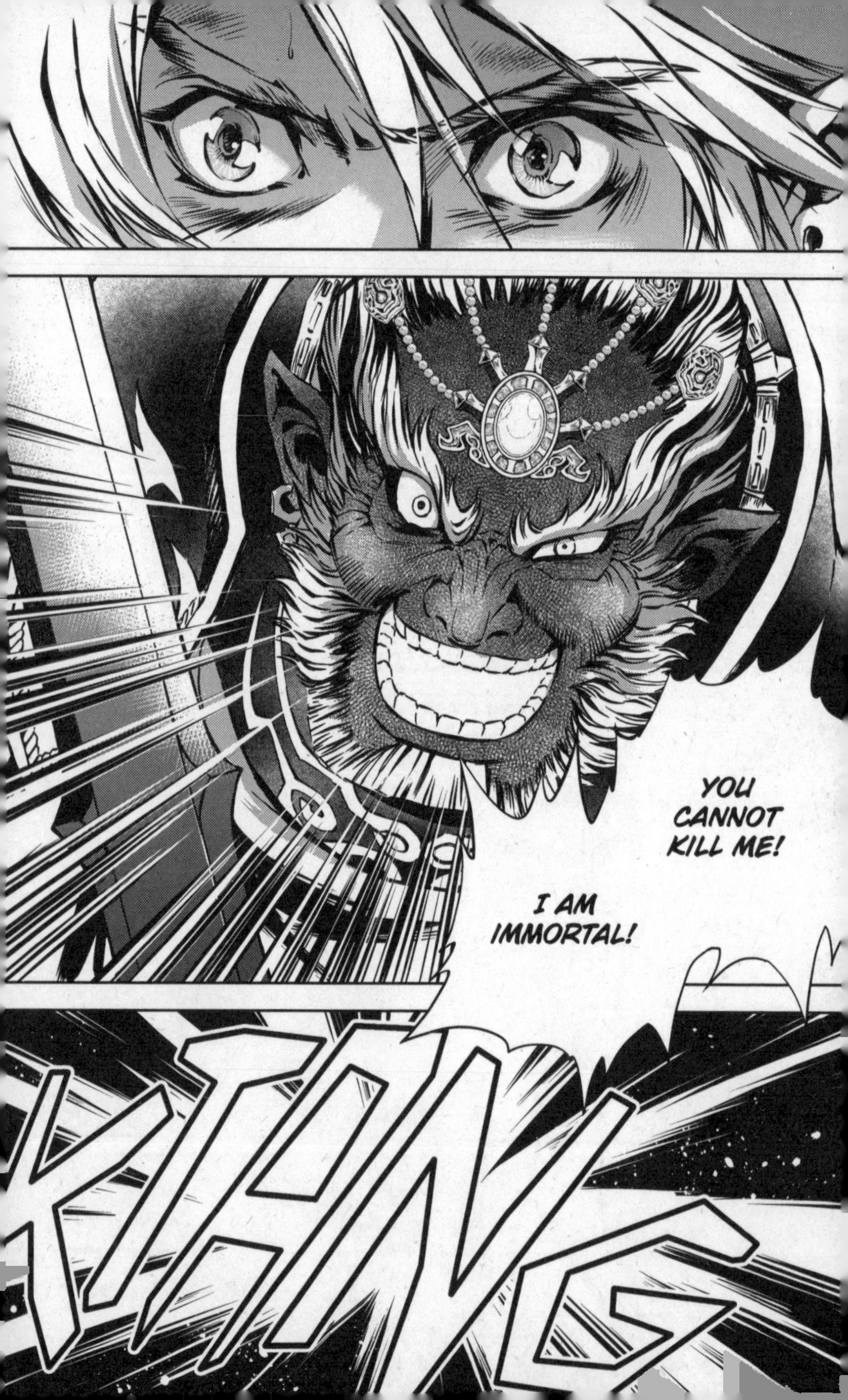
YOU CANNOT KILL ME!
I AM IMMORTAL!
KTHNG

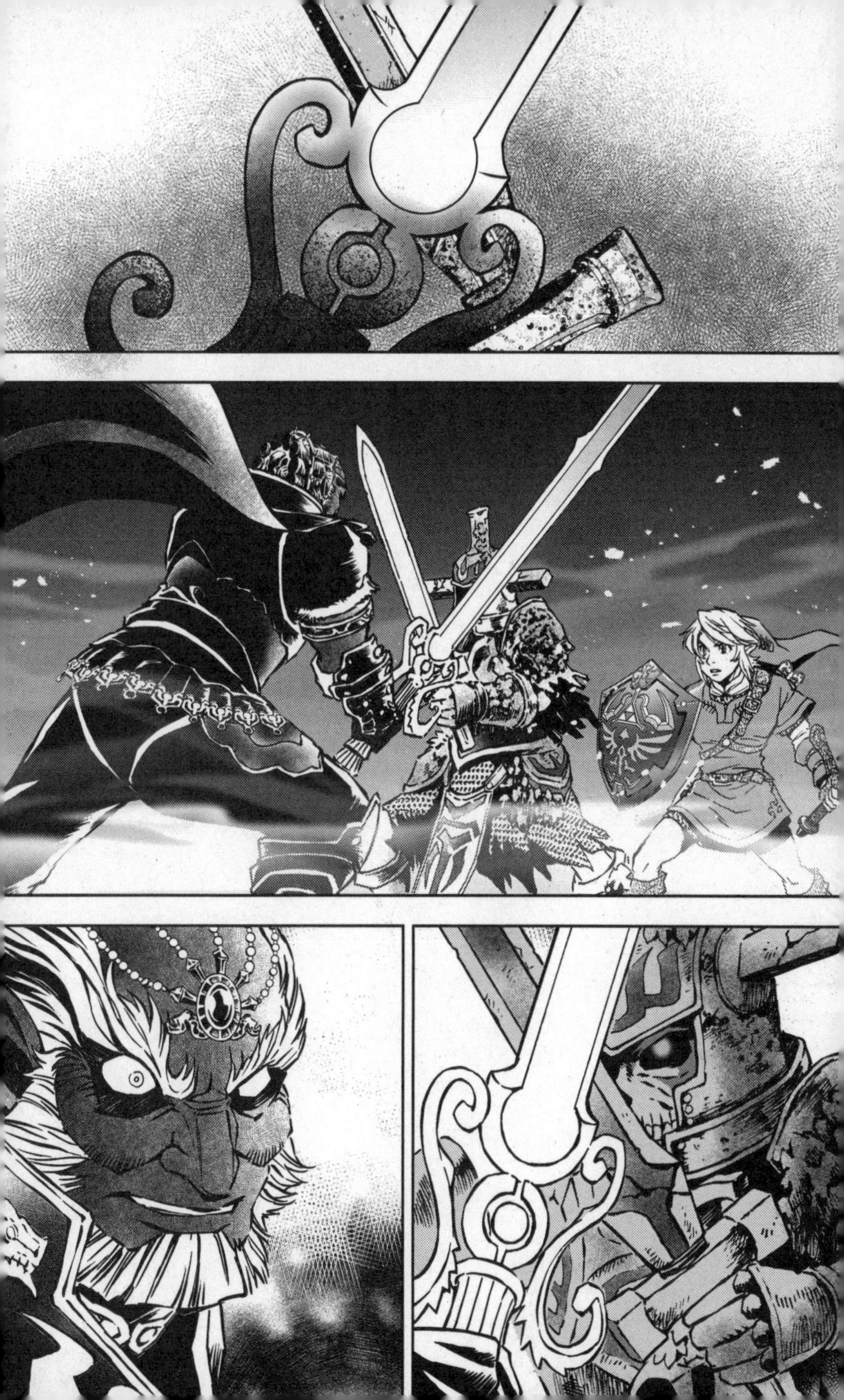

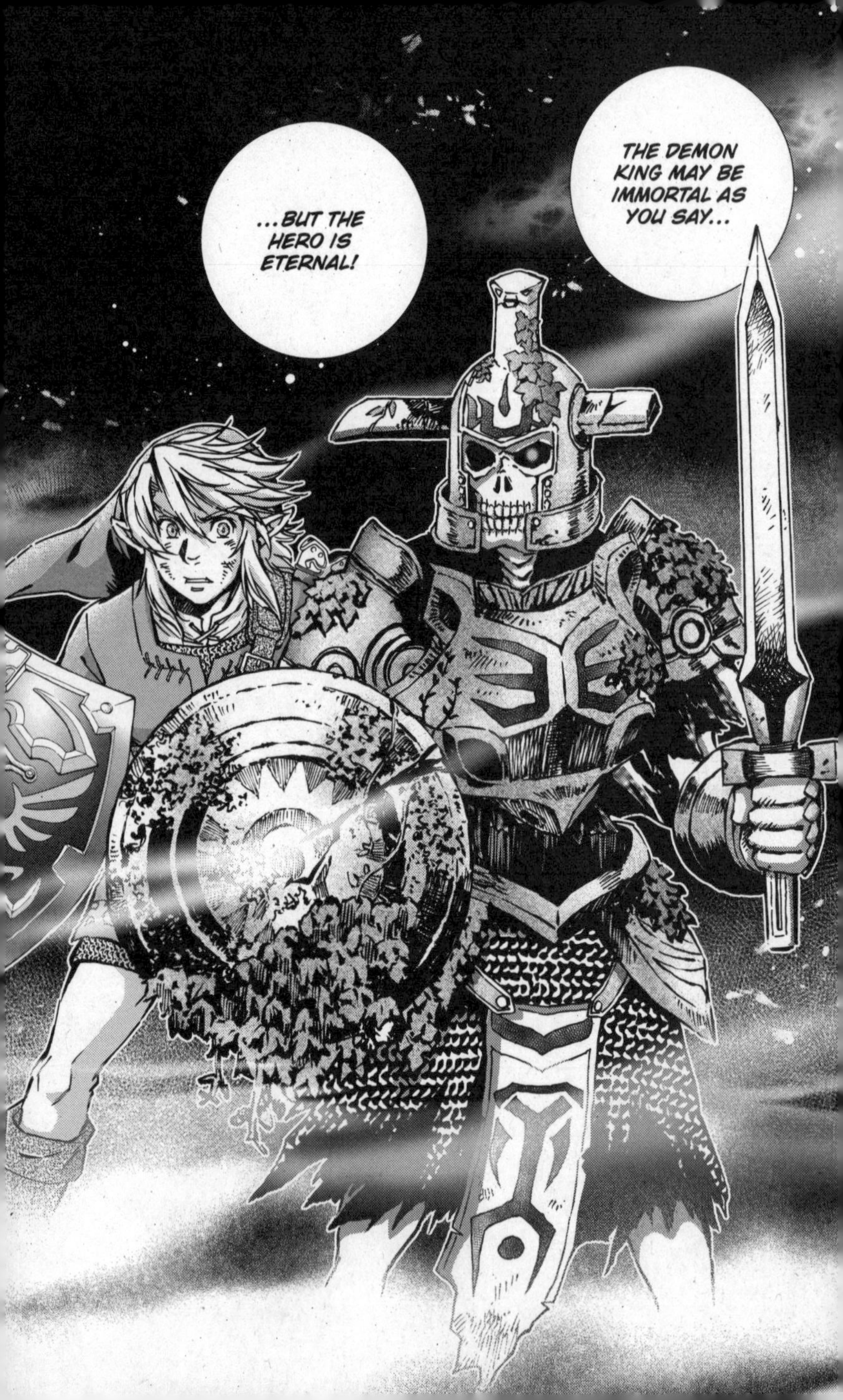
THE DEMON KING MAY BE IMMORTAL AS YOU SAY...
...BUT THE HERO IS ETERNAL!

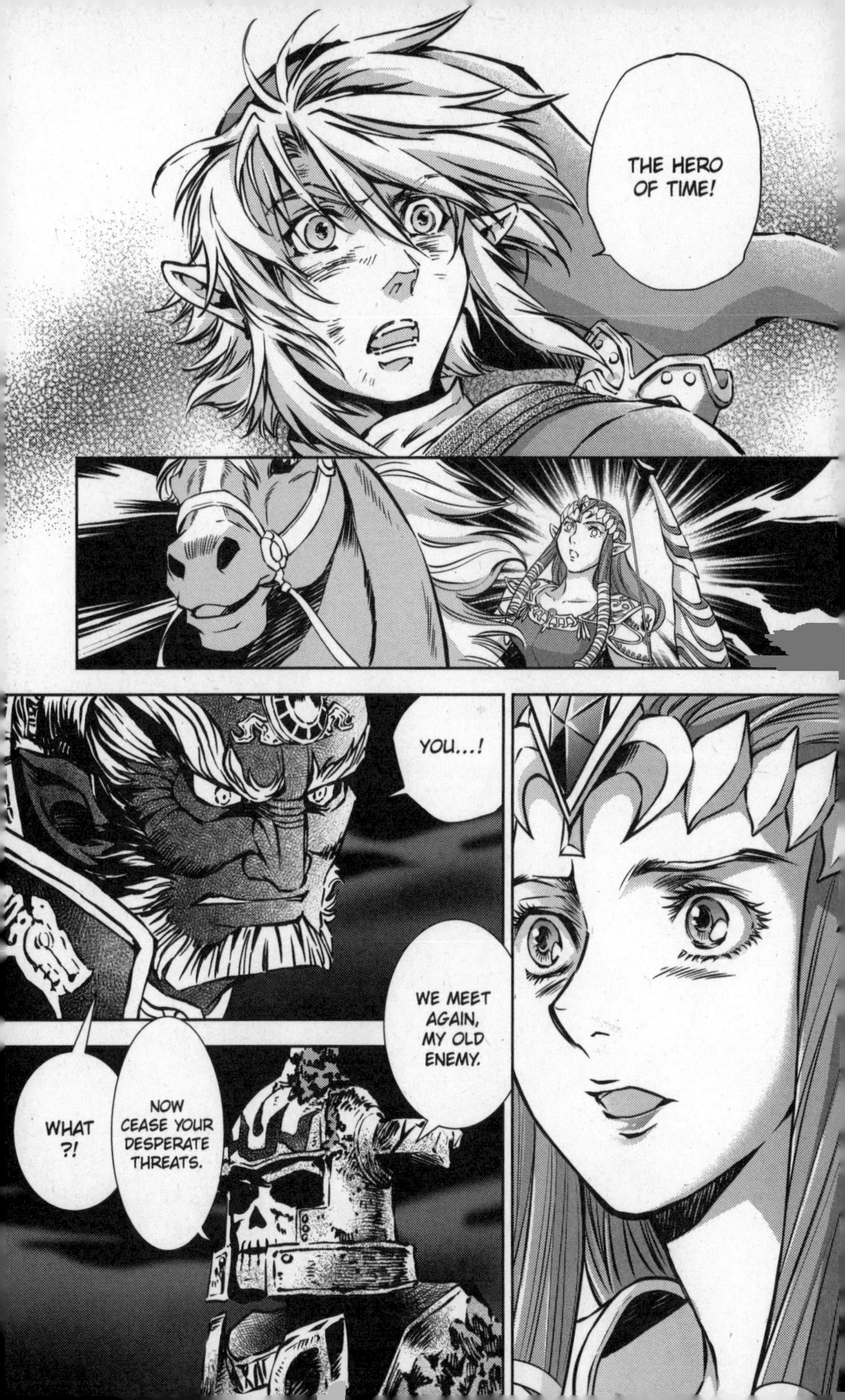
THE HERO OF TIME!
YOU...!
WE MEET AGAIN, MY OLD ENEMY.
NOW CEASE YOUR DESPERATE THREATS.
WHAT?!

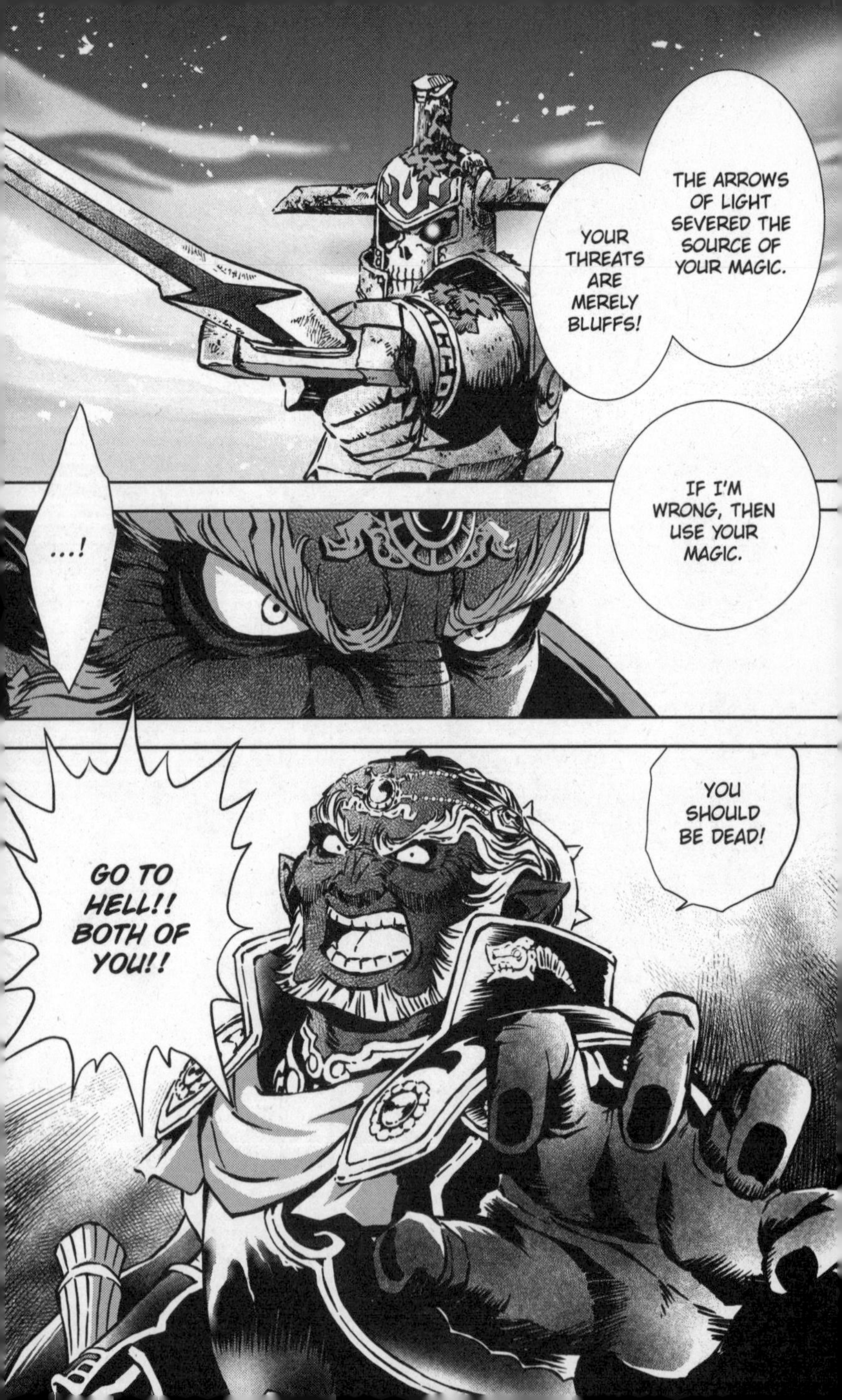
THE ARROWS OF LIGHT SEVERED THE SOURCE OF YOUR MAGIC.
YOUR THREATS ARE MERELY BLUFFS!
IF I'M WRONG, THEN USE YOUR MAGIC.
...!
YOU SHOULD BE DEAD!
GO TO HELL!! BOTH OF YOU!!

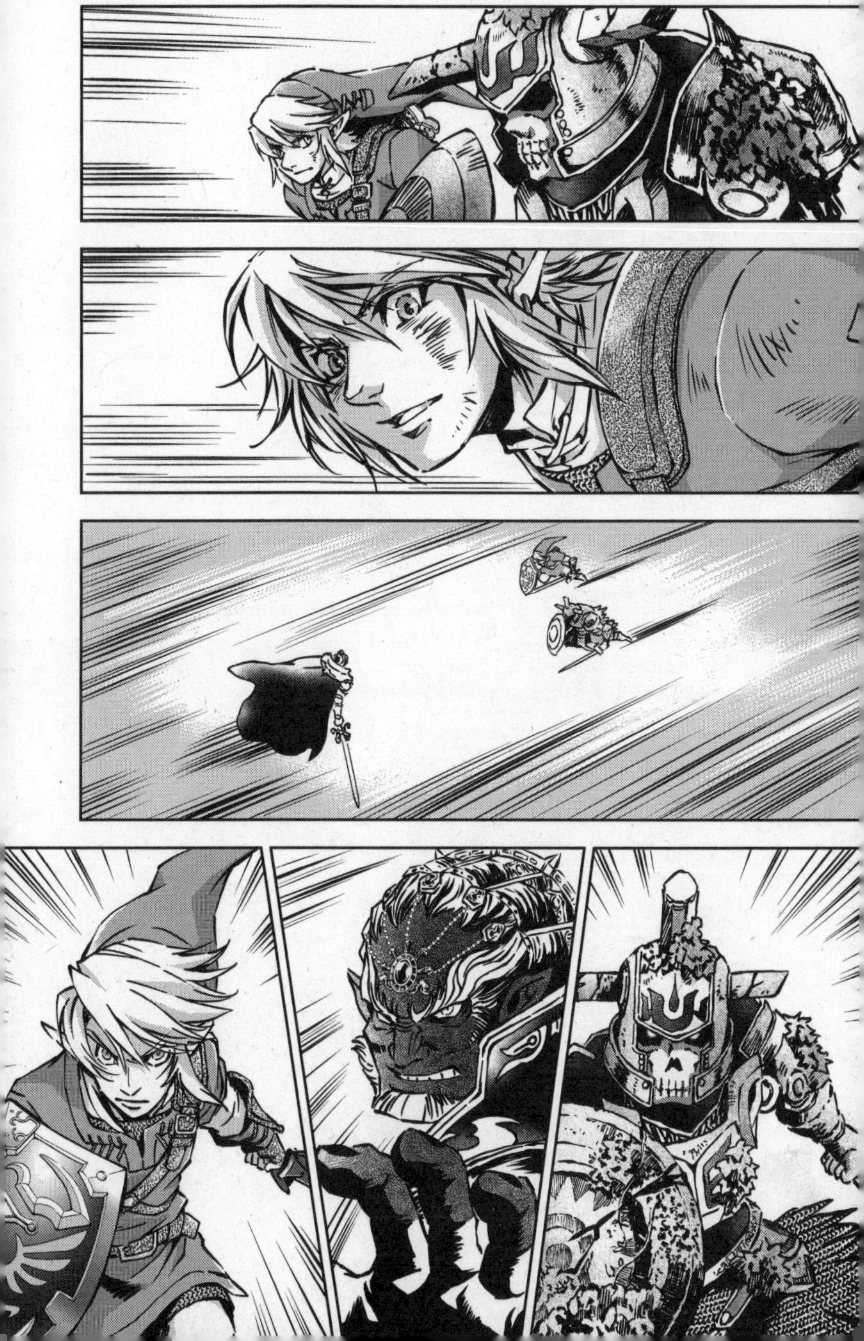

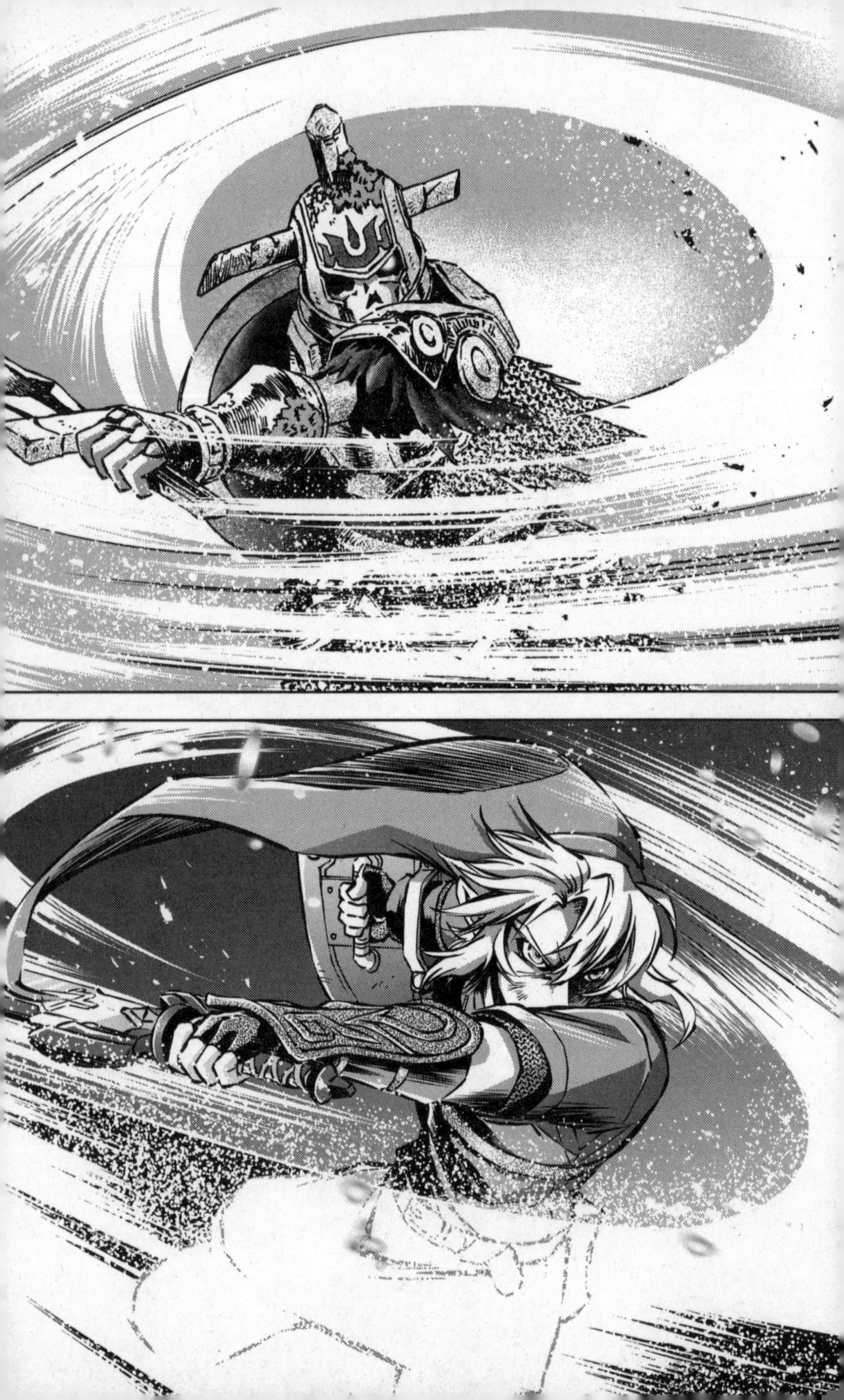

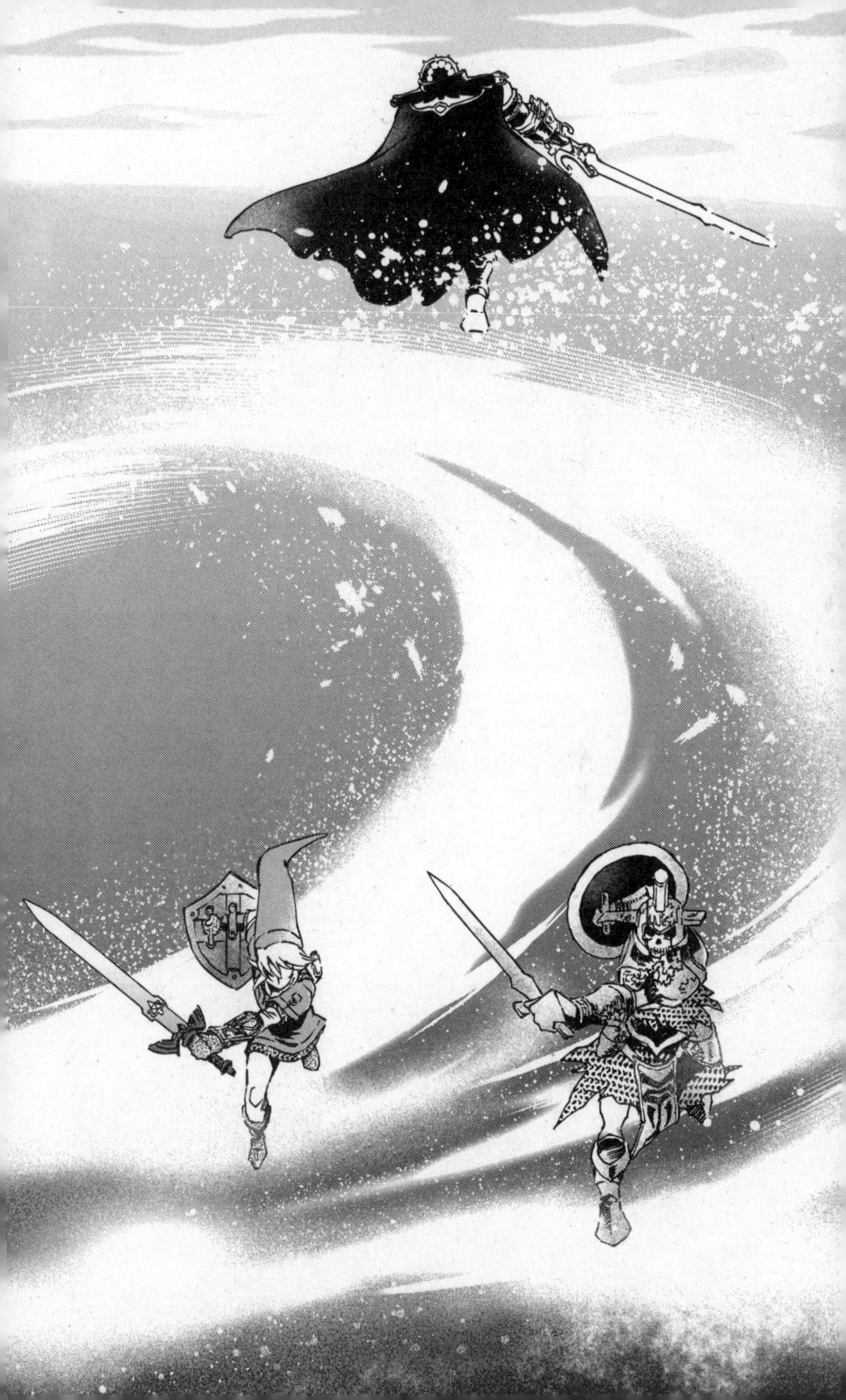

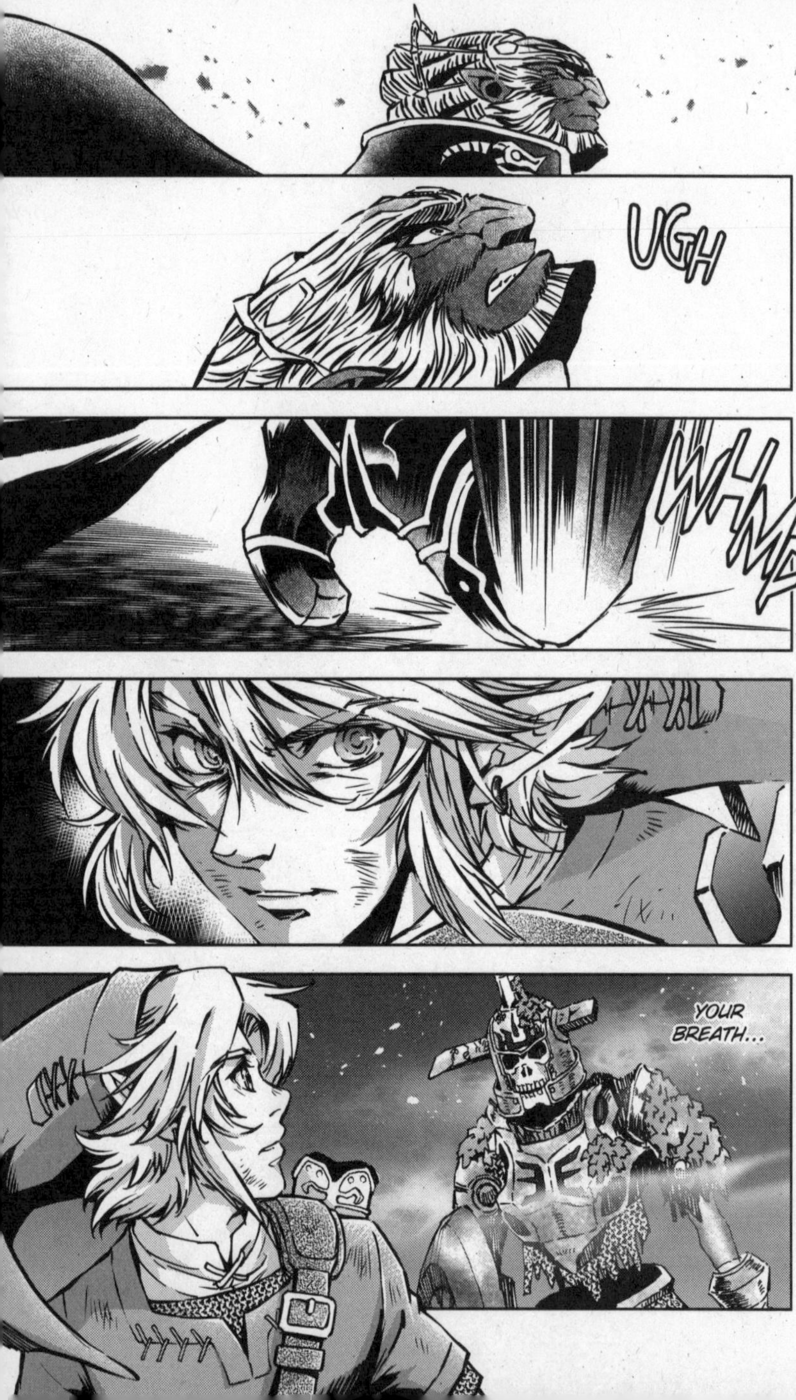
UGH
WHMP
YOUR BREATH...

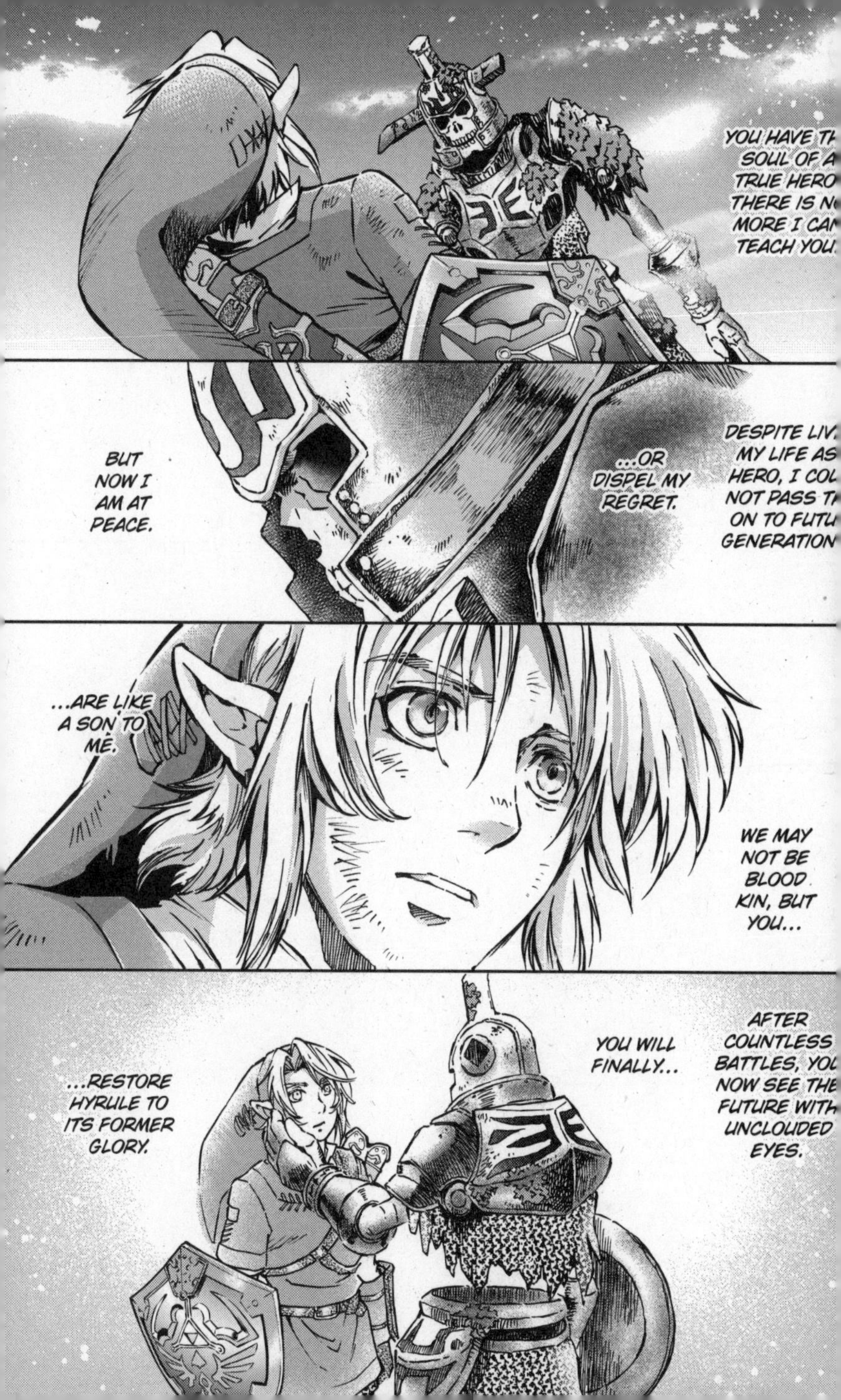
YOU HAVE TH SOUL OF A TRUE HERO THERE IS N MORE I CAN TEACH YOU.
DESPITE LIV MY LIFE AS HERO, I COL NOT PASS T ON TO FUTU GENERATION
...OR DISPEL MY REGRET.
BUT NOW I AM AT PEACE.
WE MAY NOT BE BLOOD KIN, BUT YOU...
...ARE LIKE A SON TO ME.
AFTER COUNTLESS BATTLES, YO NOW SEE THE FUTURE WITH UNCLOUDED EYES.
YOU WILL FINALLY...
...RESTORE HYRULE TO ITS FORMER GLORY.

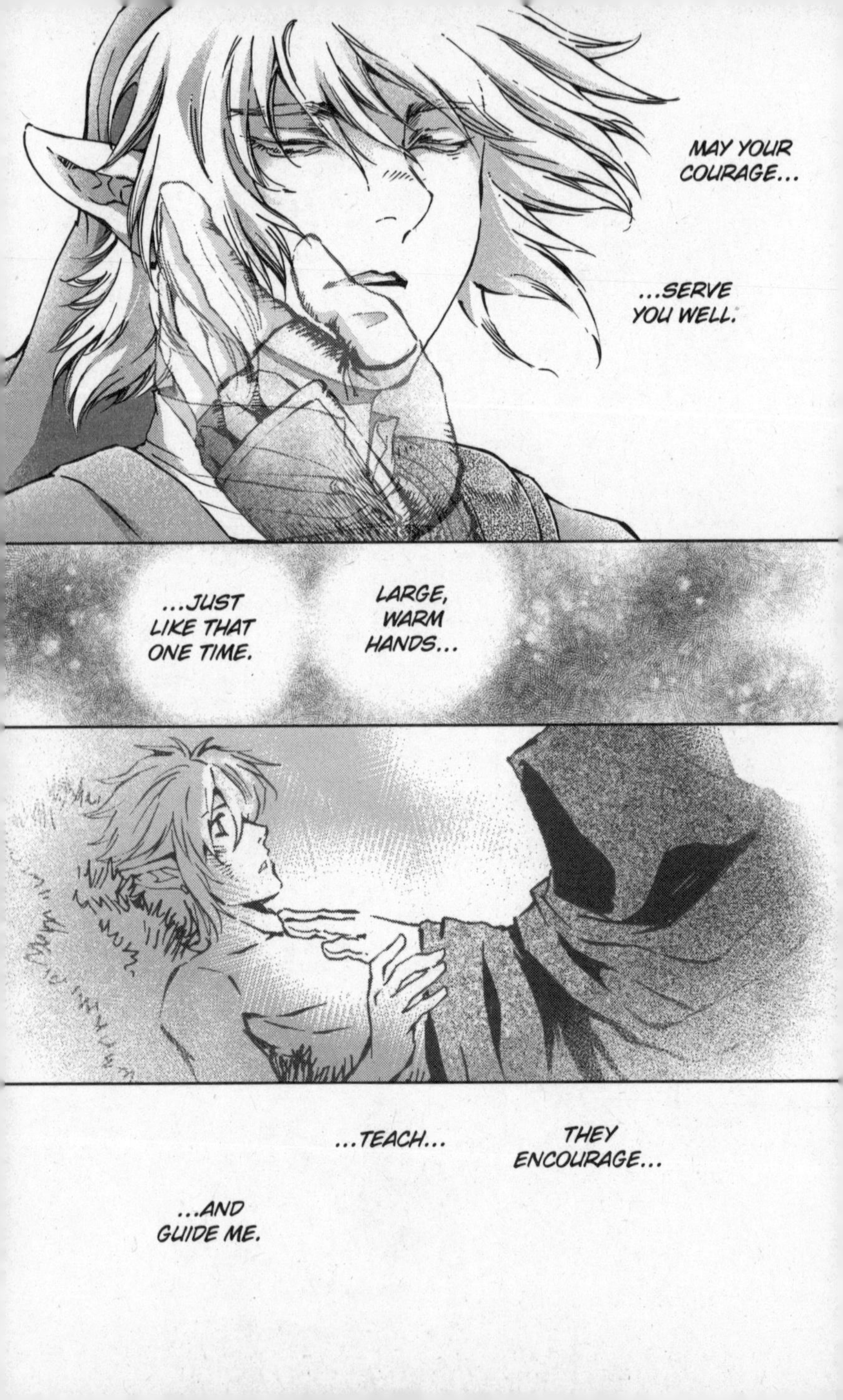
MAY YOUR COURAGE...
...SERVE YOU WELL.
LARGE, WARM HANDS...
...JUST LIKE THAT ONE TIME.
THEY ENCOURAGE...
...TEACH...
...AND GUIDE ME.

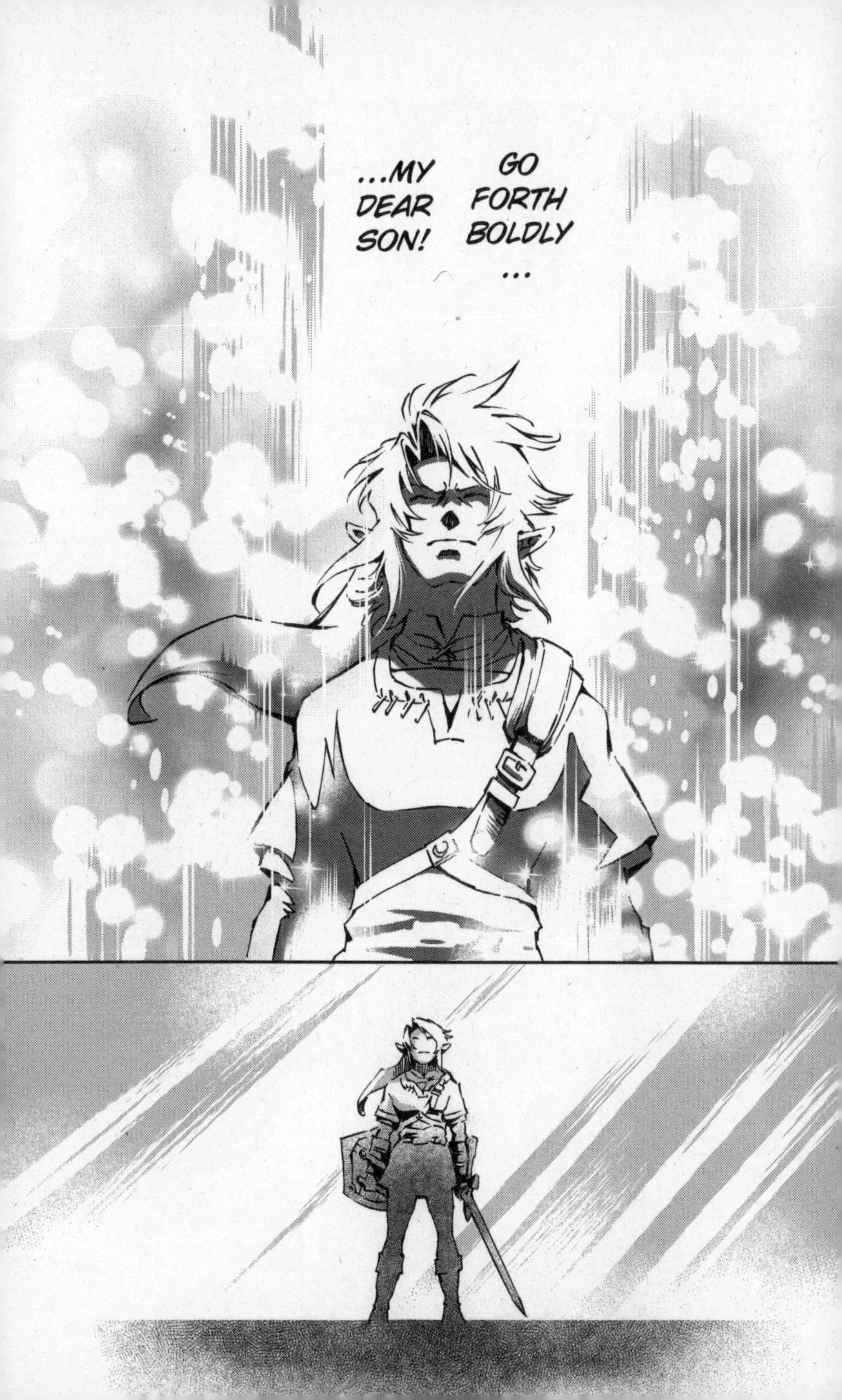
GO FORTH BOLDLY ...
...MY DEAR SON!

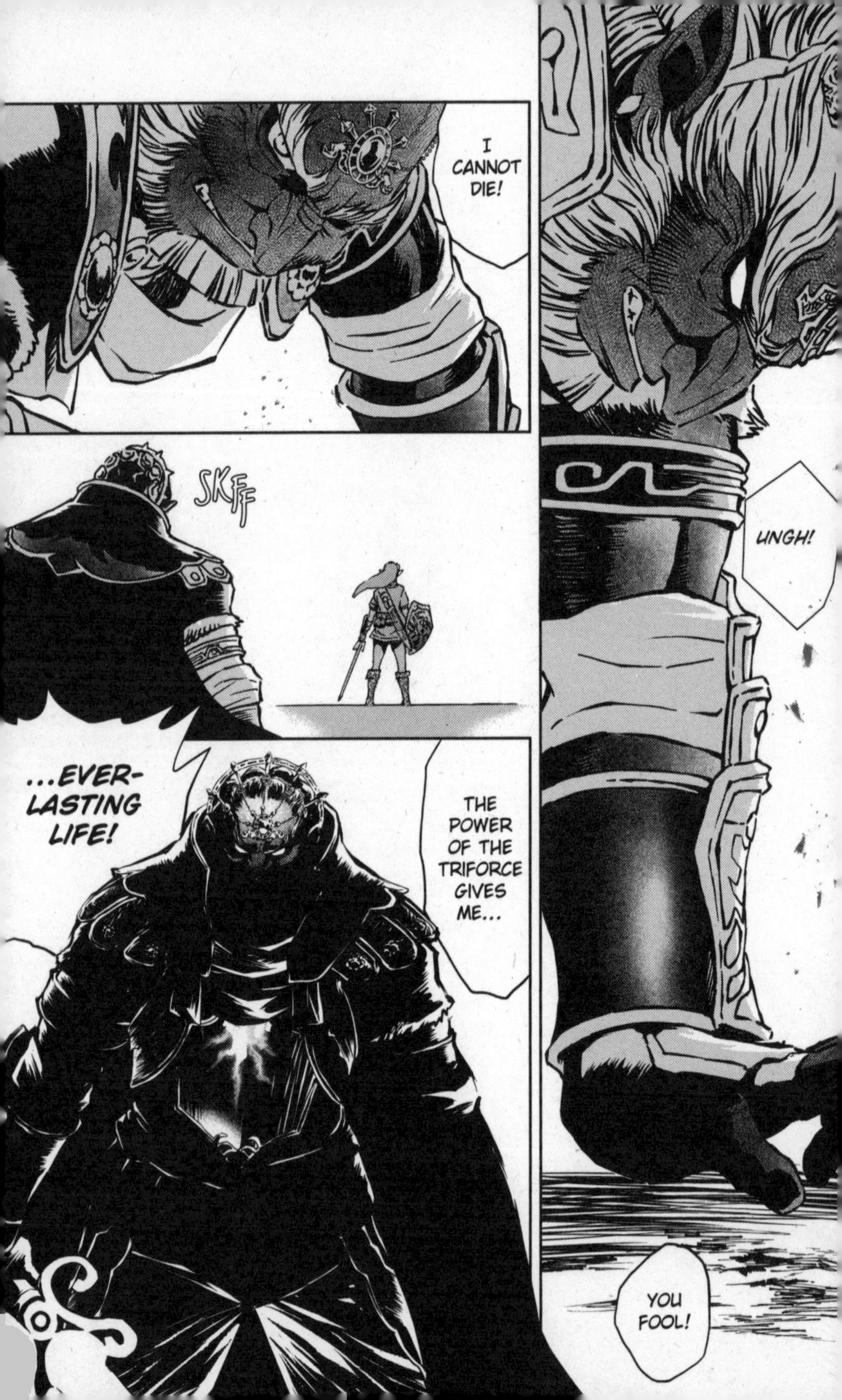
UNGH!
YOU FOOL!
I CANNOT DIE!
SKFF
THE POWER OF THE TRIFORCE GIVES ME...
...EVER-LASTING LIFE!

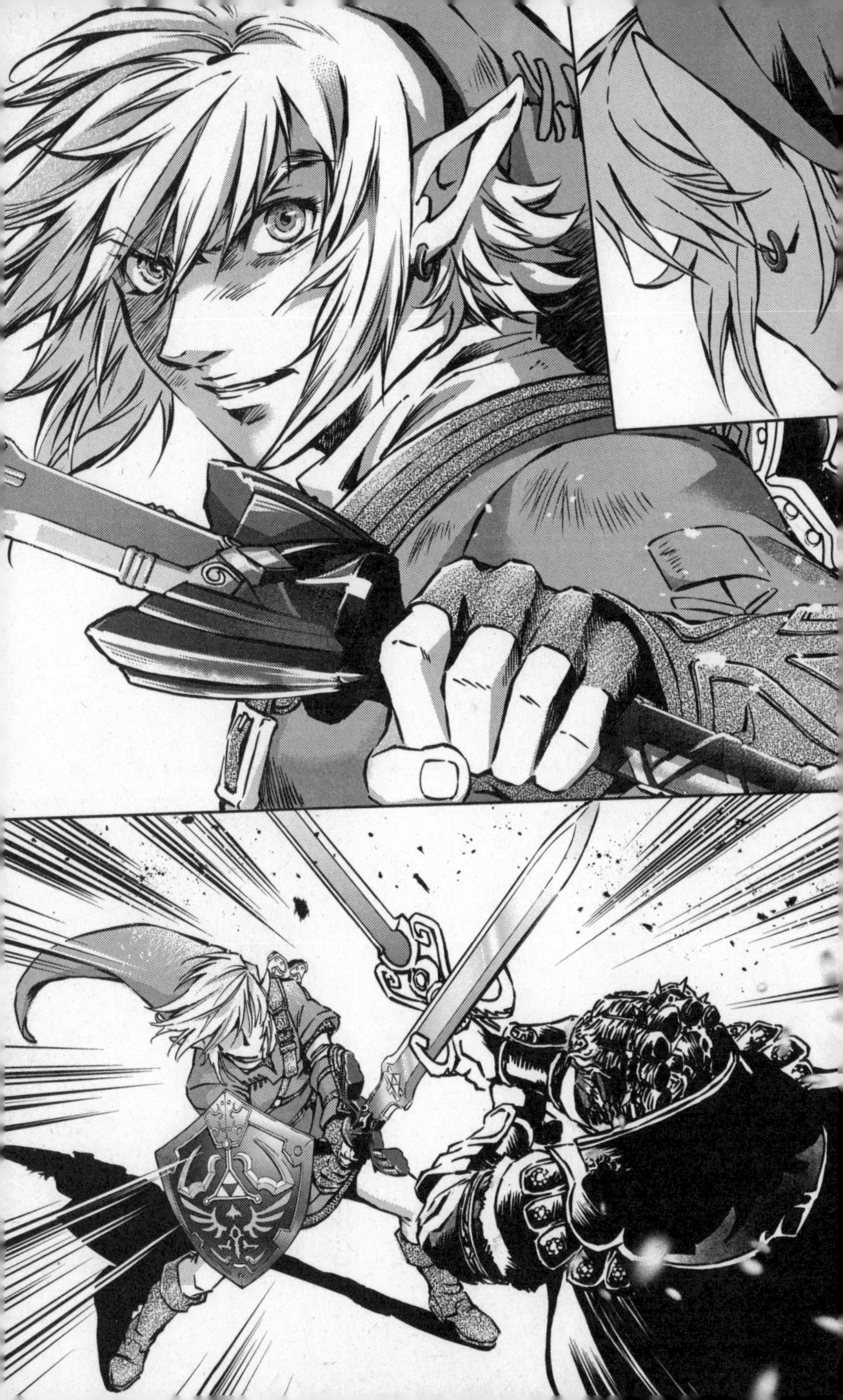

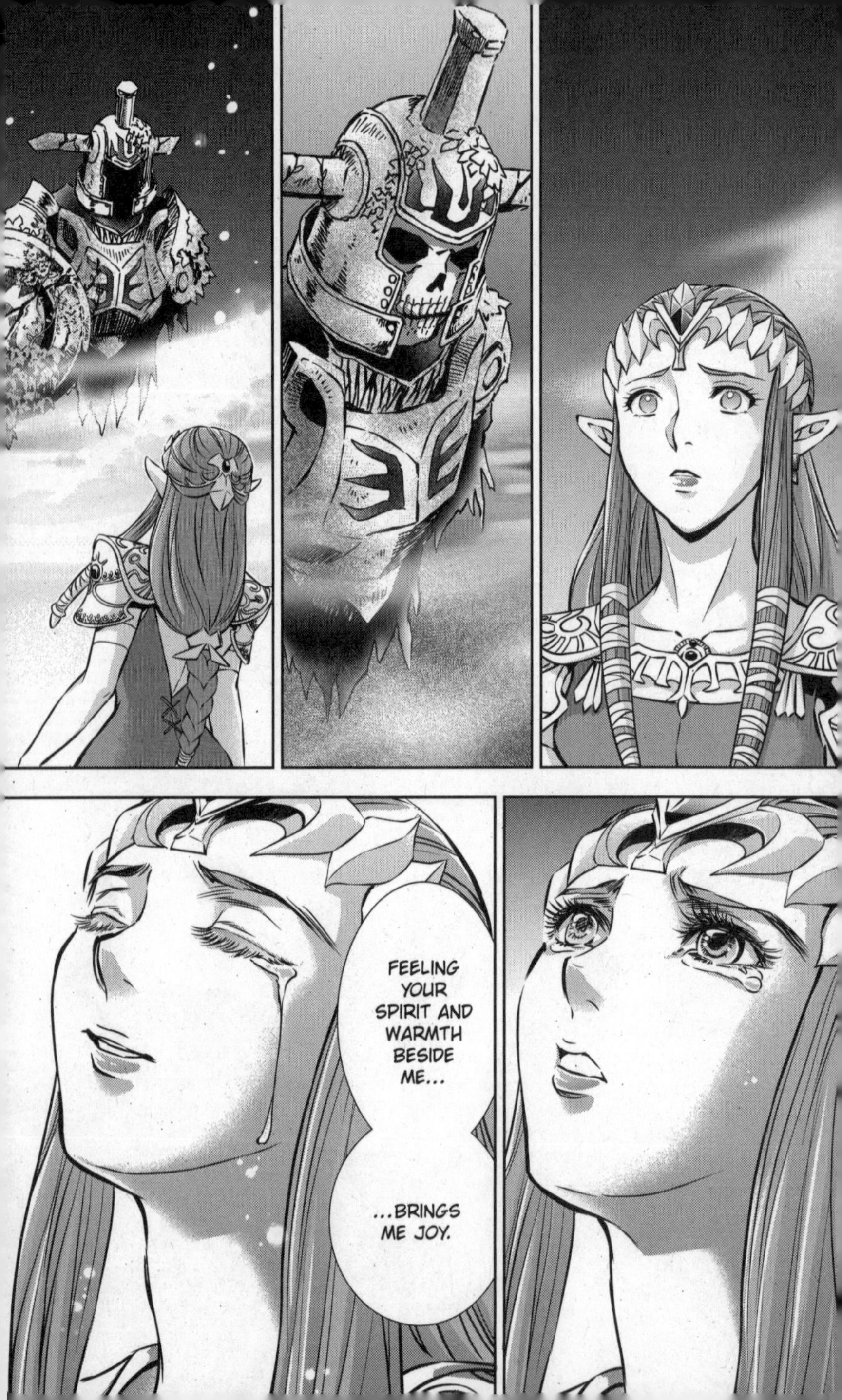
FEELING YOUR SPIRIT AND WARMTH BESIDE ME...
...BRINGS ME JOY.

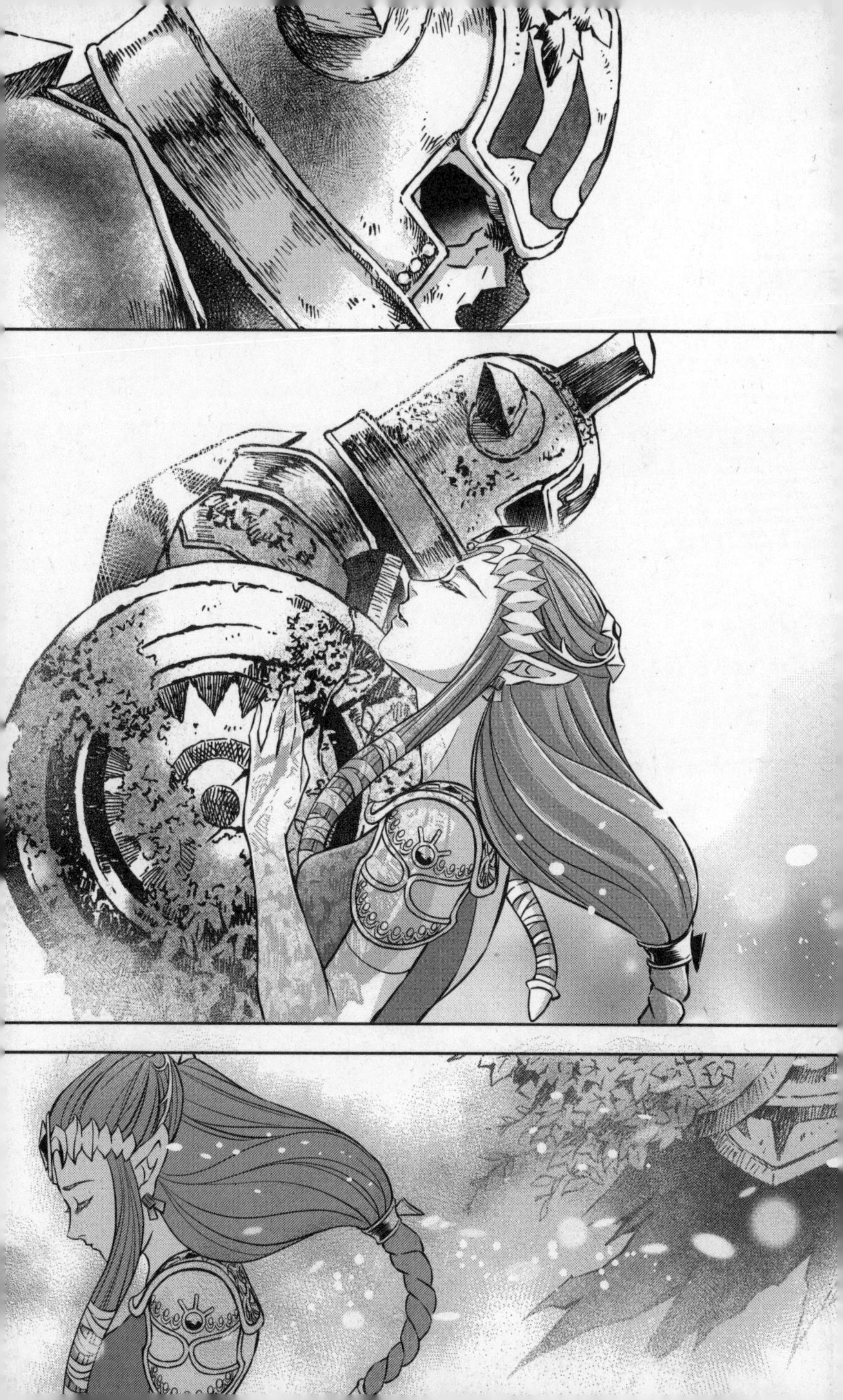

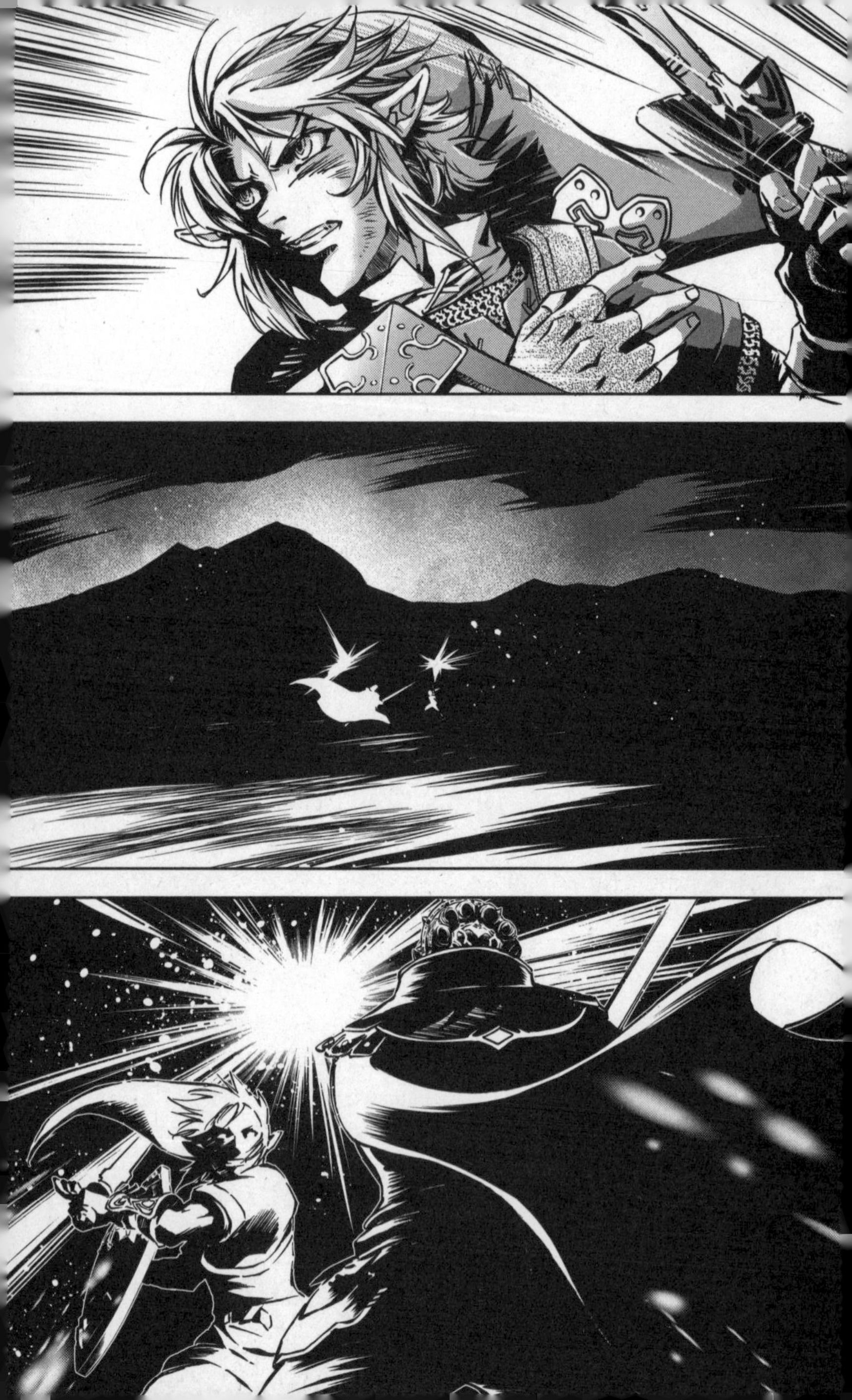

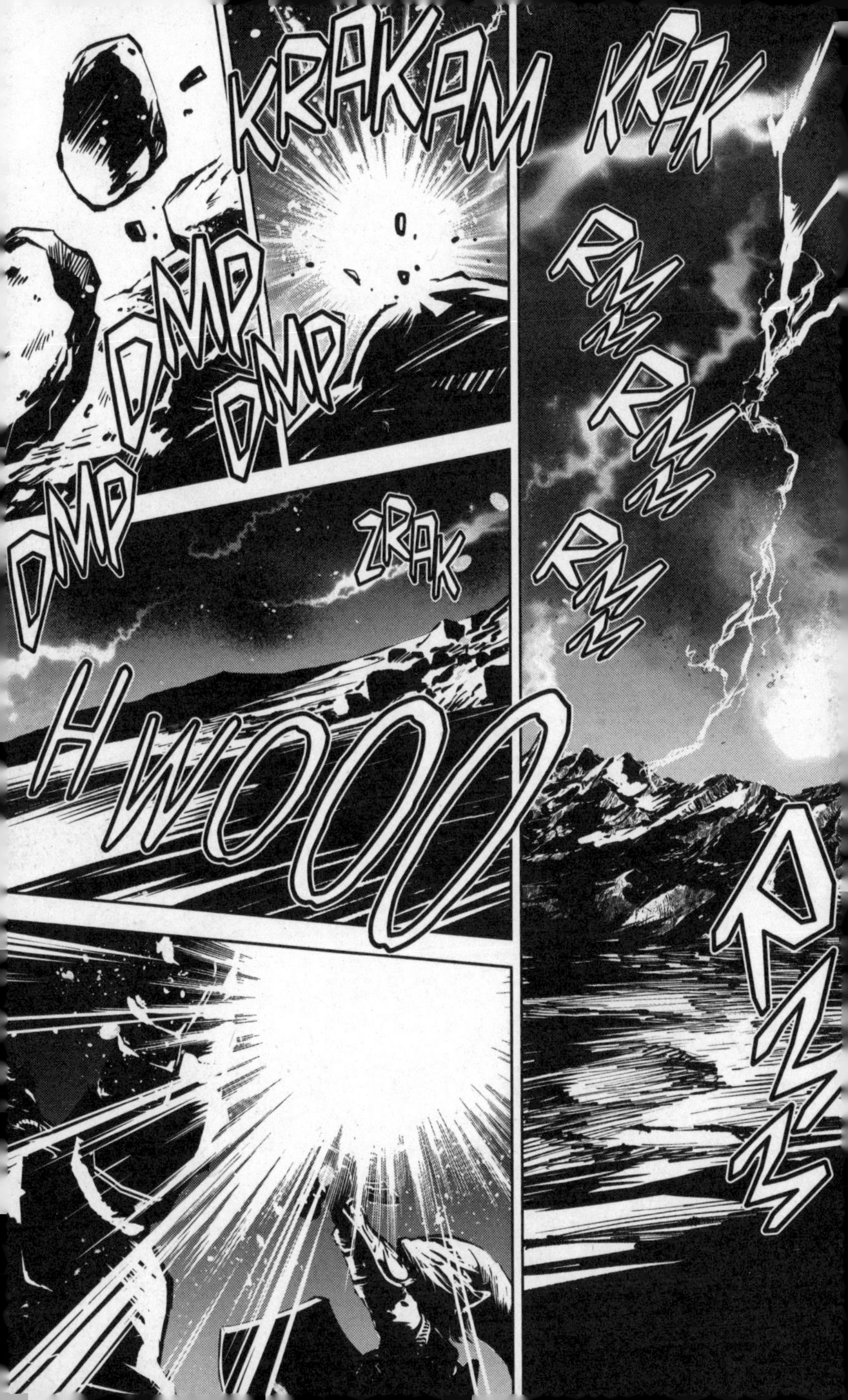
KRAK
RMMMRMMM
RMM
KRAKAM
DMP DMP DMP DMP
ZRAK
HWOOO

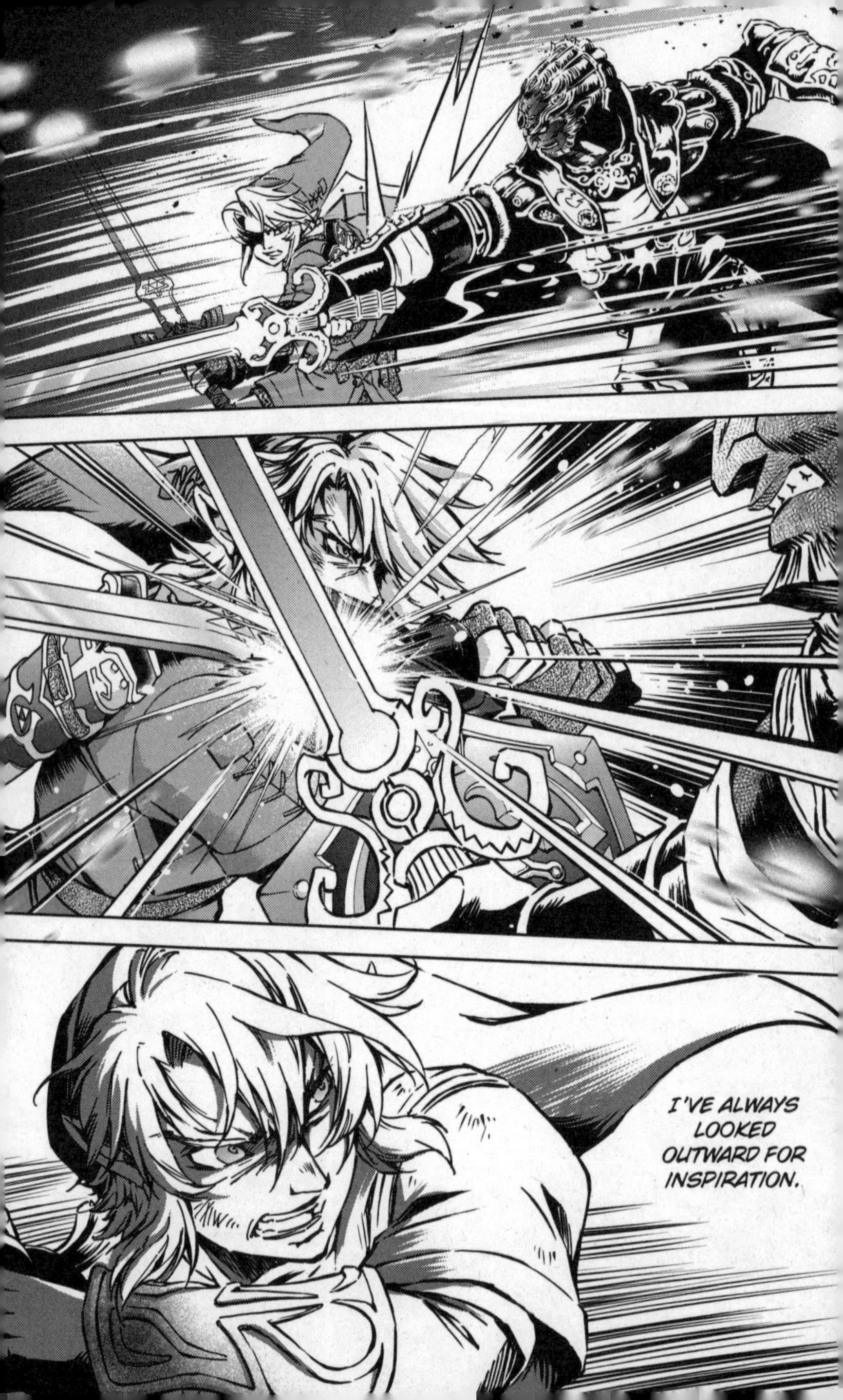
I'VE ALWAYS LOOKED OUTWARD FOR INSPIRATION.

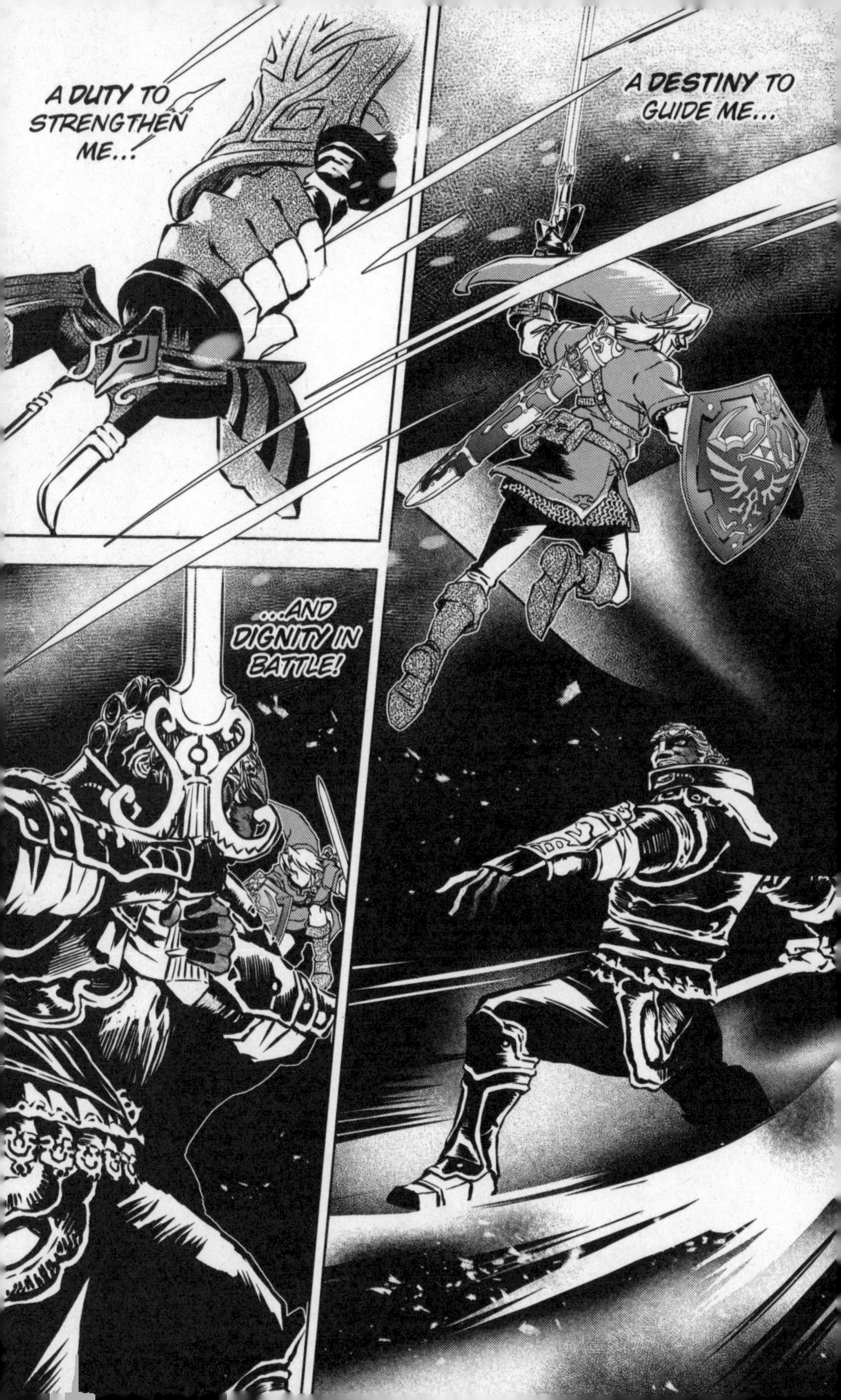
A DESTINY TO GUIDE ME...
A DUTY TO STRENGTHEN ME..!
...AND DIGNITY IN BATTLE!

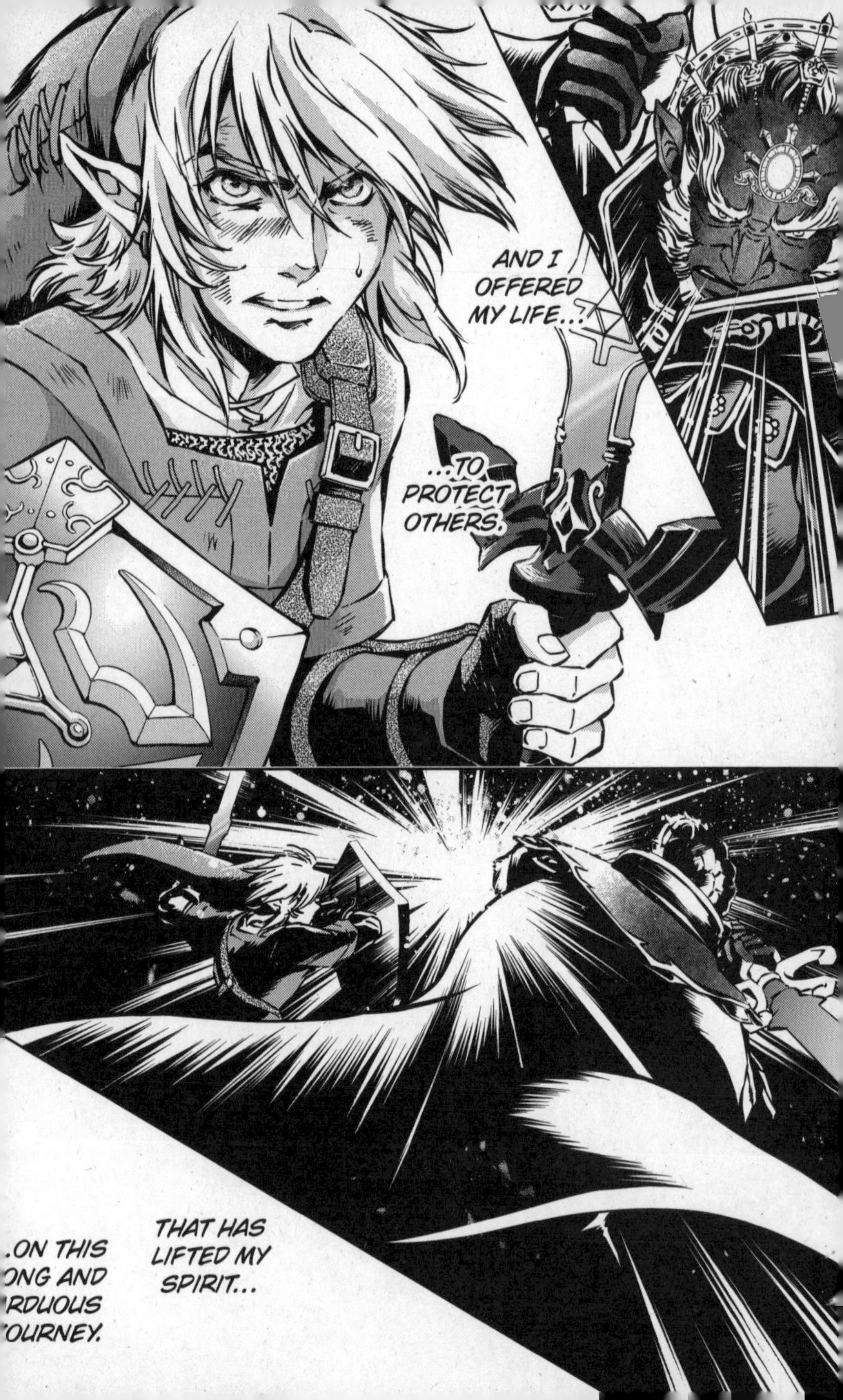
AND I OFFERED MY LIFE...?
...TO PROTECT OTHERS.
THAT HAS LIFTED MY SPIRIT...
.ON THIS ONG AND RDUOUS OURNEY.

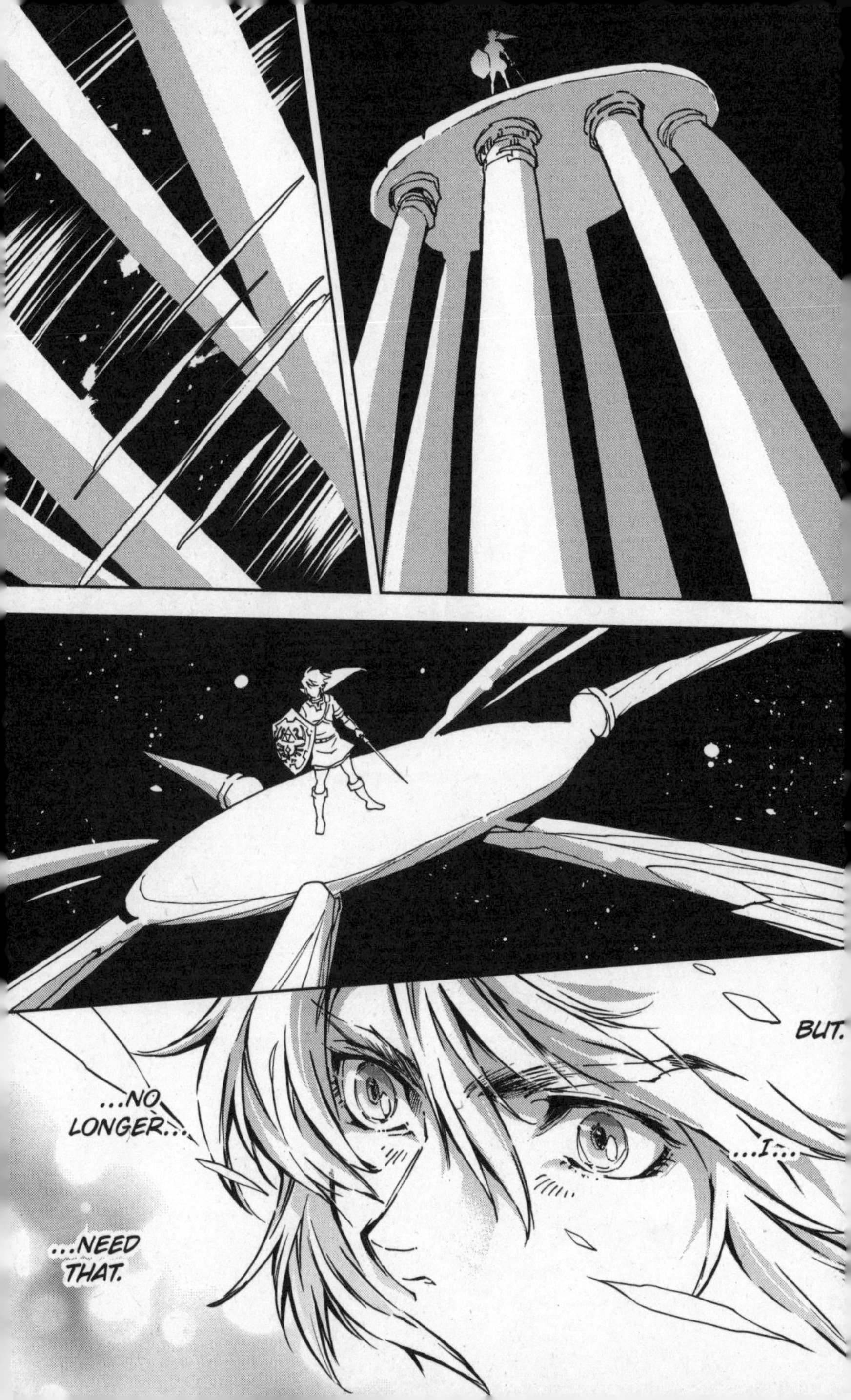
BUT.
...I...
...NO LONGER...
...NEED THAT.

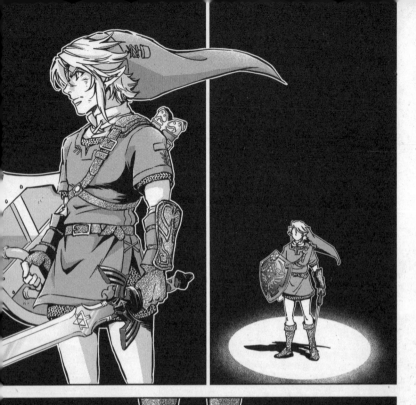

PERHAPS THIS IS WHAT IT MEANS...
...TO FIND YOUR TRUE SELF.
TO STAND ON YOUR OWN...
...TWO FEET.

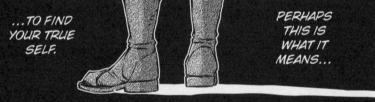

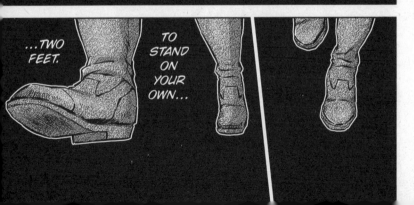

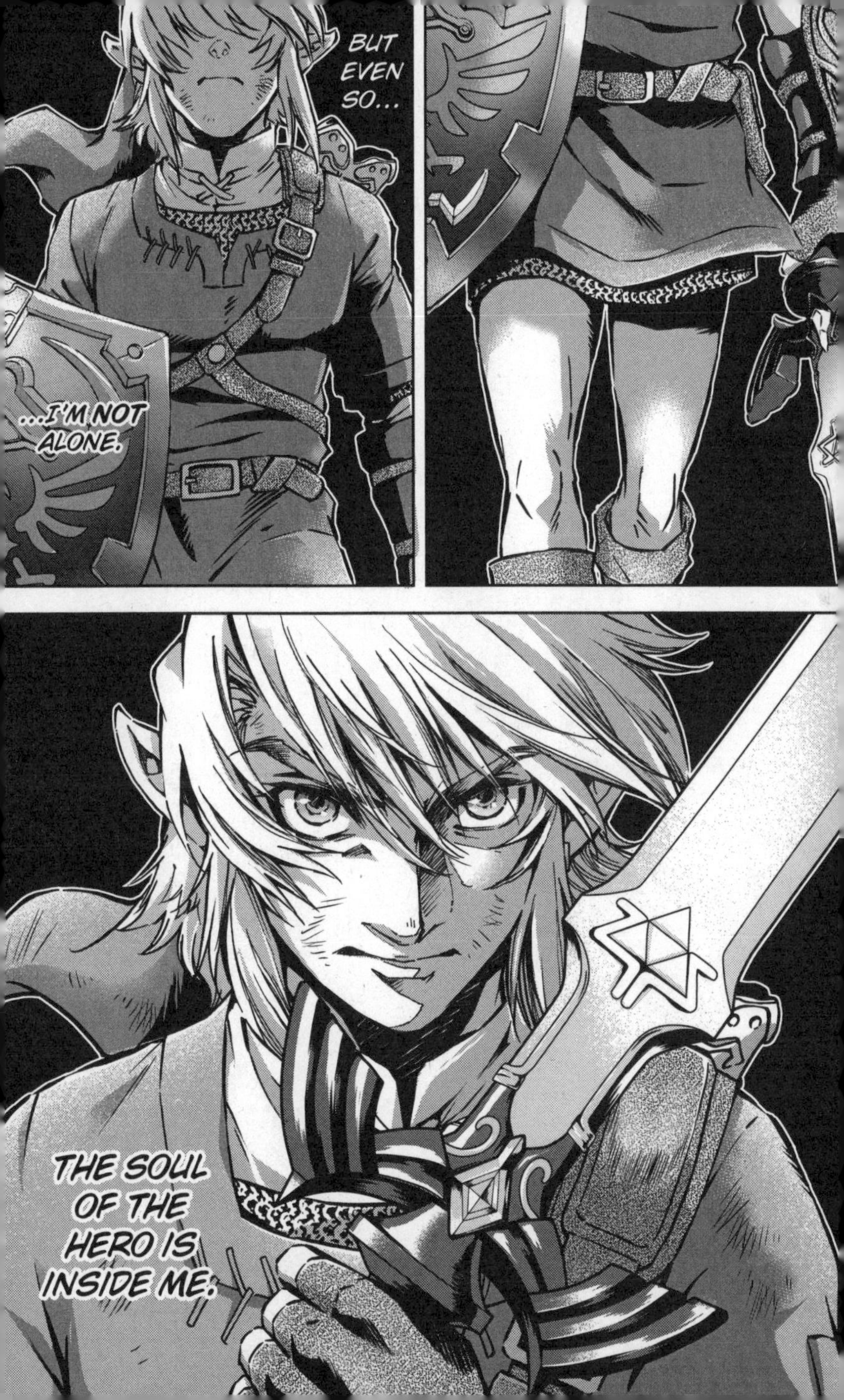
BUT EVEN SO...
...I'M NOT ALONE.
THE SOUL OF THE HERO IS INSIDE ME.

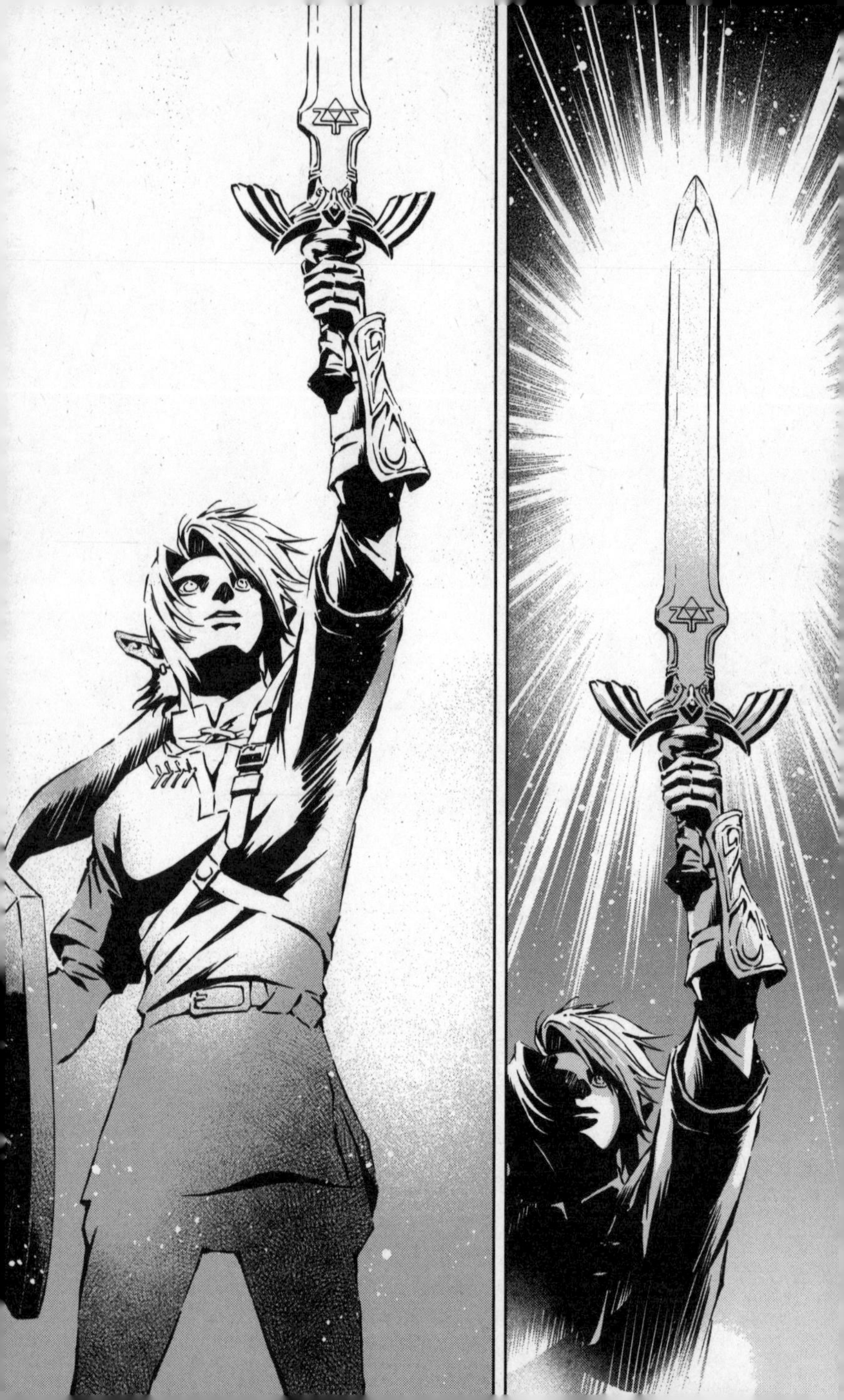

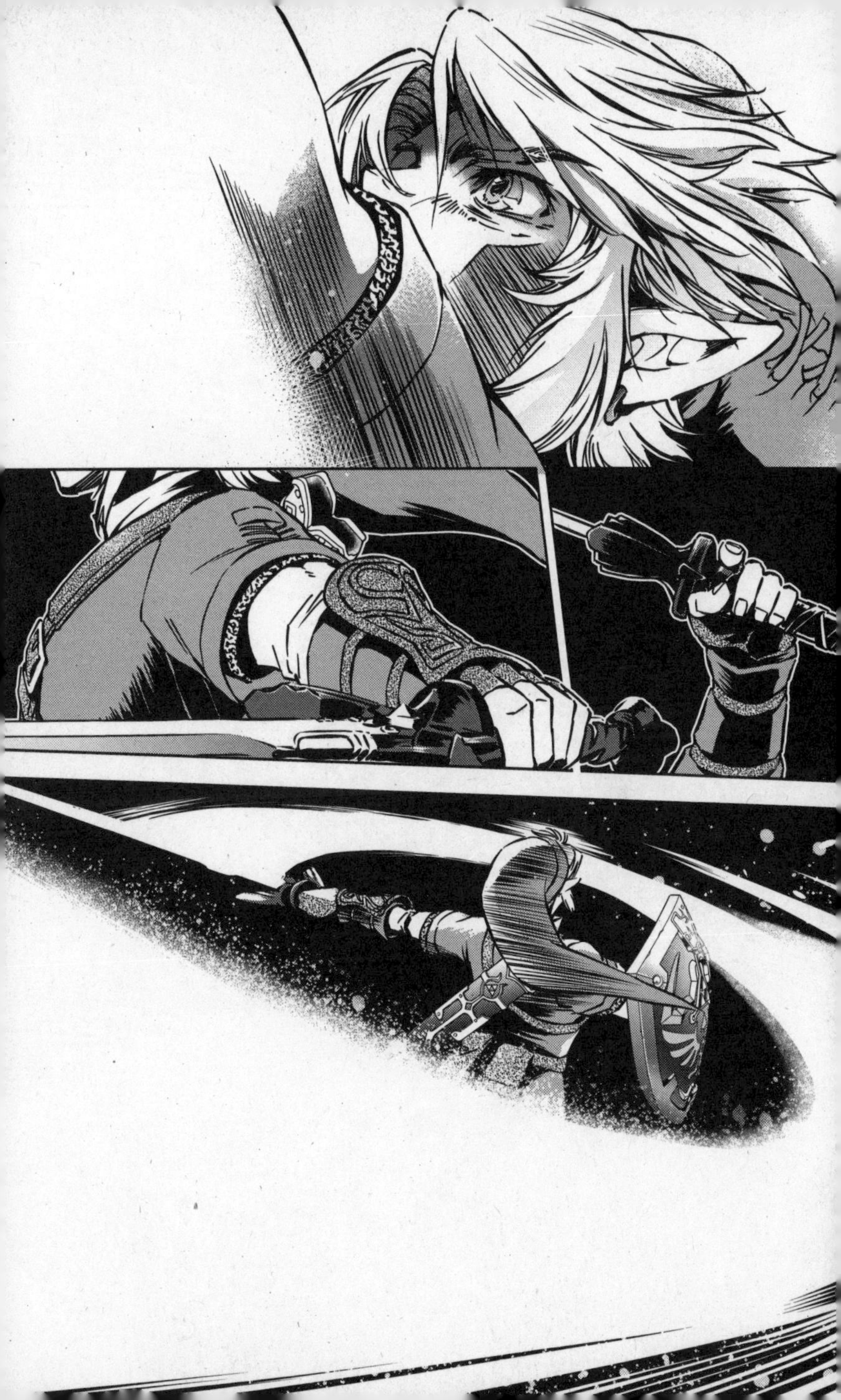

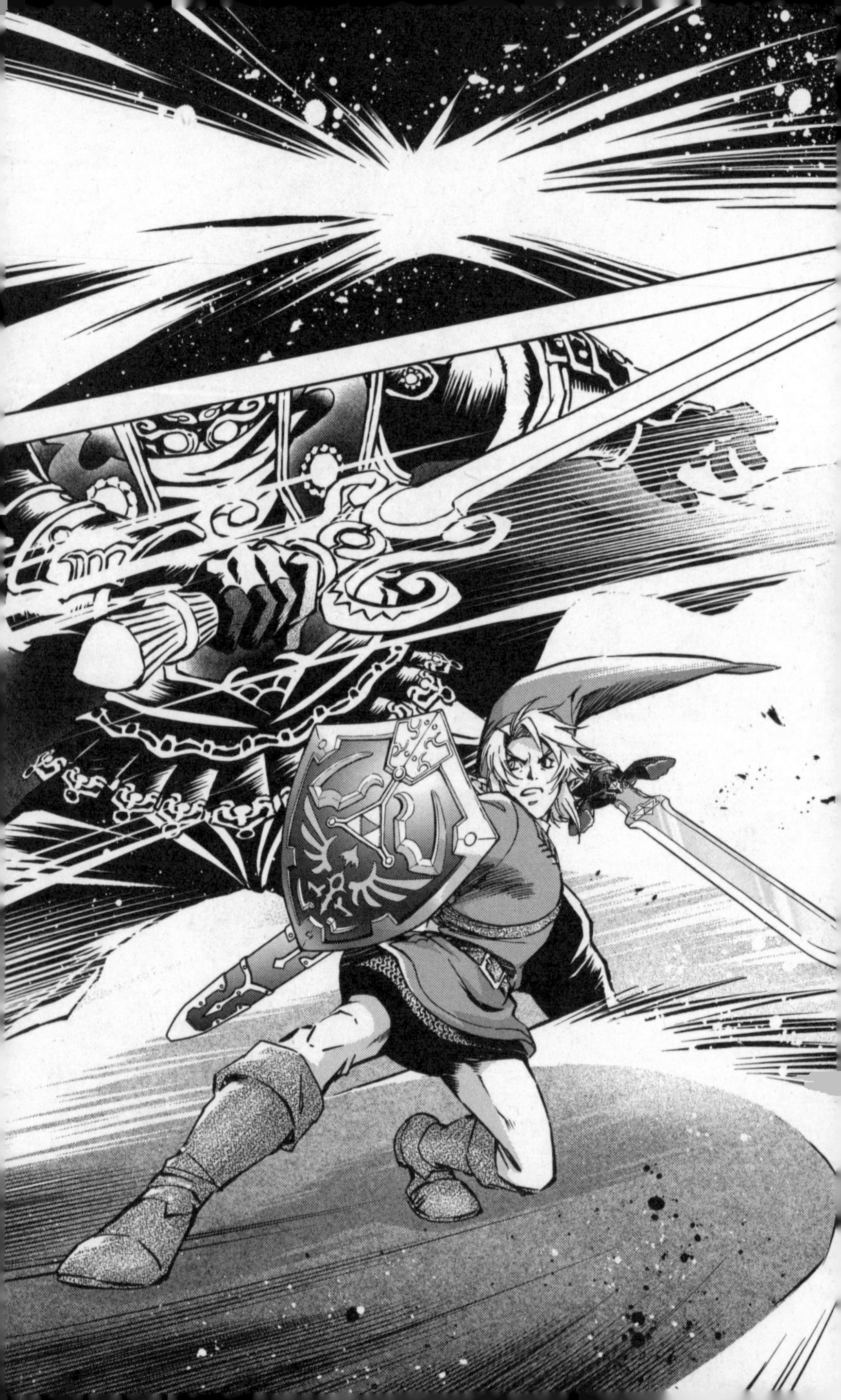

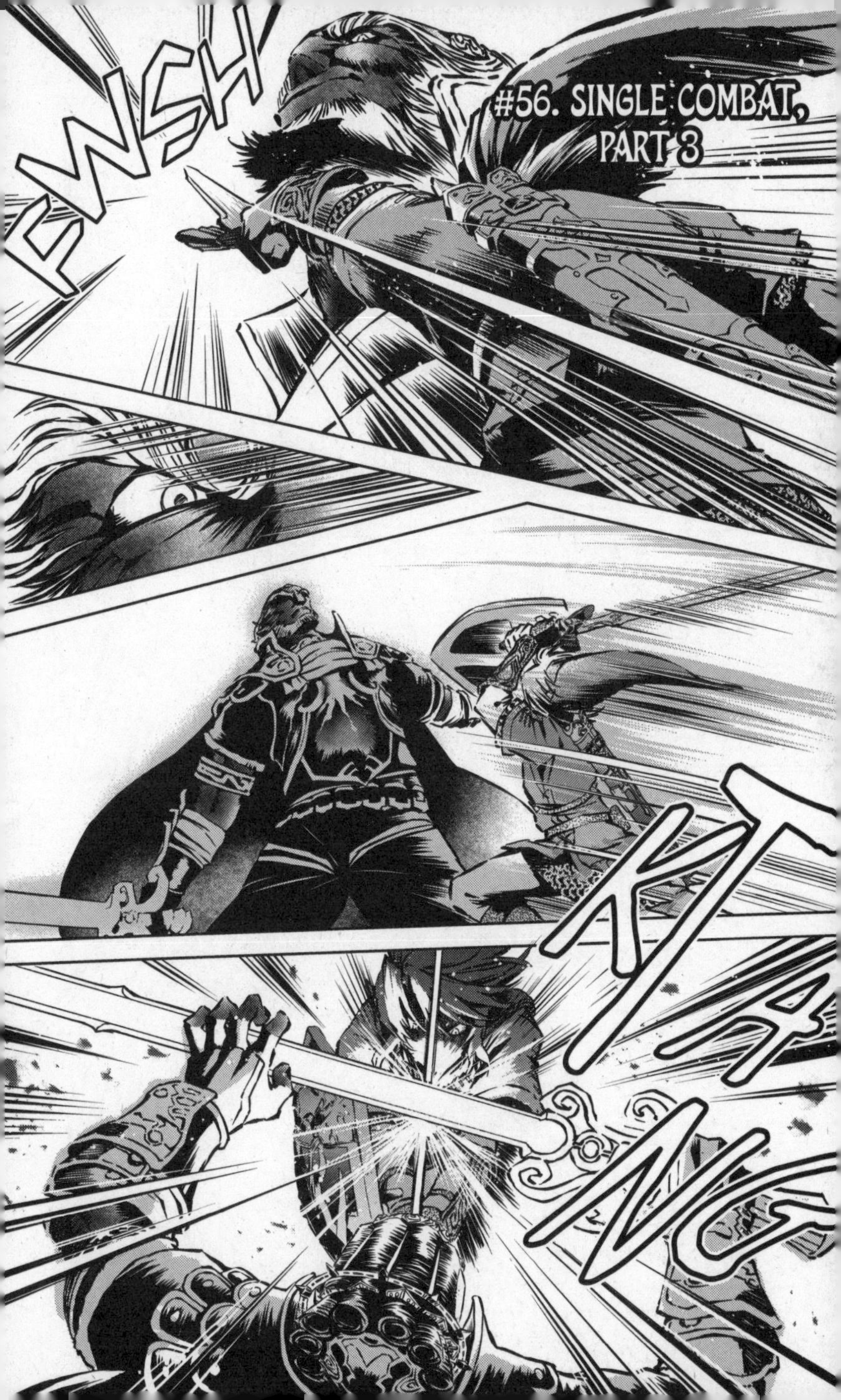
#56. SINGLE COMBAT, PART 3
FWSH
KTANG

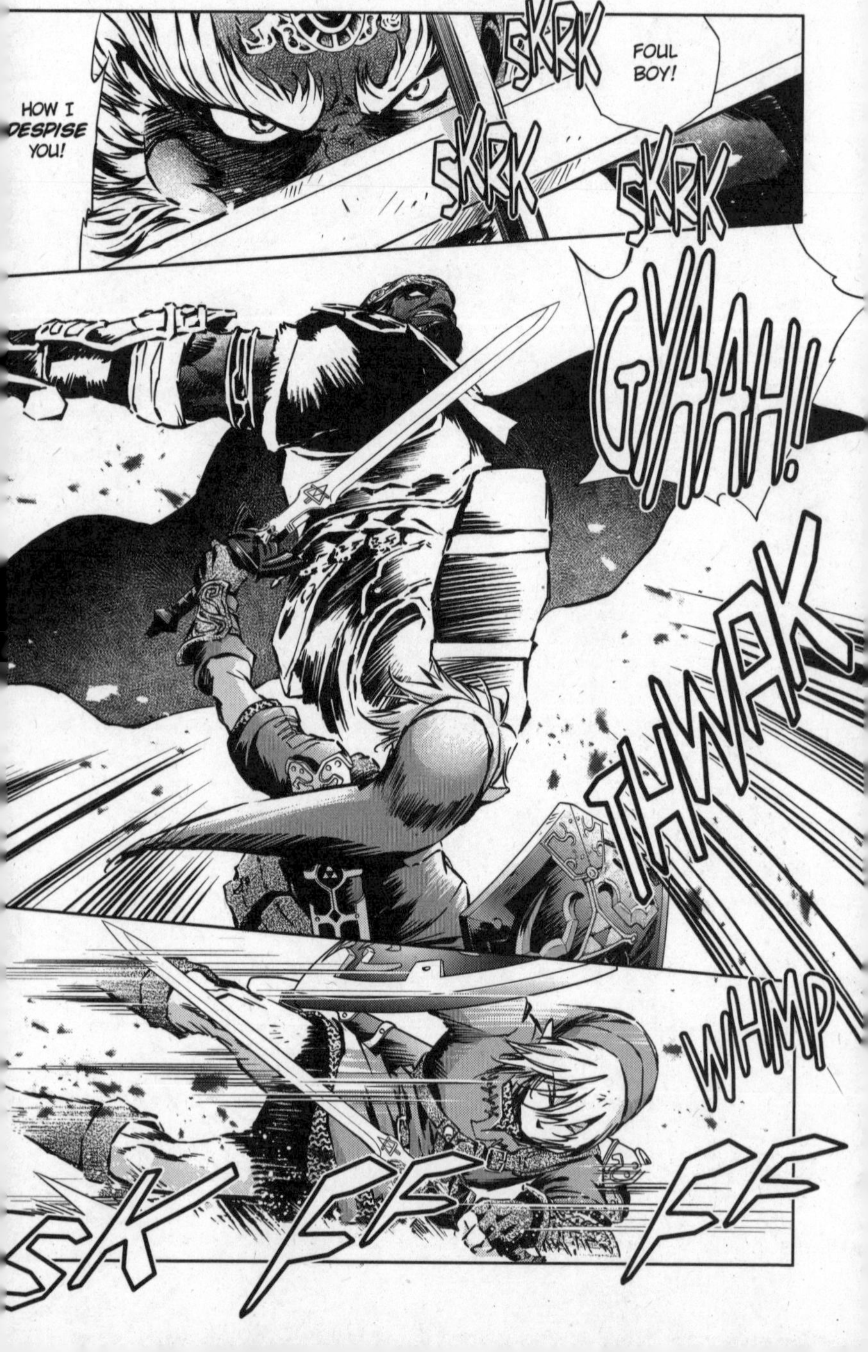
FOUL BOY!
SKRK
HOW I DESPISE YOU!
SKRK
SKRK
GYAAH!
THWAK
WHMP
SK FFF FFF

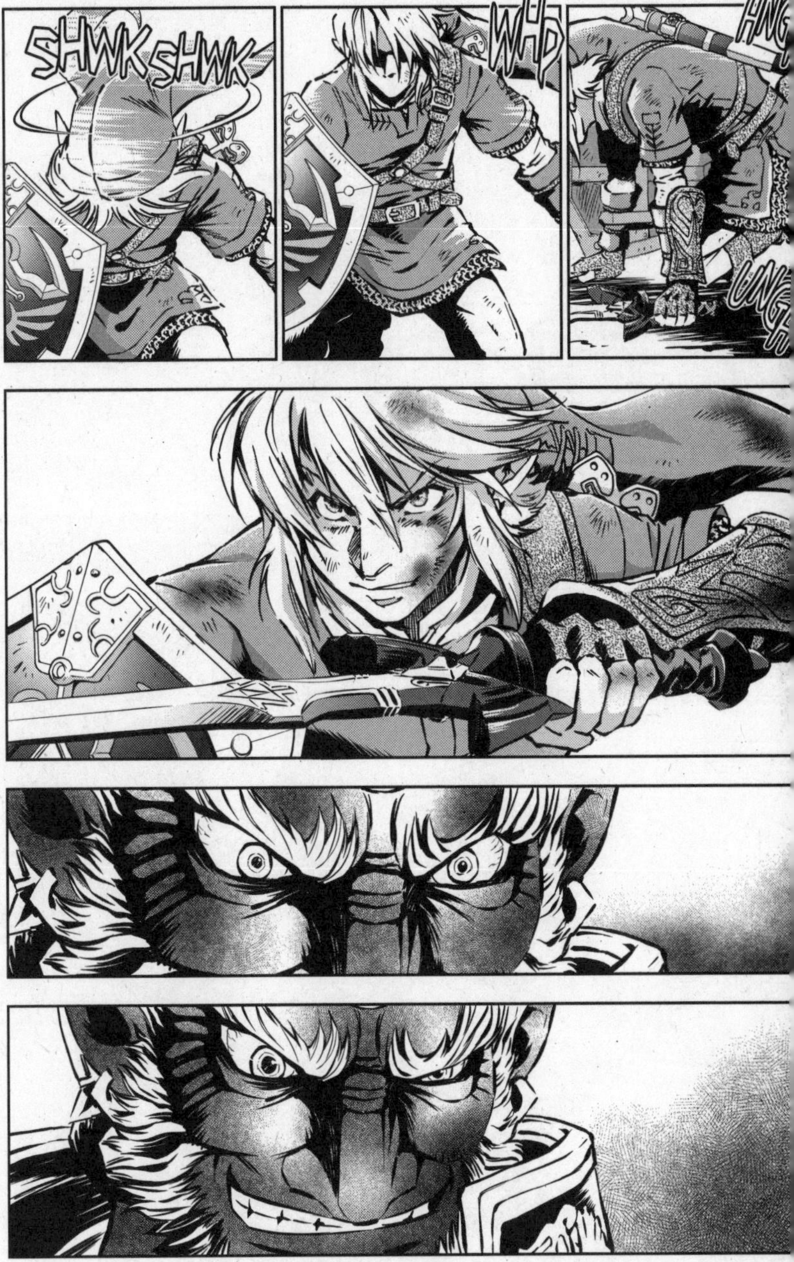
HNG
UNGH
WHD
SHWK SHWK

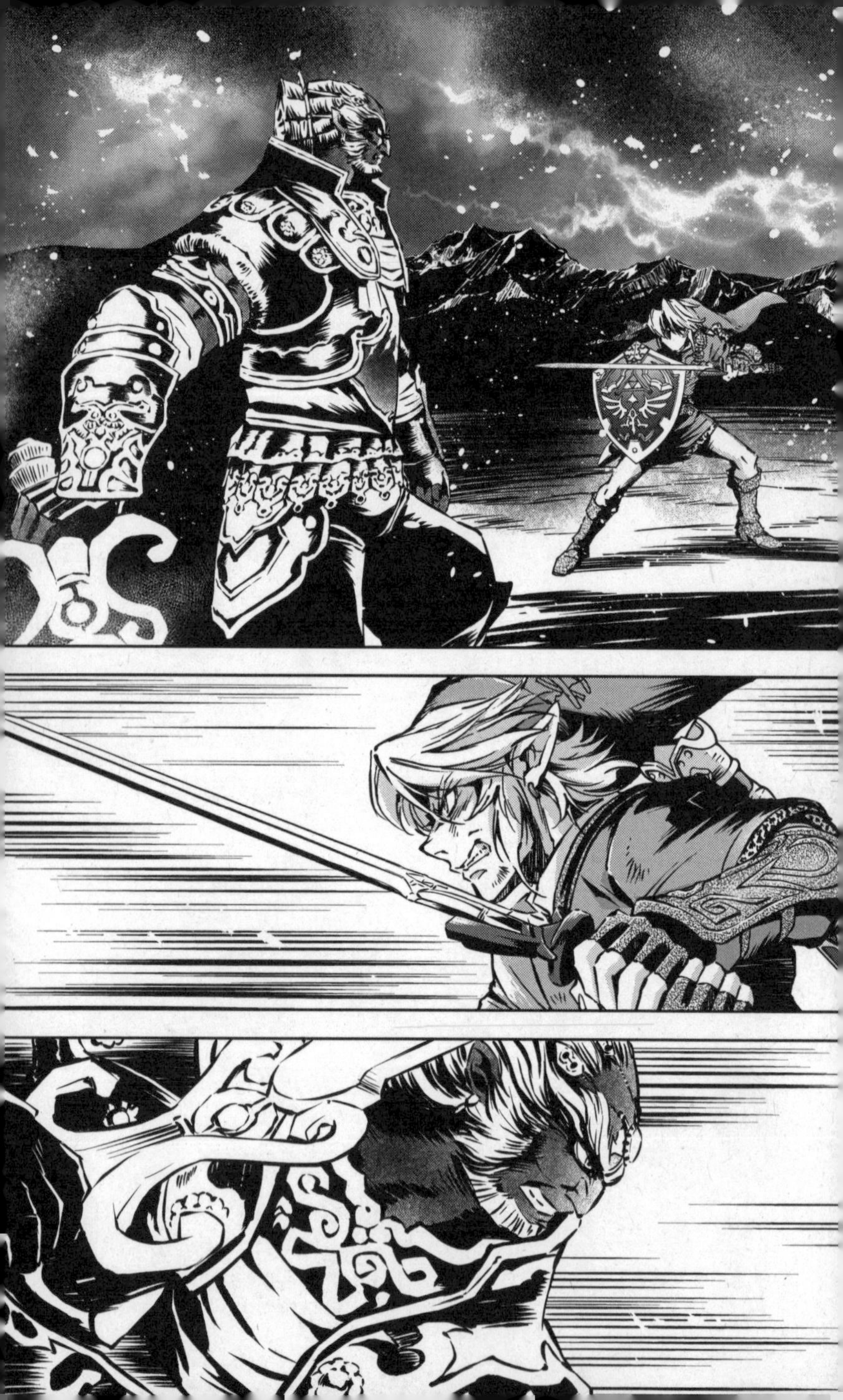

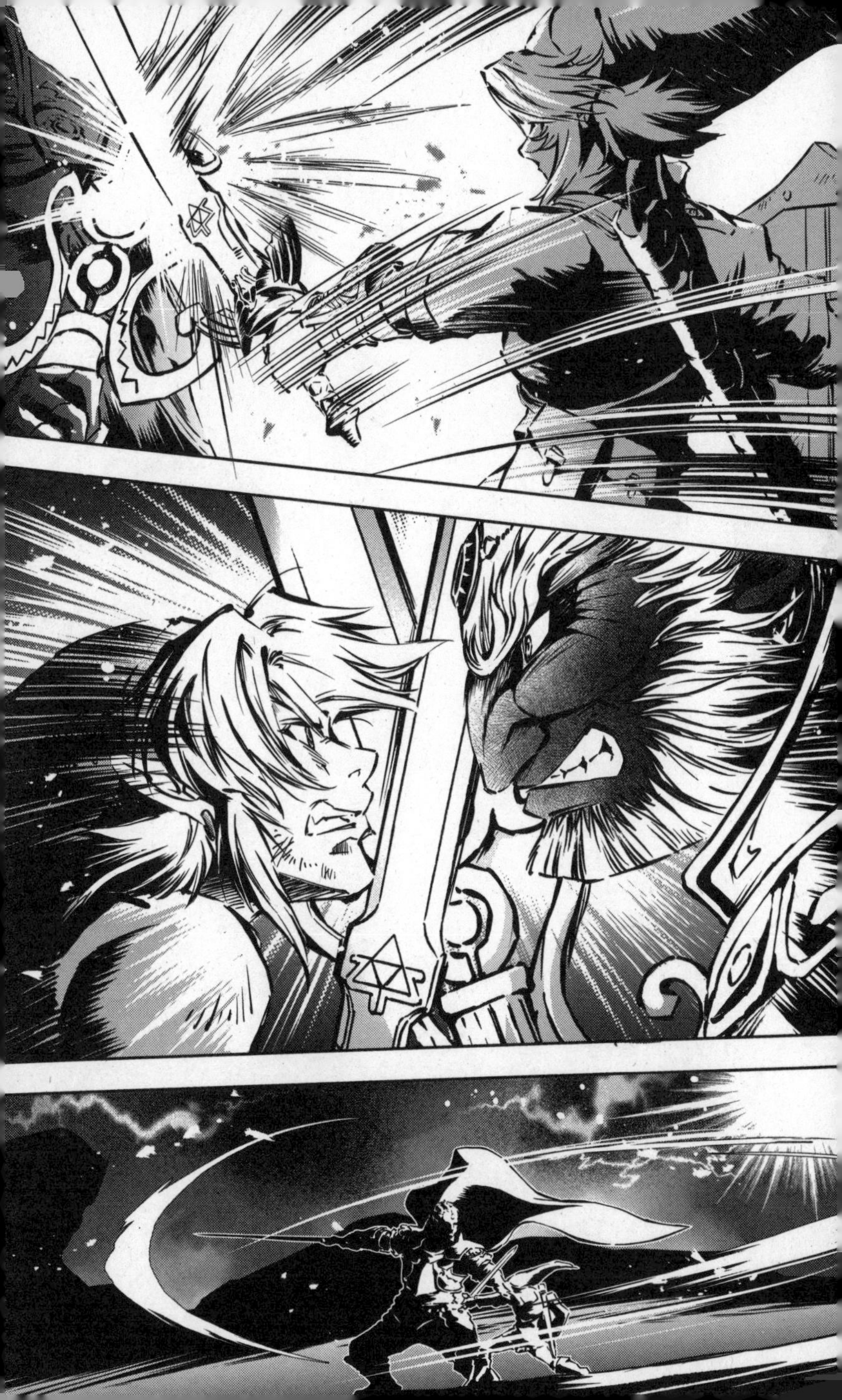

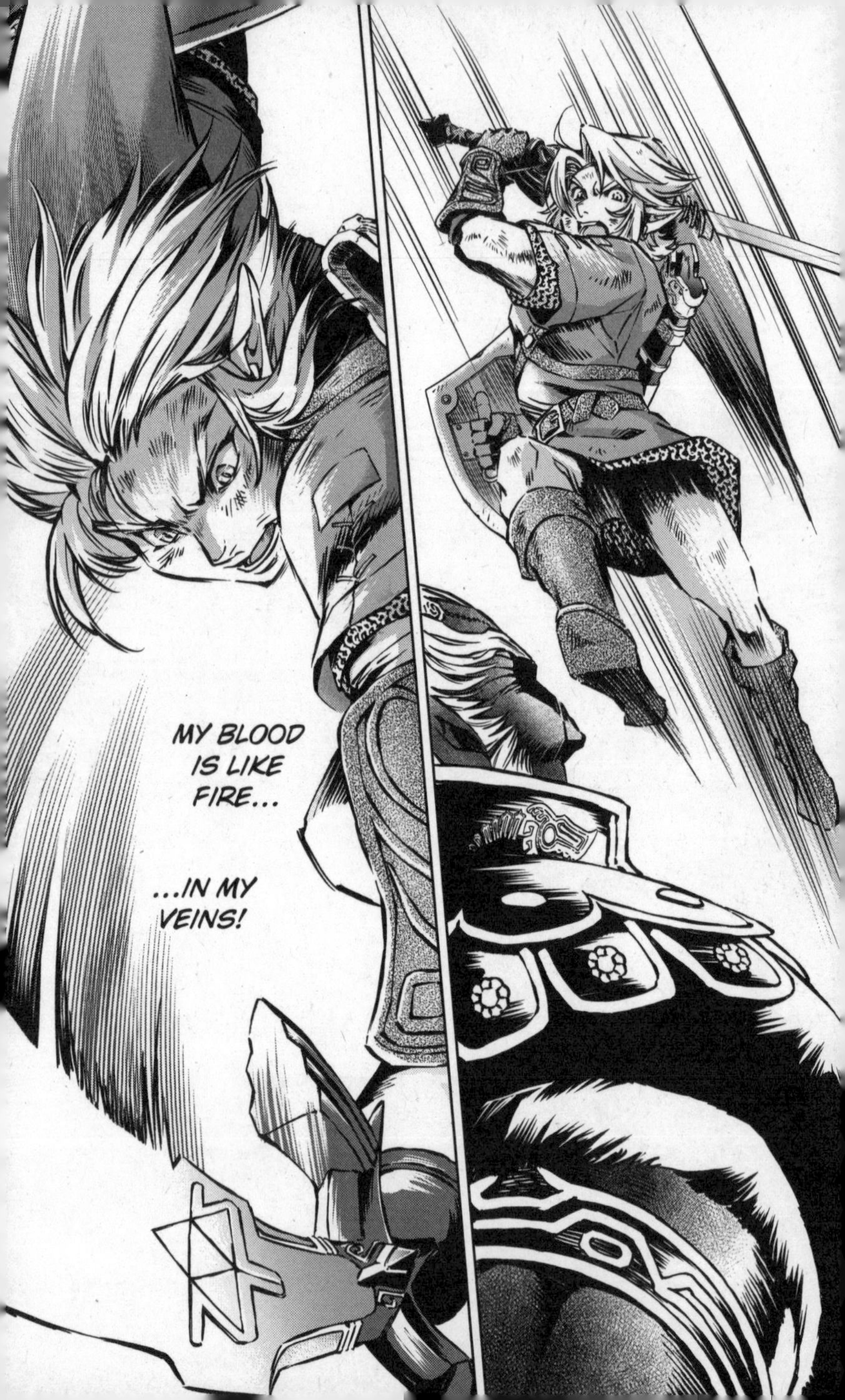
MY BLOOD IS LIKE FIRE...
...IN MY VEINS!

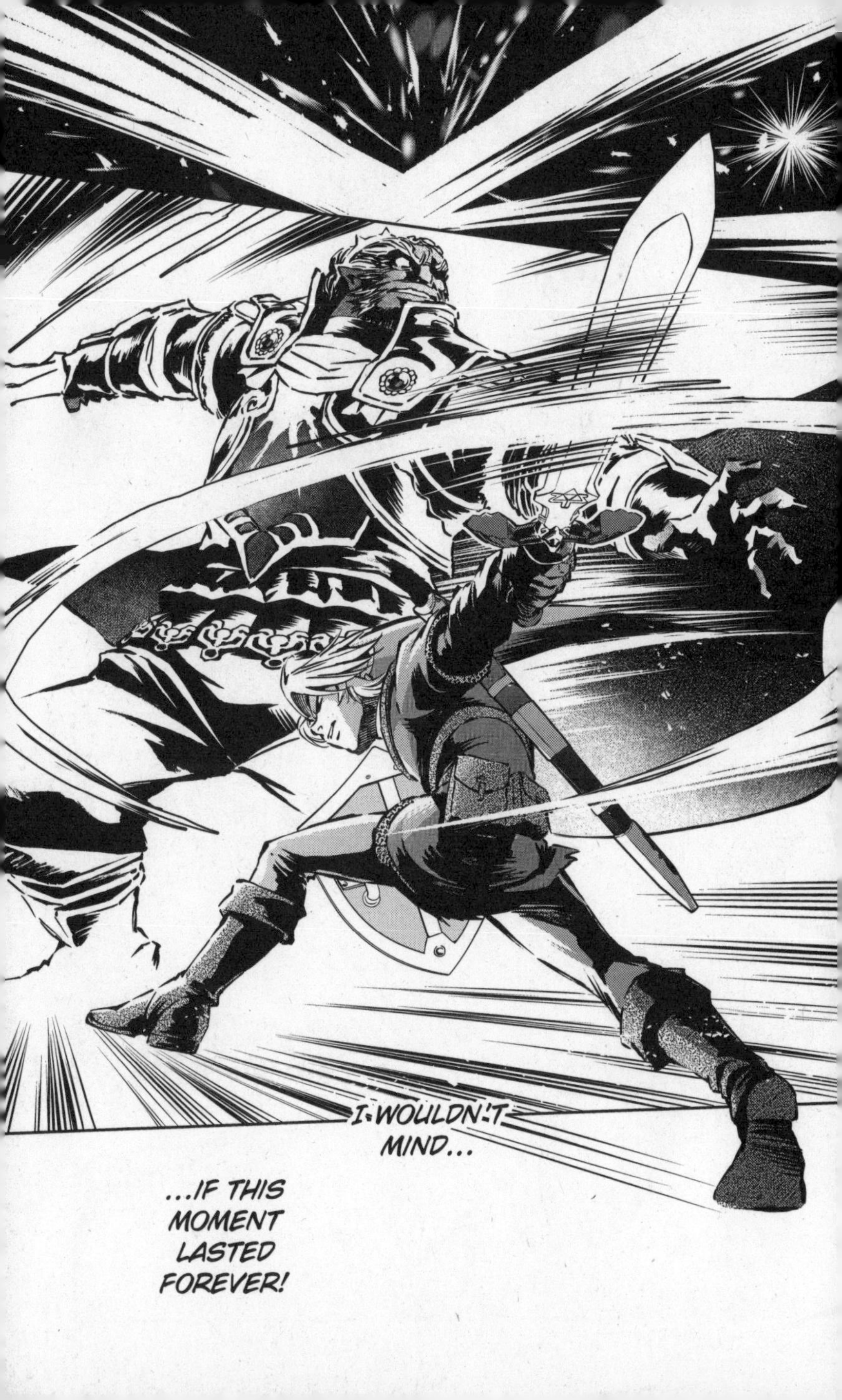
I WOULDN'T MIND...
...IF THIS MOMENT LASTED FOREVER!

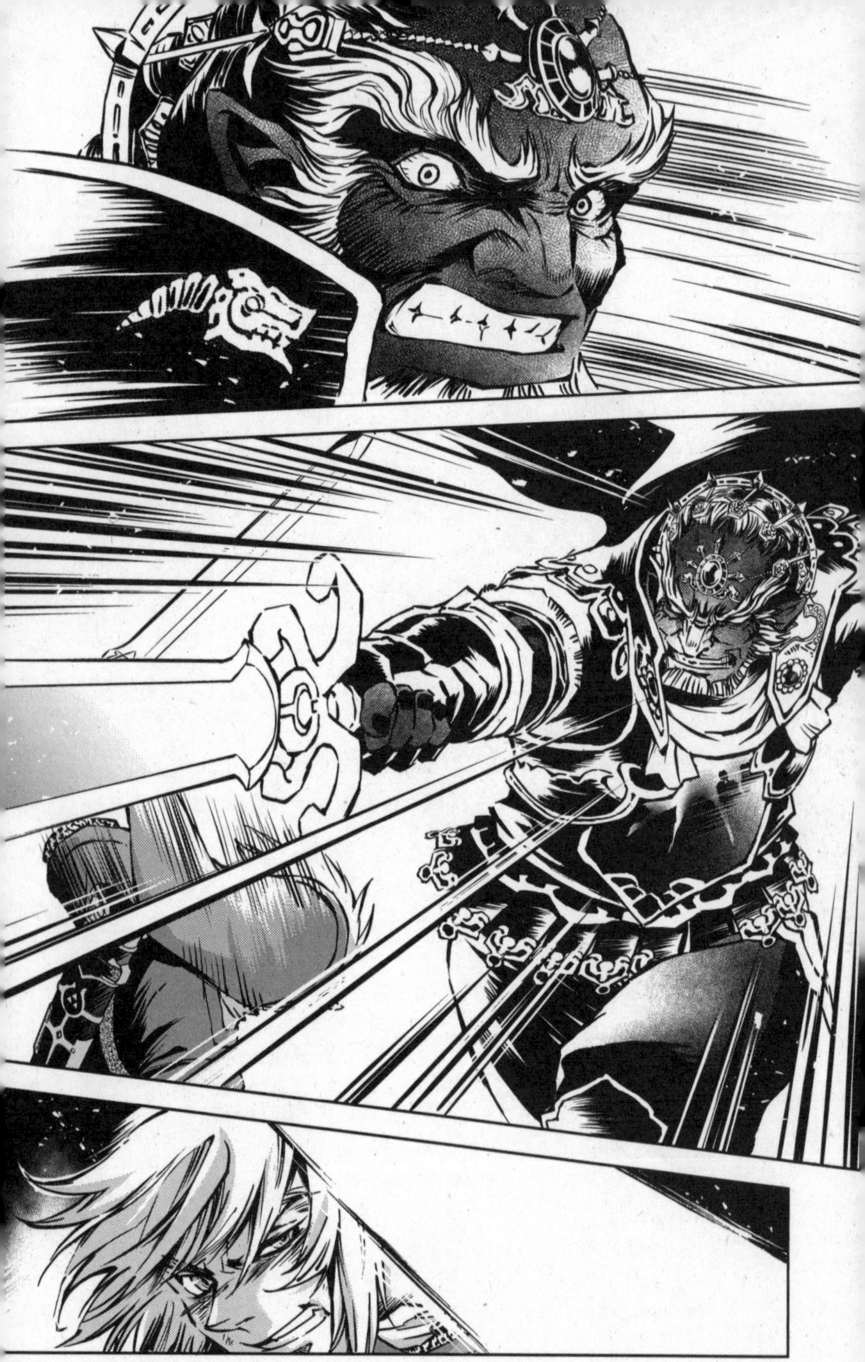

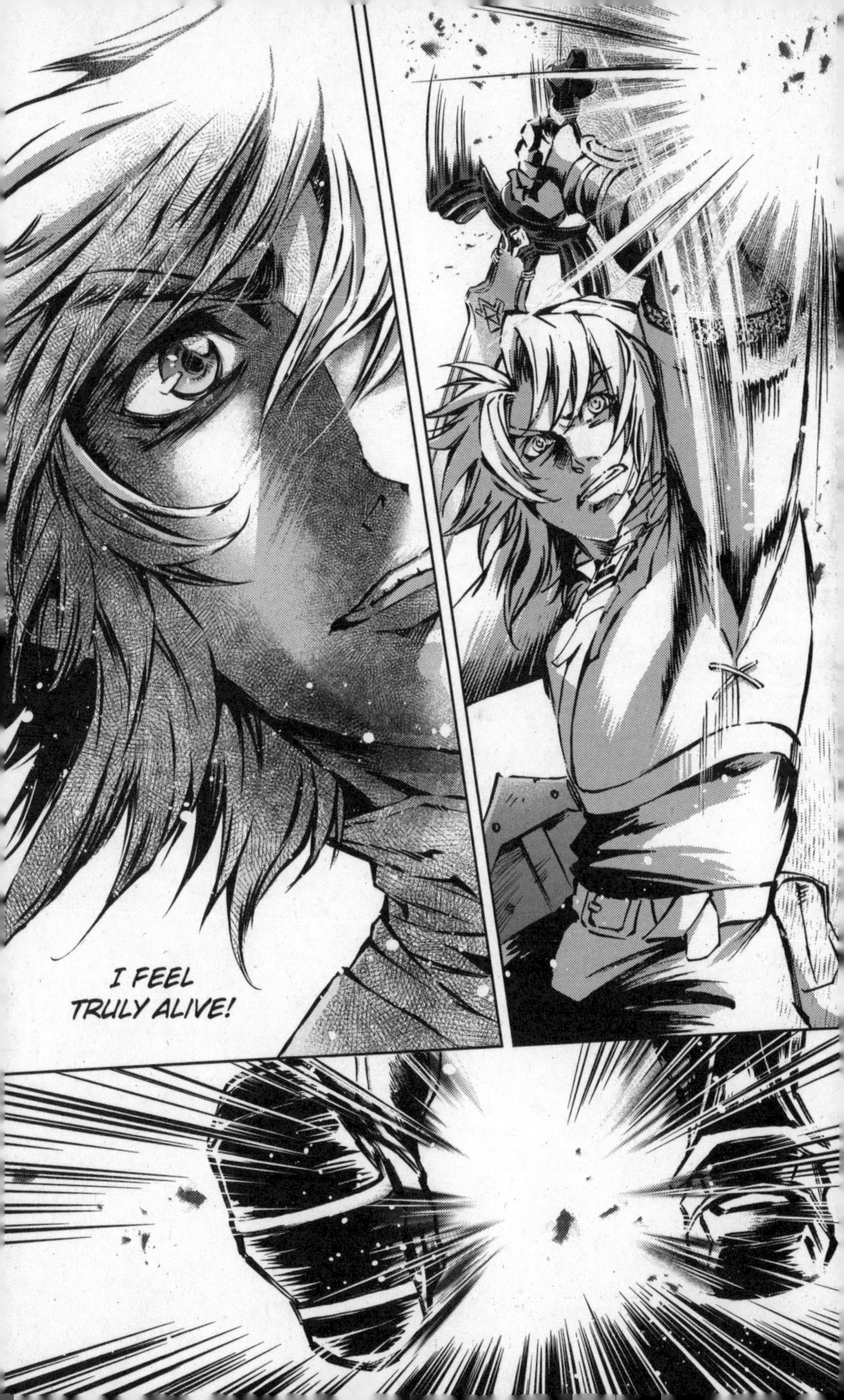
I FEEL TRULY ALIVE!

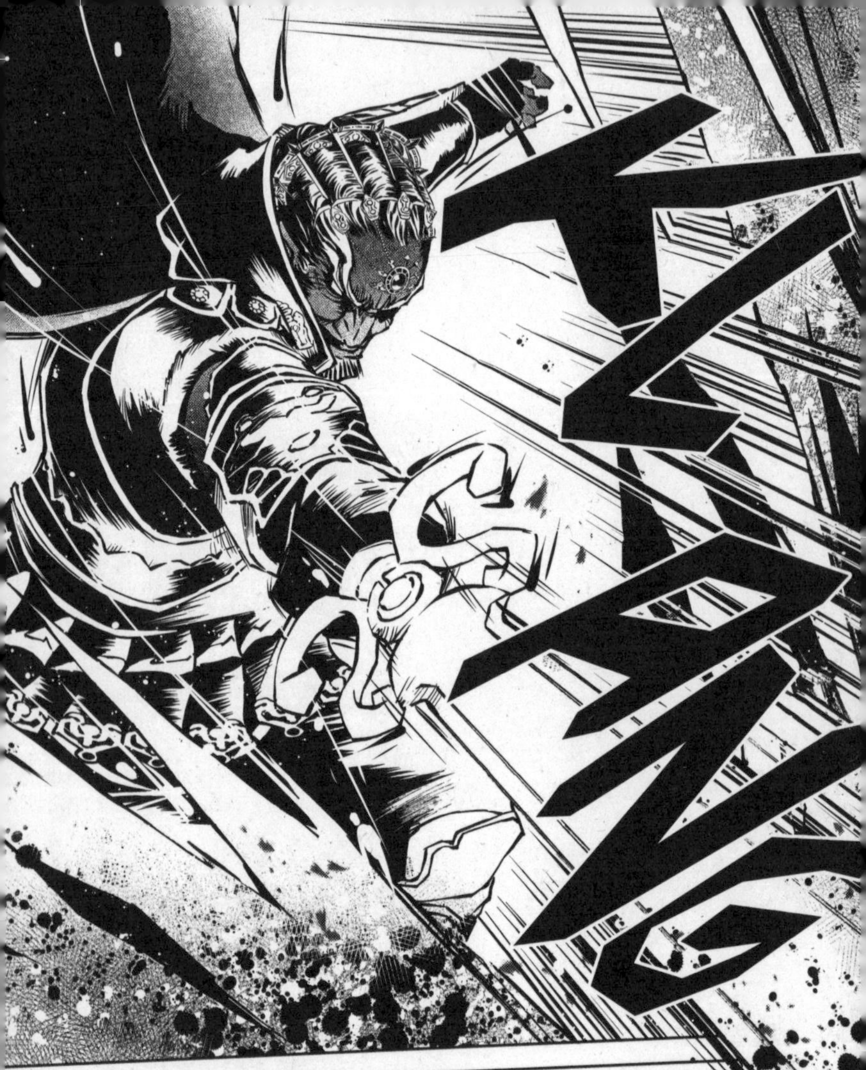
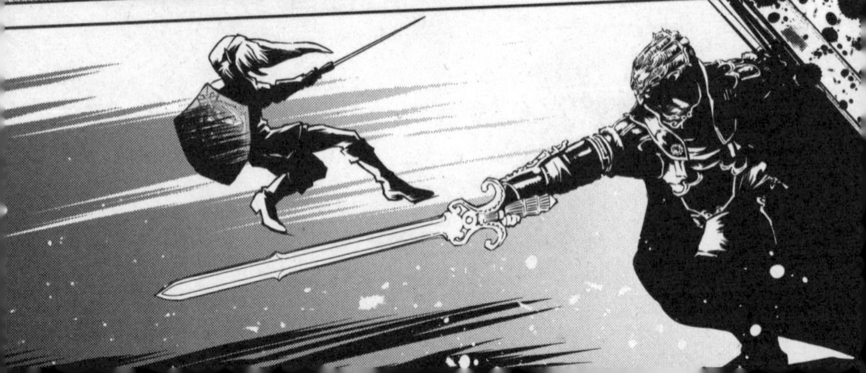

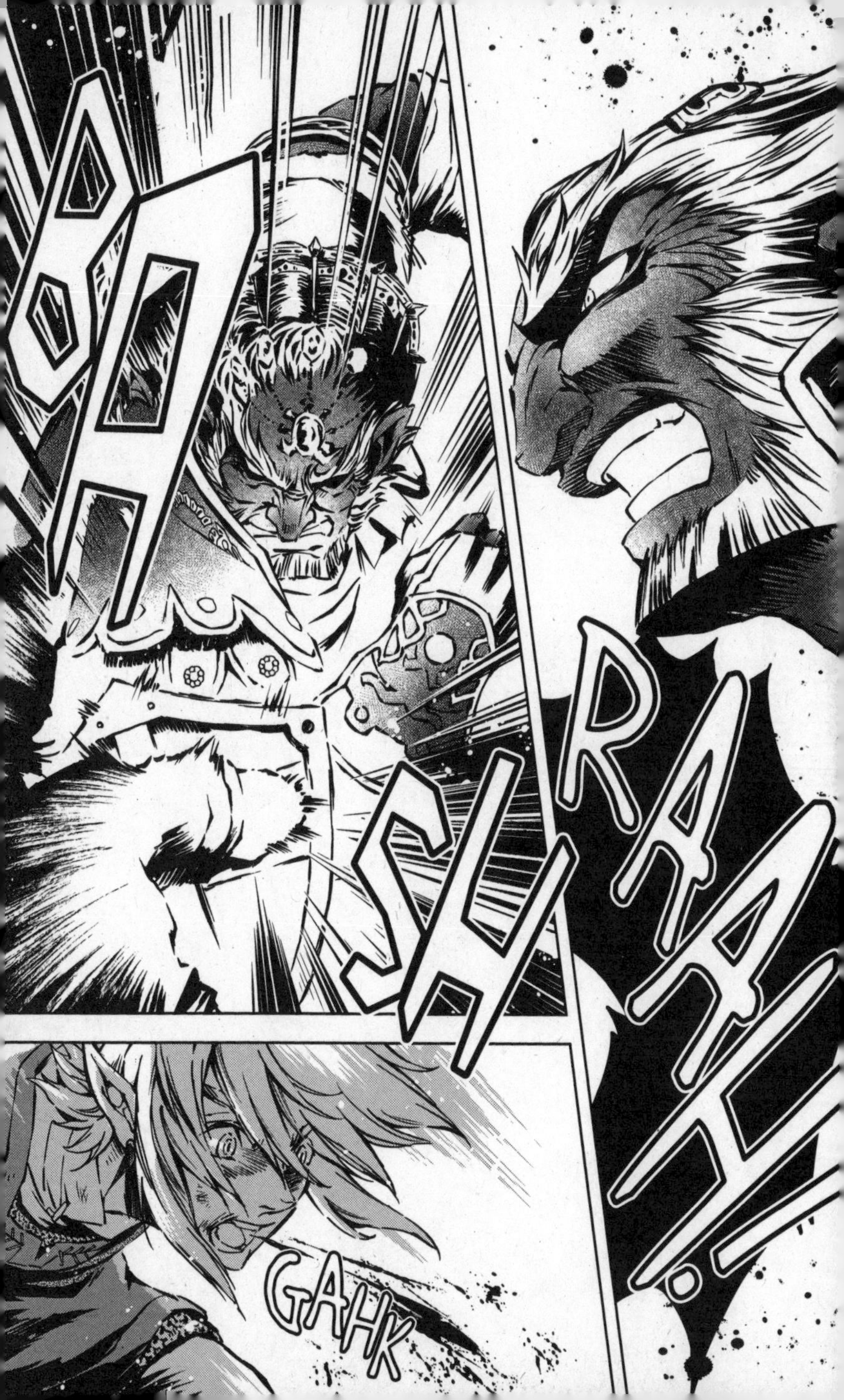
SHRAAHH!
GAHK

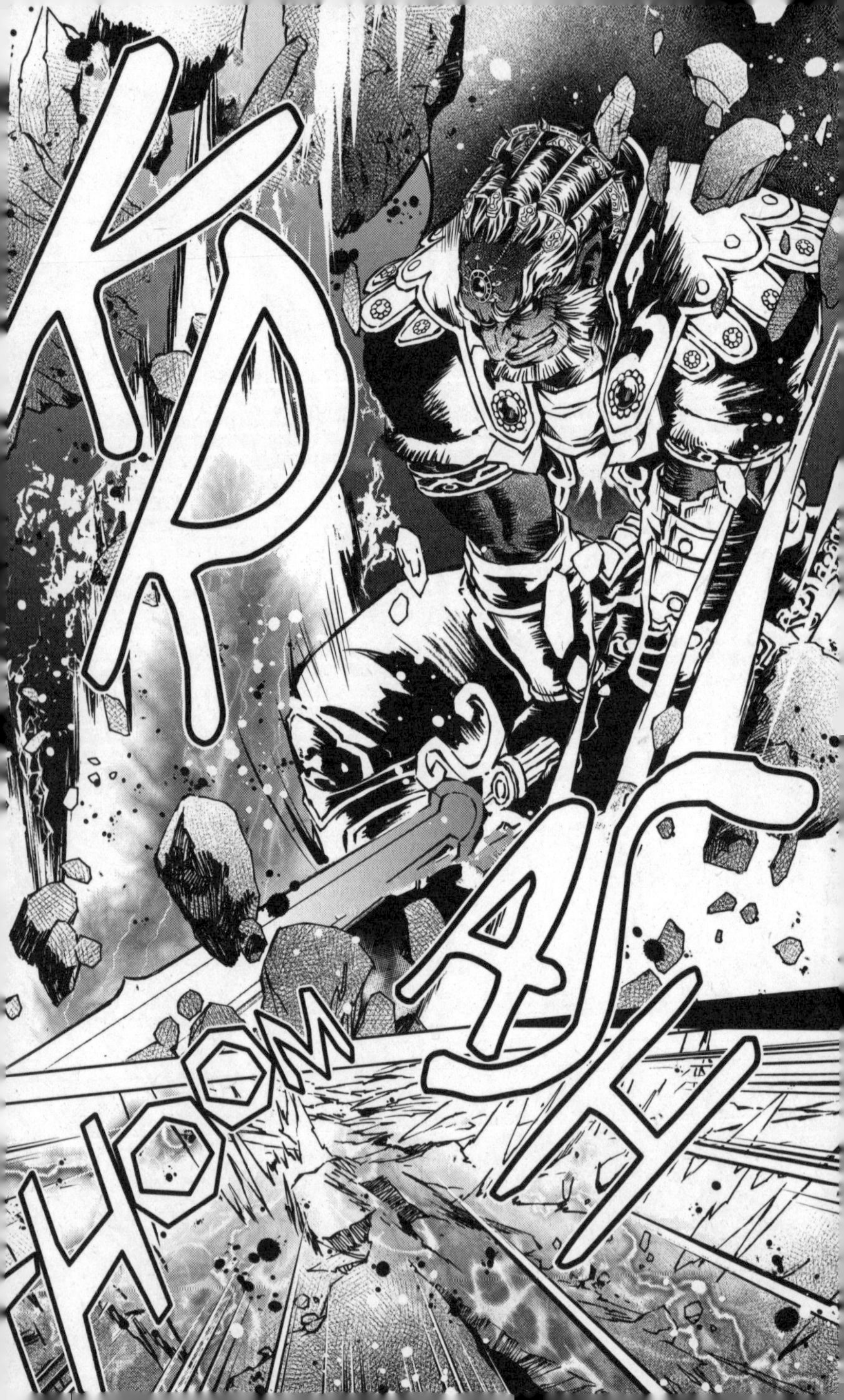
KRASH
KOOM

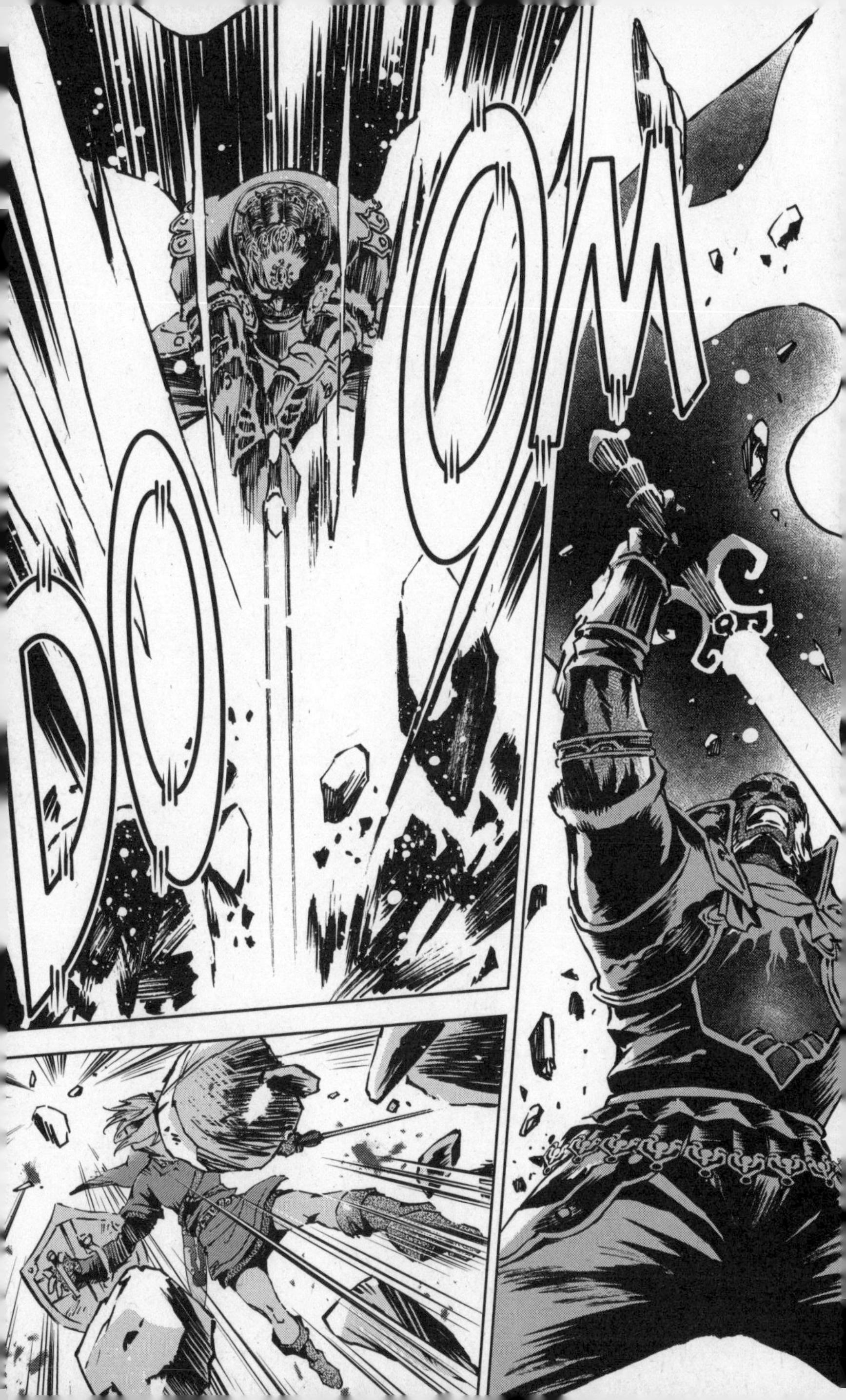
DOOM

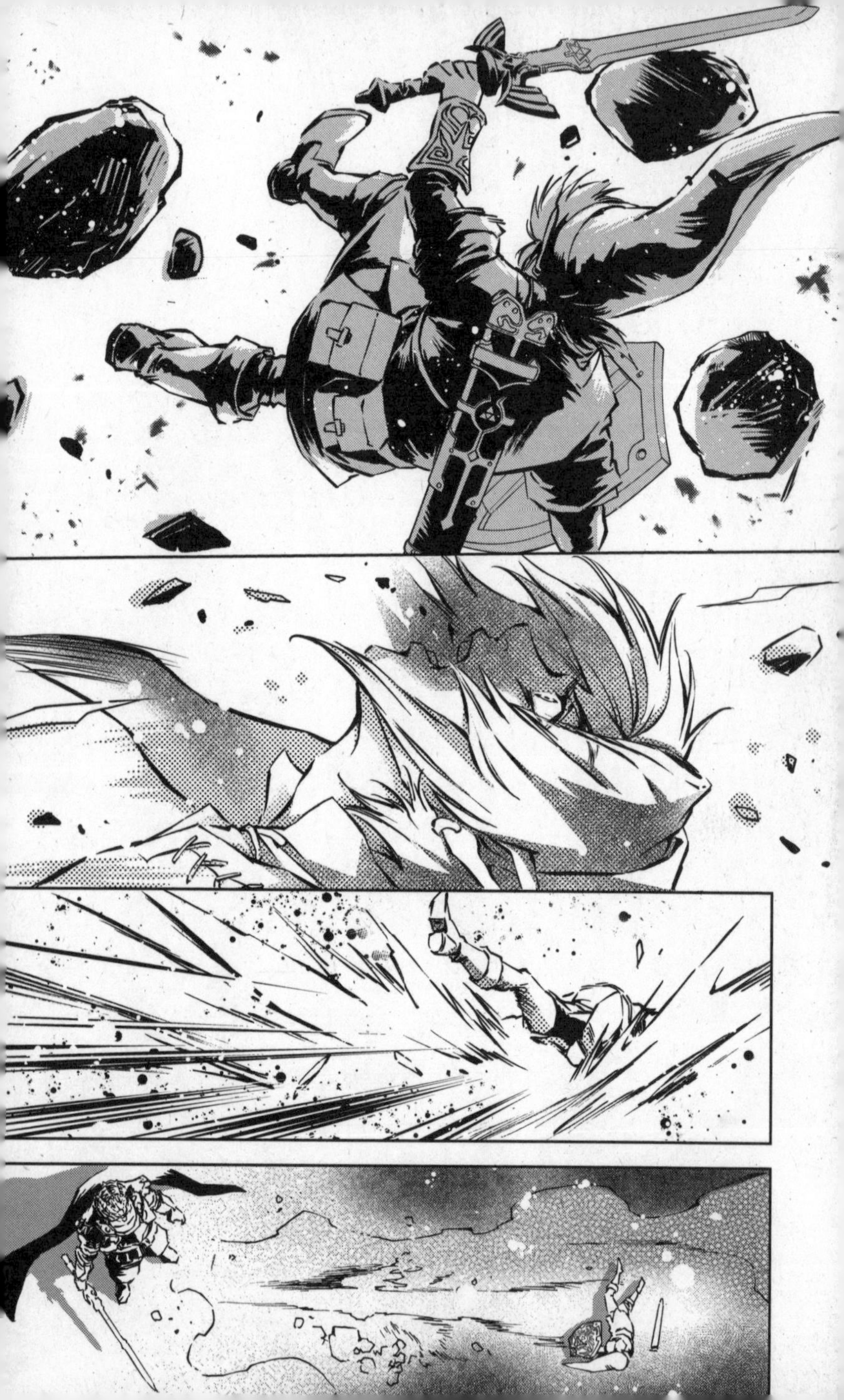

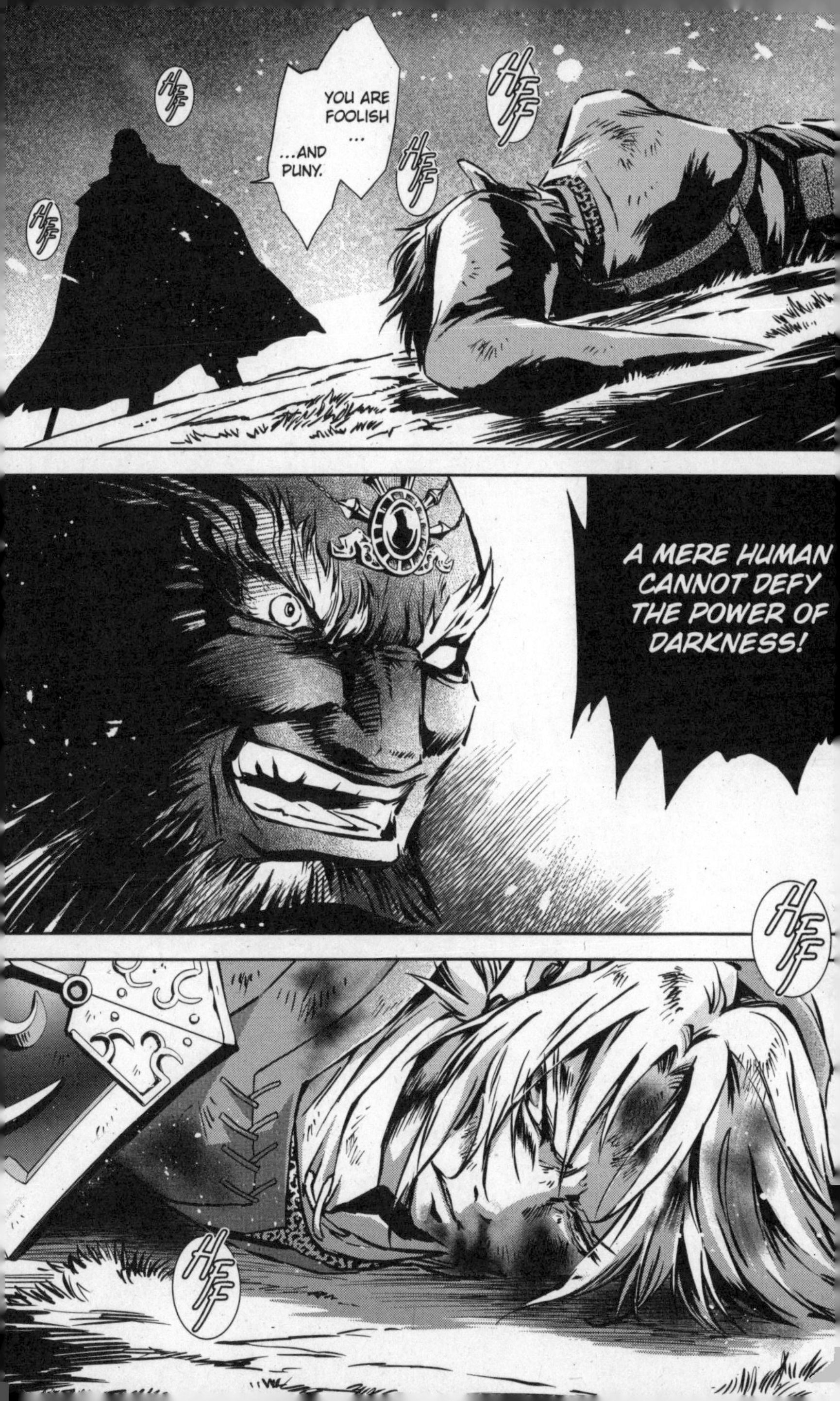
HFF
YOU ARE FOOLISH ...
...AND PUNY.
HFF
HFF
HFF
A MERE HUMAN CANNOT DEFY THE POWER OF DARKNESS!
HFF
HFF

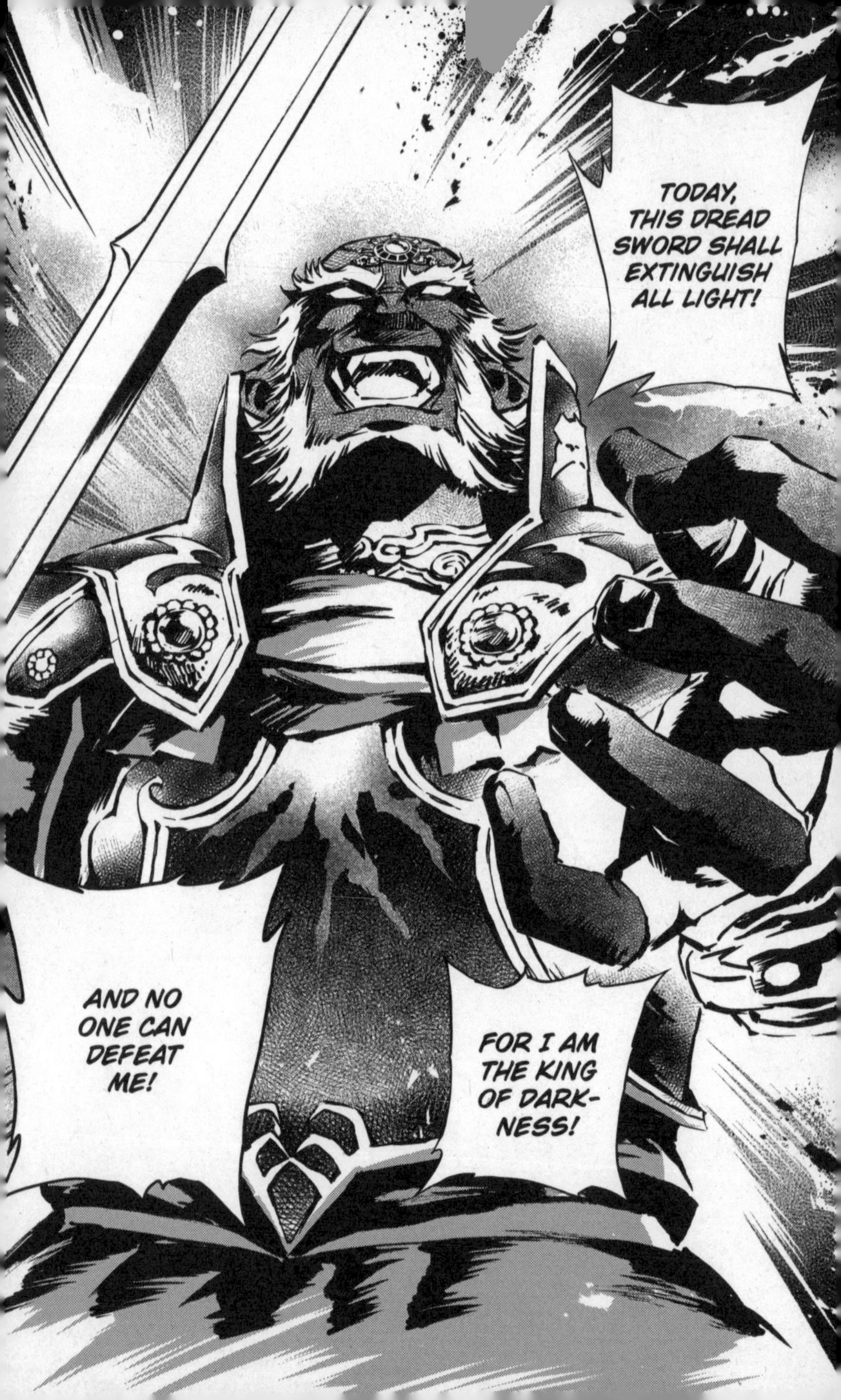
TODAY, THIS DREAD SWORD SHALL EXTINGUISH ALL LIGHT!
FOR I AM THE KING OF DARK- NESS!
AND NO ONE CAN DEFEAT ME!

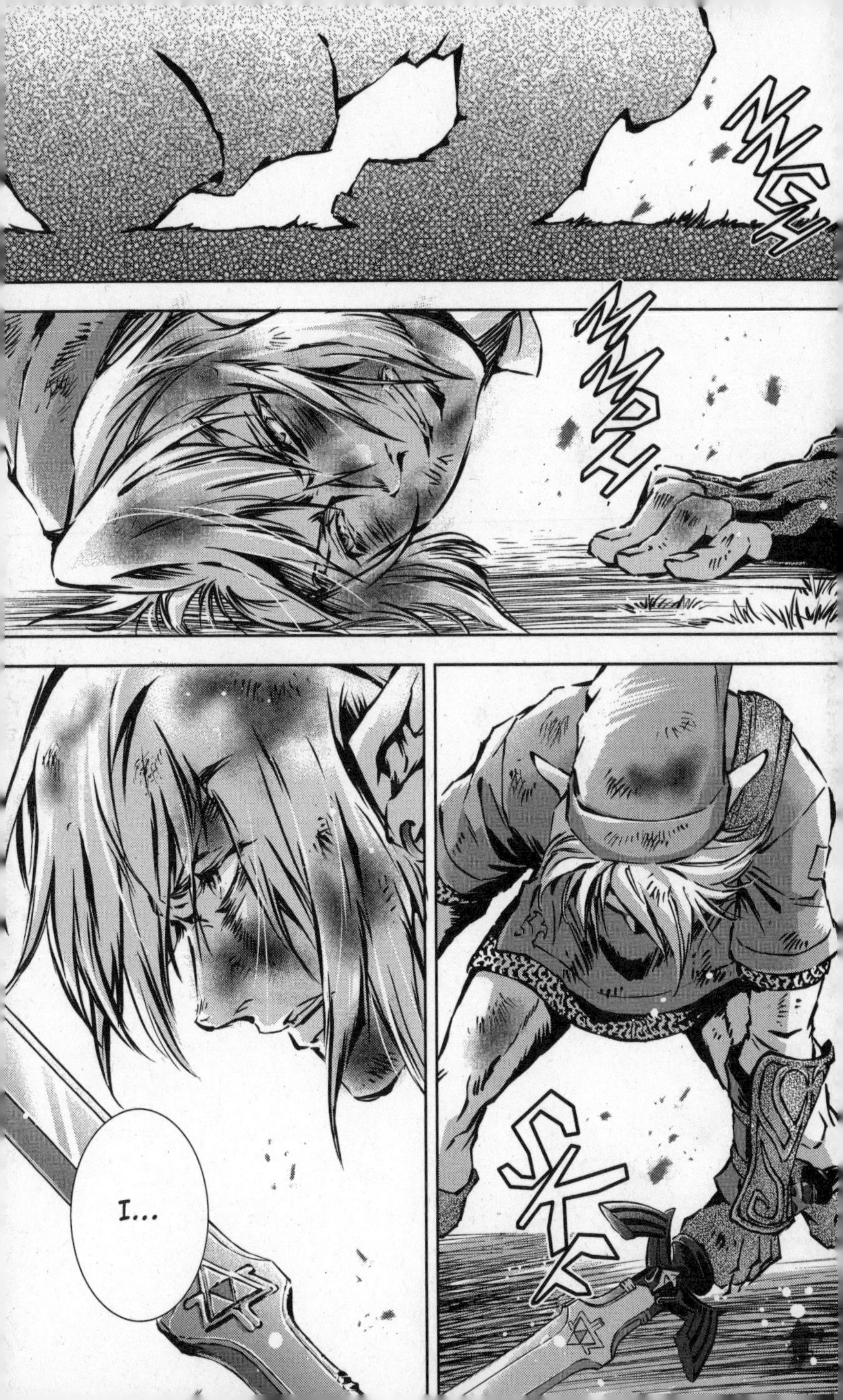
NNGH
MMPH
SKK
I...

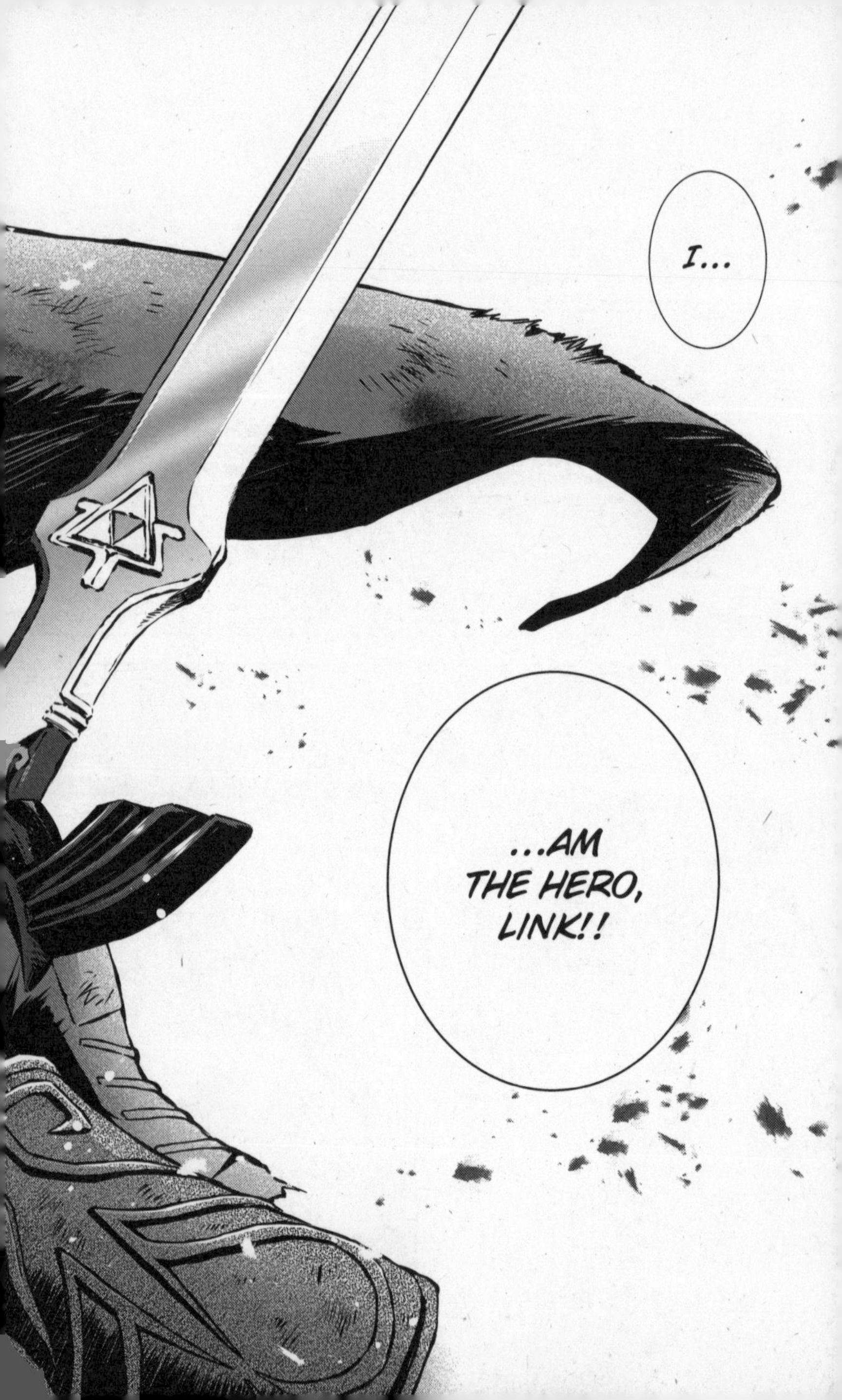
I...
...AM THE HERO, LINK!!

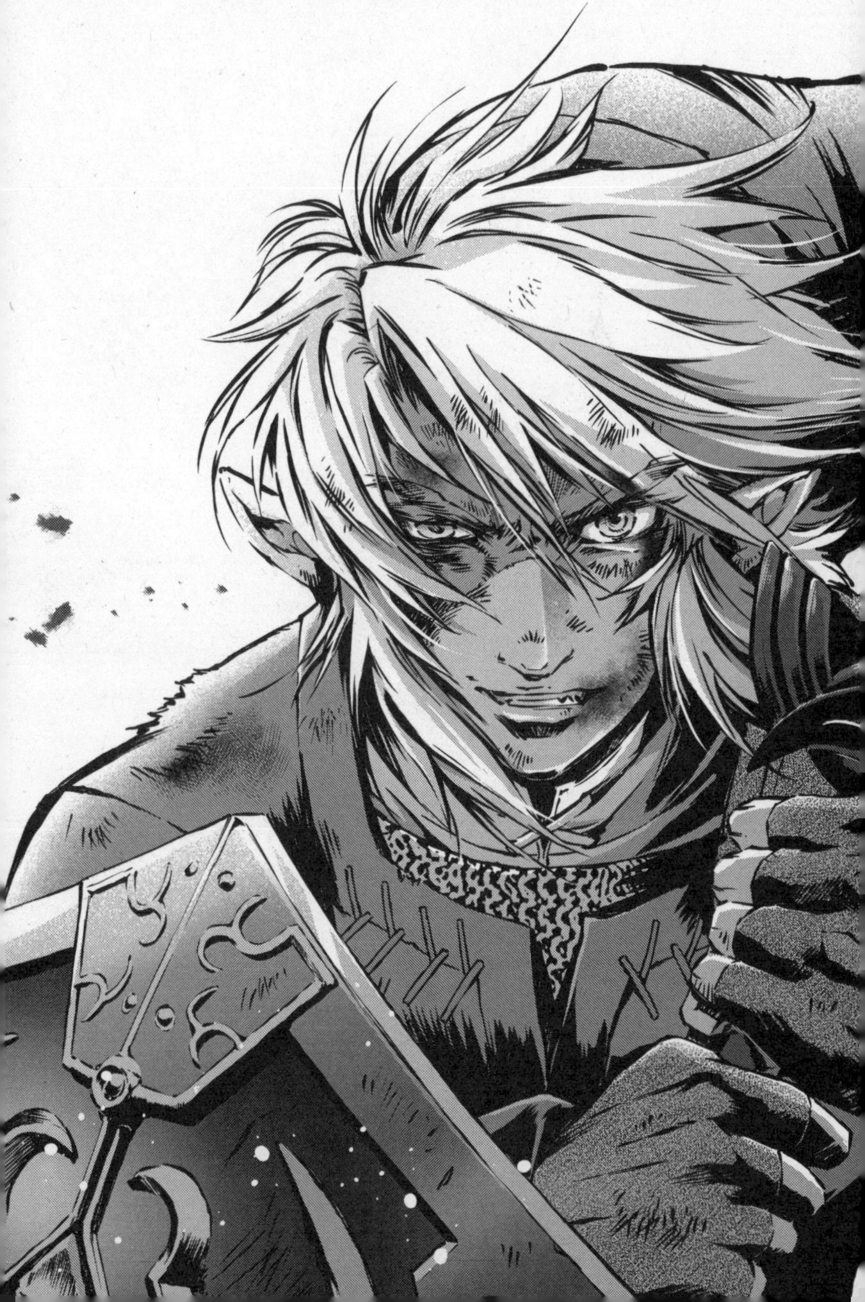

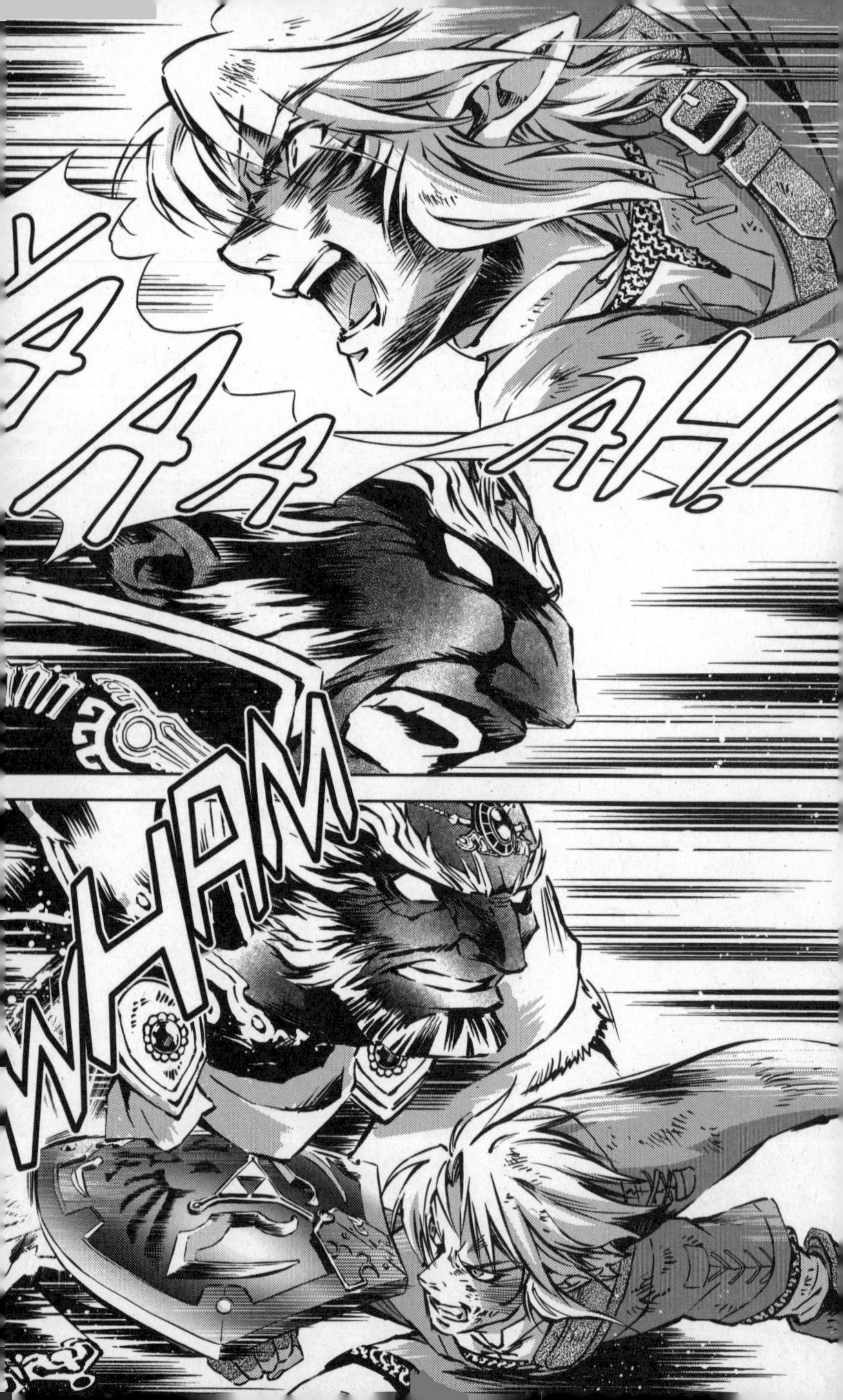
YAAAAH!!
WHAM

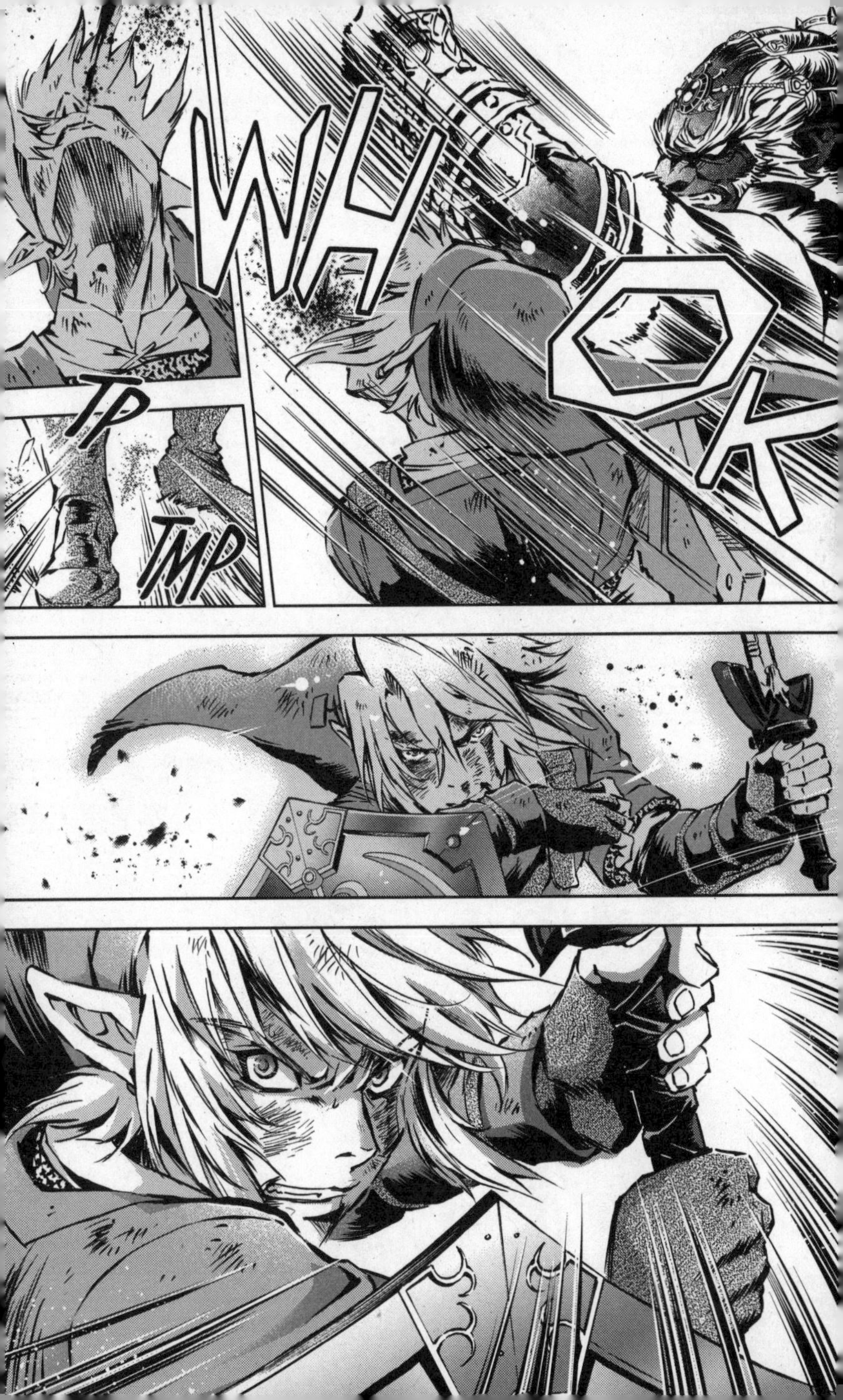
WHOK
TP
TMP

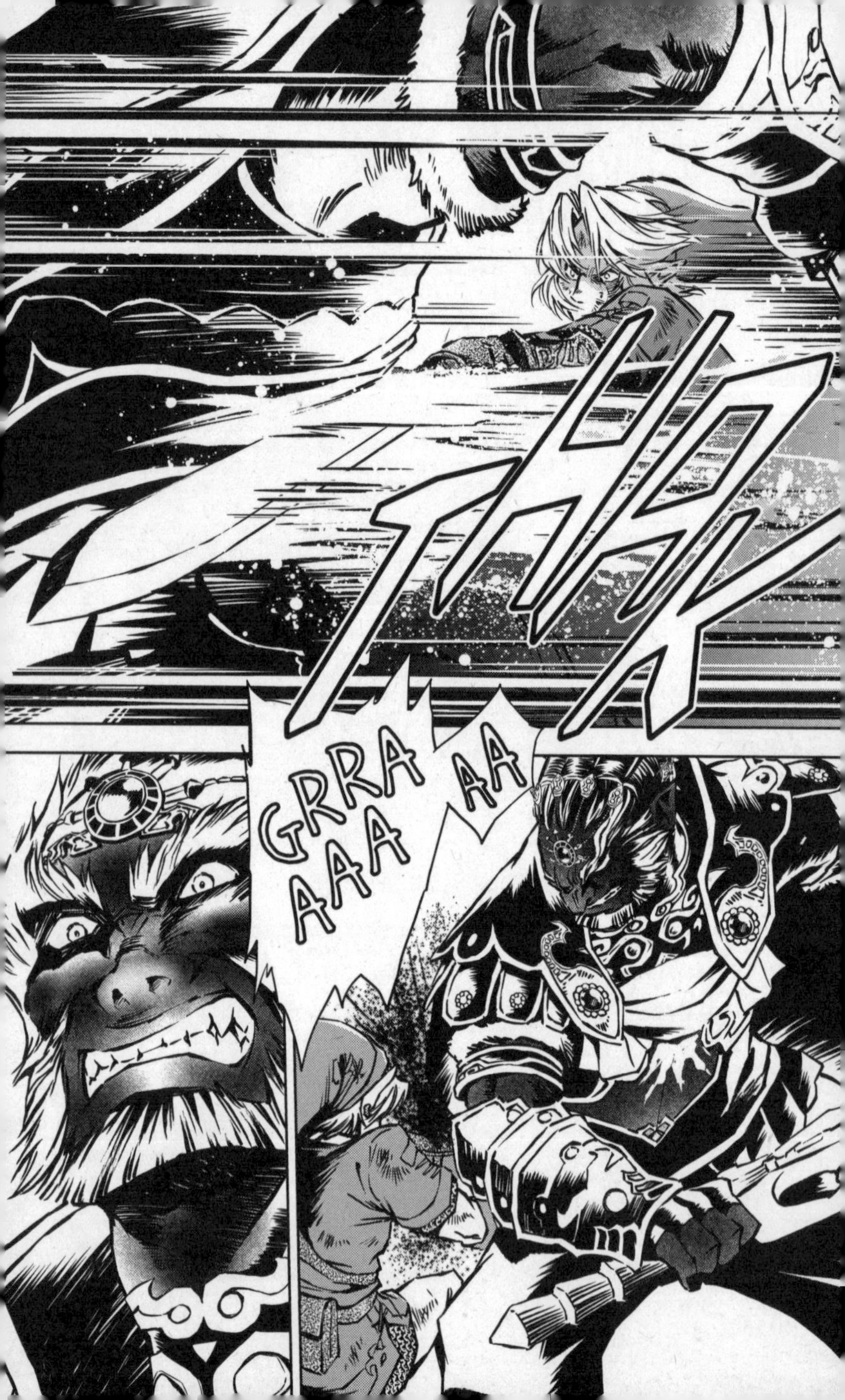
SHK
GRRA AAA AA

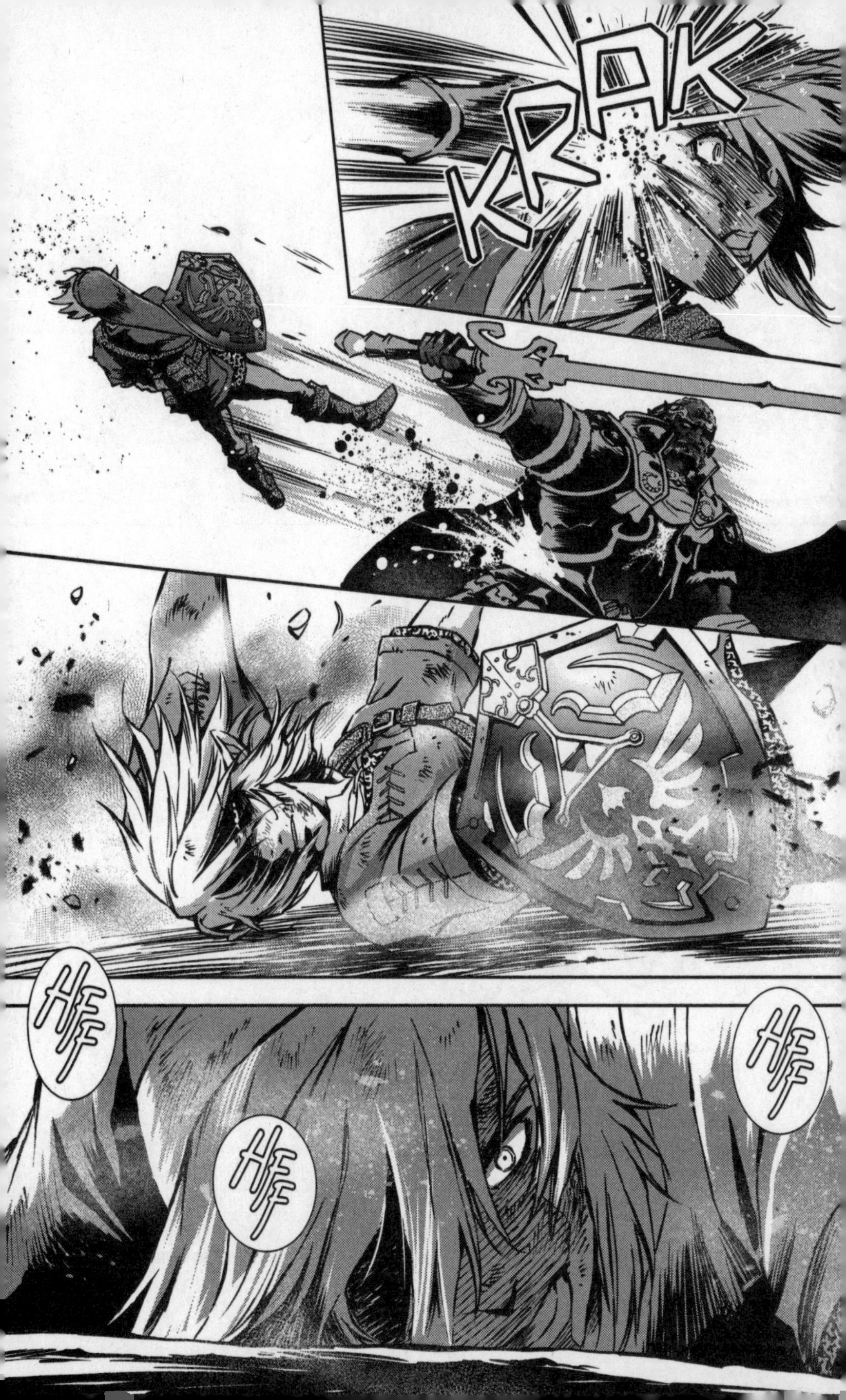
KRAK
HFF
HFF
HFF

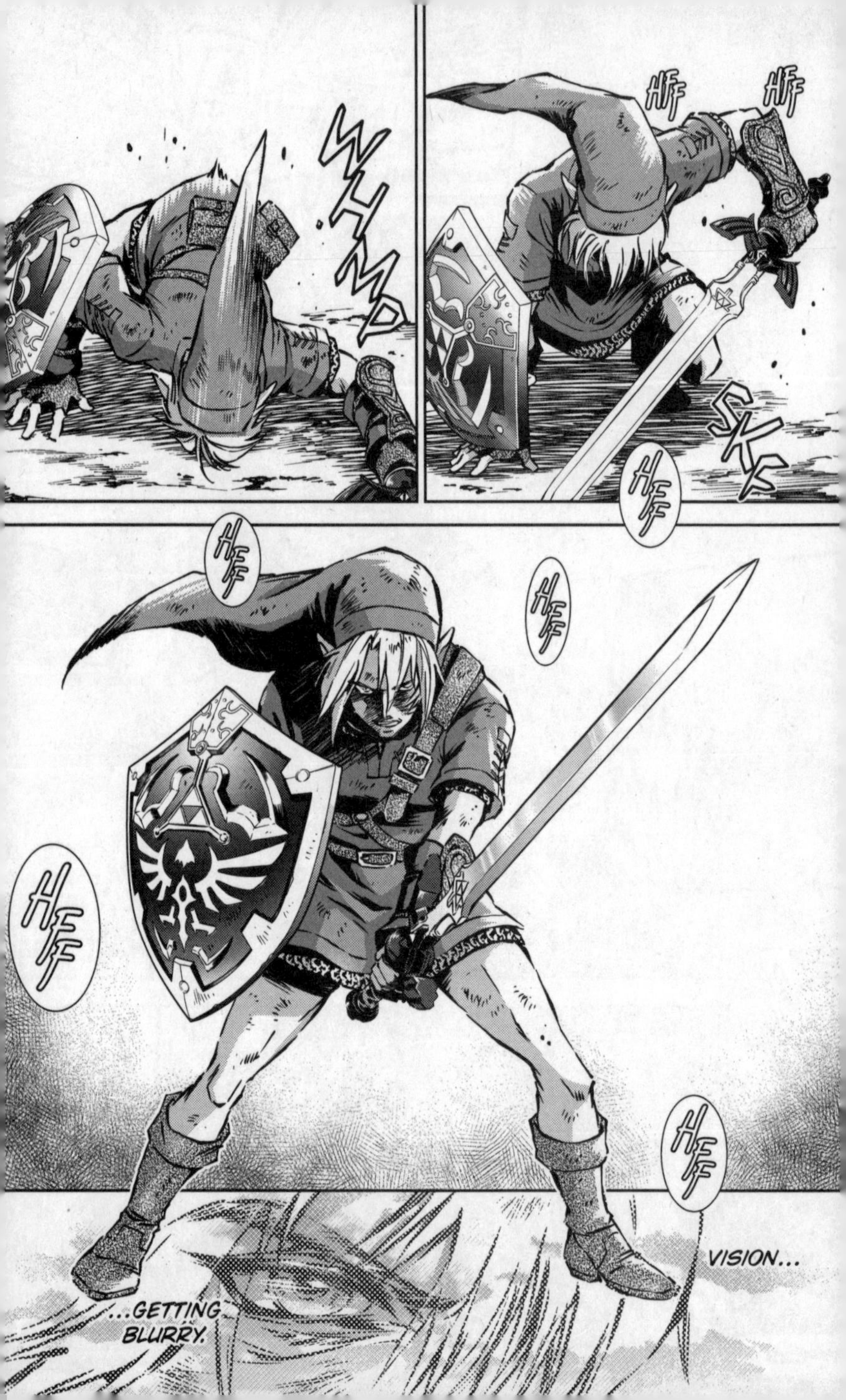
HFF
HFF
SKK
HFF
WHMP
HFF
HFF
HFF
HFF
VISION...
...GETTING BLURRY.

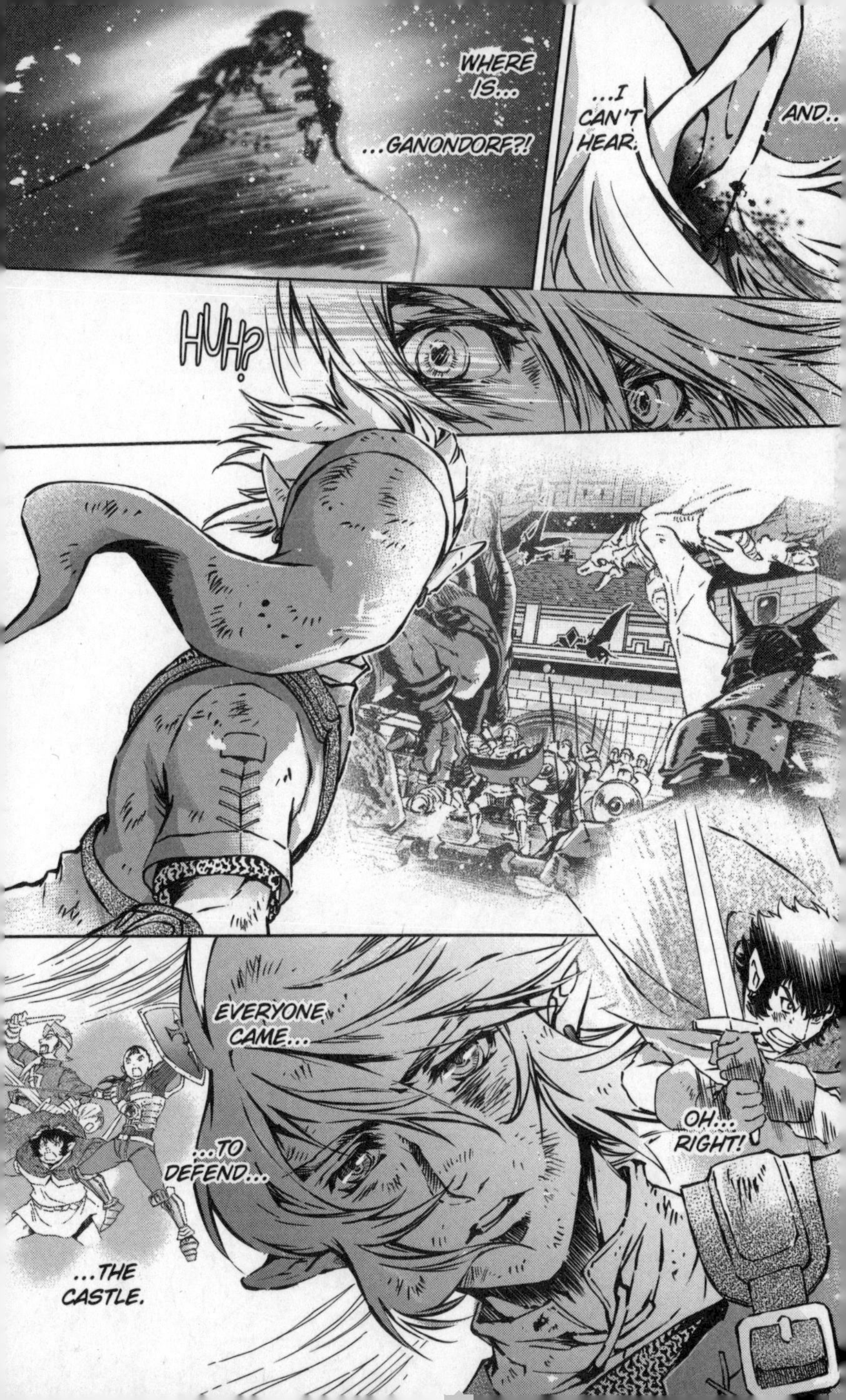
...I CAN'T HEAR.
AND...
WHERE IS...
...GANONDORF?!
HUH?
OH... RIGHT!
EVERYONE CAME...
...TO DEFEND...
...THE CASTLE.

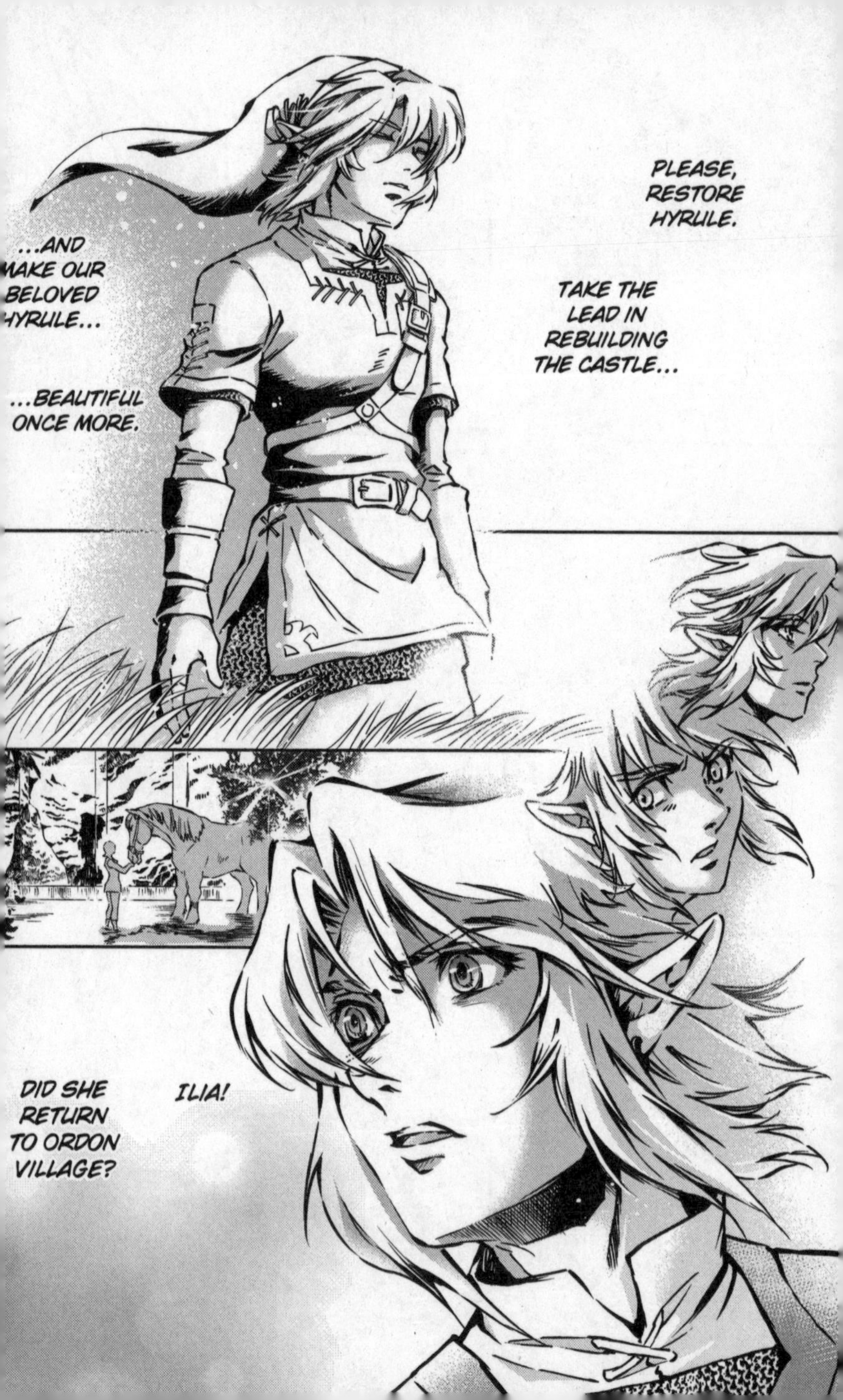
PLEASE, RESTORE HYRULE.
TAKE THE LEAD IN REBUILDING THE CASTLE...
...AND MAKE OUR BELOVED HYRULE...
...BEAUTIFUL ONCE MORE.
ILIA!
DID SHE RETURN TO ORDON VILLAGE?

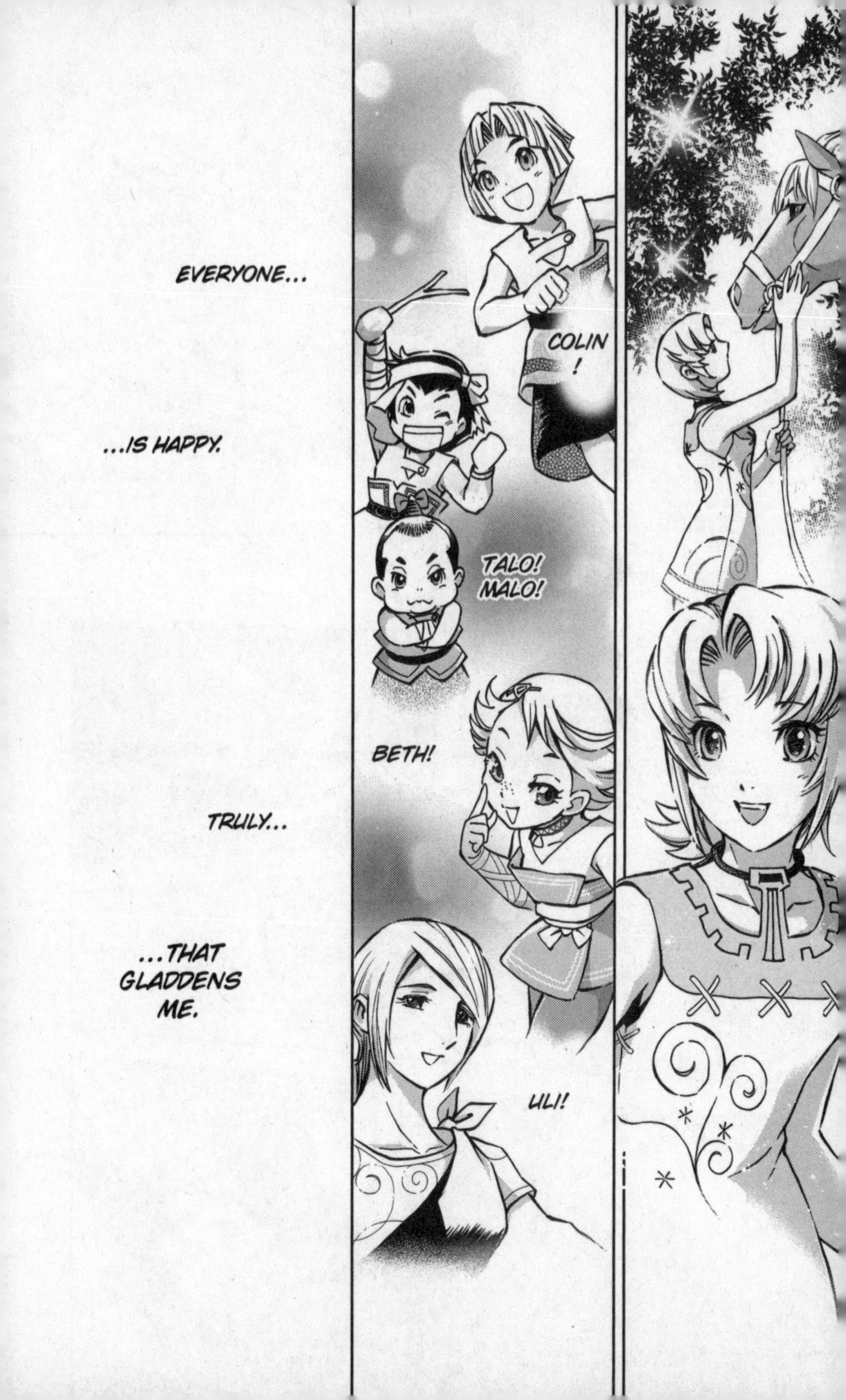
COLIN!
TALO! MALO!
BETH!
ULI!
EVERYONE...
...IS HAPPY.
TRULY...
...THAT GLADDENS ME.

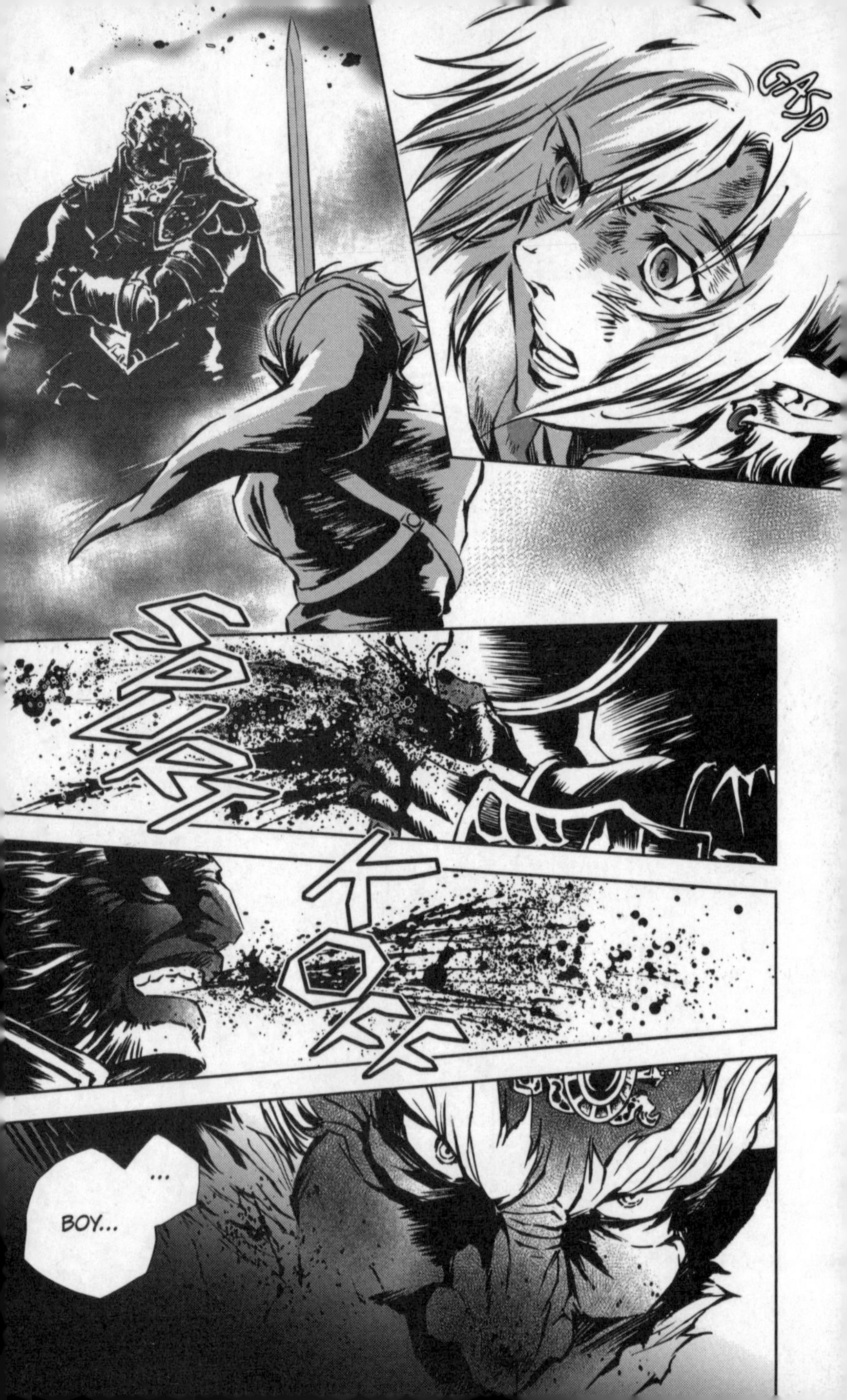
GASP
SPLURT
KOFF
... BOY...

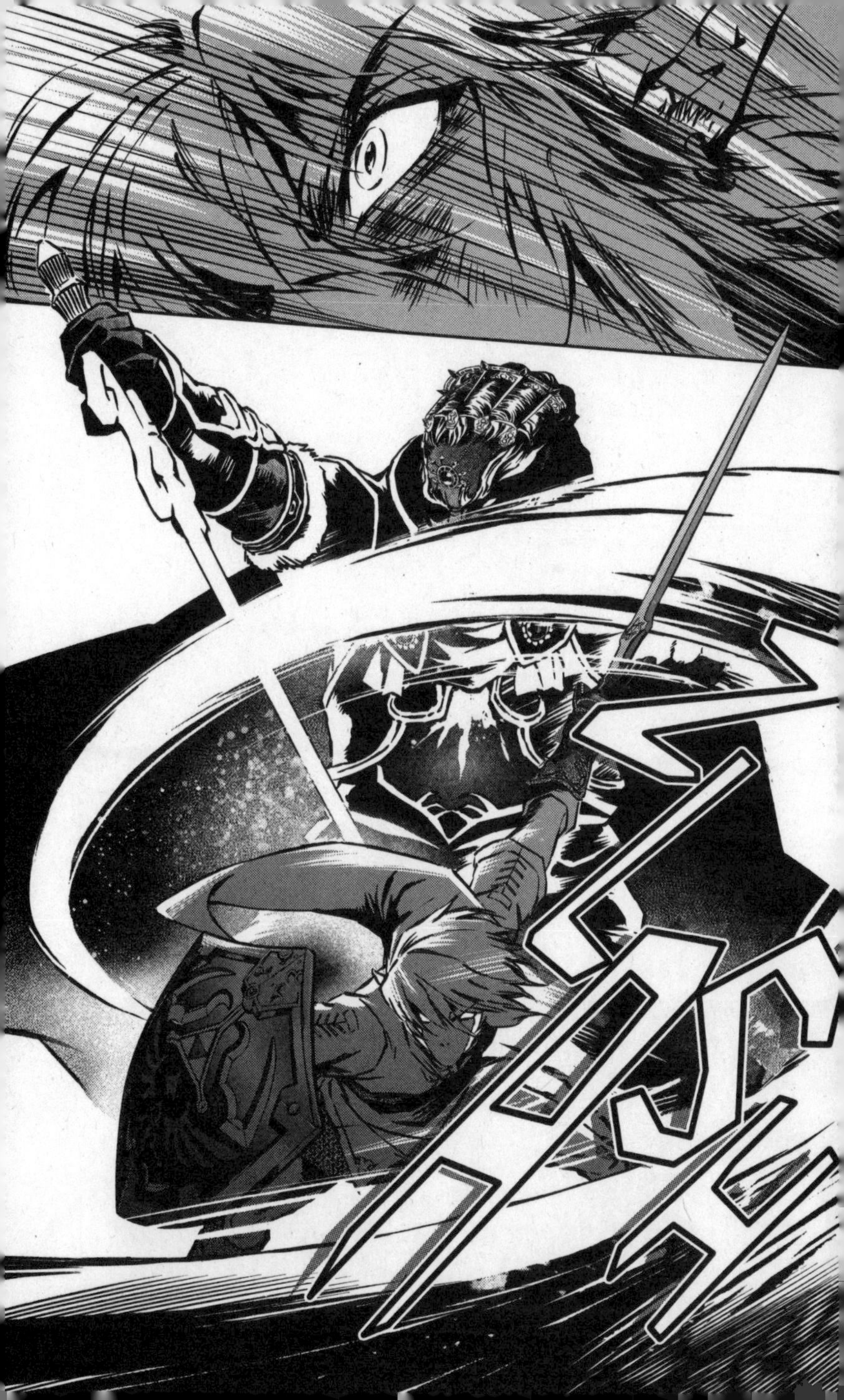

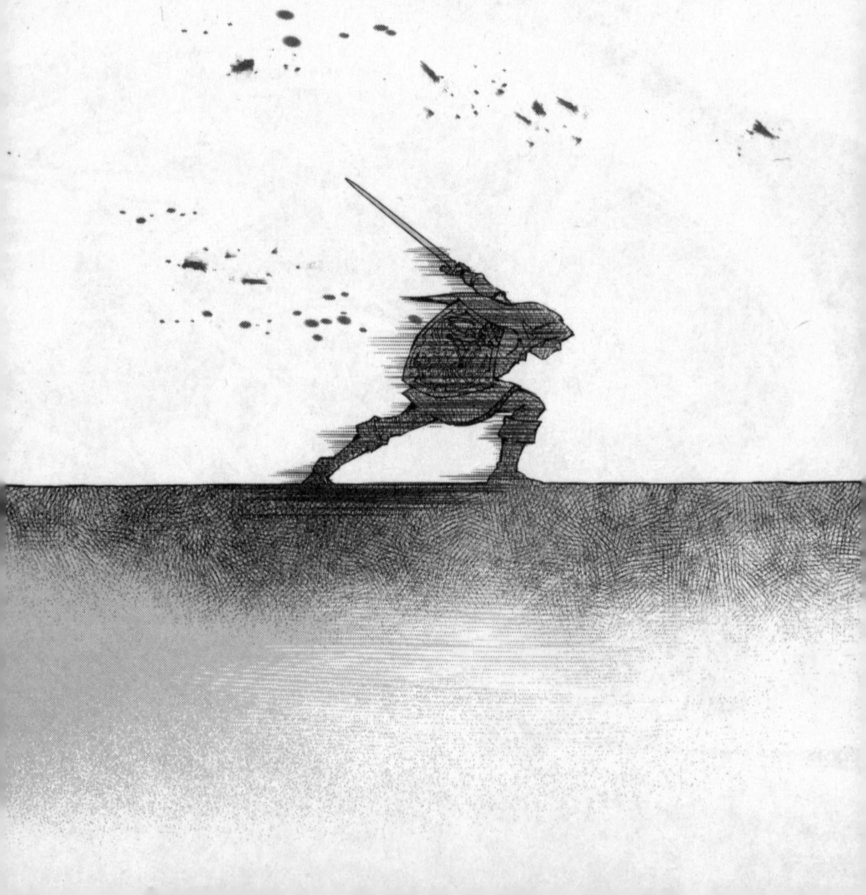

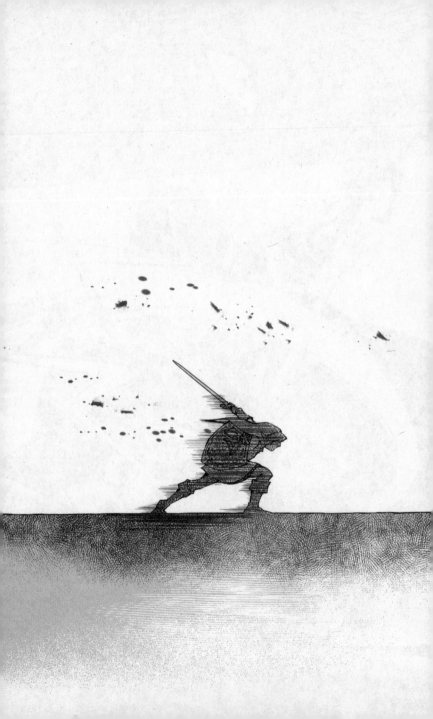

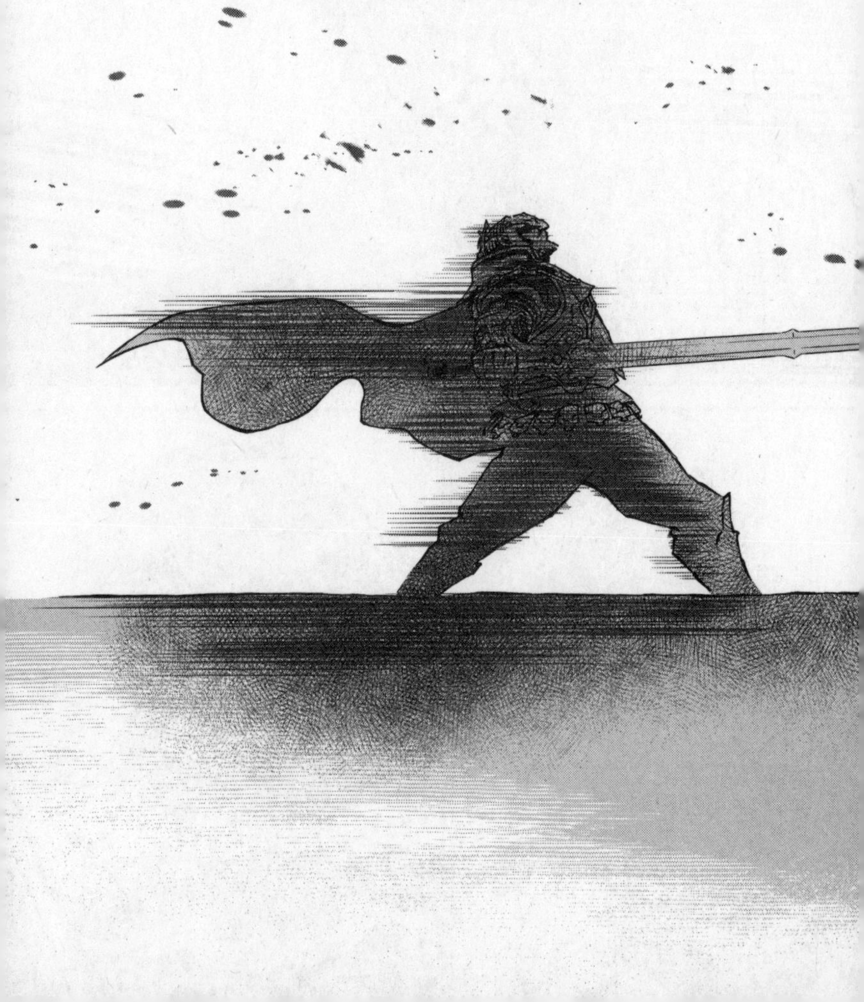

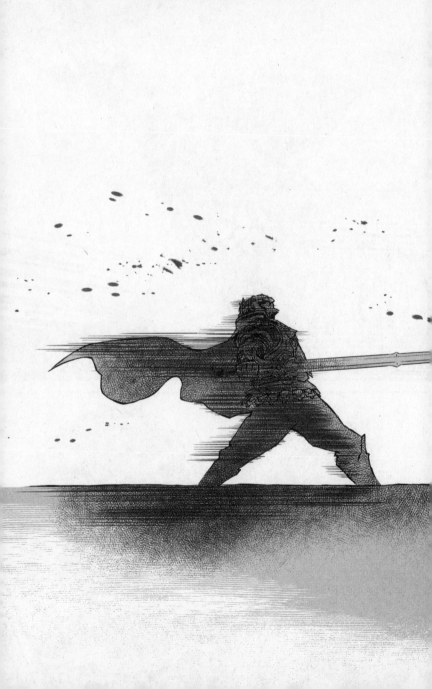

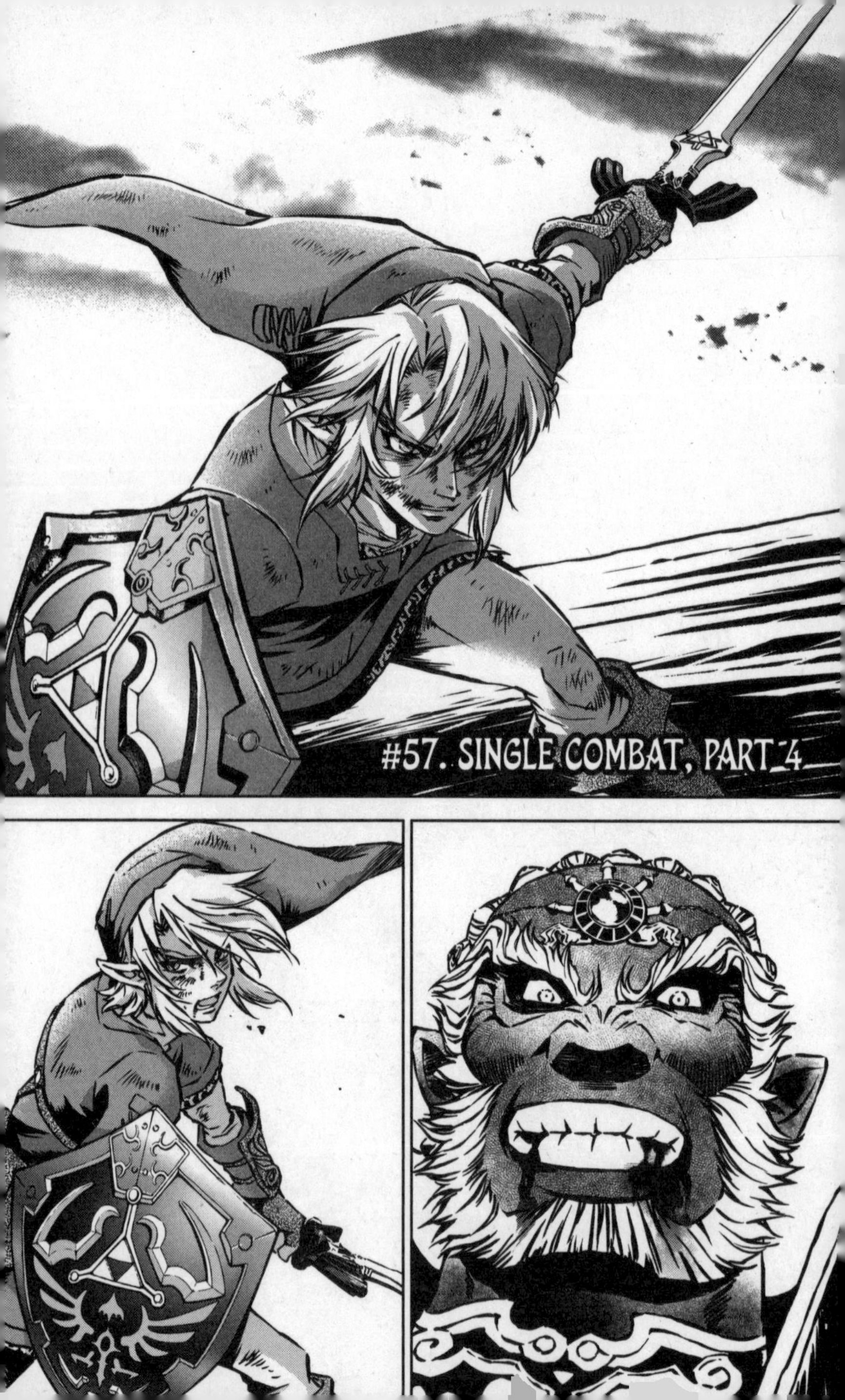
#57. SINGLE COMBAT, PART 4

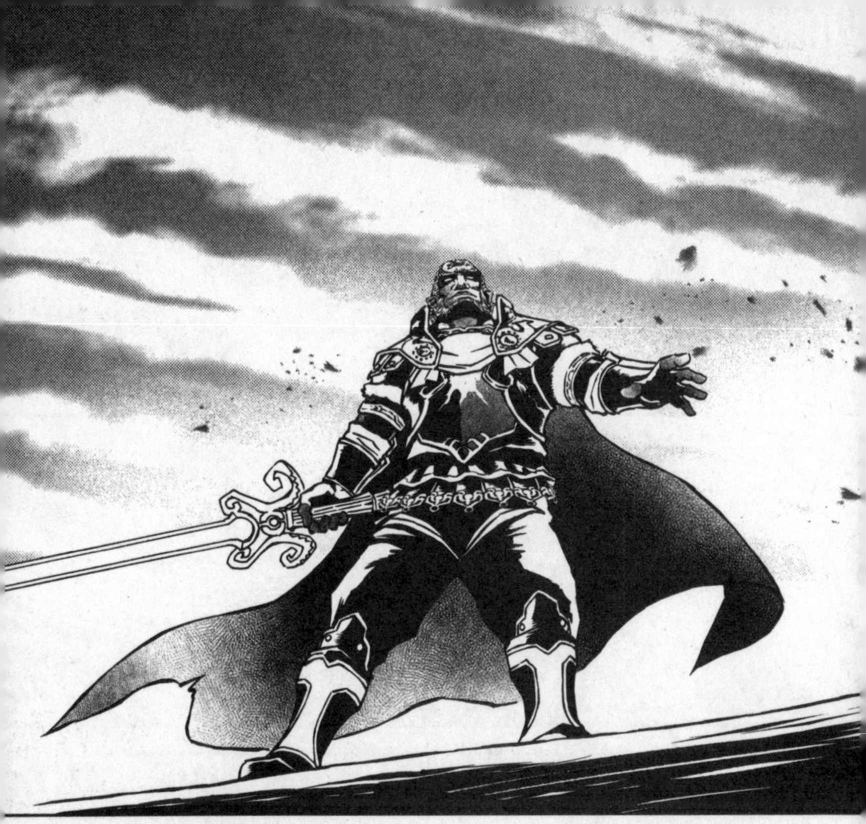
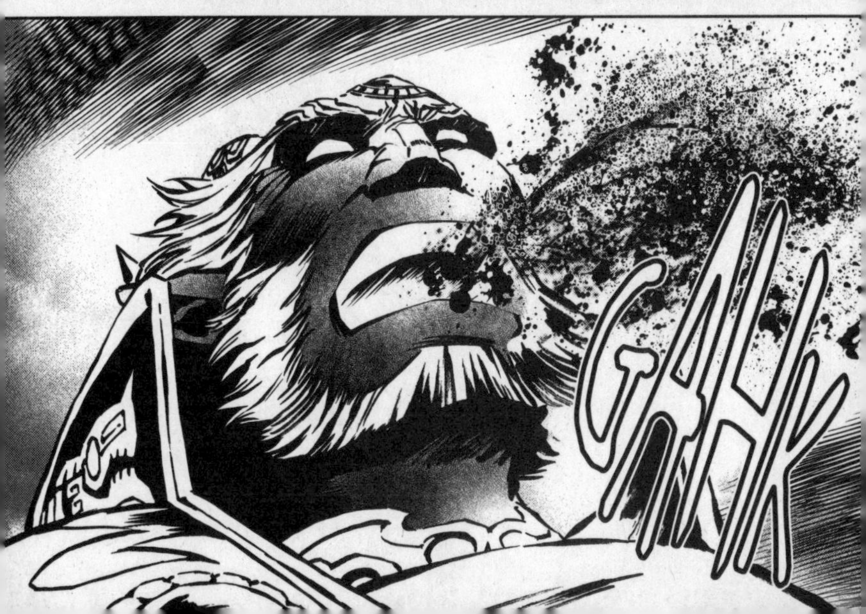
GAHK

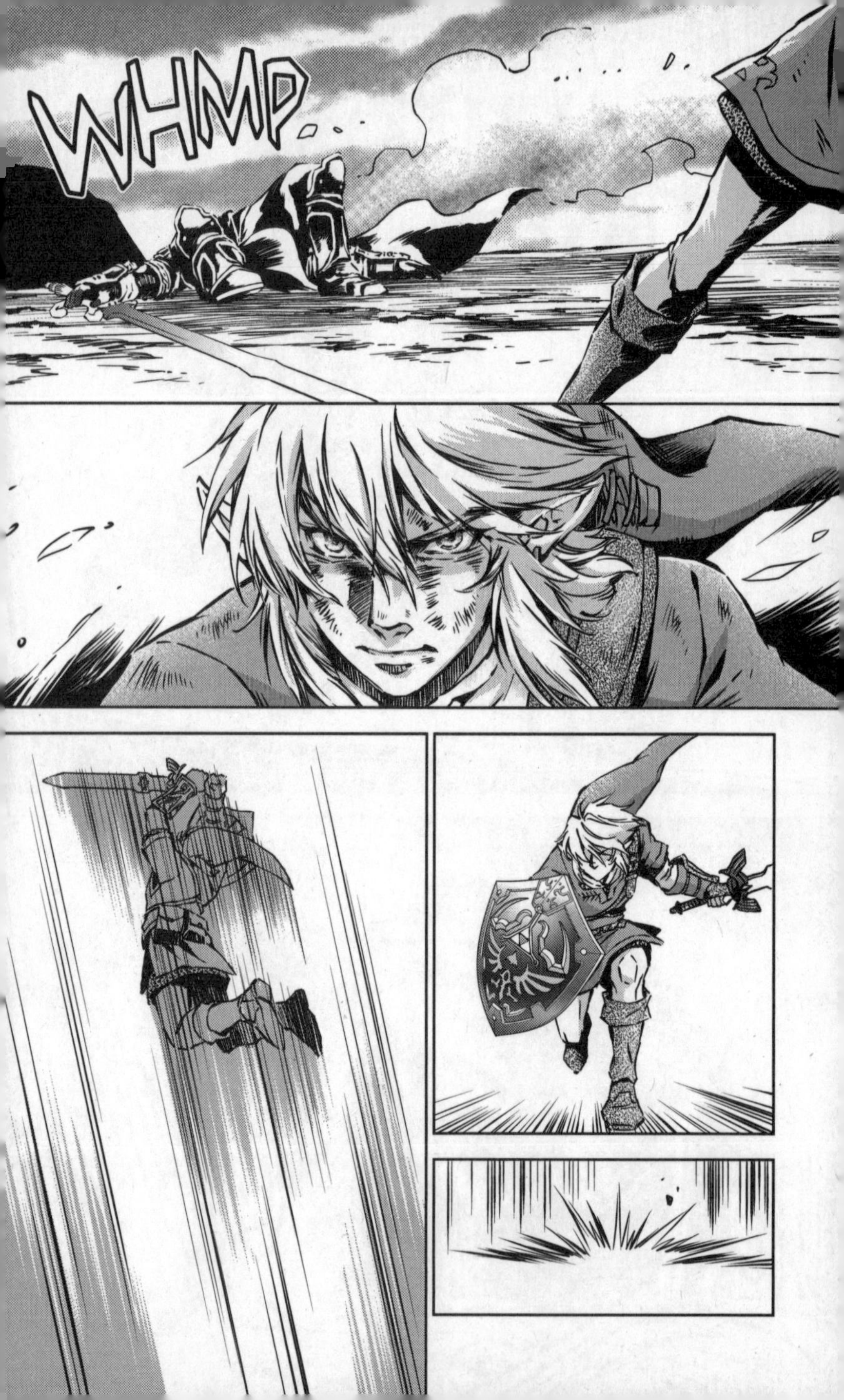
WHMP

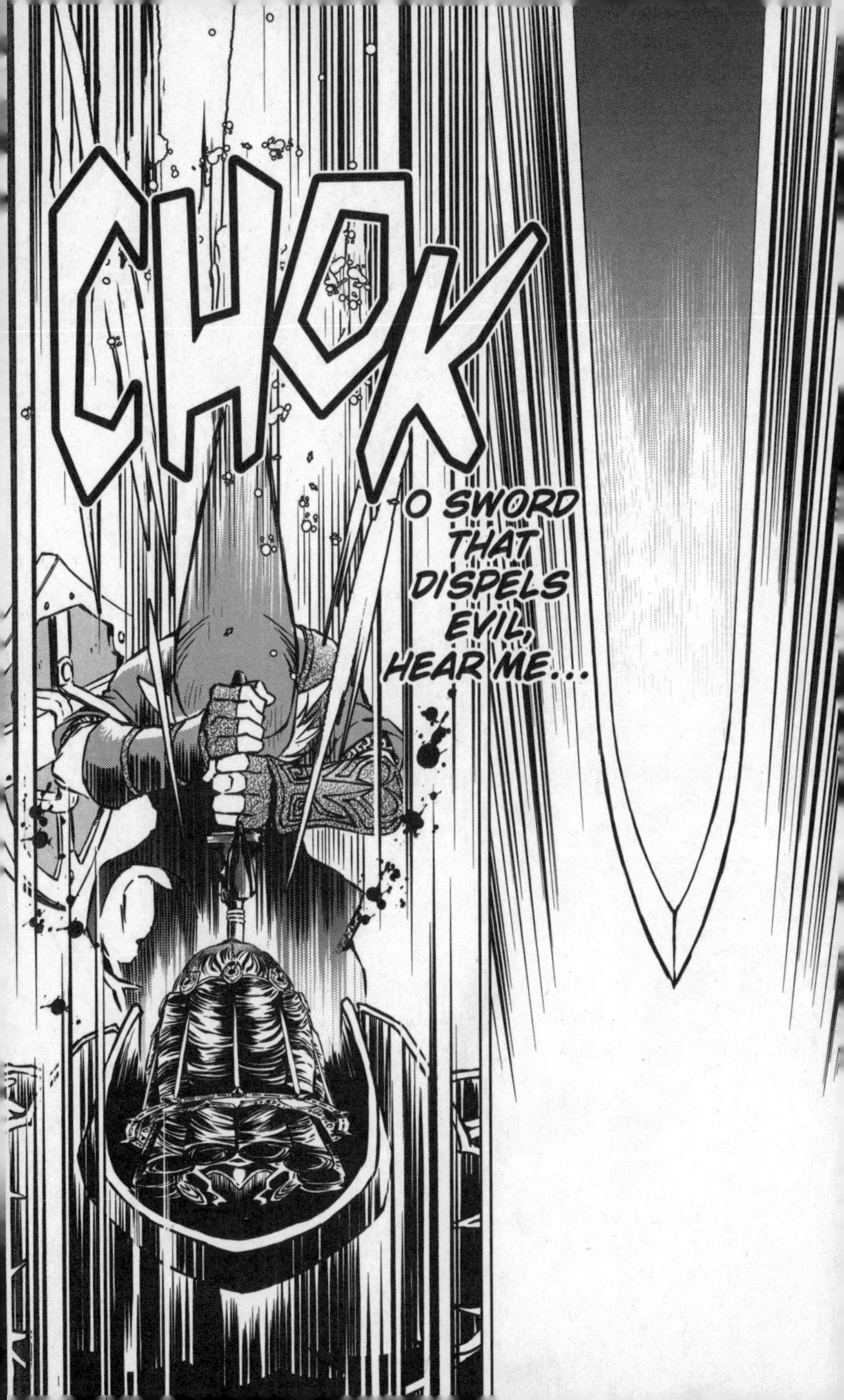
CHOK
O SWORD THAT DISPELS EVIL, HEAR ME...

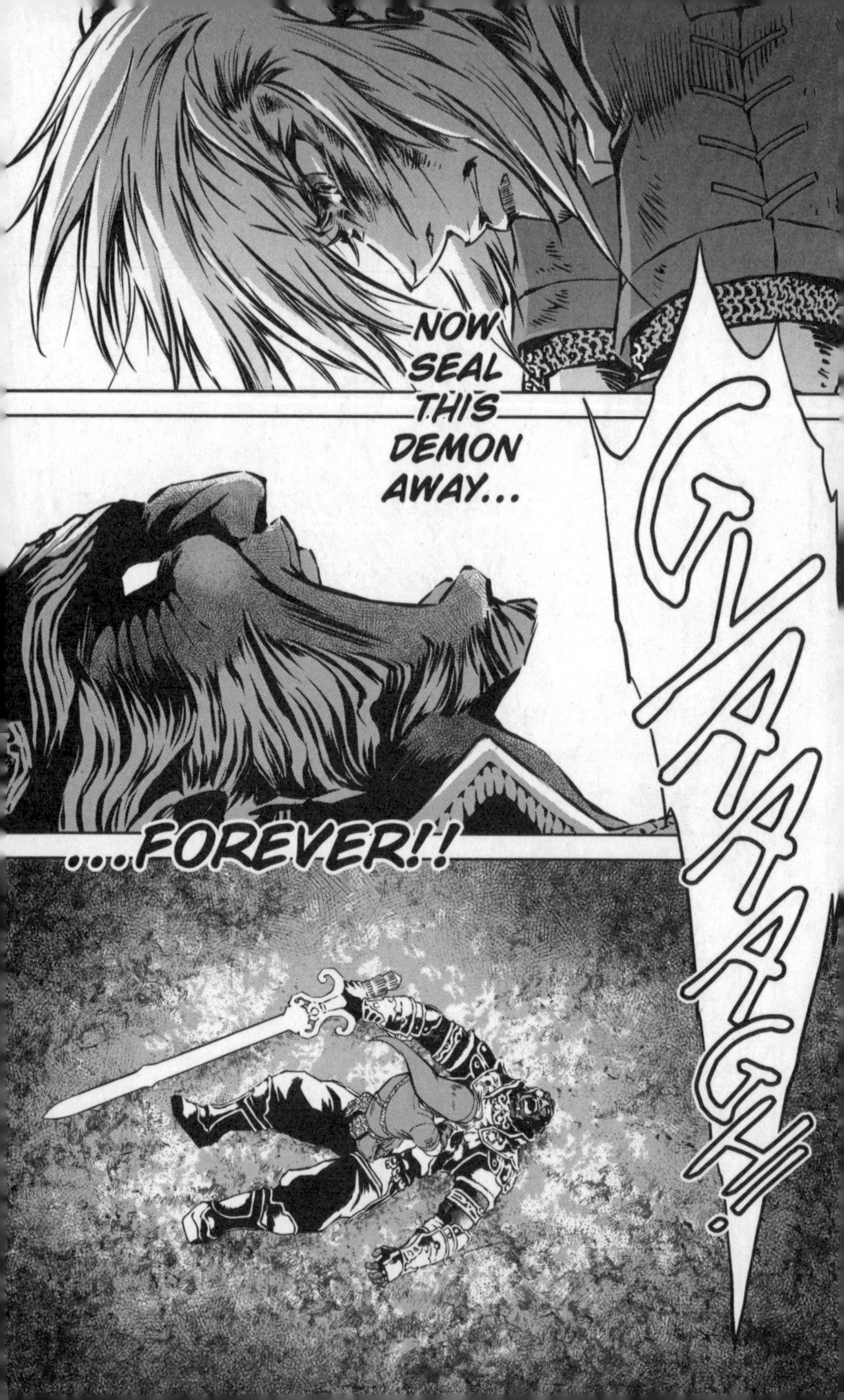
NOW SEAL THIS DEMON AWAY...
GYAAAAGH!!
...FOREVER!!

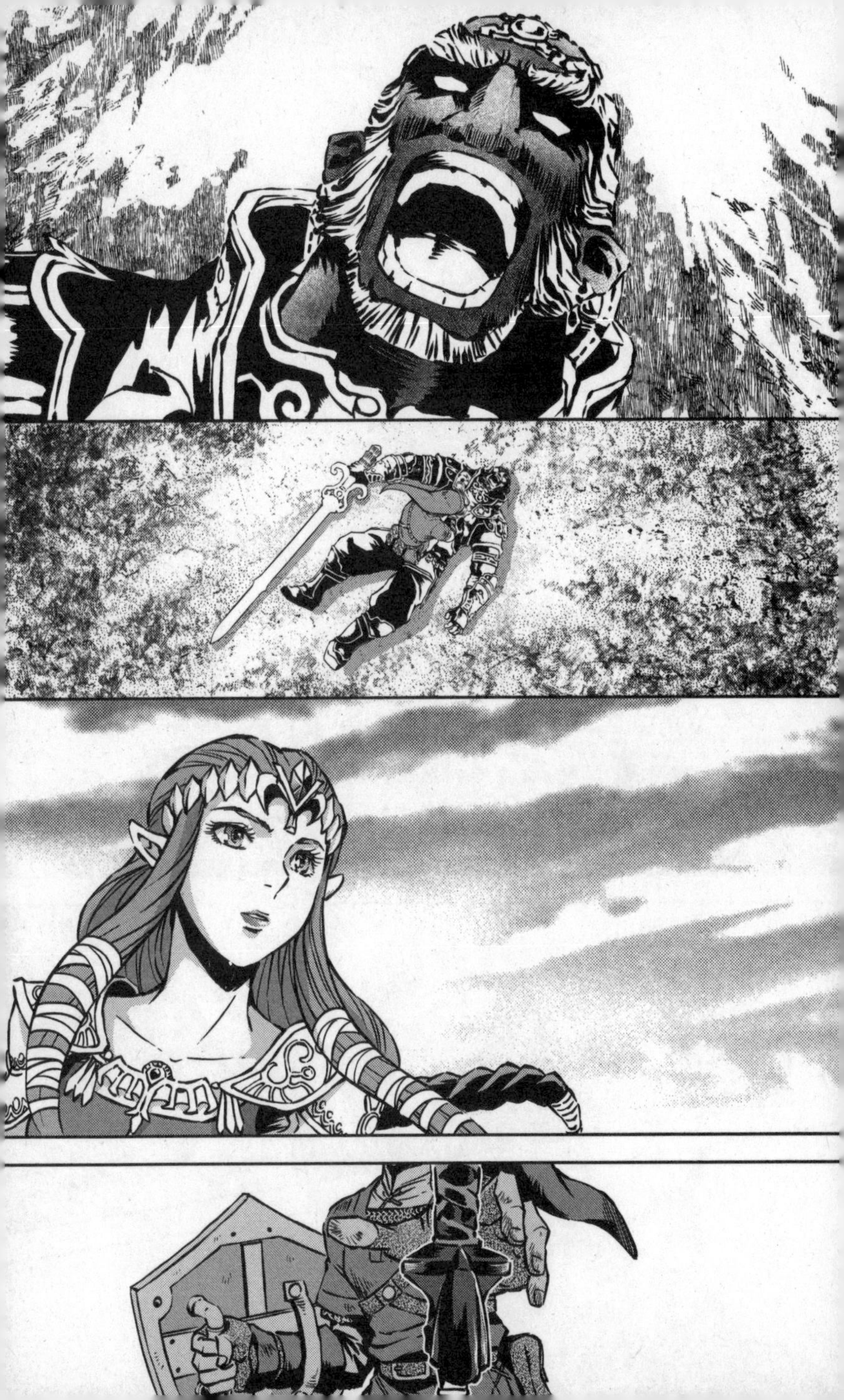

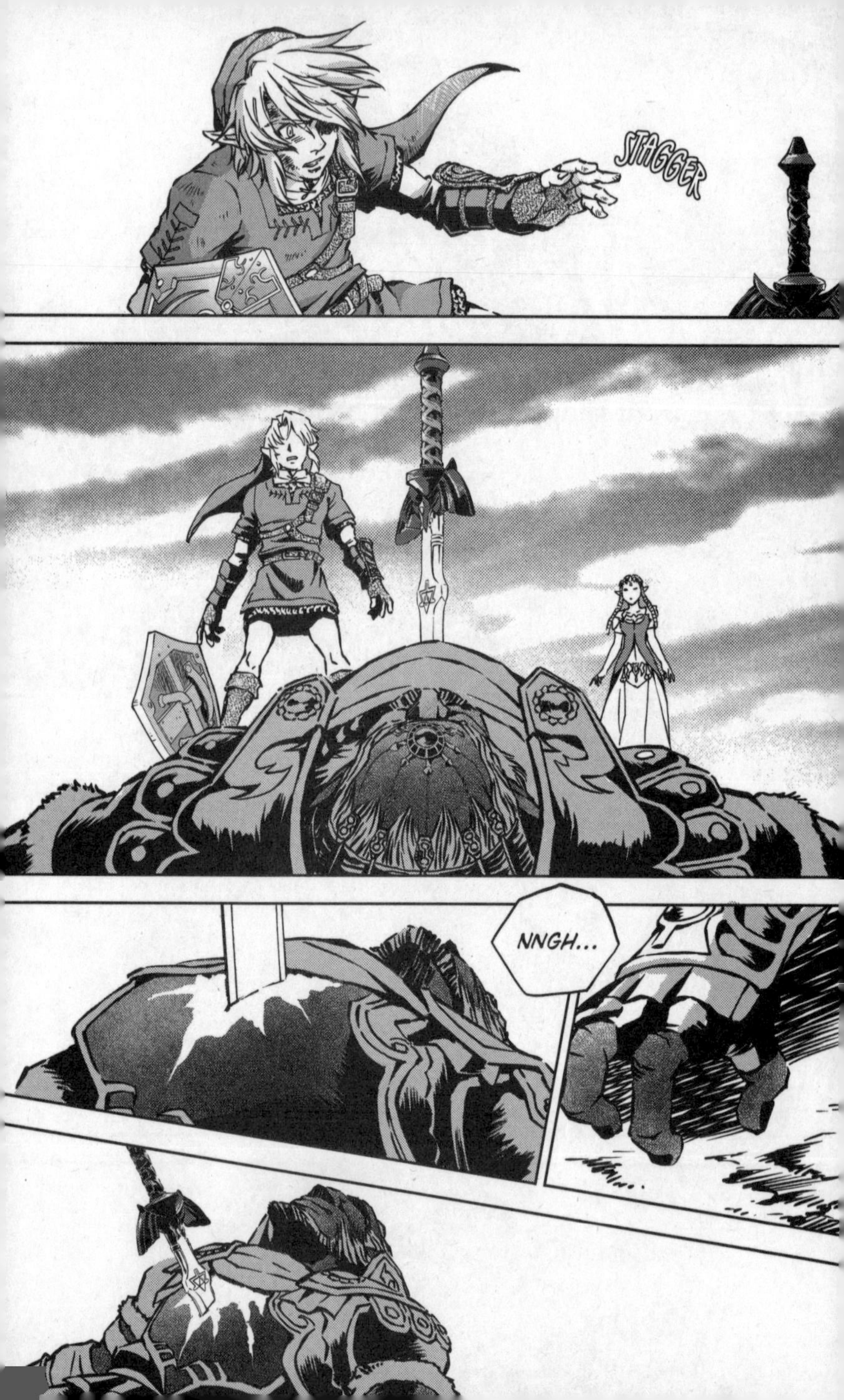
STAGGER
NNGH...

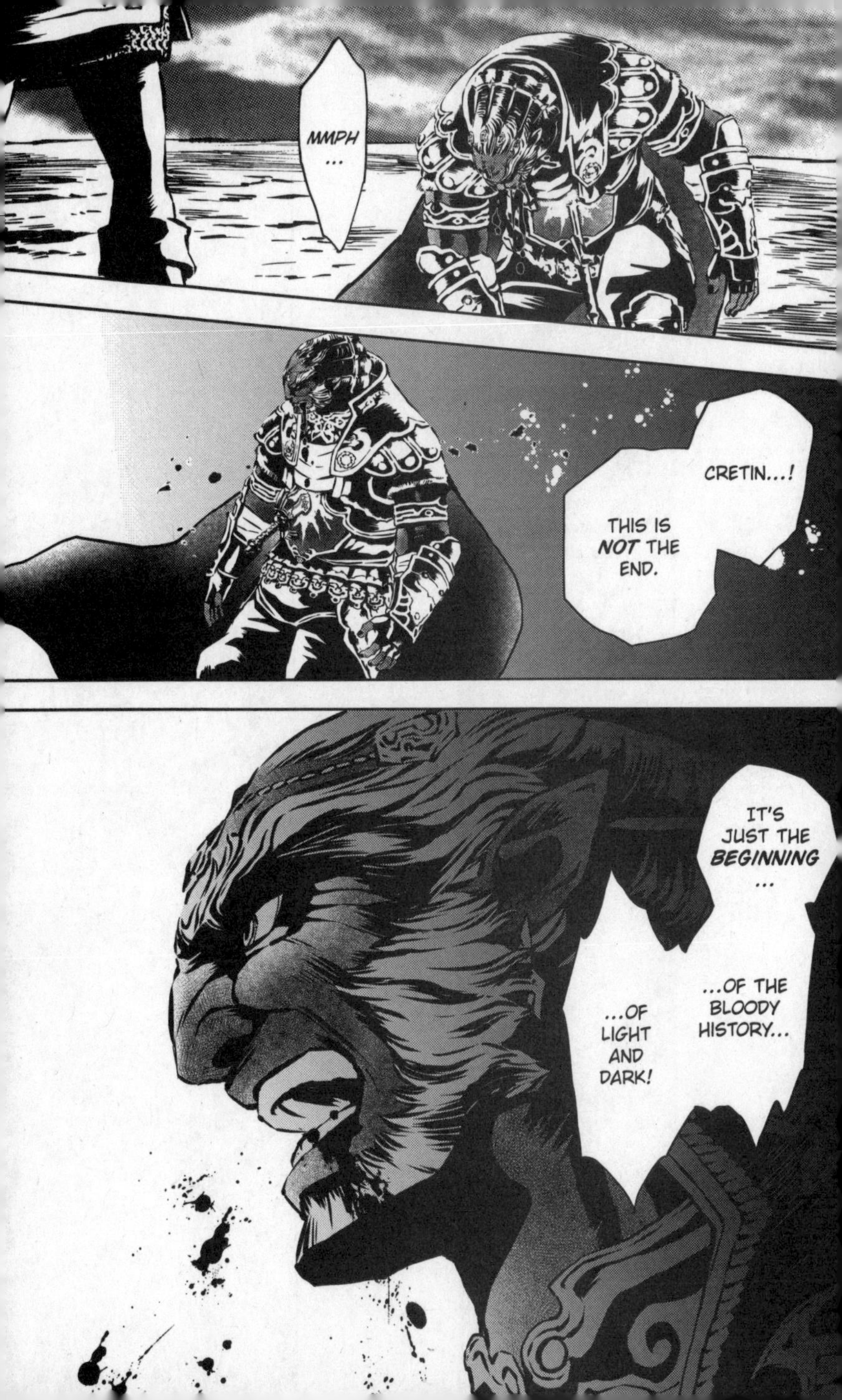
MMPH ...
CRETIN...!
THIS IS NOT THE END.
IT'S JUST THE BEGINNING ...
...OF THE BLOODY HISTORY...
...OF LIGHT AND DARK!

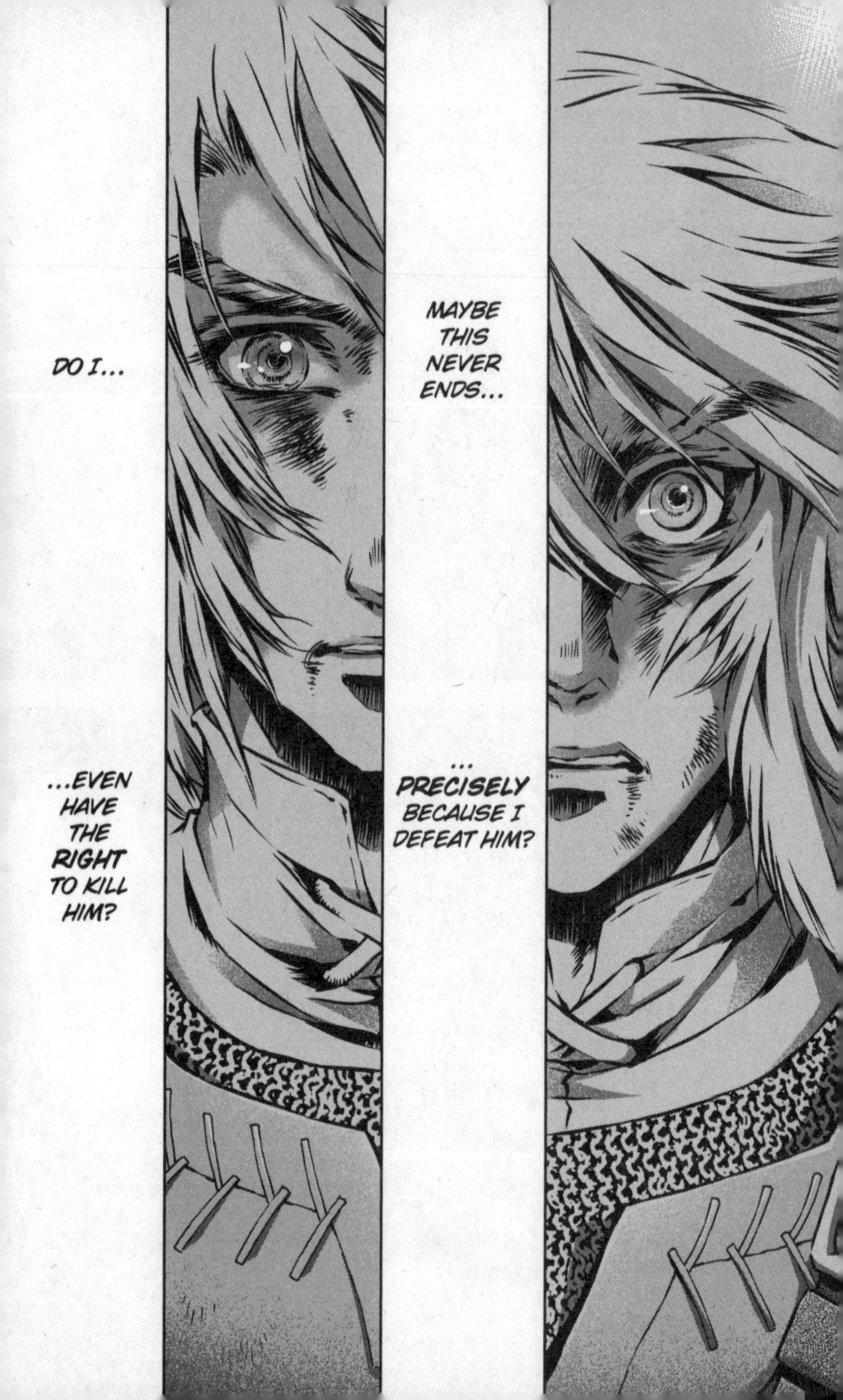
MAYBE THIS NEVER ENDS...
...PRECISELY BECAUSE I DEFEAT HIM?
DO I...
...EVEN HAVE THE RIGHT TO KILL HIM?

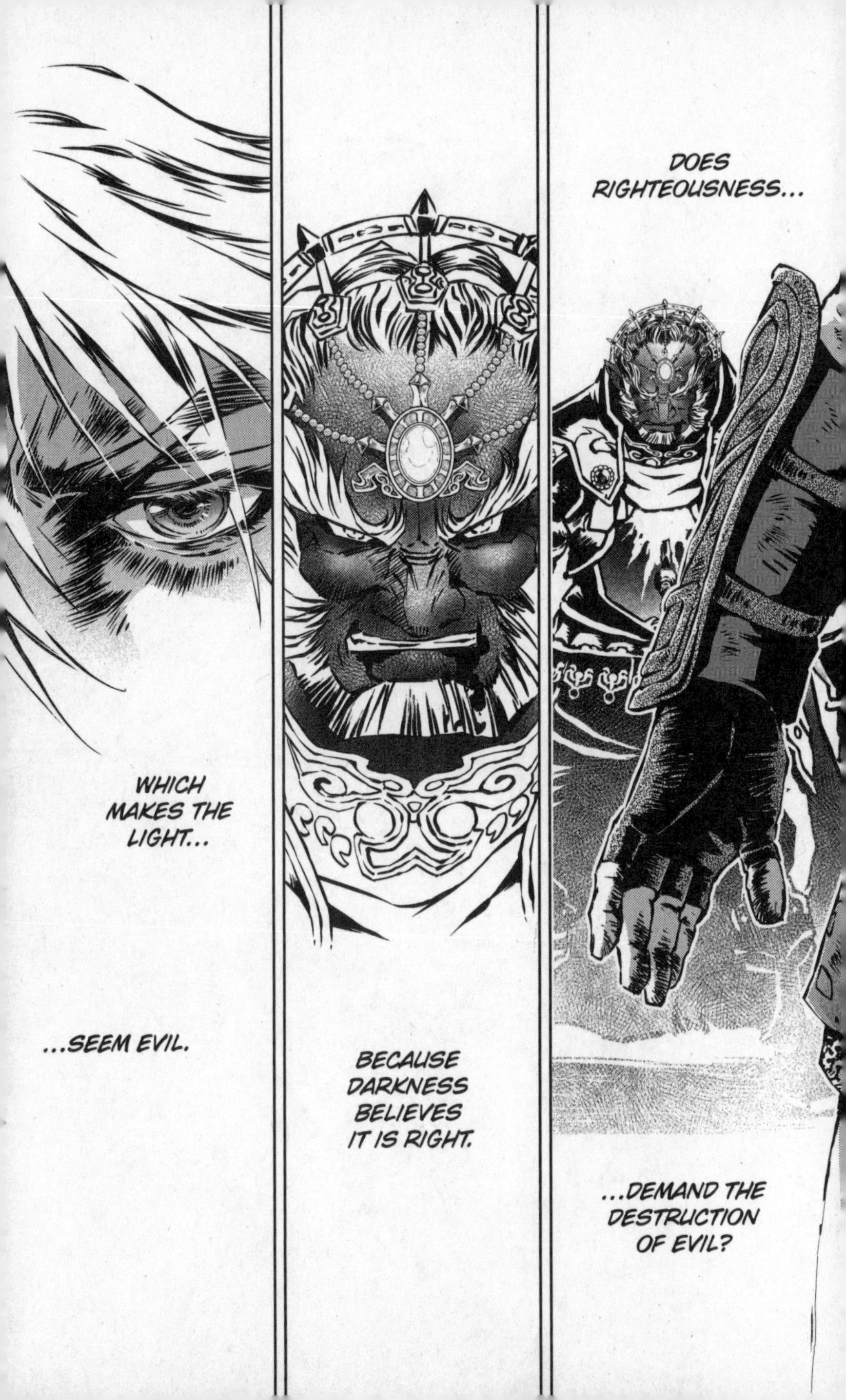
DOES RIGHTEOUSNESS...
...DEMAND THE DESTRUCTION OF EVIL?
BECAUSE DARKNESS BELIEVES IT IS RIGHT.
WHICH MAKES THE LIGHT...
...SEEM EVIL.

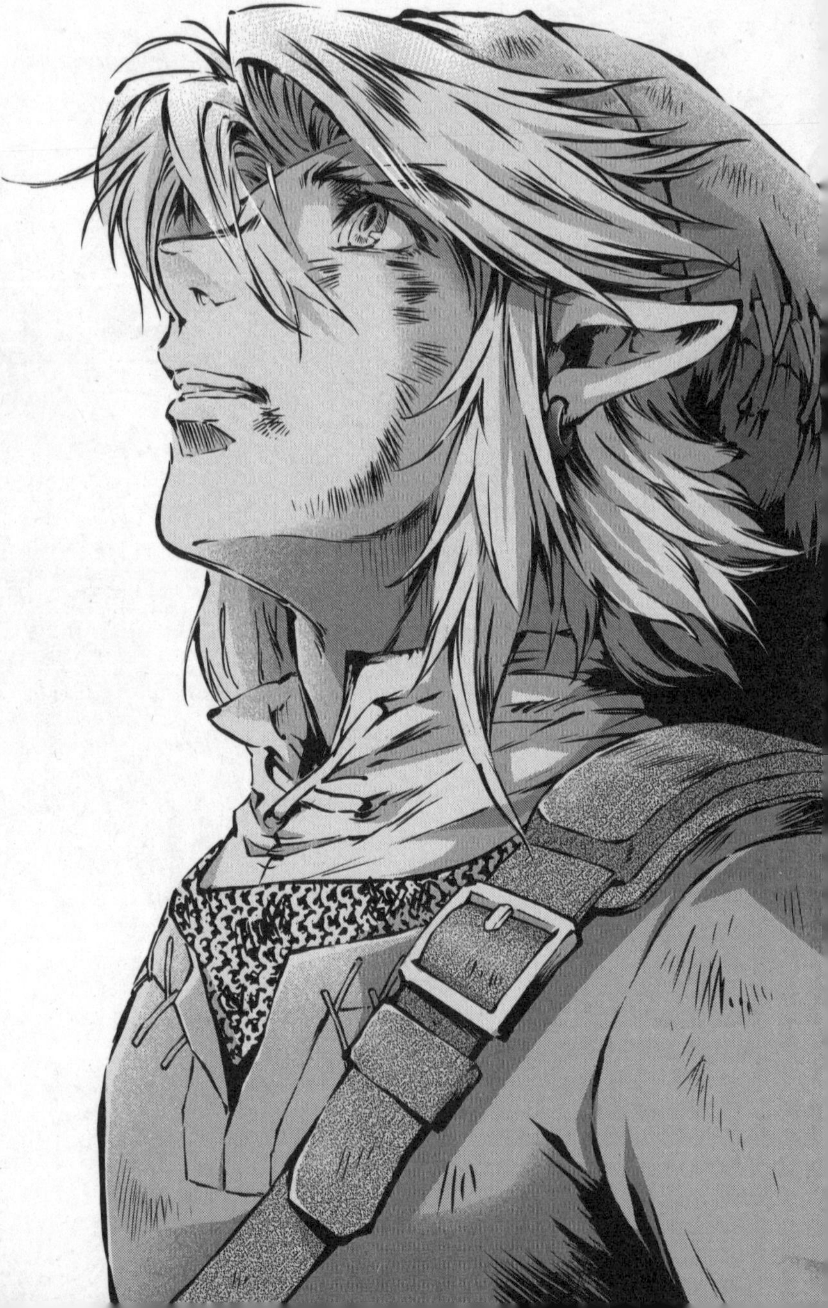

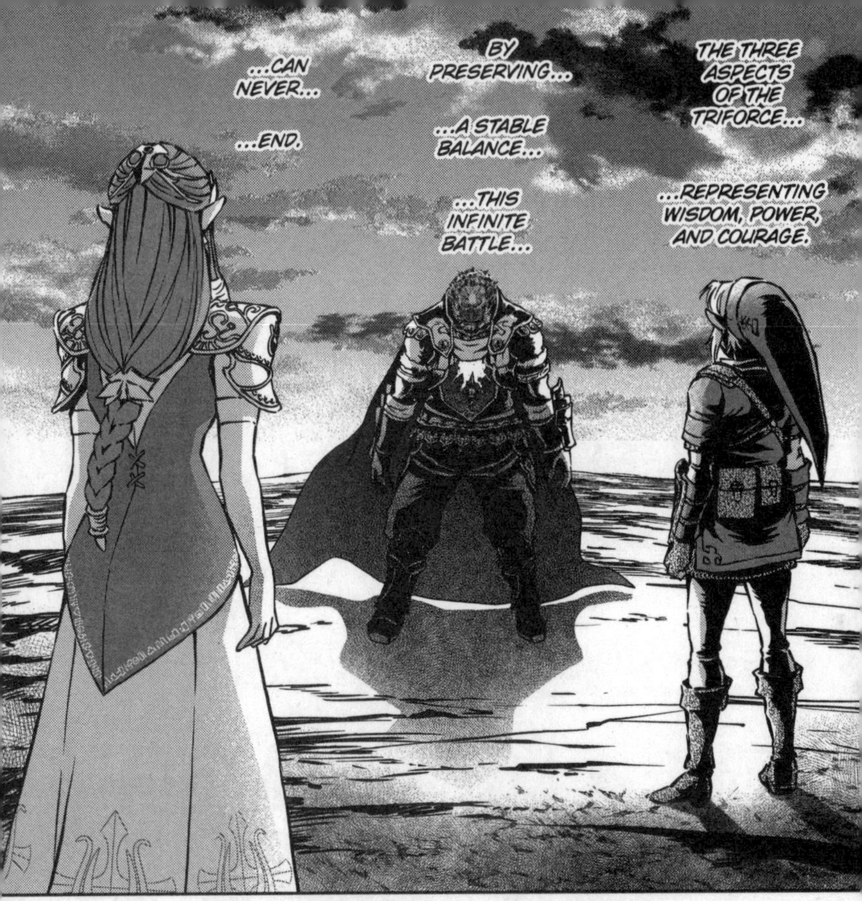
THE THREE ASPECTS OF THE TRIFORCE...
...REPRESENTING WISDOM, POWER, AND COURAGE.
BY PRESERVING...
...A STABLE BALANCE...
...THIS INFINITE BATTLE...
...CAN NEVER...
...END.

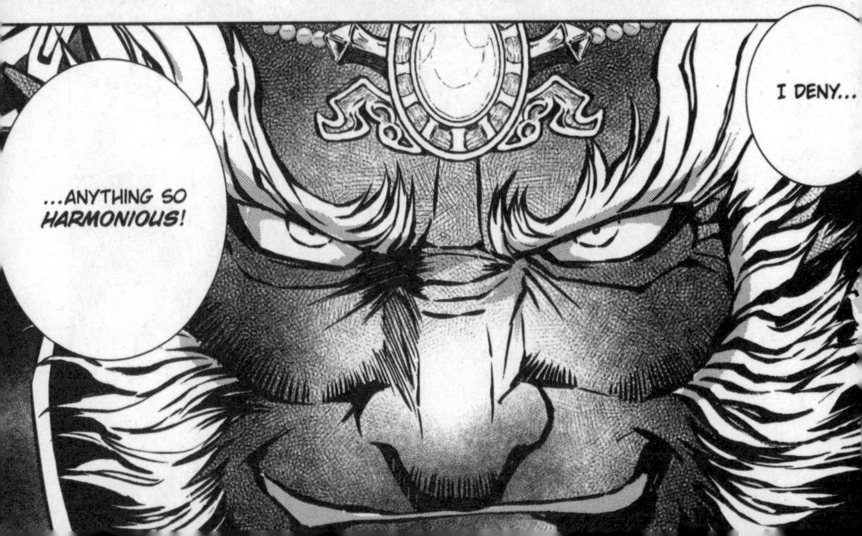
I DENY...
...ANYTHING SO *HARMONIOUS!*

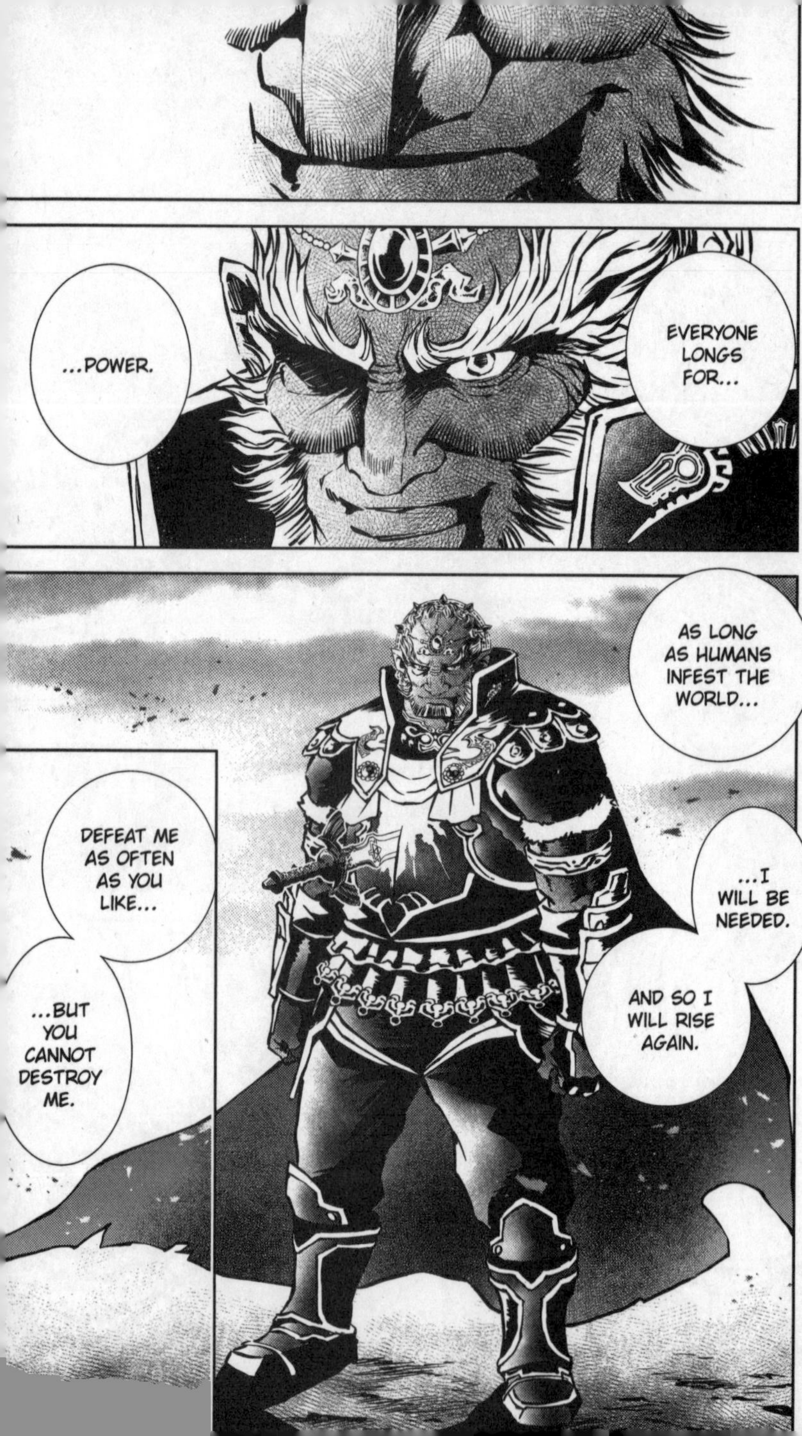
EVERYONE LONGS FOR...
...POWER.
AS LONG AS HUMANS INFEST THE WORLD...
...I WILL BE NEEDED.
AND SO I WILL RISE AGAIN.
DEFEAT ME AS OFTEN AS YOU LIKE...
...BUT YOU CANNOT DESTROY ME.

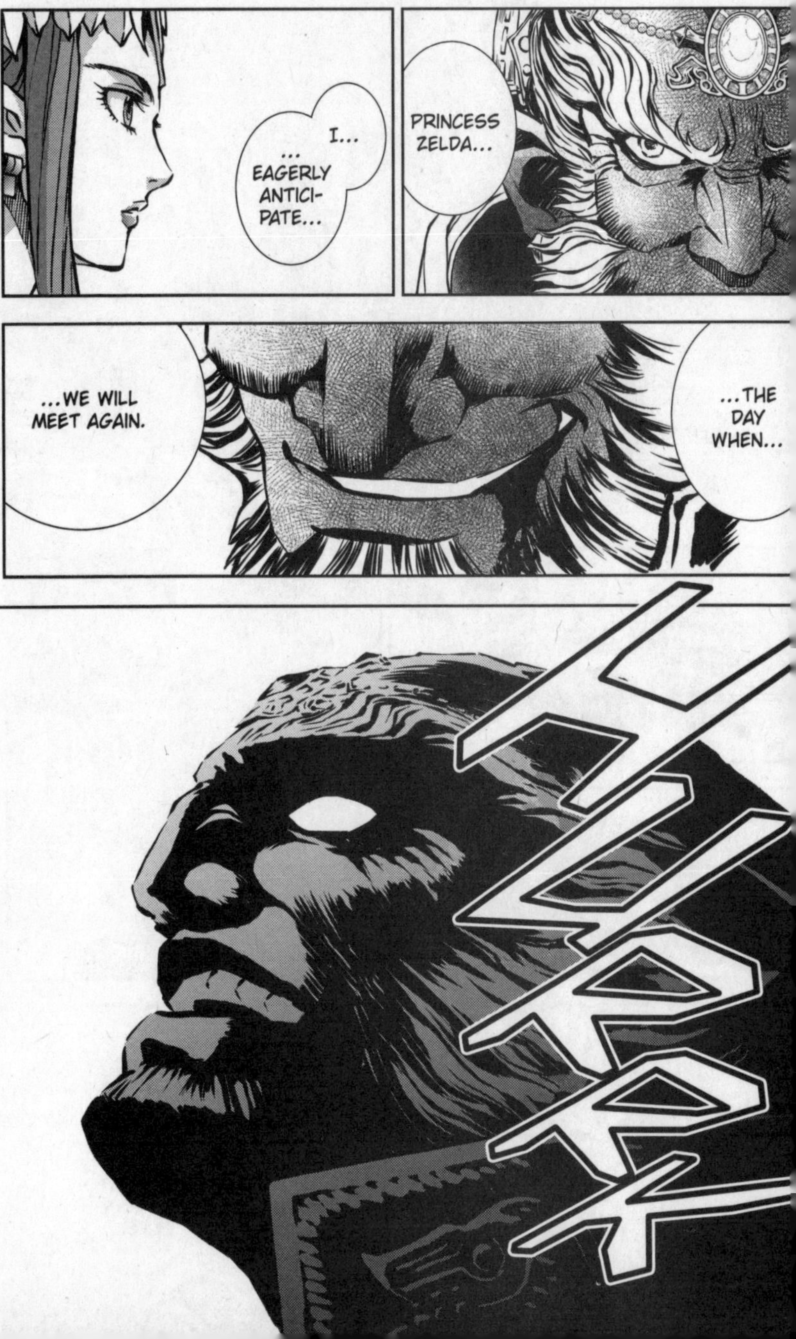
PRINCESS ZELDA...
I... ... EAGERLY ANTICIPATE...
...THE DAY WHEN...
...WE WILL MEET AGAIN.

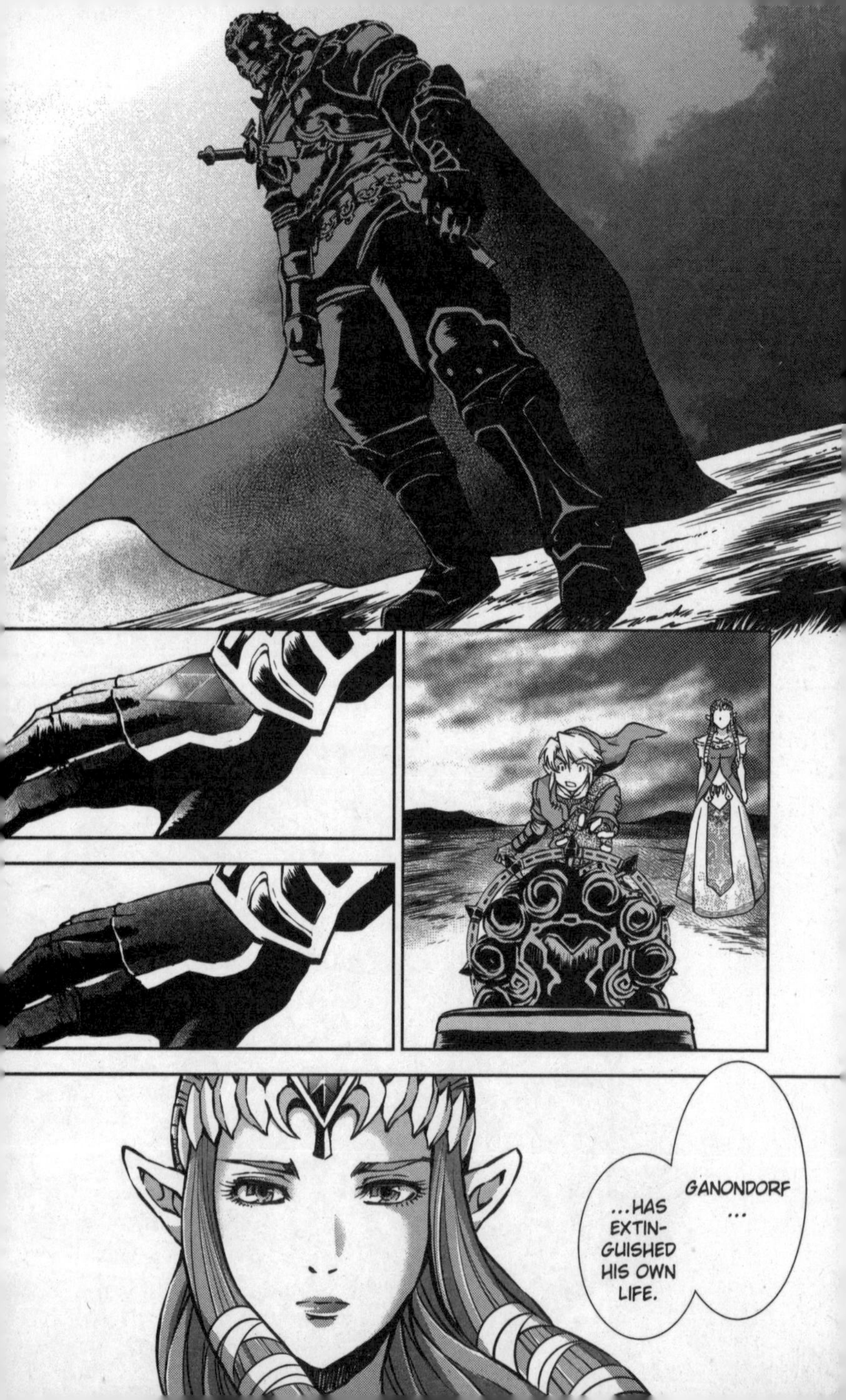
GANONDORF ...
...HAS EXTIN-GUISHED HIS OWN LIFE.

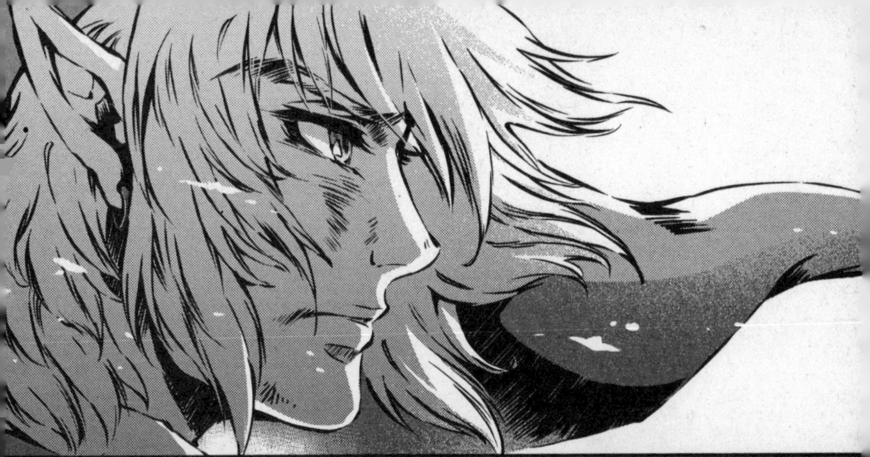
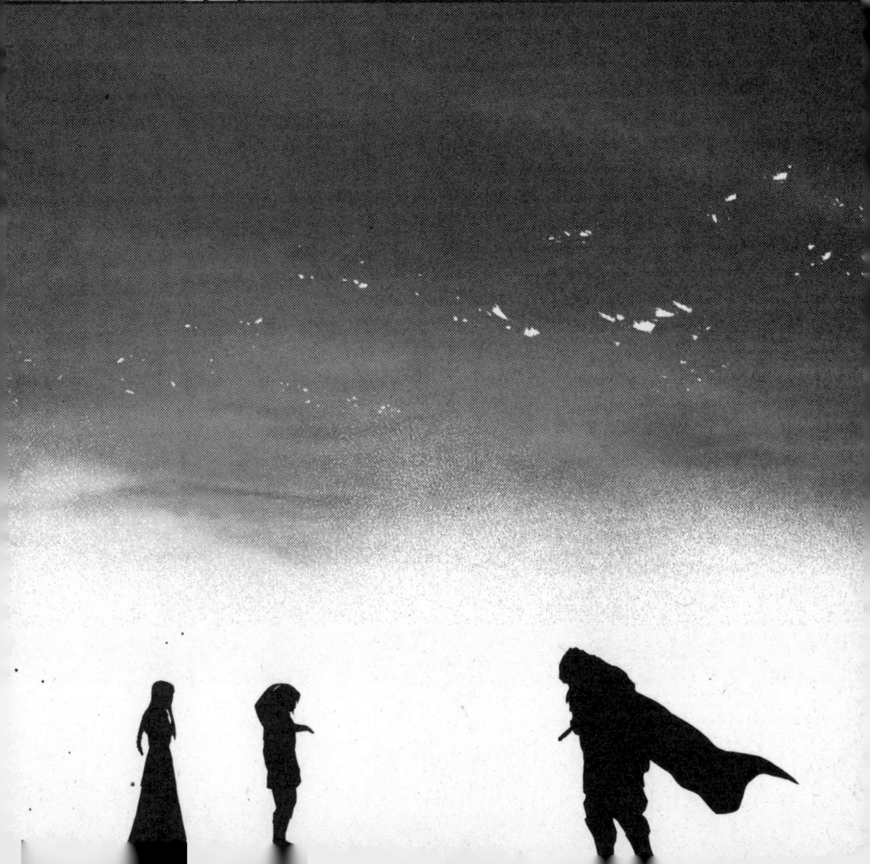

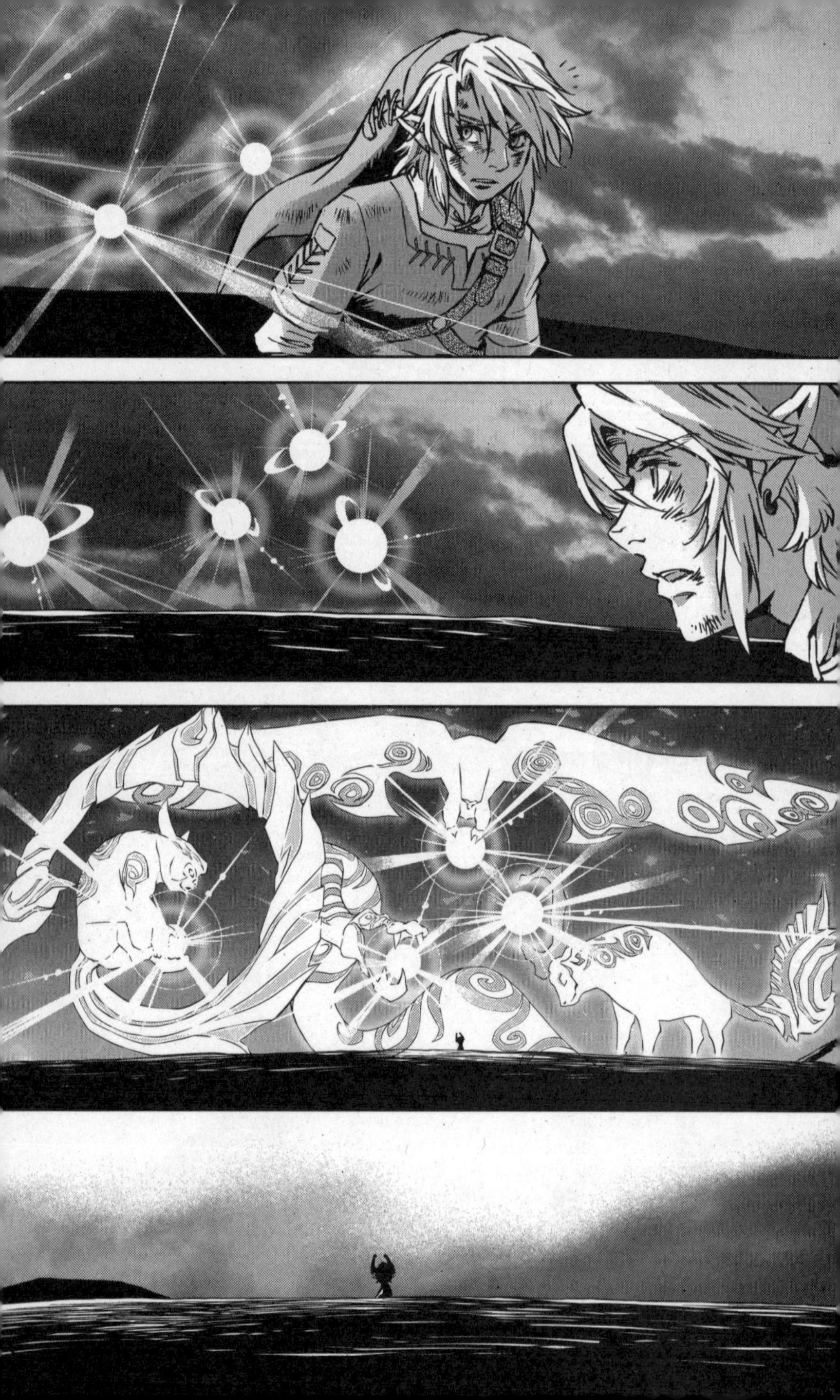

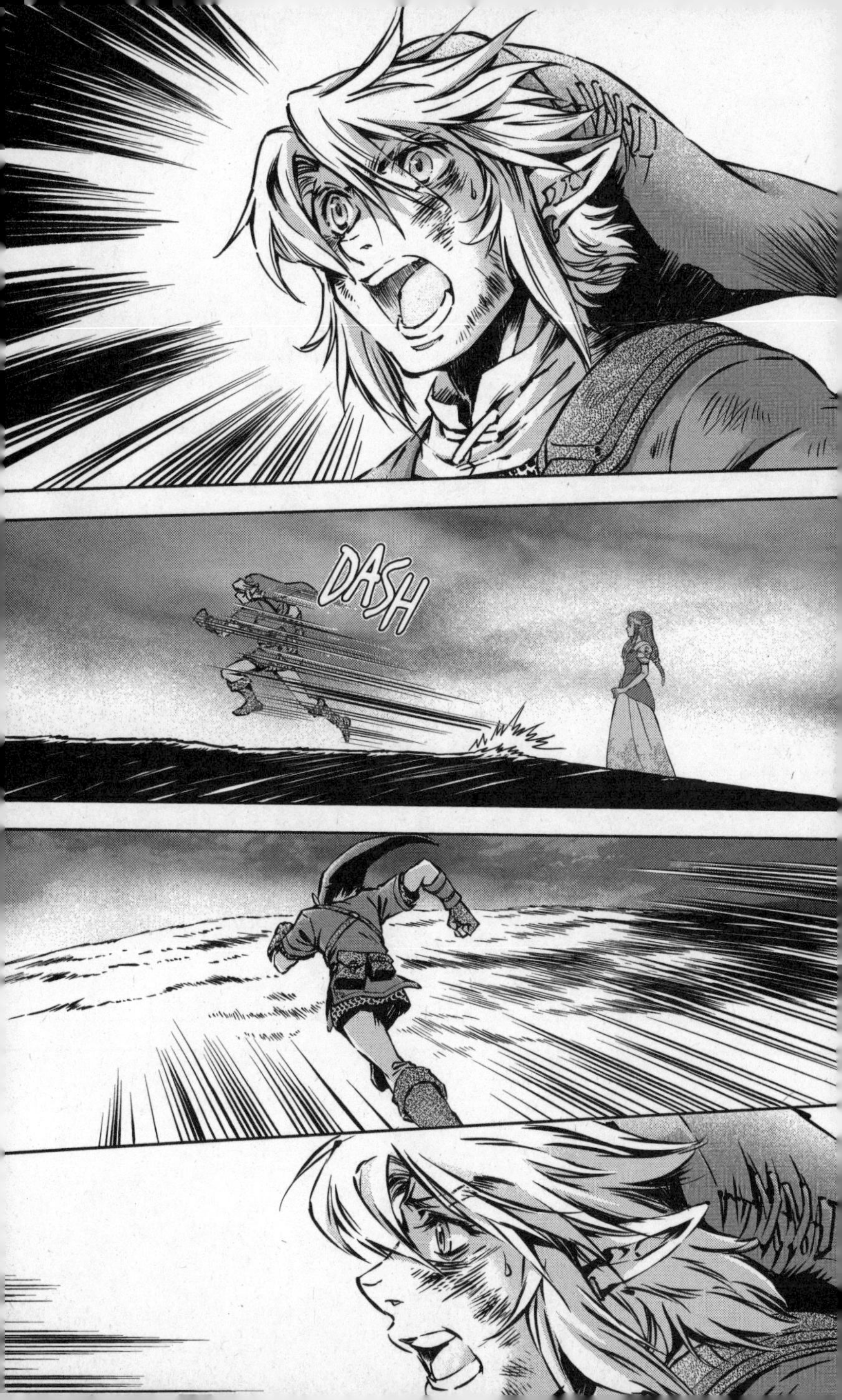
DASH

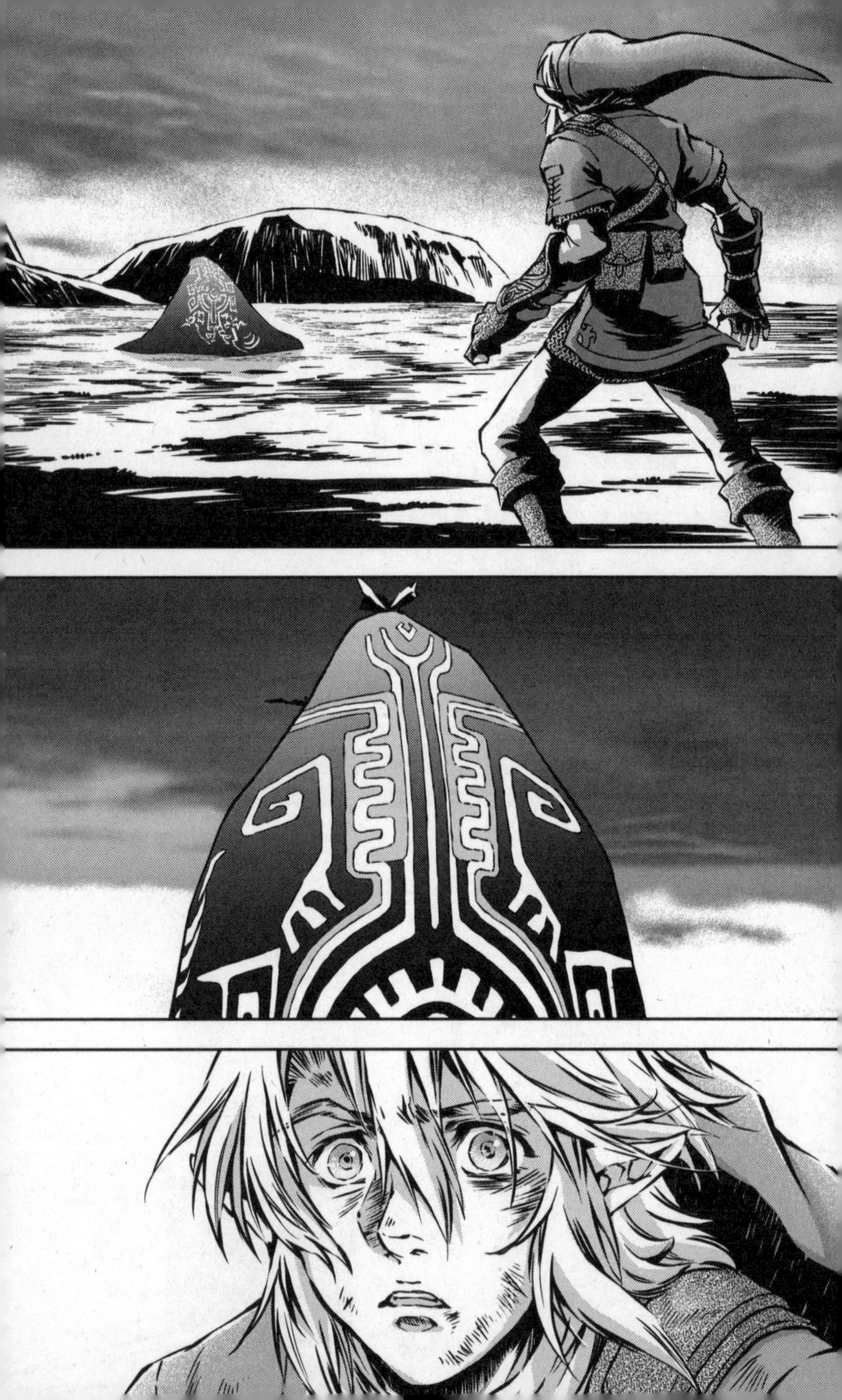

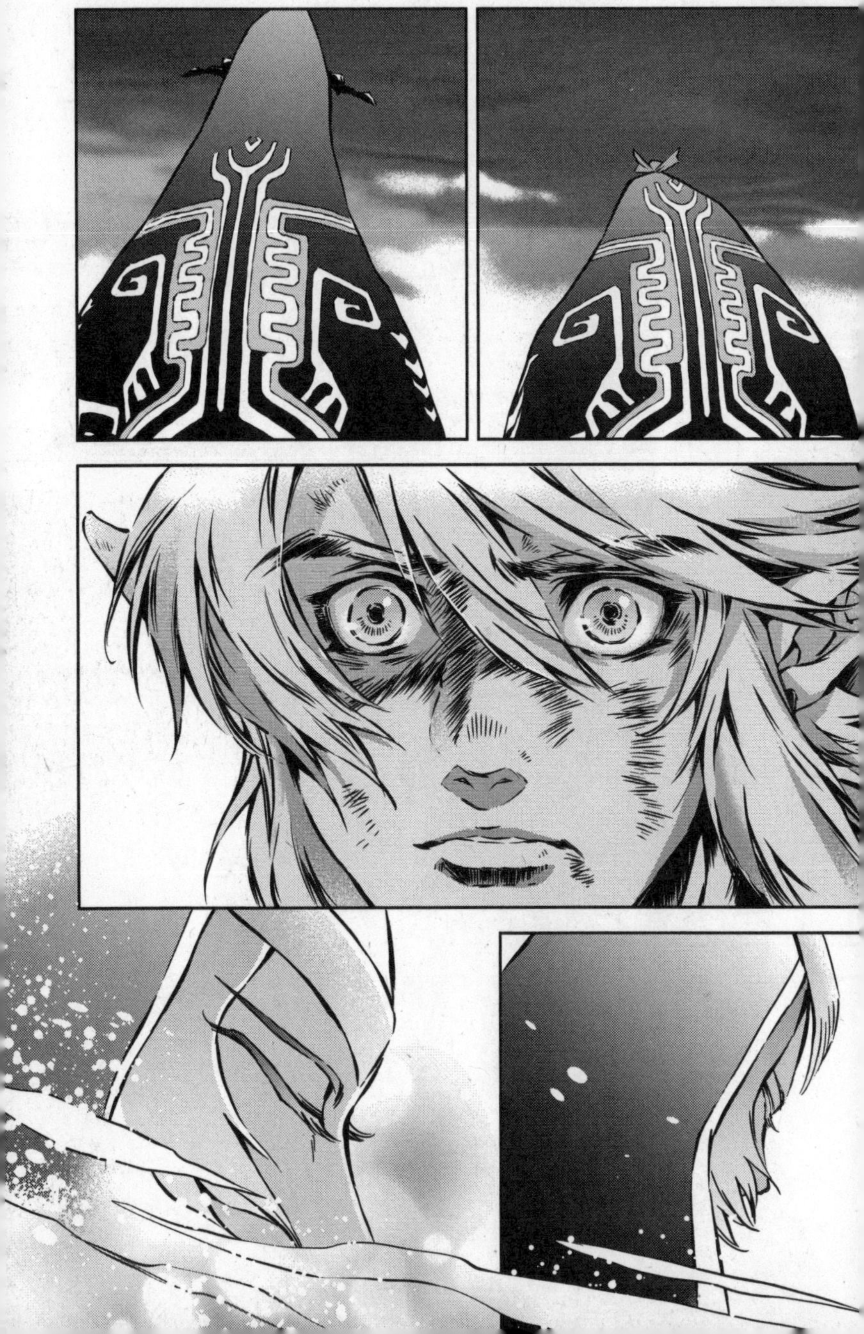

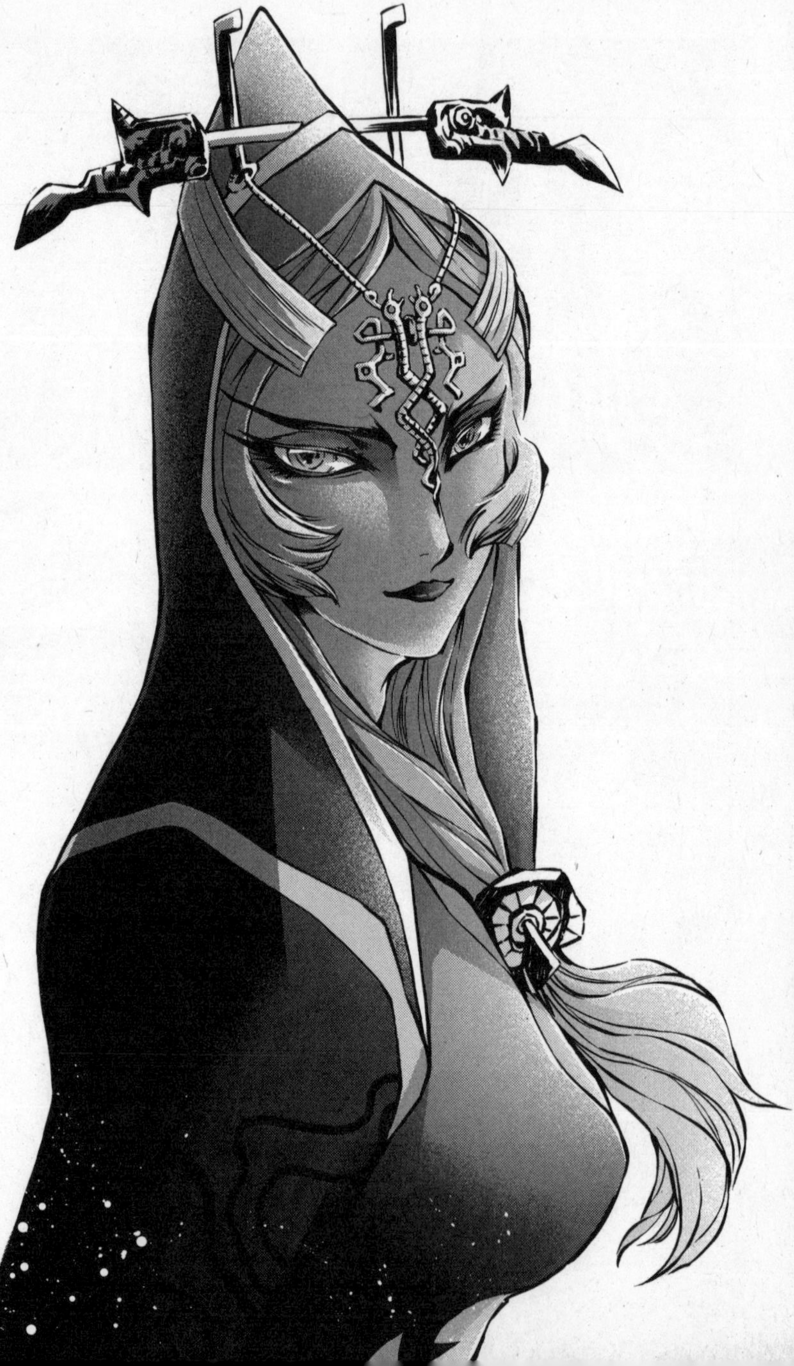

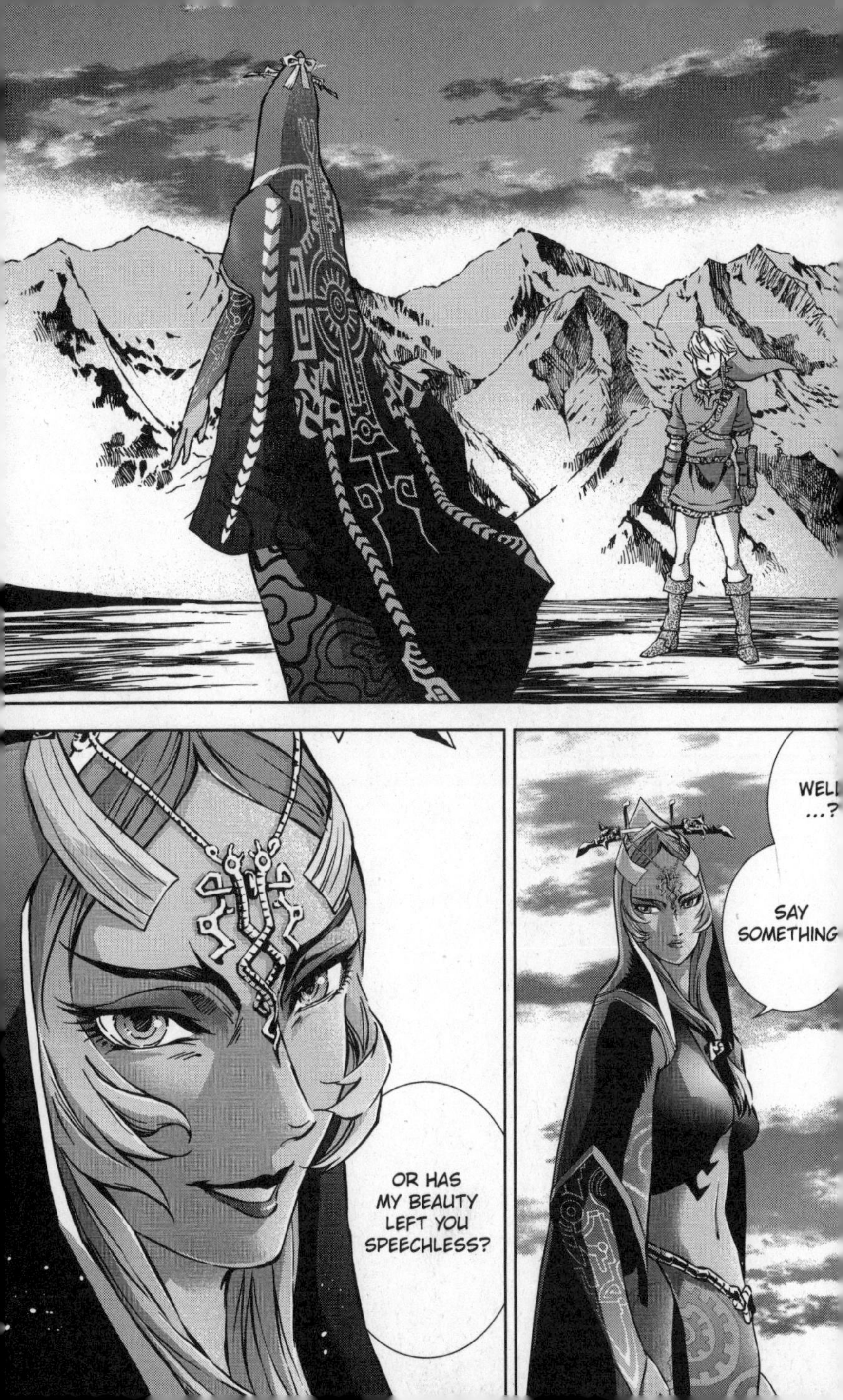
WELL ...?
SAY SOMETHING
OR HAS MY BEAUTY LEFT YOU SPEECHLESS?

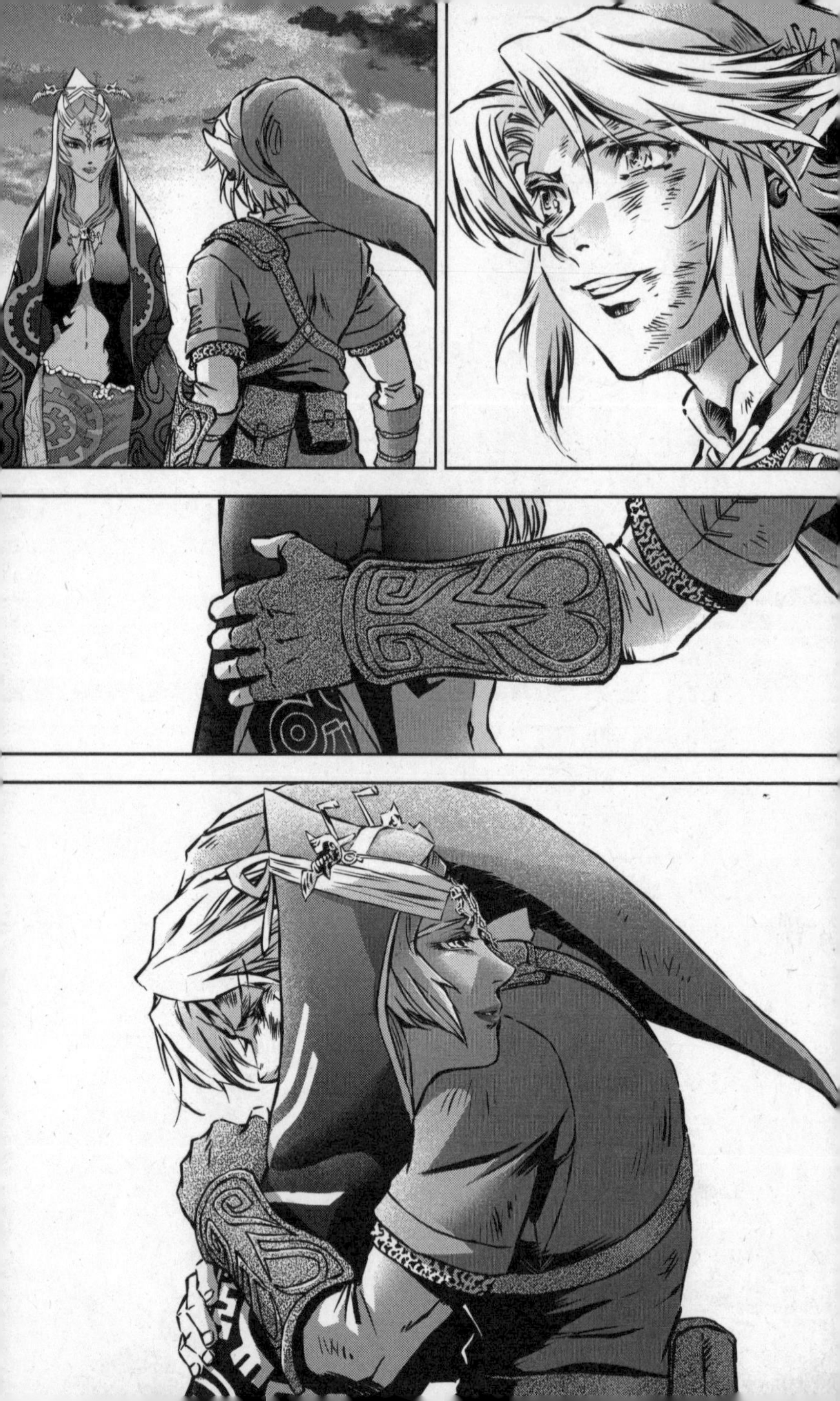

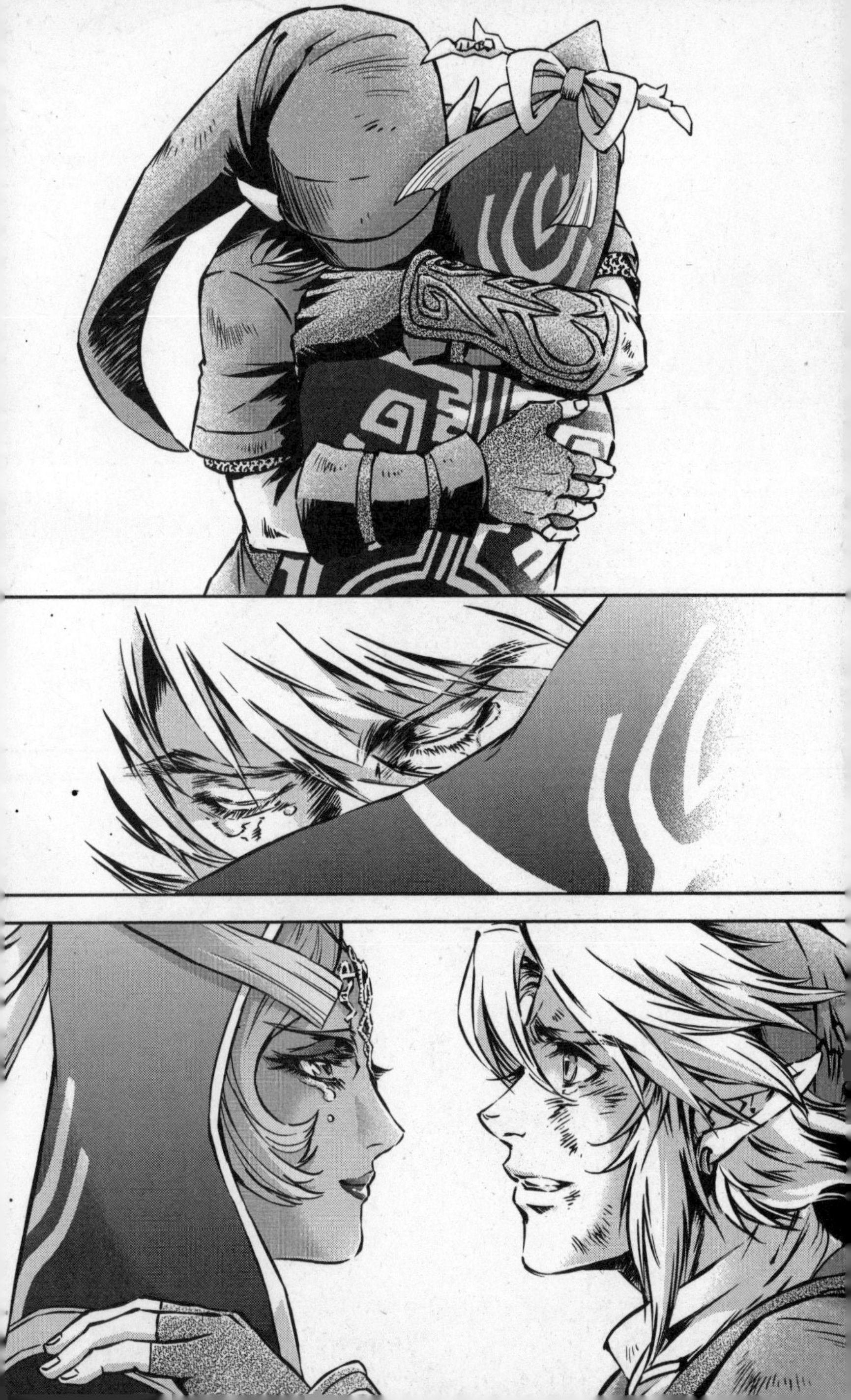

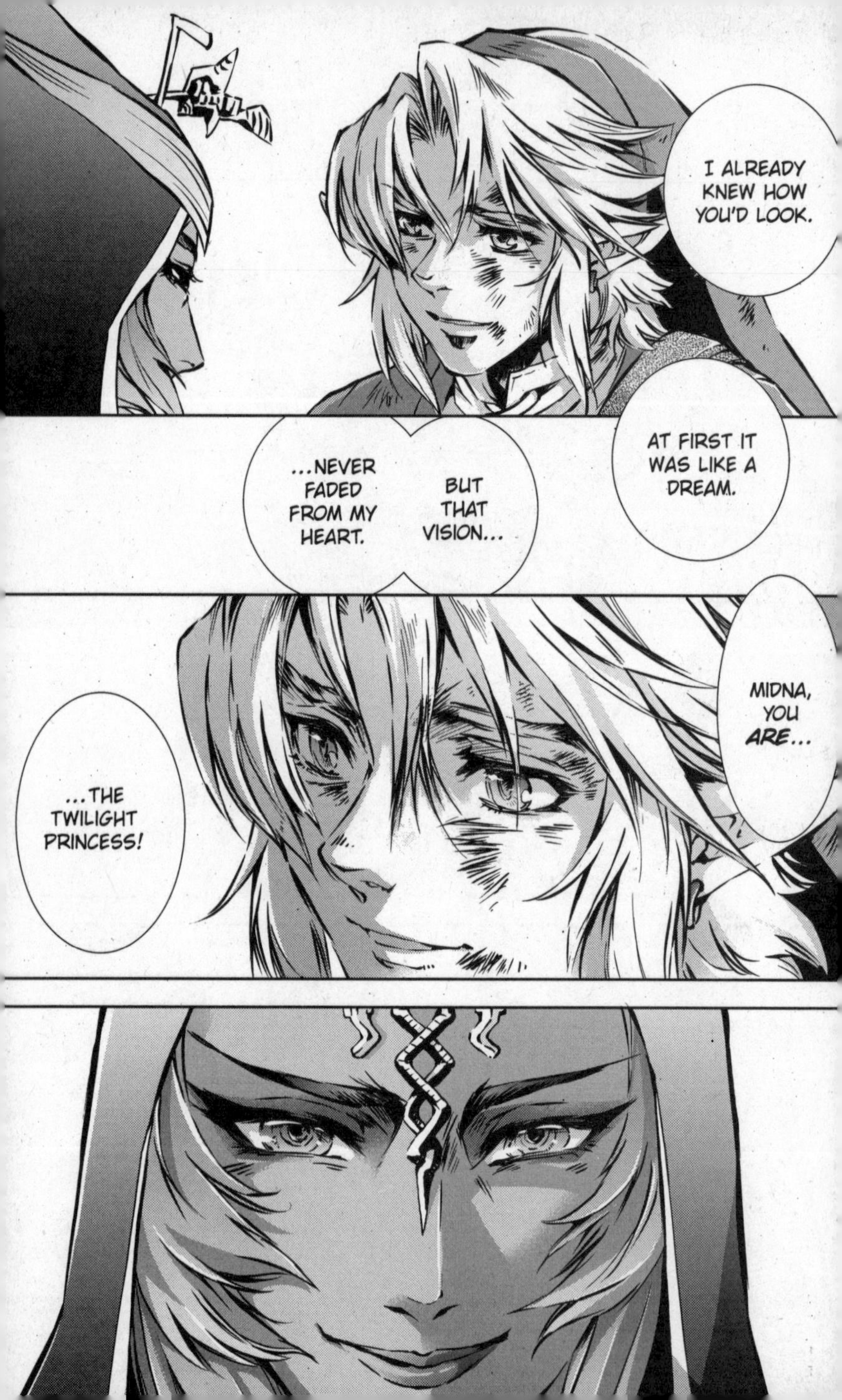
I ALREADY KNEW HOW YOU'D LOOK.
AT FIRST IT WAS LIKE A DREAM.
BUT THAT VISION...
...NEVER FADED FROM MY HEART.
MIDNA, YOU *ARE*...
...THE TWILIGHT PRINCESS!

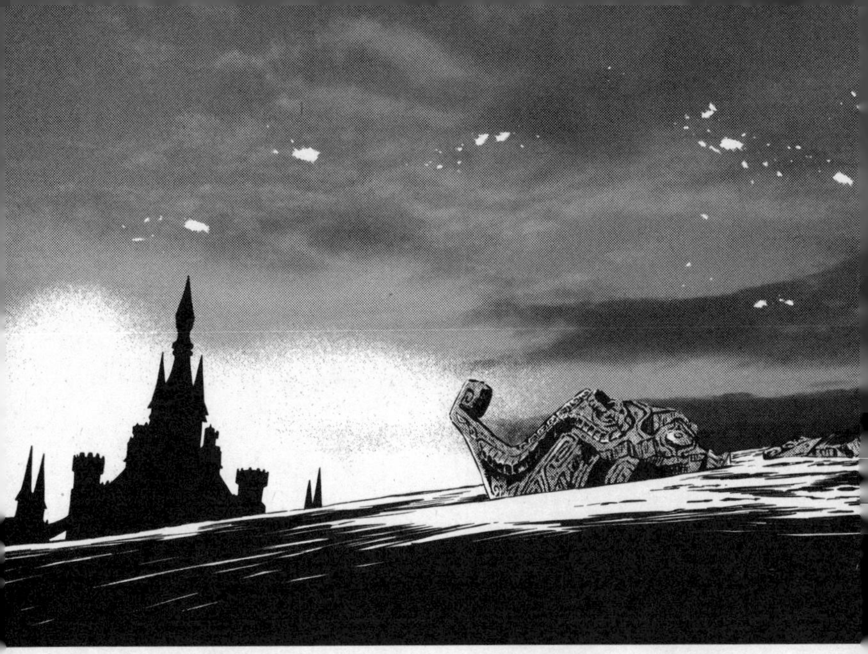
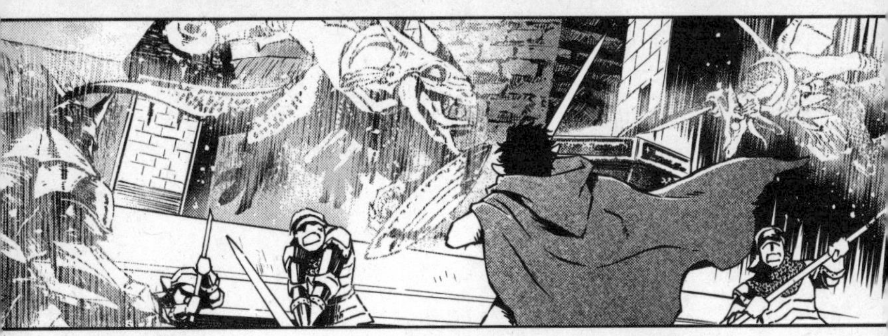
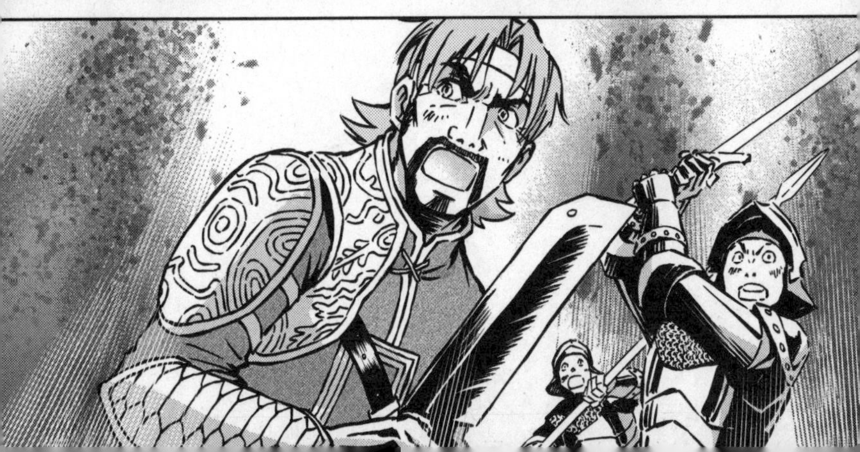

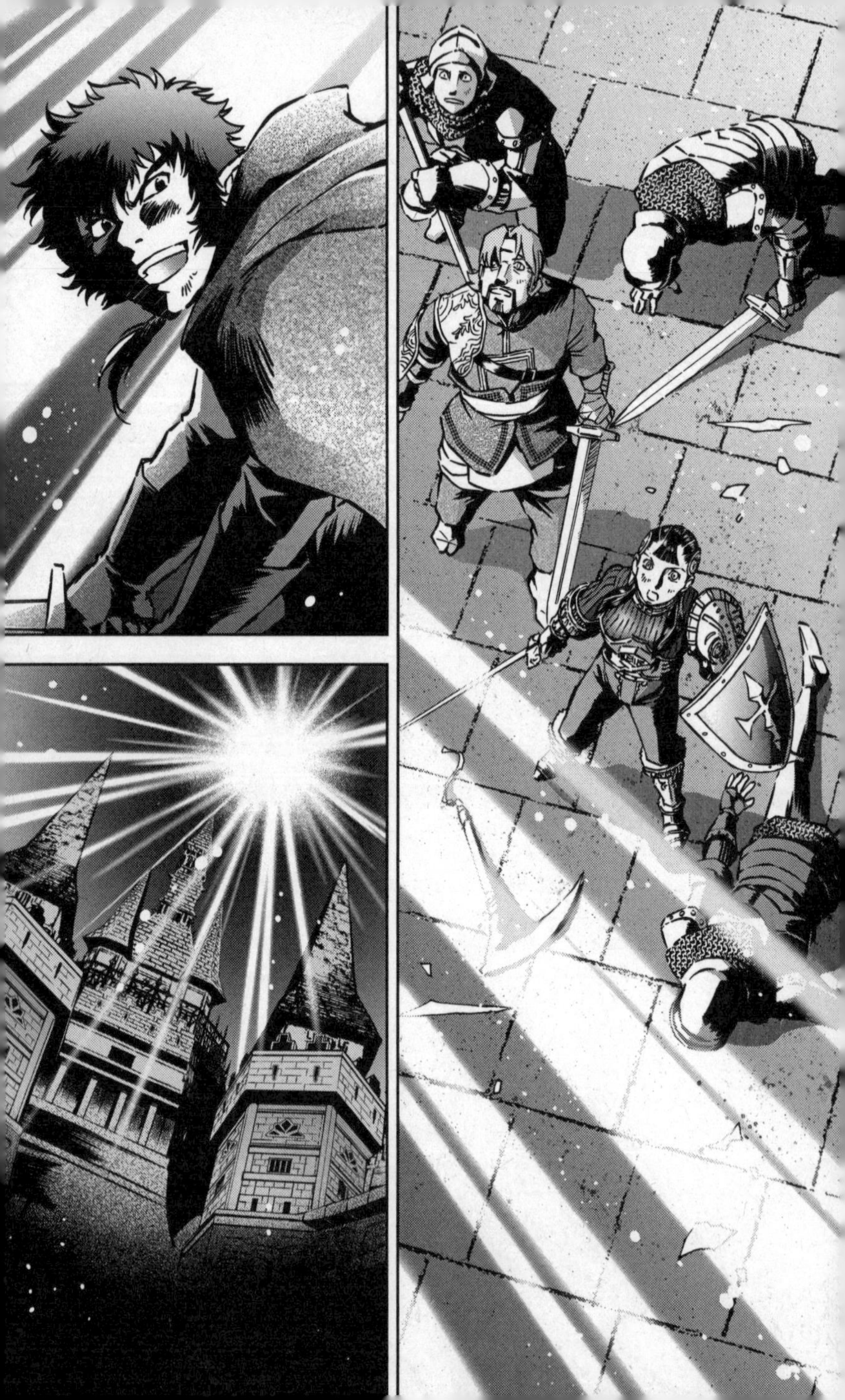

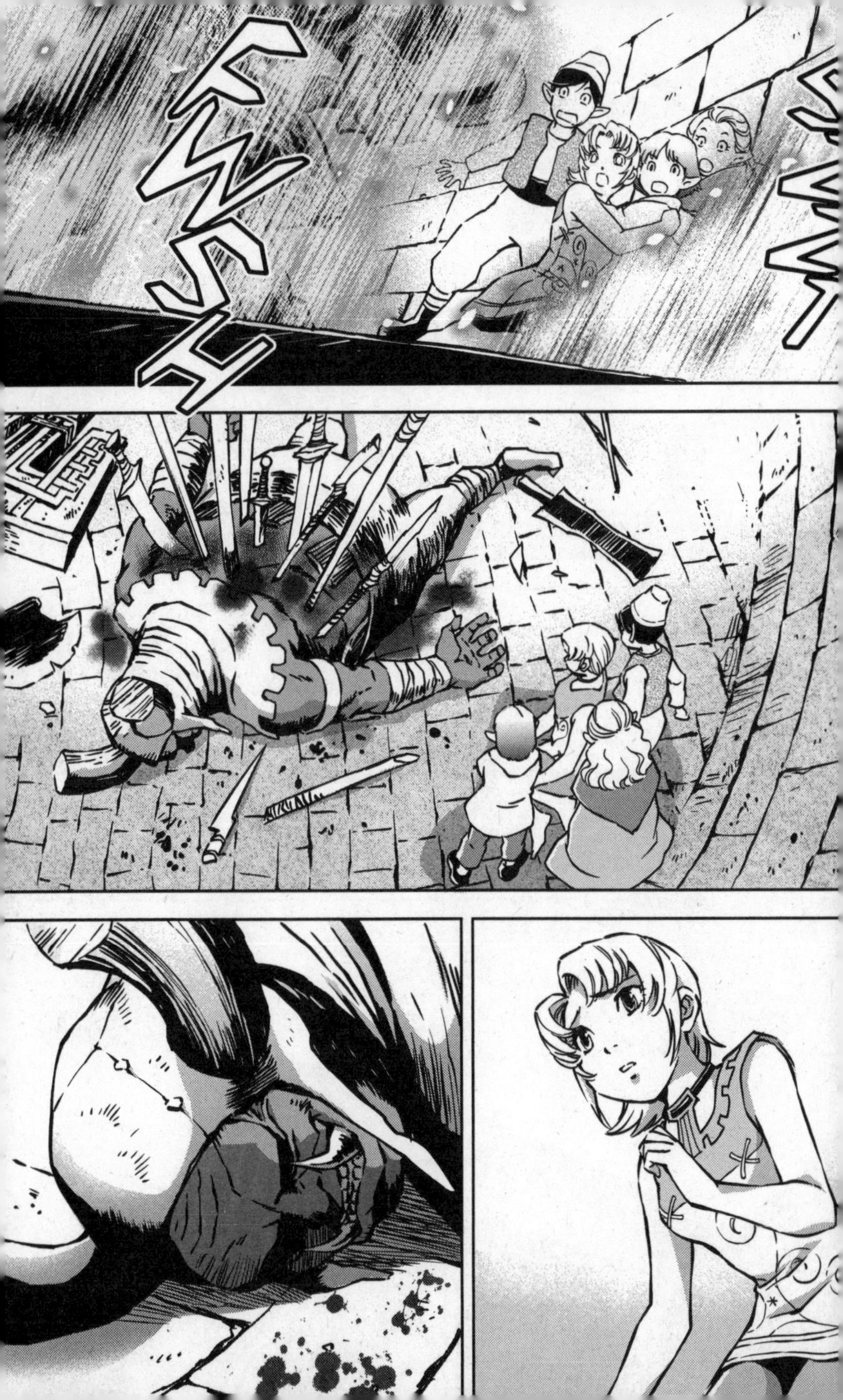
KWSSH

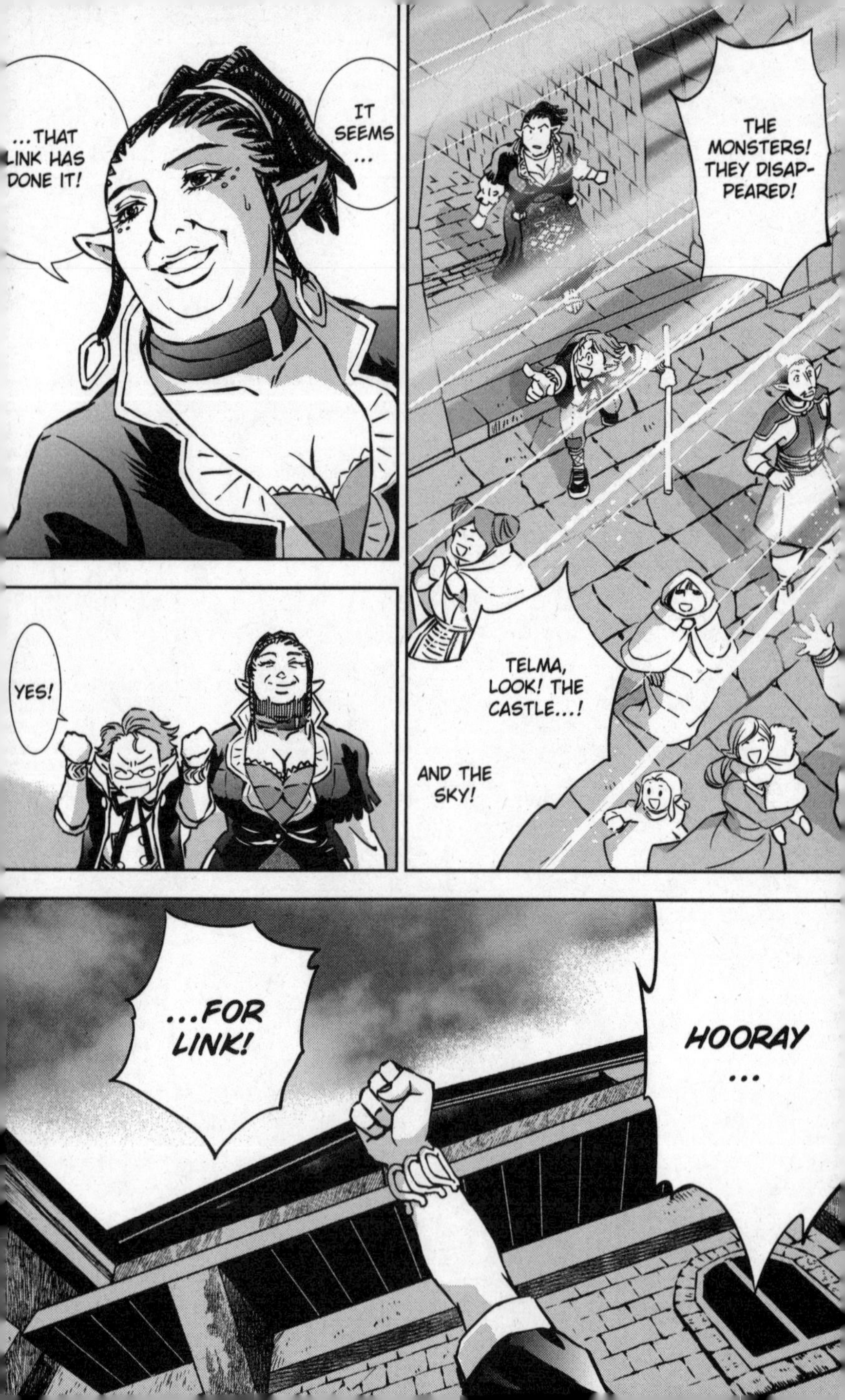
THE MONSTERS! THEY DISAP-PEARED!
TELMA, LOOK! THE CASTLE...!
AND THE SKY!
IT SEEMS...
...THAT LINK HAS DONE IT!
YES!
HOORAY...
...FOR LINK!

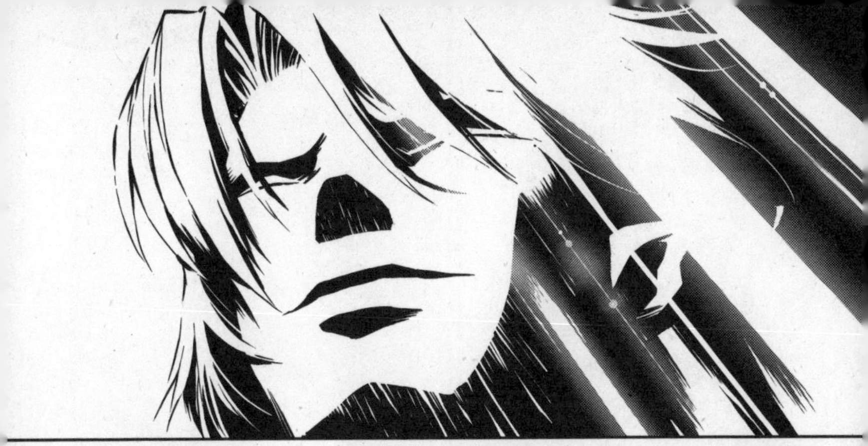
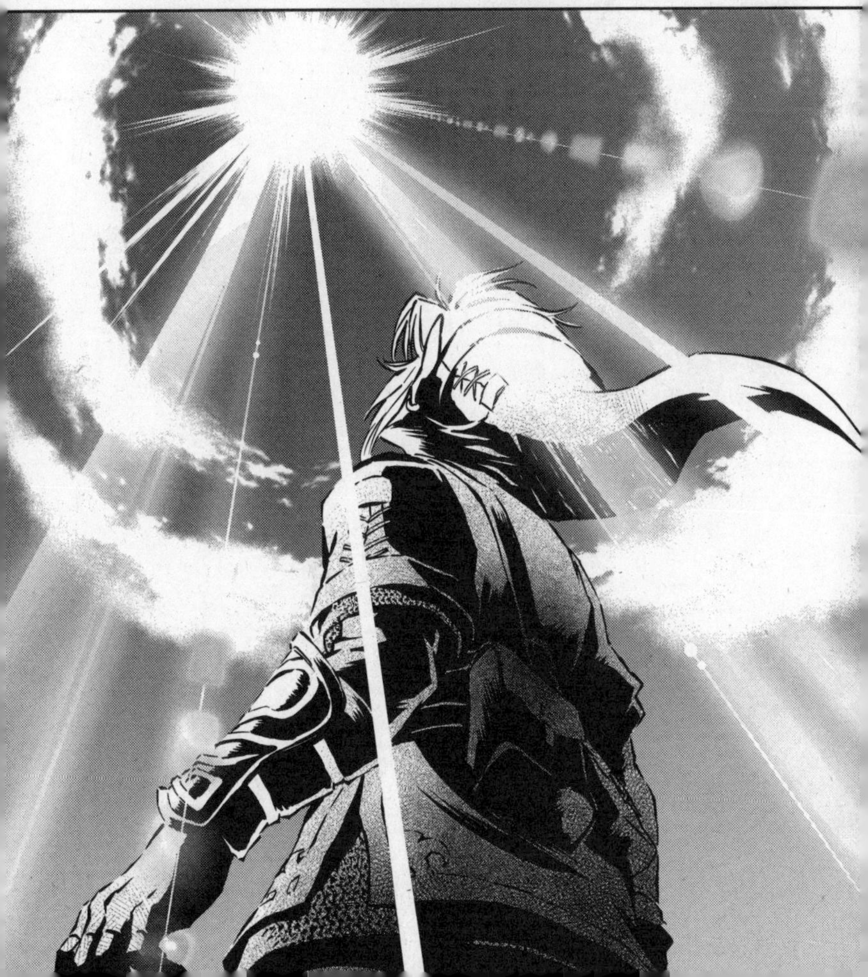

#58. A NEW DEPARTURE

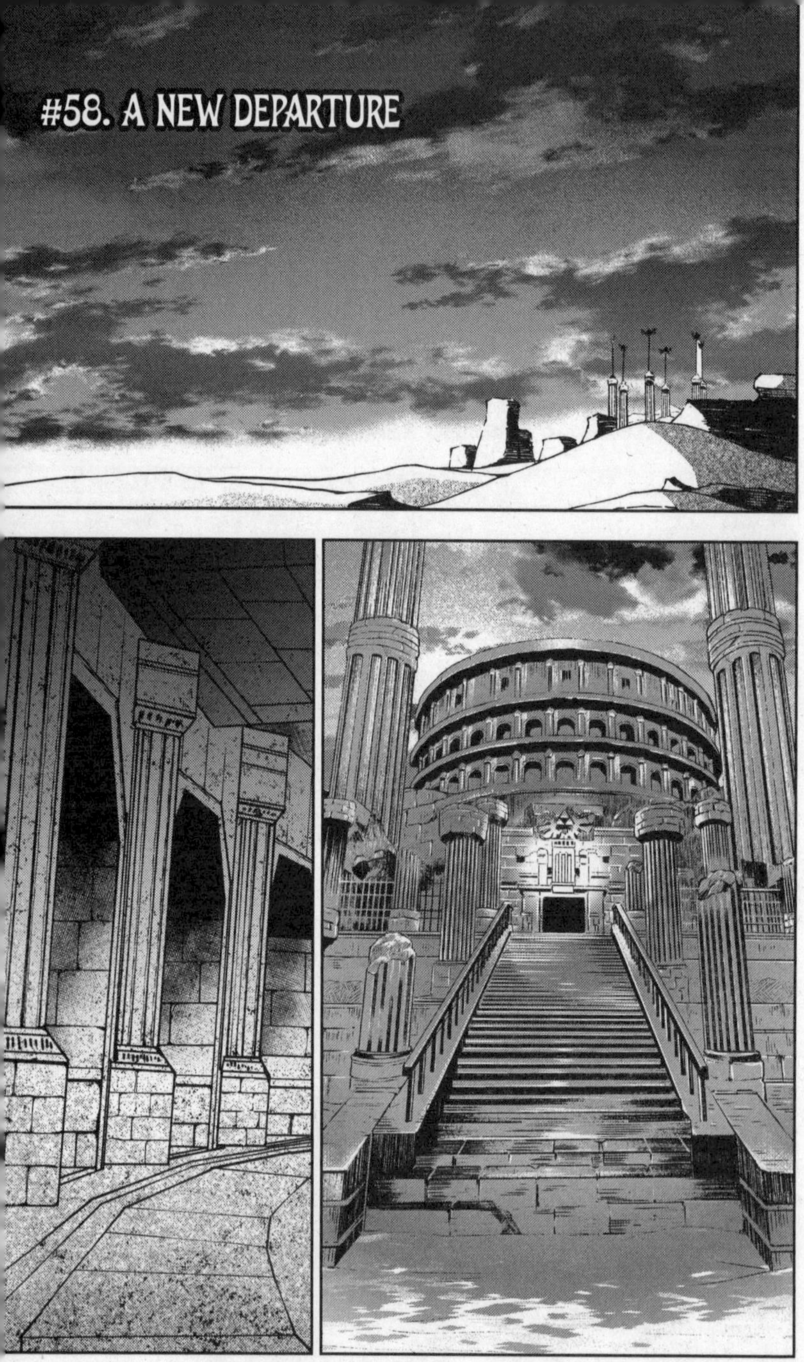

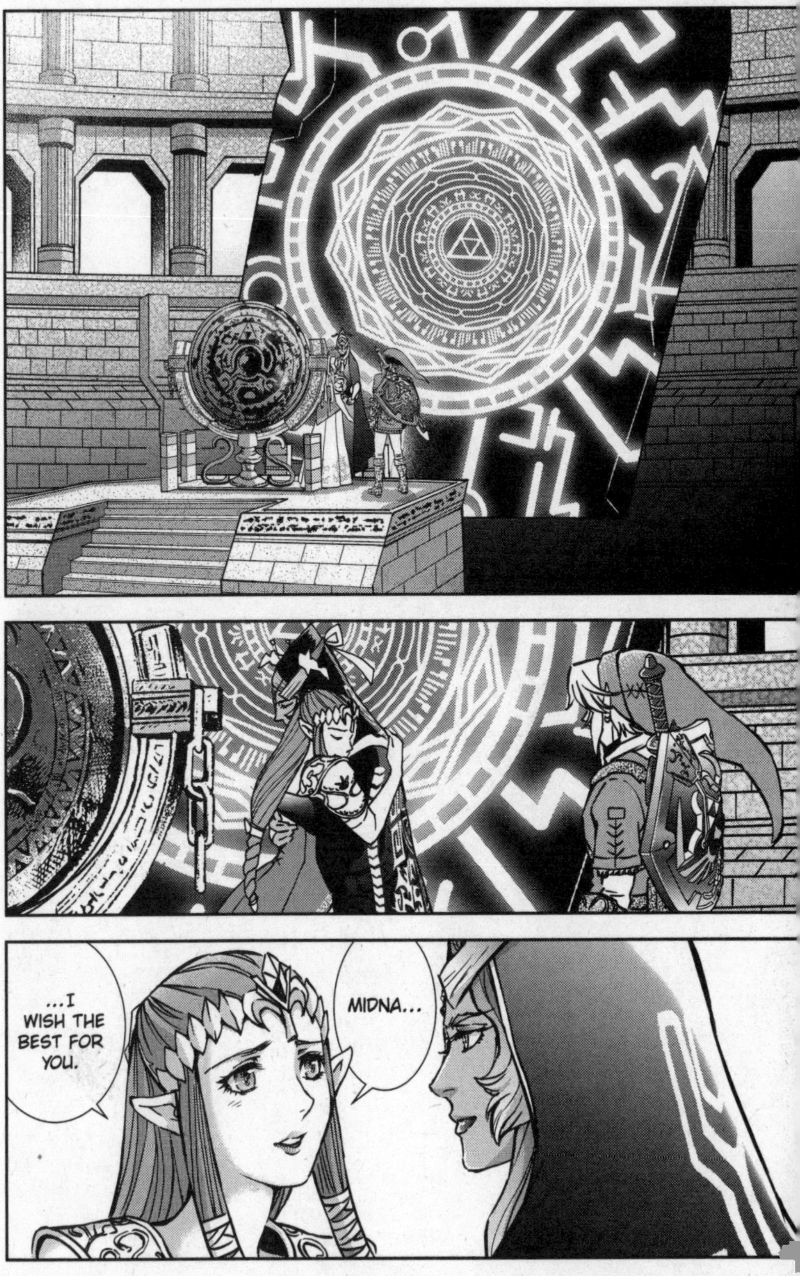
MIDNA...
...I WISH THE BEST FOR YOU.

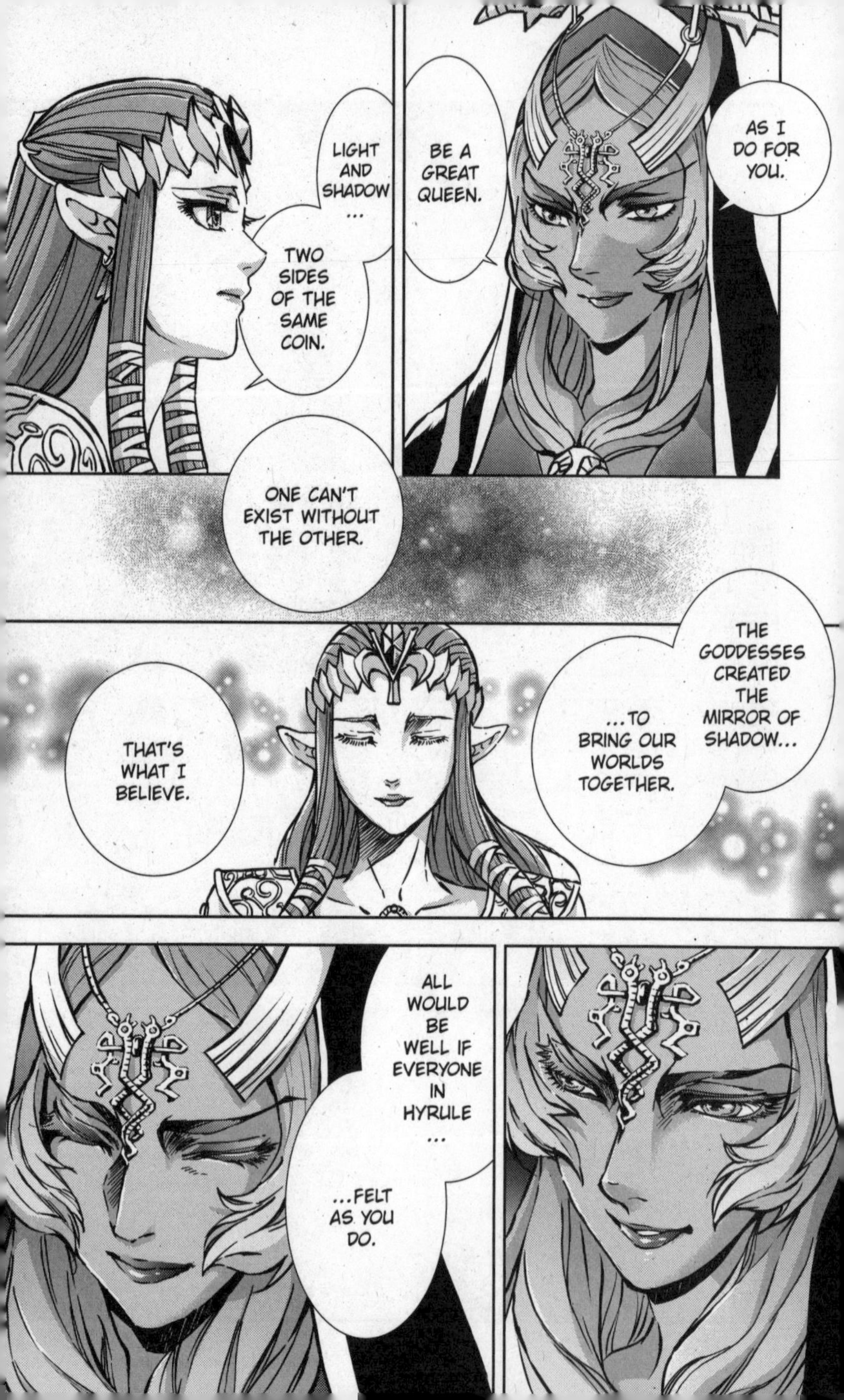
AS I DO FOR YOU.
BE A GREAT QUEEN.
LIGHT AND SHADOW ...
TWO SIDES OF THE SAME COIN.
ONE CAN'T EXIST WITHOUT THE OTHER.
THE GODDESSES CREATED THE MIRROR OF SHADOW...
...TO BRING OUR WORLDS TOGETHER.
THAT'S WHAT I BELIEVE.
ALL WOULD BE WELL IF EVERYONE IN HYRULE ...
...FELT AS YOU DO.

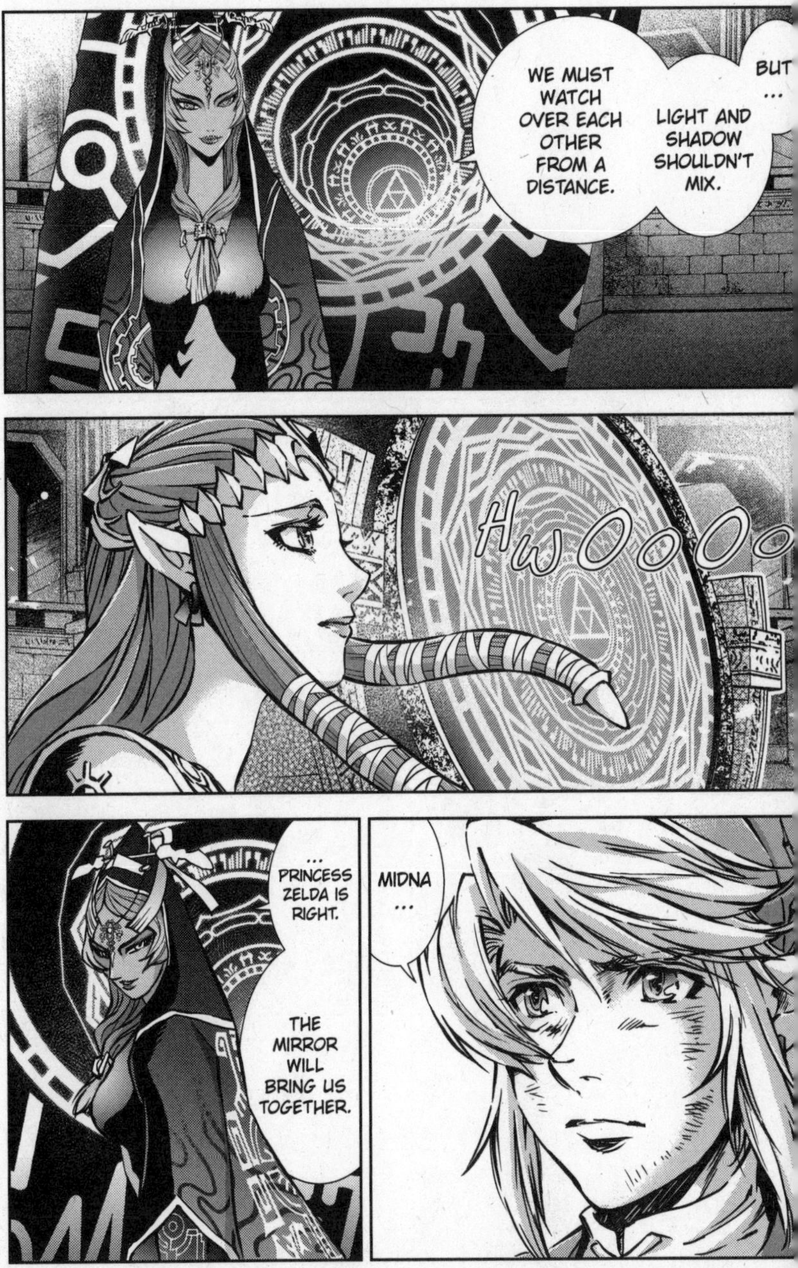
BUT ...
LIGHT AND SHADOW SHOULDN'T MIX.
WE MUST WATCH OVER EACH OTHER FROM A DISTANCE.
HWOOOO
MIDNA ...
... PRINCESS ZELDA IS RIGHT.
THE MIRROR WILL BRING US TOGETHER.

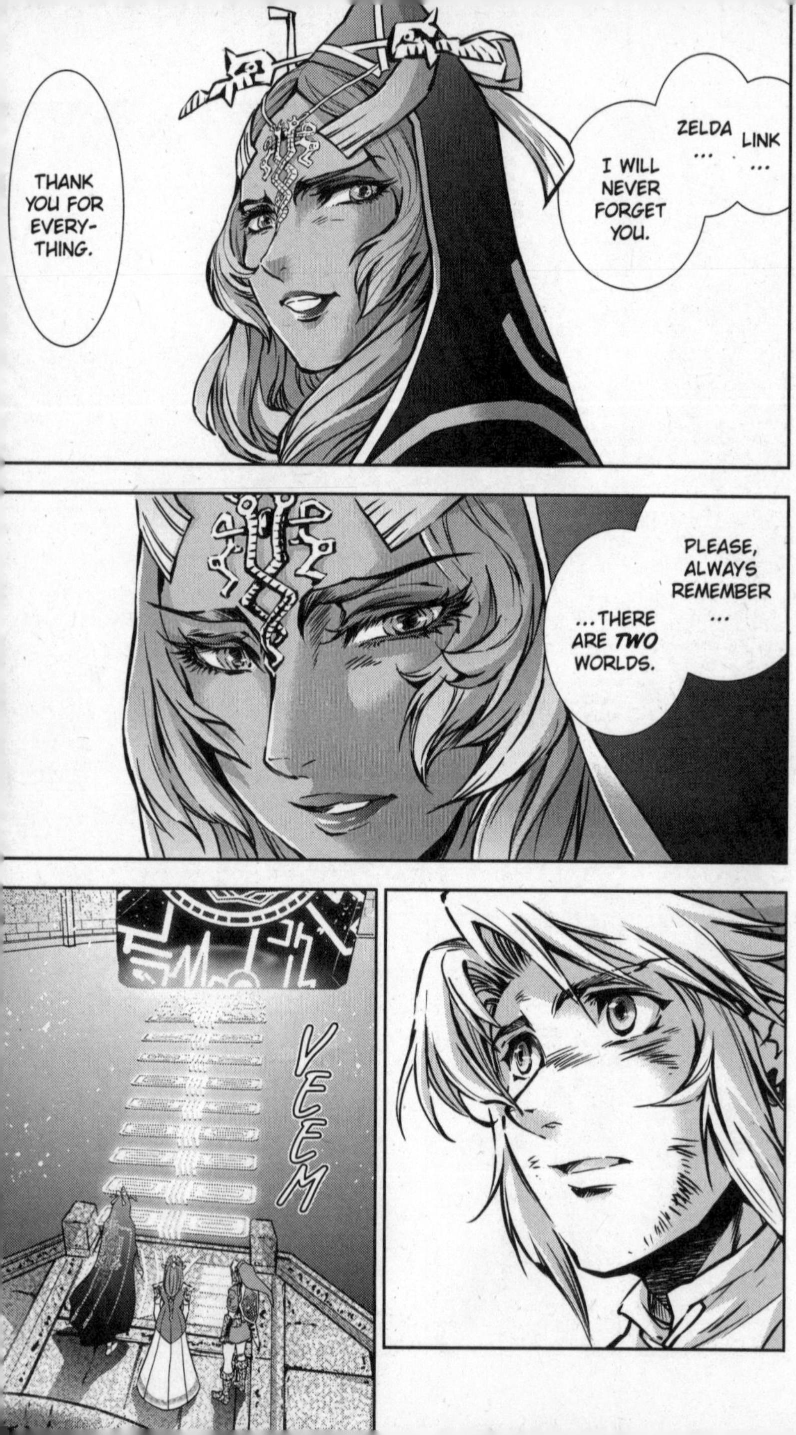
LINK ... ZELDA ... I WILL NEVER FORGET YOU.
THANK YOU FOR EVERY-THING.
PLEASE, ALWAYS REMEMBER ... ...THERE ARE *TWO* WORLDS.
VEEM

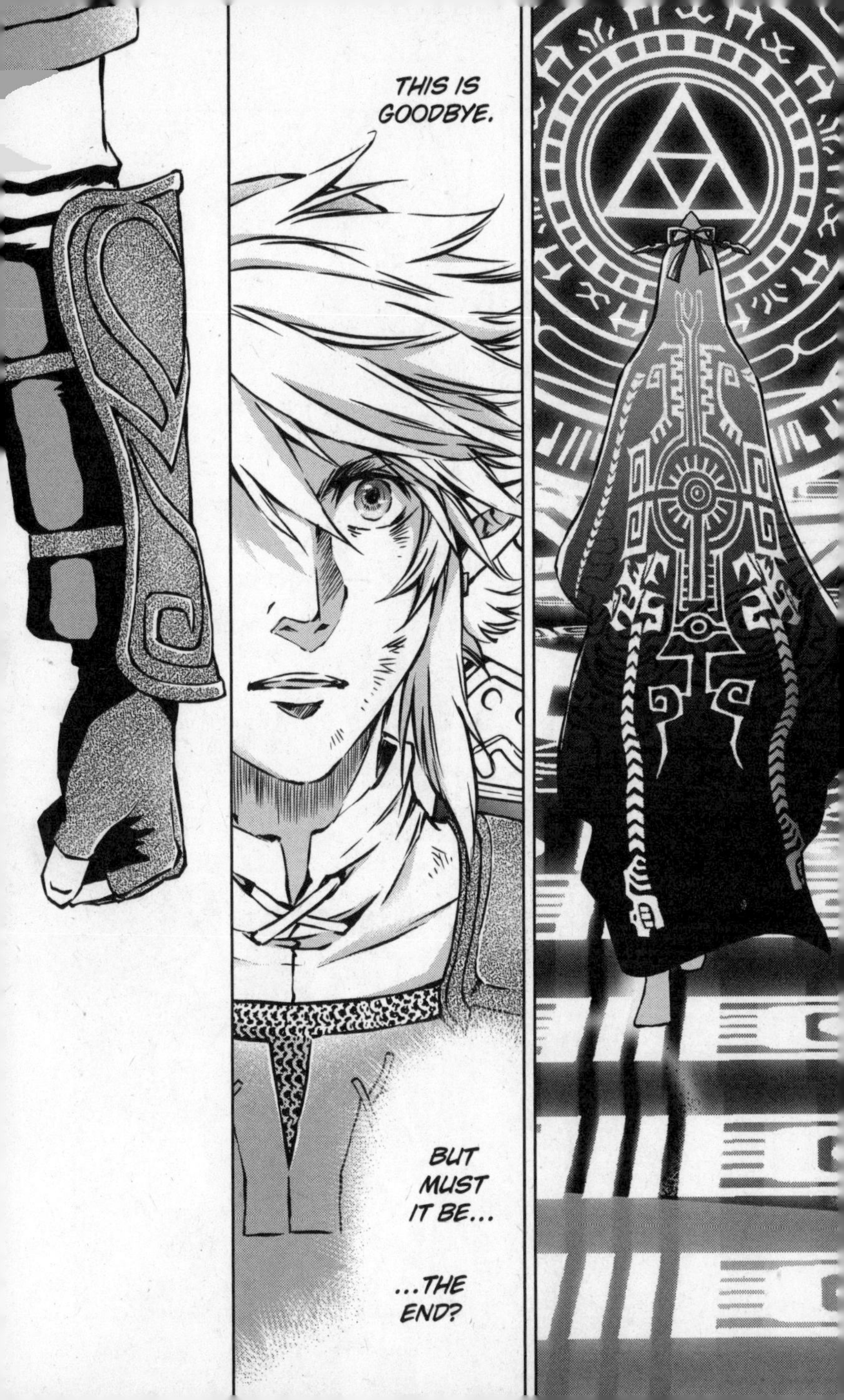
THIS IS GOODBYE.
BUT MUST IT BE...
...THE END?

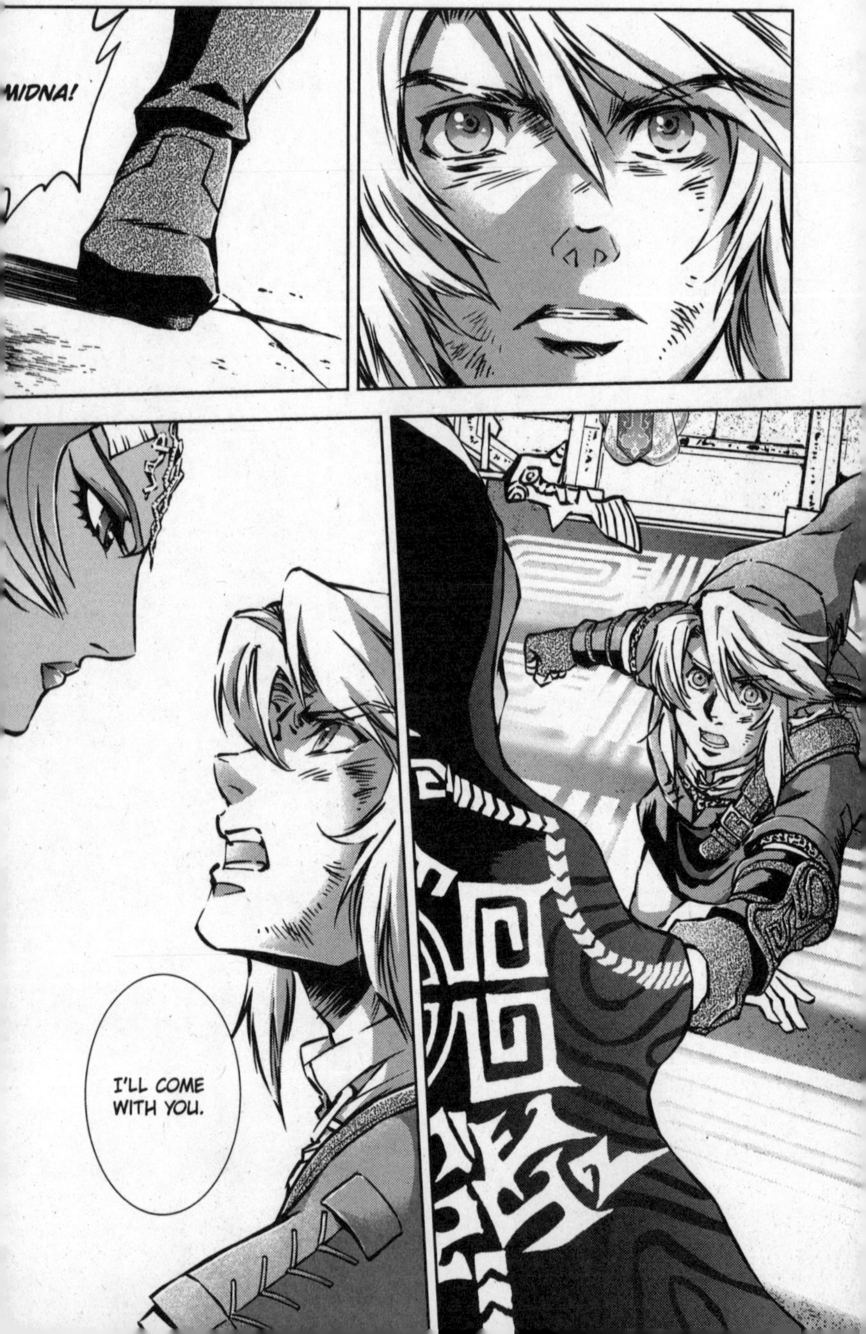
MIDNA!
I'LL COME WITH YOU.

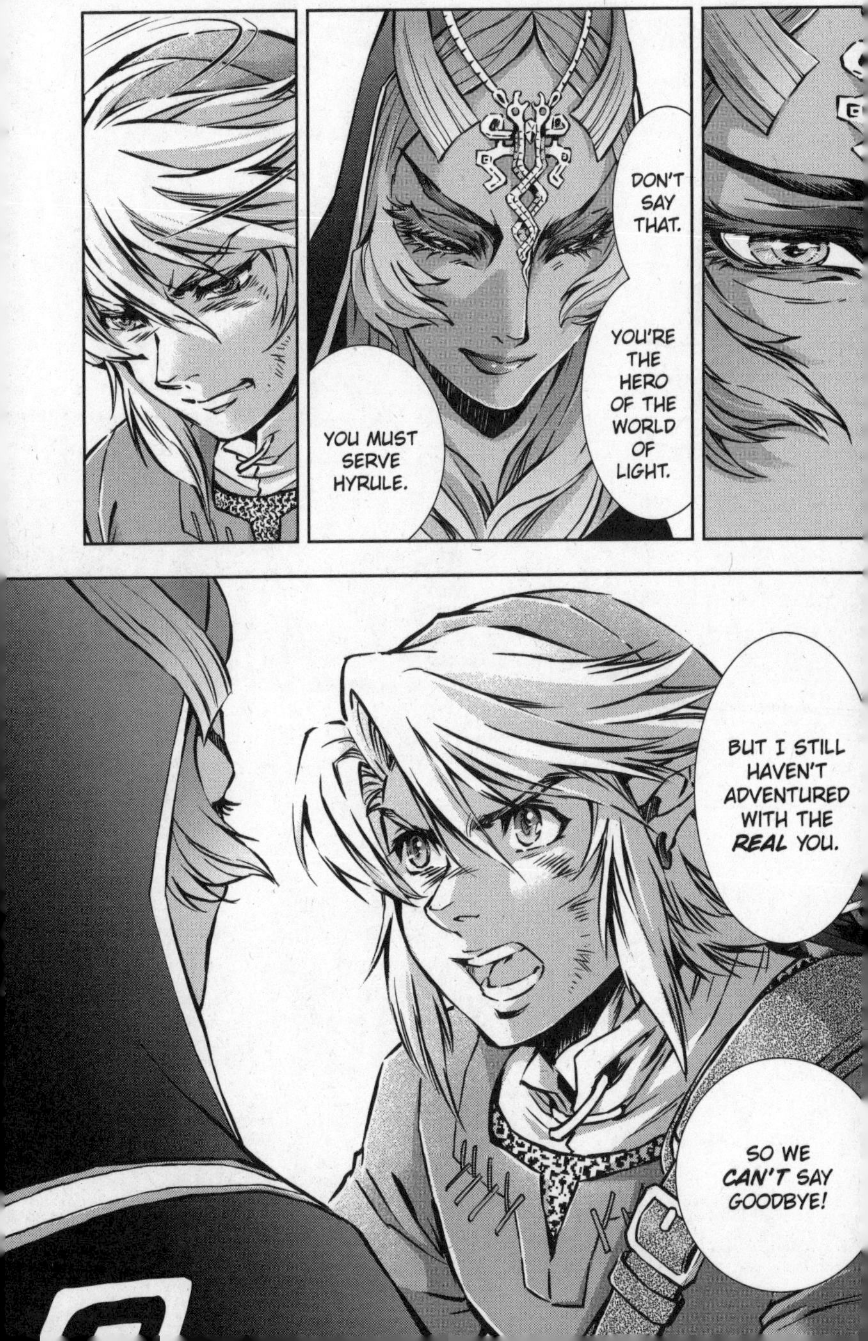
DON'T SAY THAT.
YOU'RE THE HERO OF THE WORLD OF LIGHT.
YOU MUST SERVE HYRULE.
BUT I STILL HAVEN'T ADVENTURED WITH THE REAL YOU.
SO WE CAN'T SAY GOODBYE!

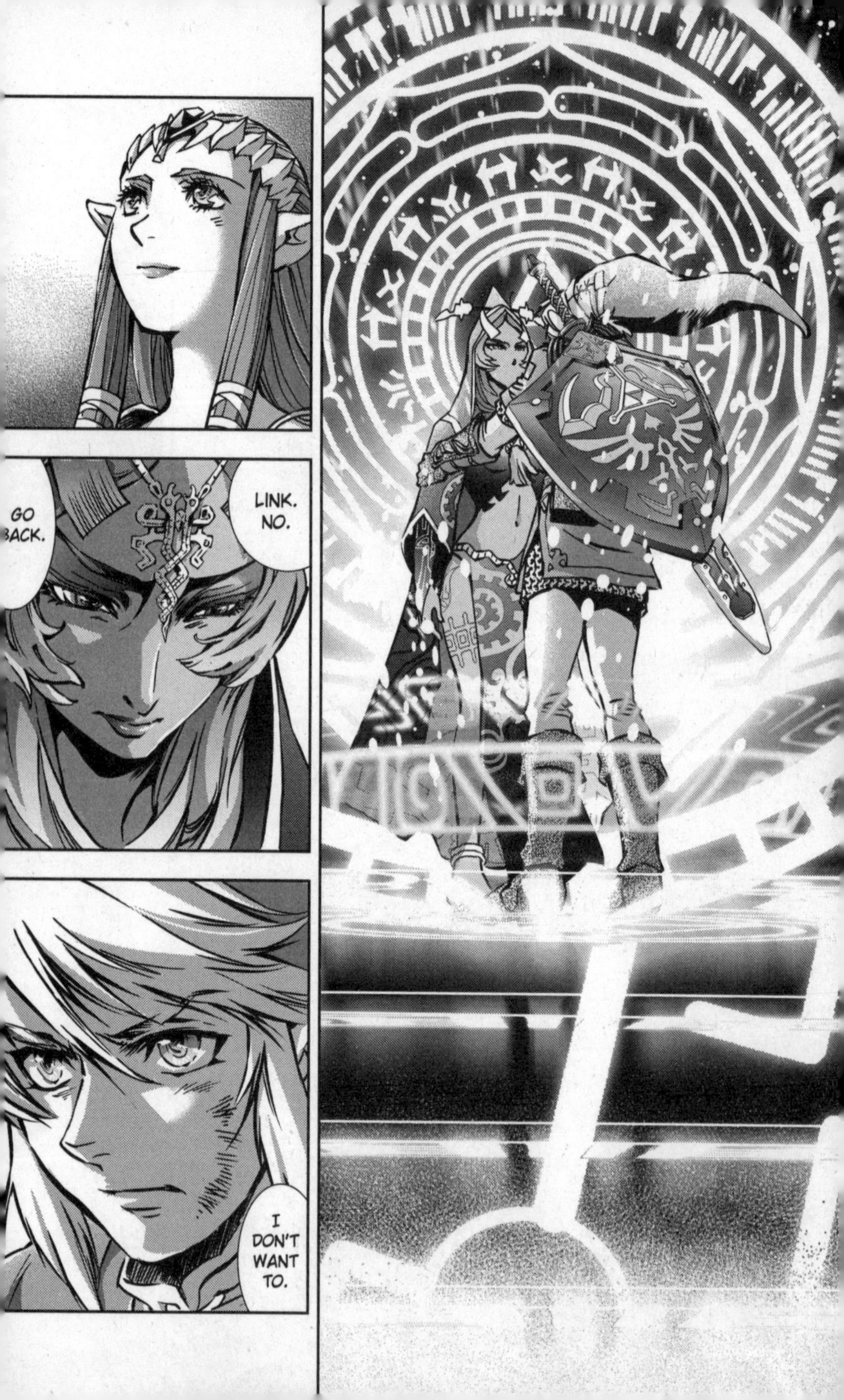
LINK. NO.
GO BACK.
I DON'T WANT TO.

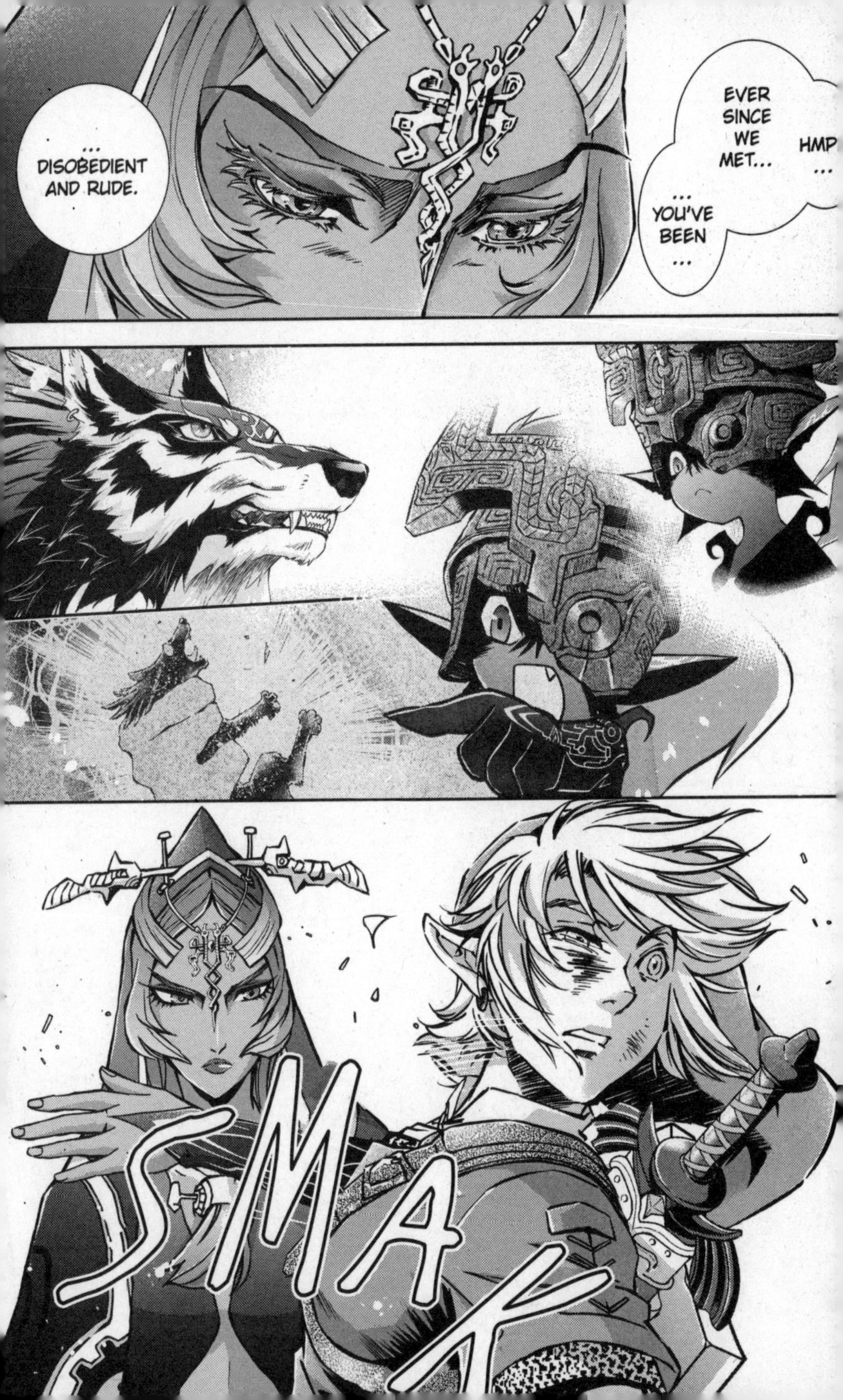
HMP...
EVER SINCE WE MET...
...YOU'VE BEEN...
...DISOBEDIENT AND RUDE.
SMAK

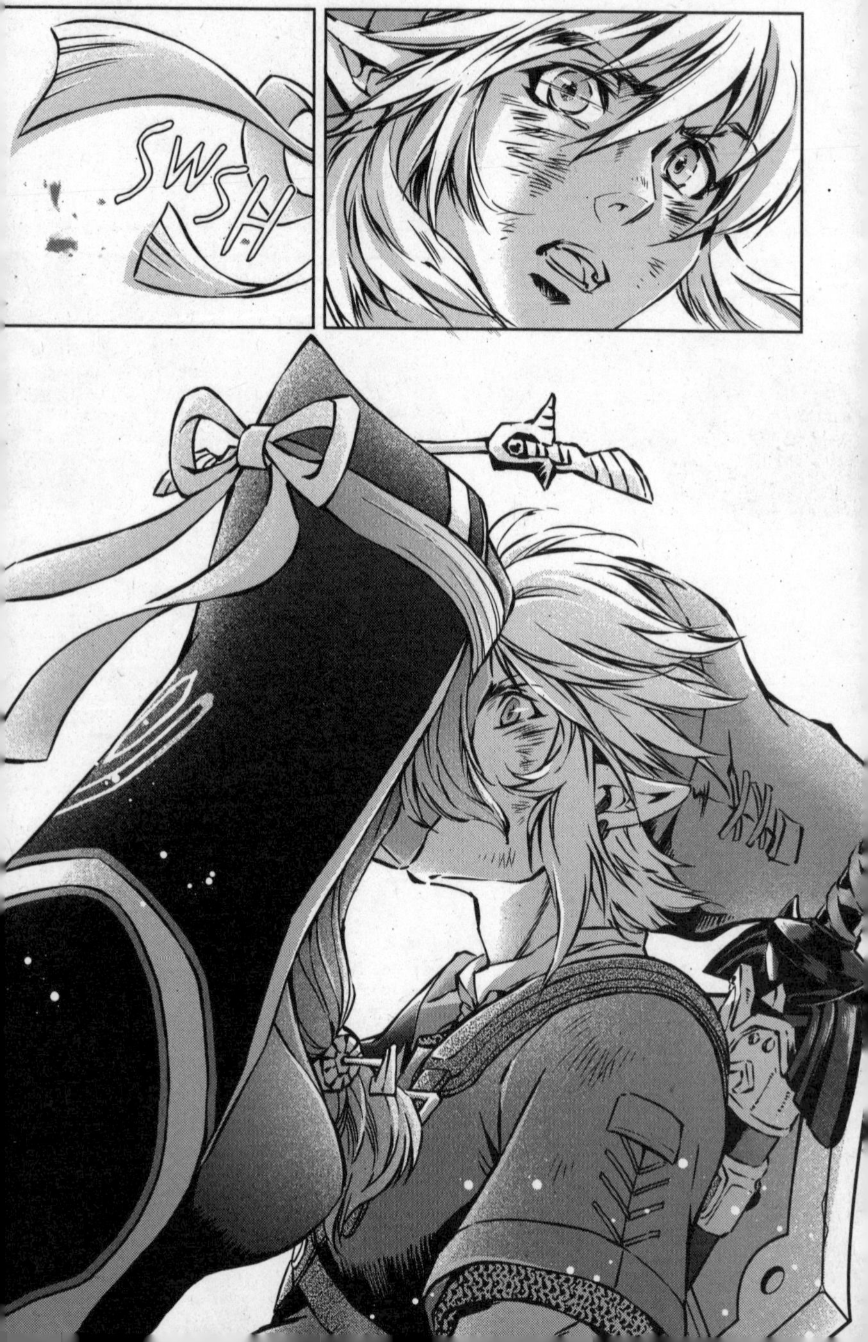
SWSH

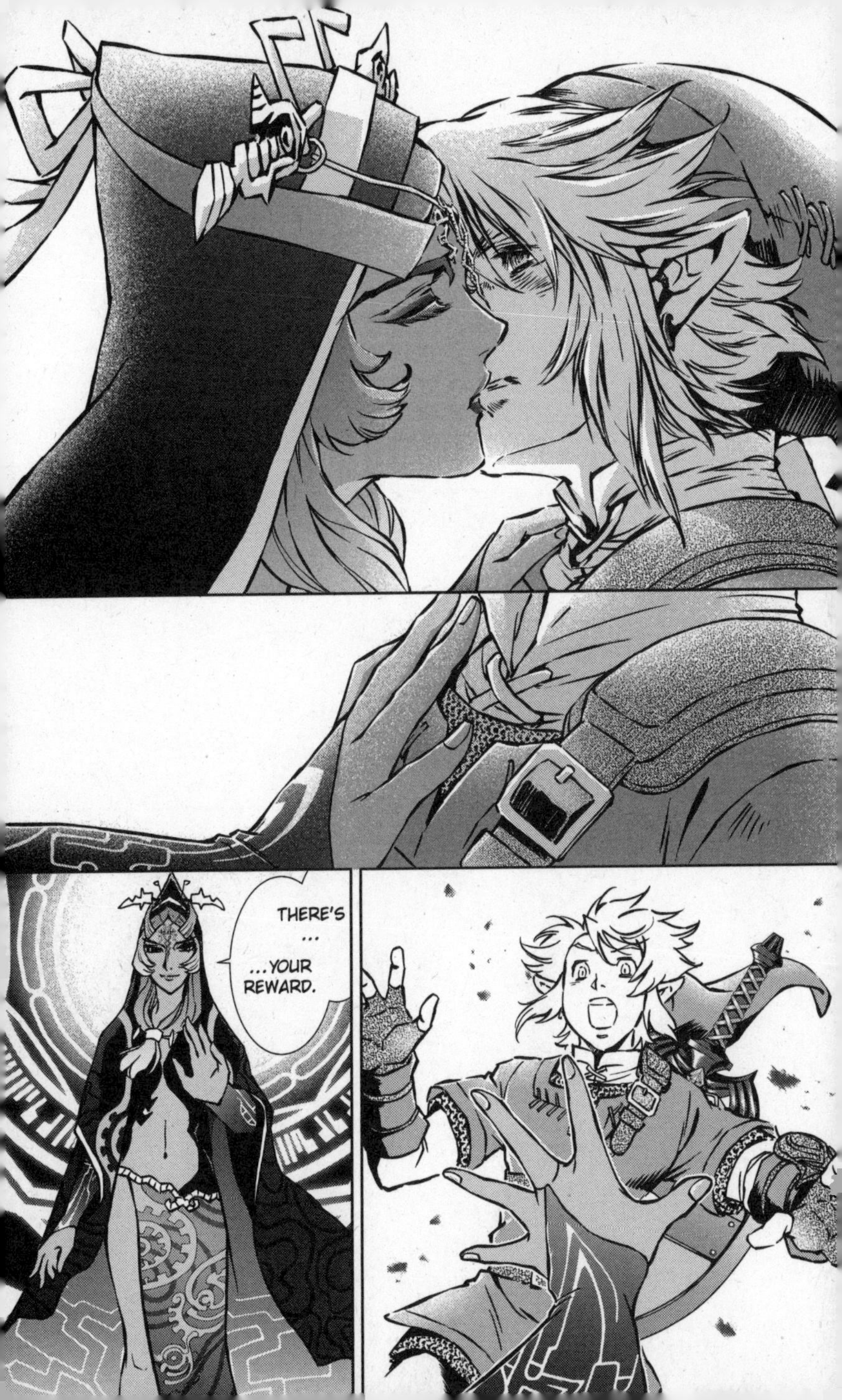
THERE'S ... ...YOUR REWARD.

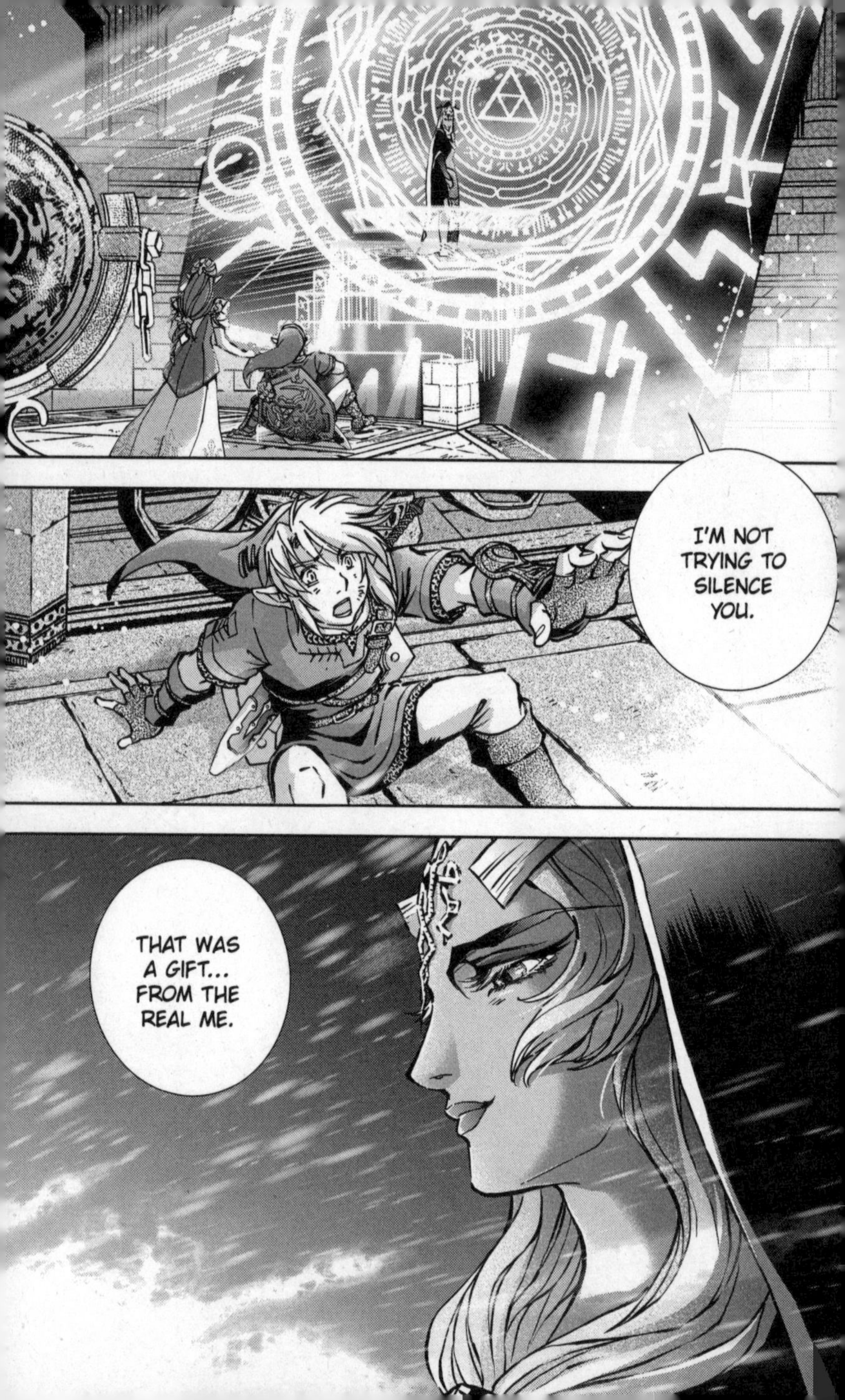
I'M NOT TRYING TO SILENCE YOU.
THAT WAS A GIFT... FROM THE REAL ME.

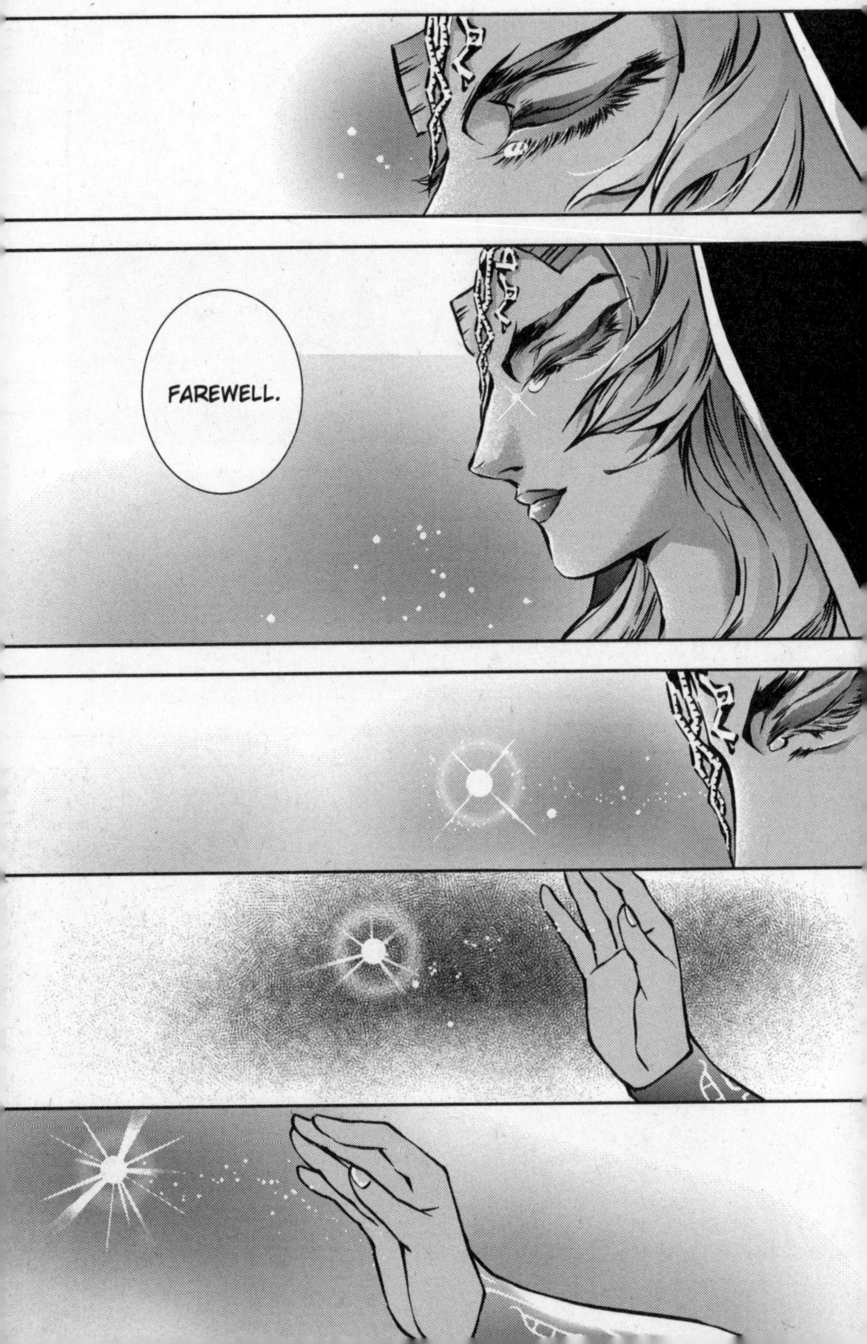
FAREWELL.

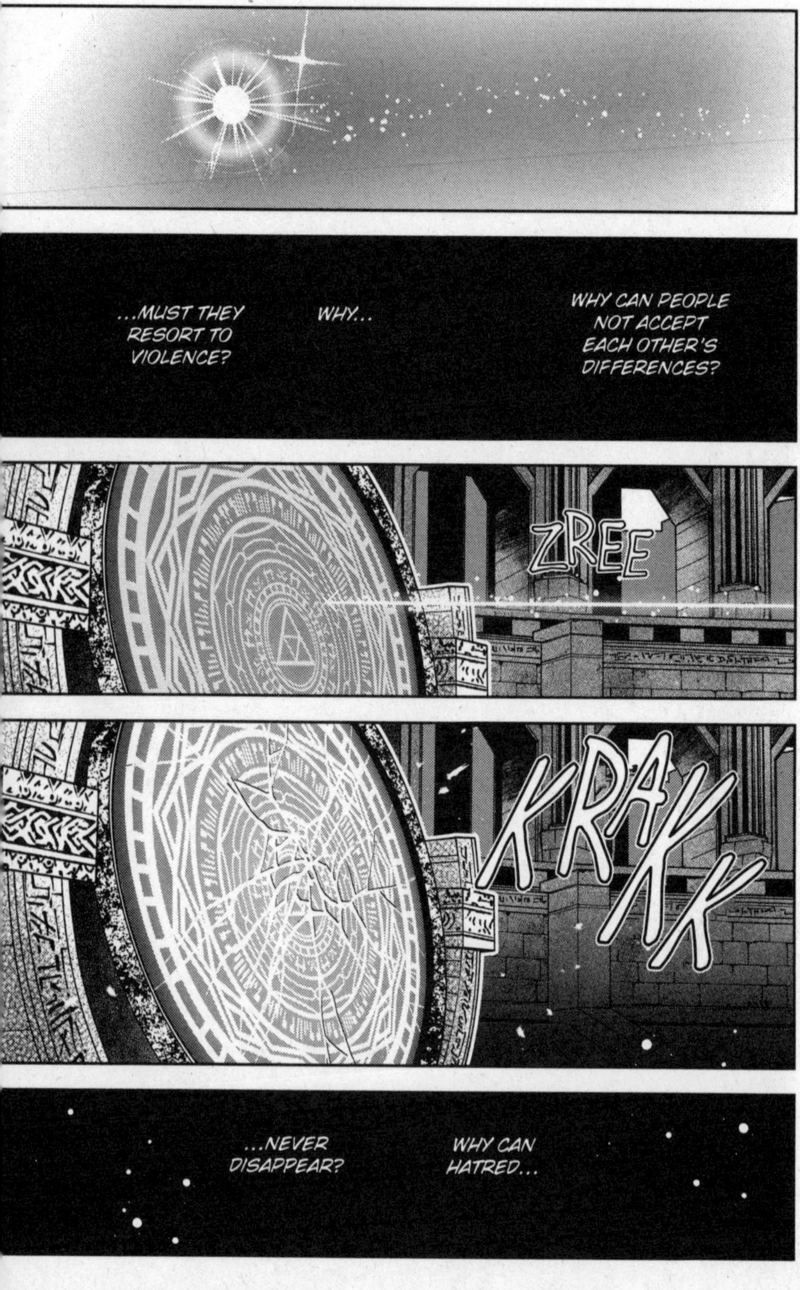
WHY CAN PEOPLE NOT ACCEPT EACH OTHER'S DIFFERENCES?
WHY...
...MUST THEY RESORT TO VIOLENCE?
ZREE
KRAKK
WHY CAN HATRED...
...NEVER DISAPPEAR?

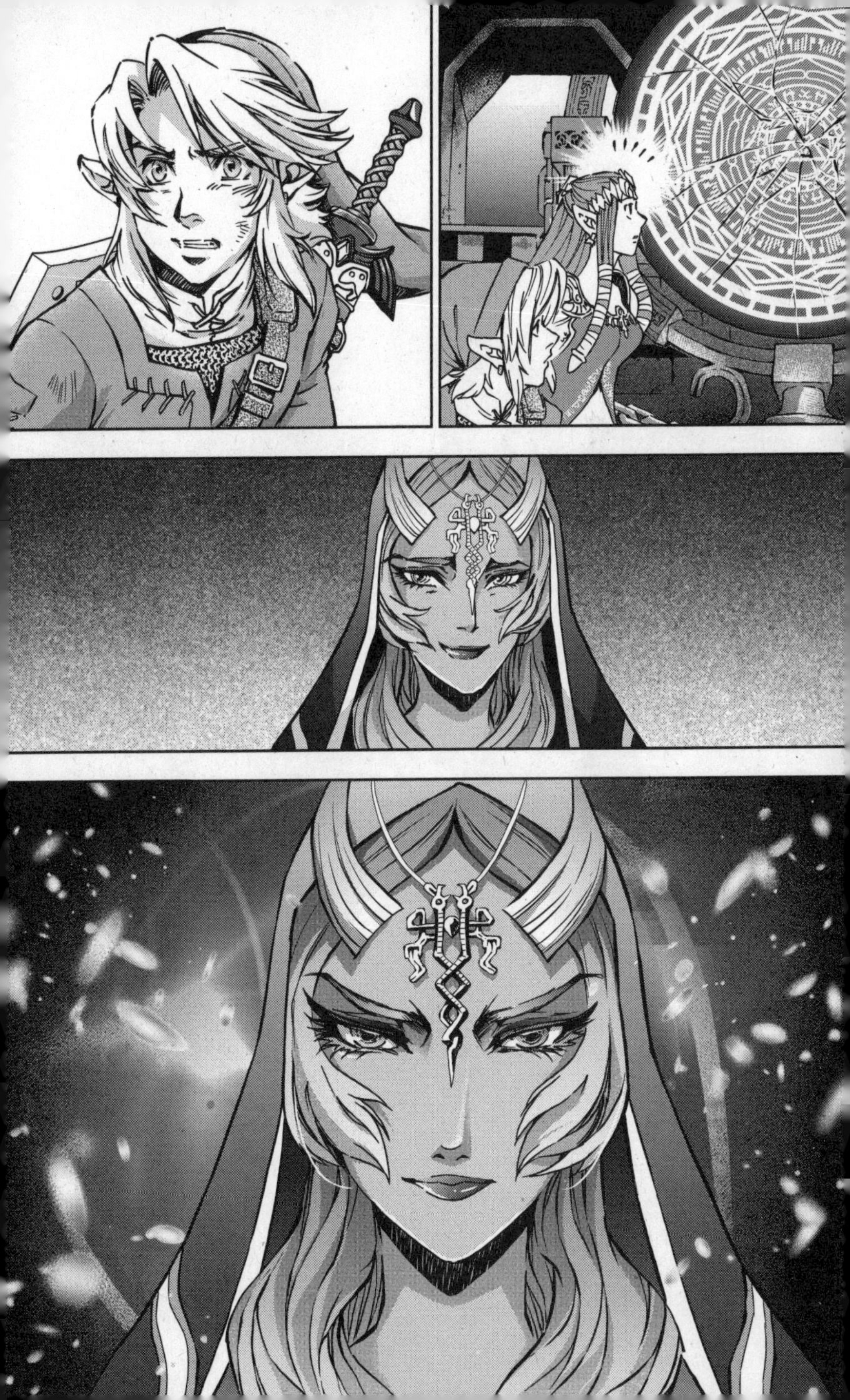

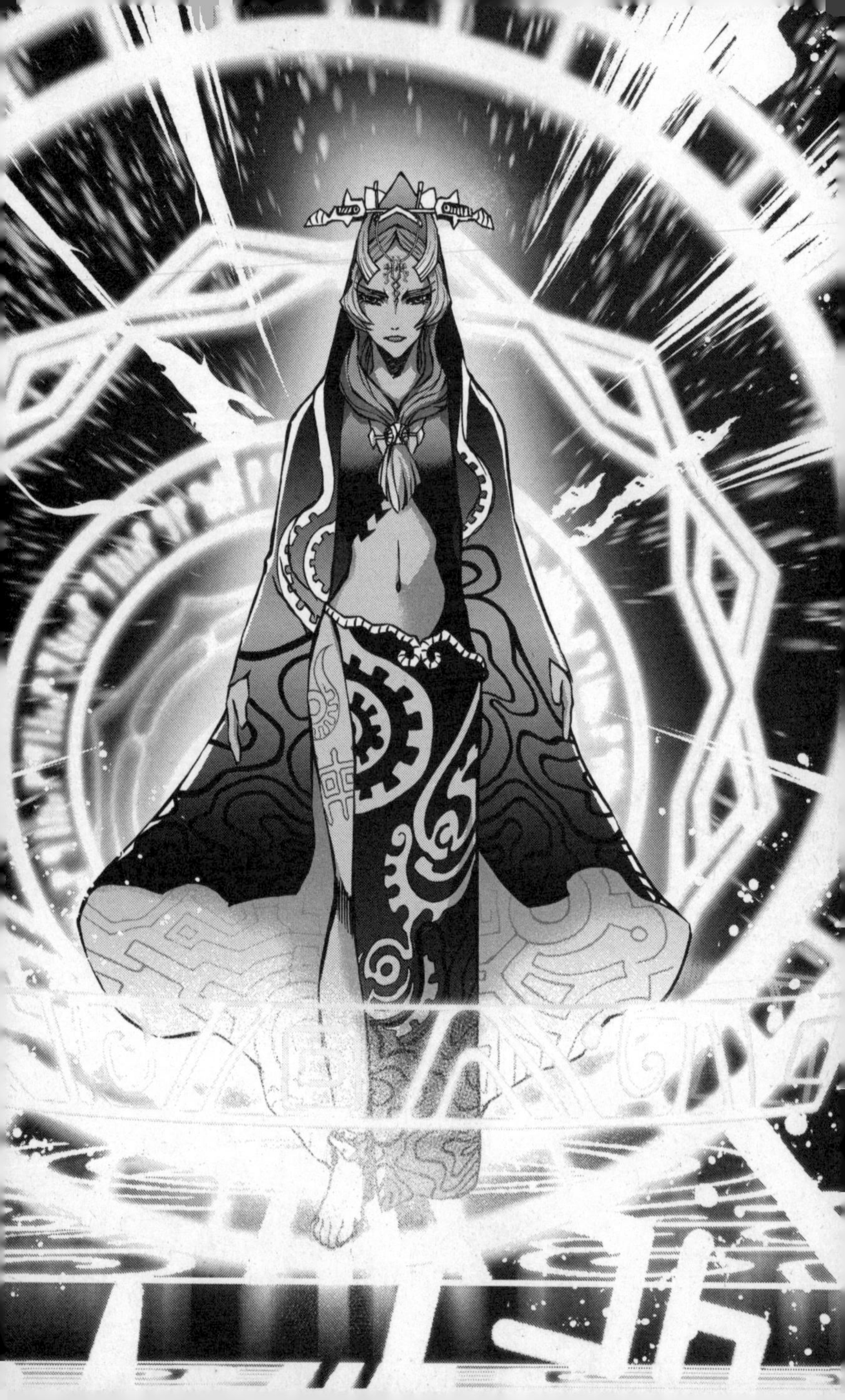

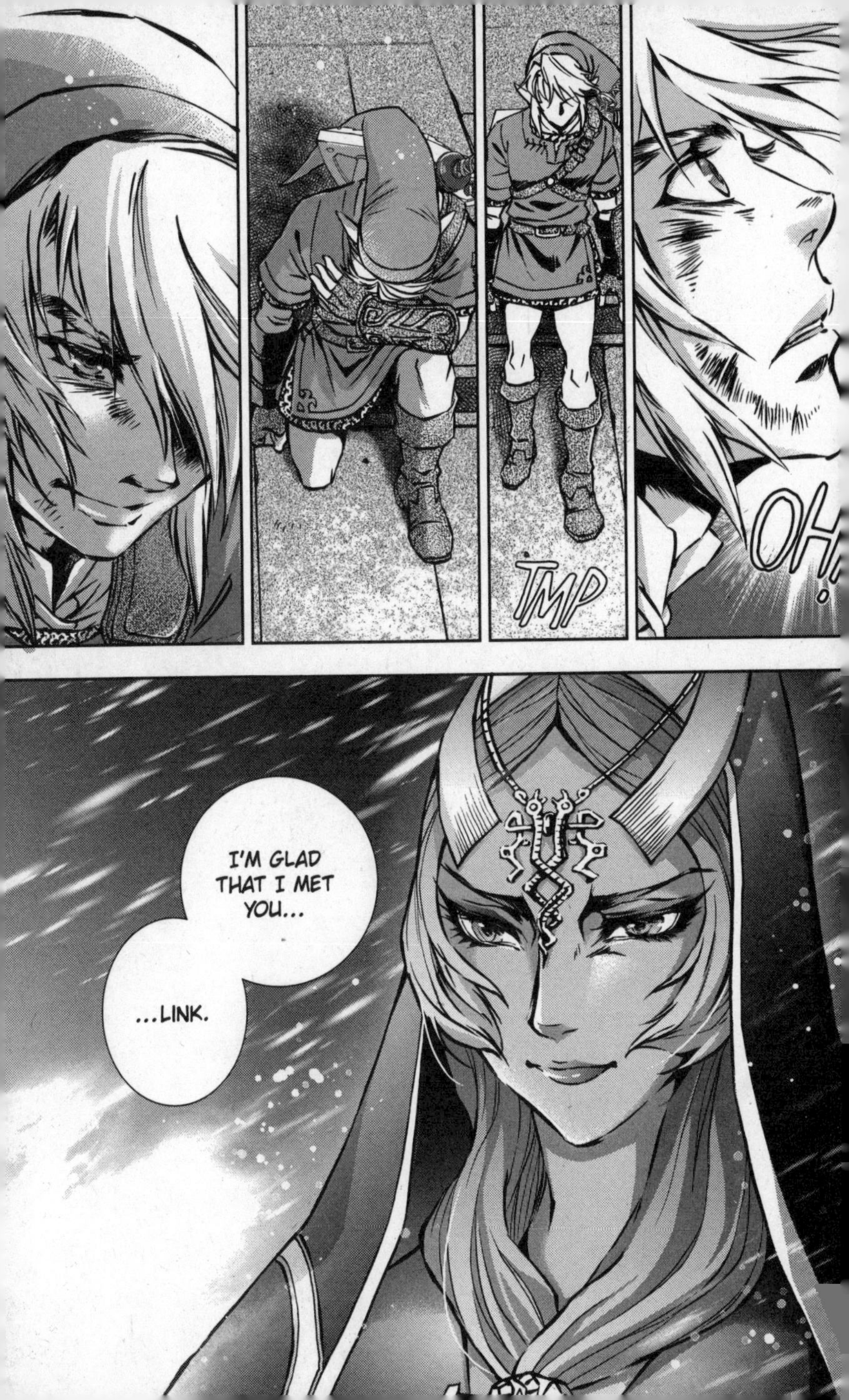
OH!
TMP
I'M GLAD THAT I MET YOU...
...LINK.

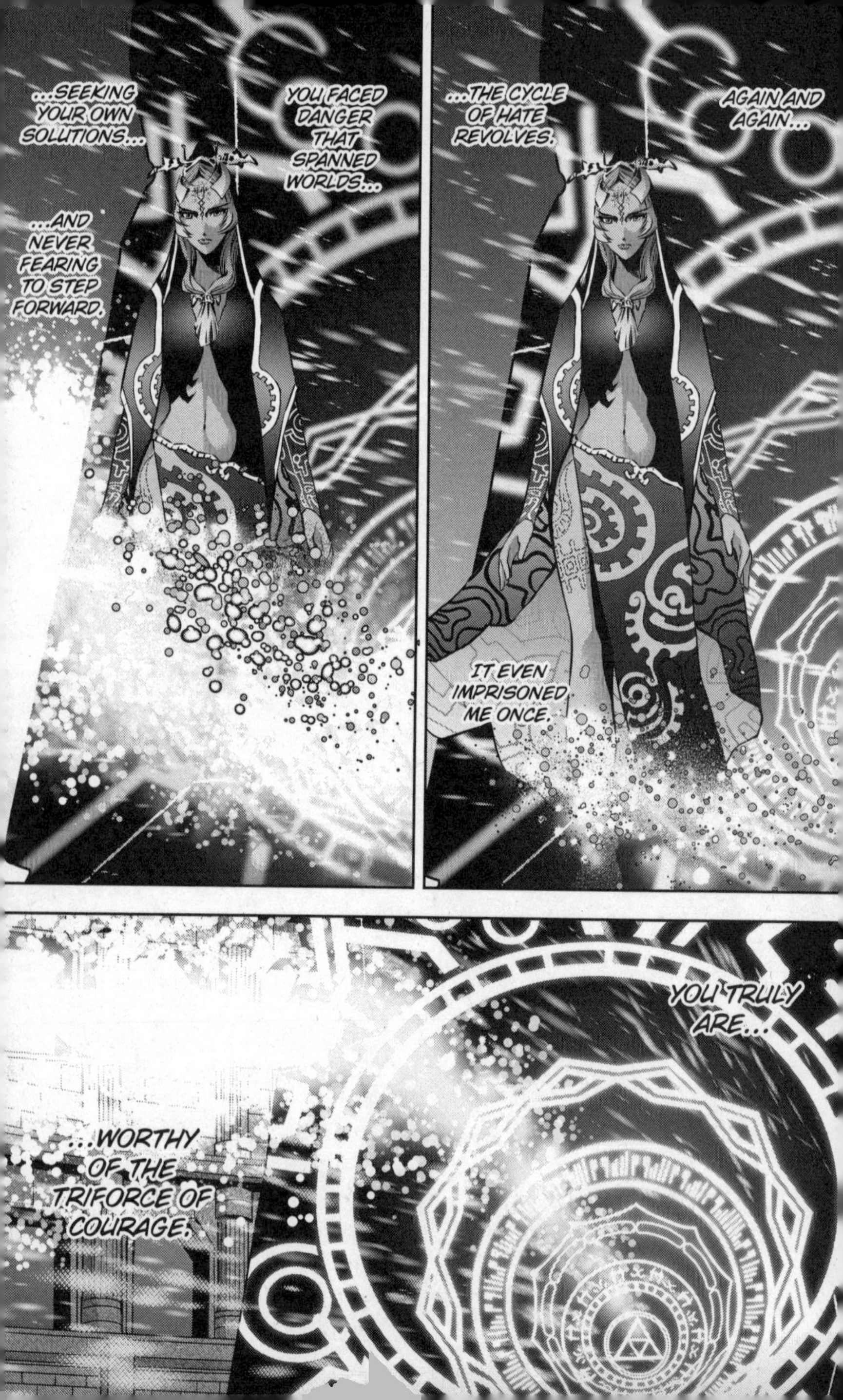
AGAIN AND AGAIN...
...THE CYCLE OF HATE REVOLVES.
IT EVEN IMPRISONED ME ONCE.
YOU FACED DANGER THAT SPANNED WORLDS...
...SEEKING YOUR OWN SOLUTIONS...
...AND NEVER FEARING TO STEP FORWARD.
YOU TRULY ARE...
...WORTHY OF THE TRIFORCE OF COURAGE.

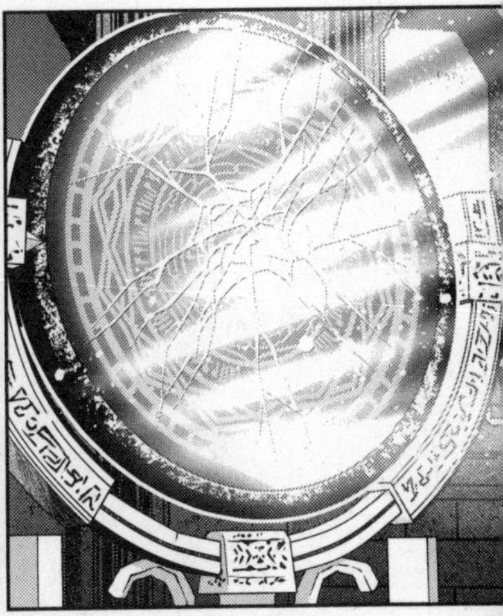

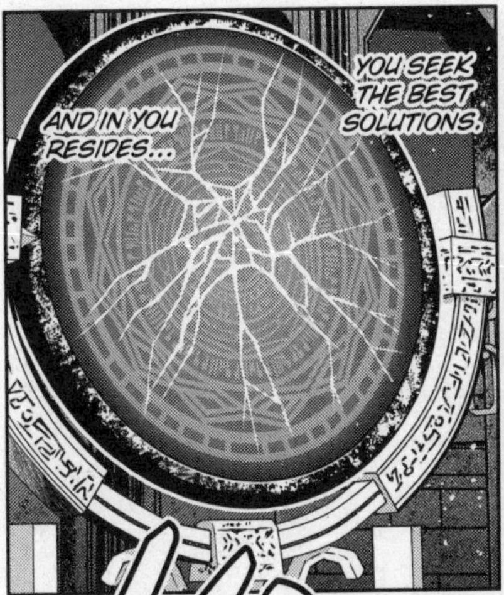
YOU SEEK THE BEST SOLUTIONS.
AND IN YOU RESIDES...

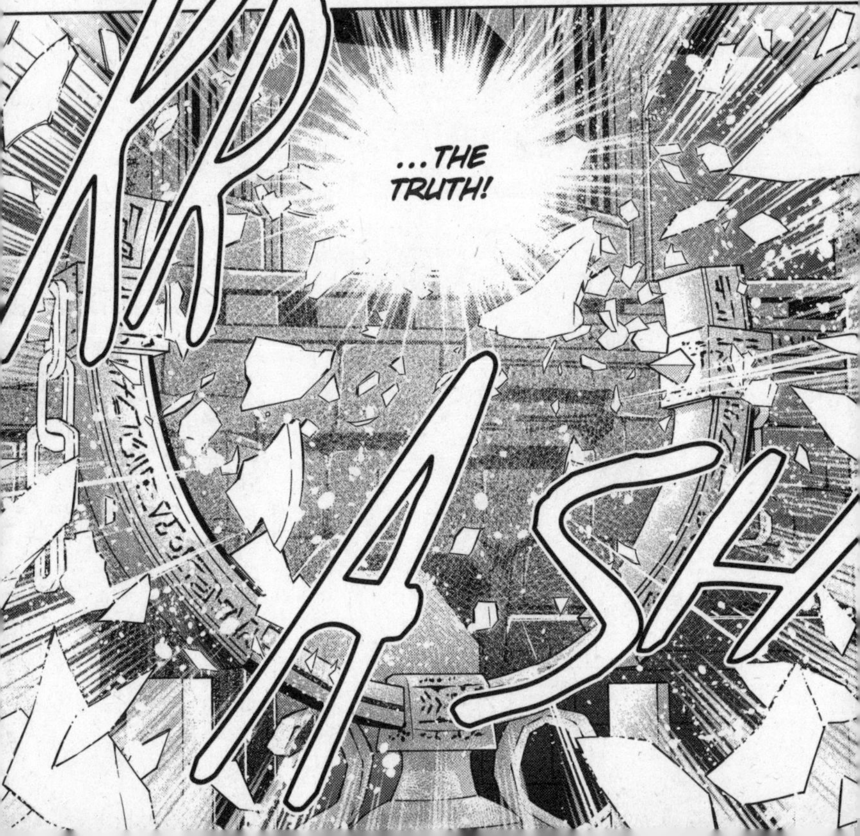
...THE TRUTH!
KRASH

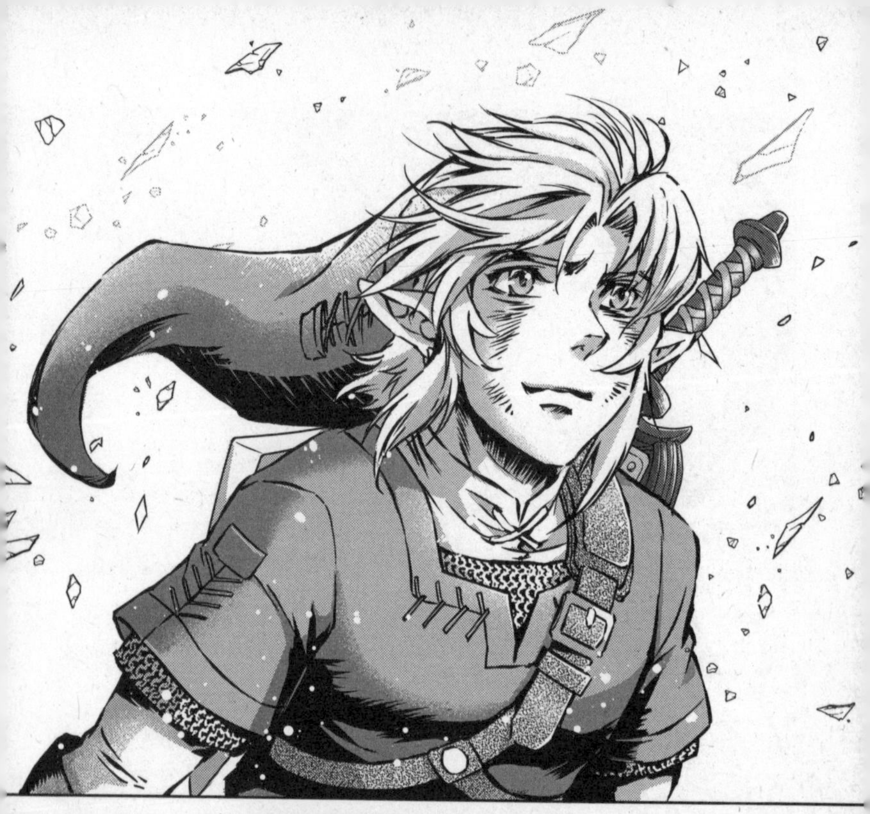
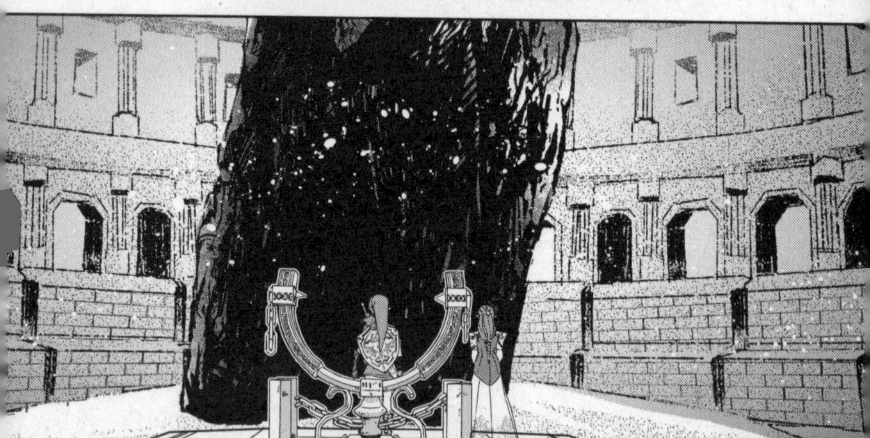
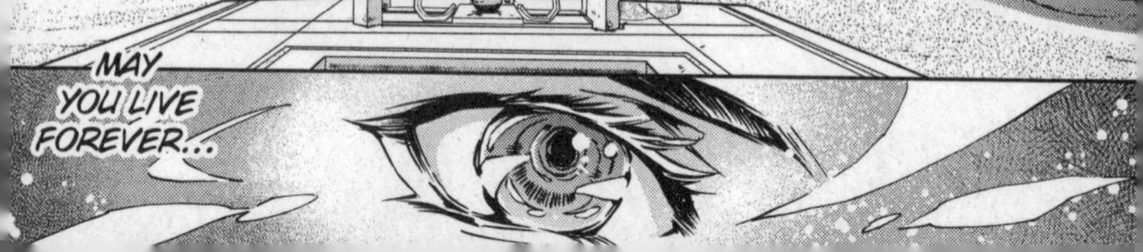
MAY YOU LIVE FOREVER...

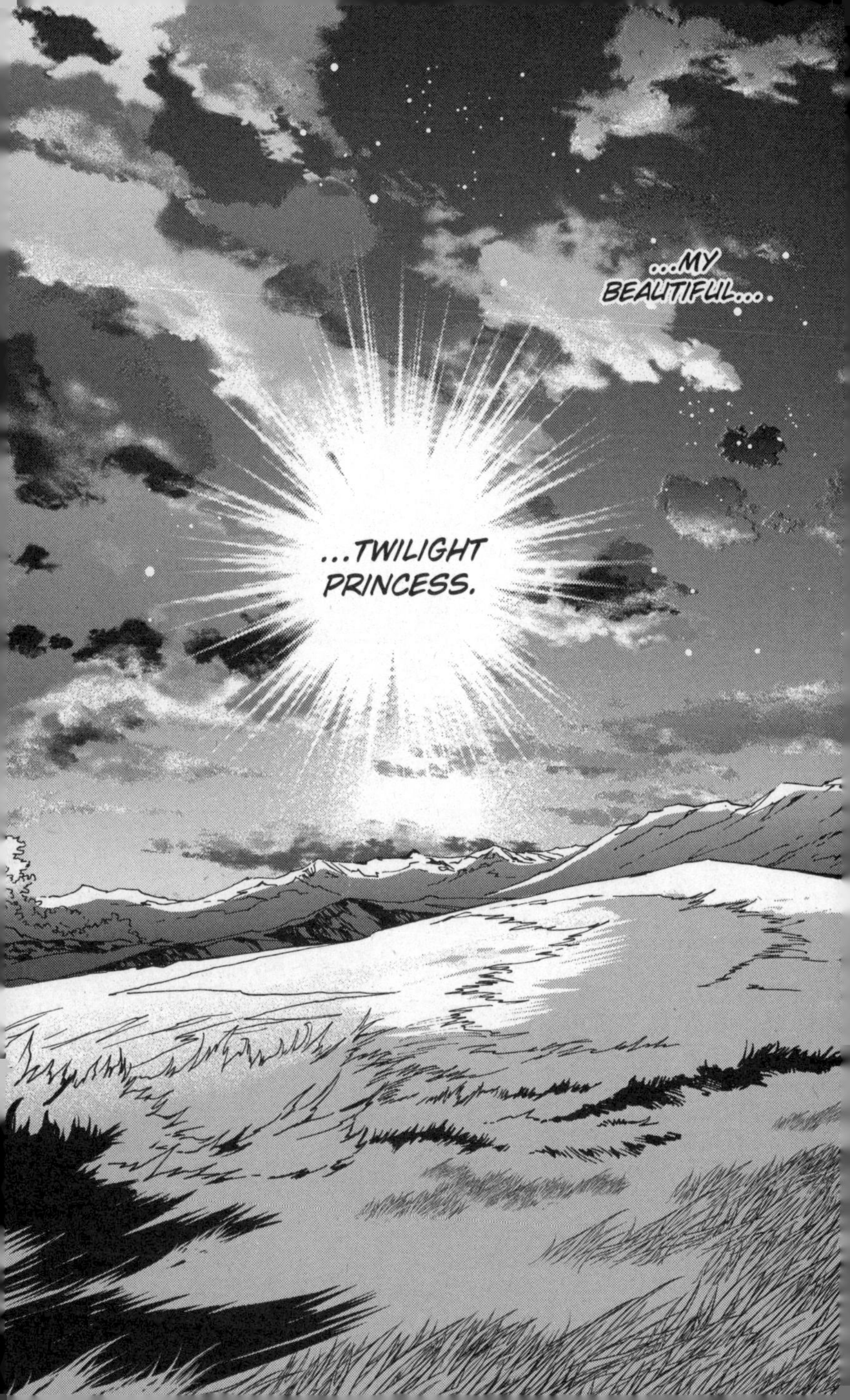
...MY BEAUTIFUL...
...TWILIGHT PRINCESS.

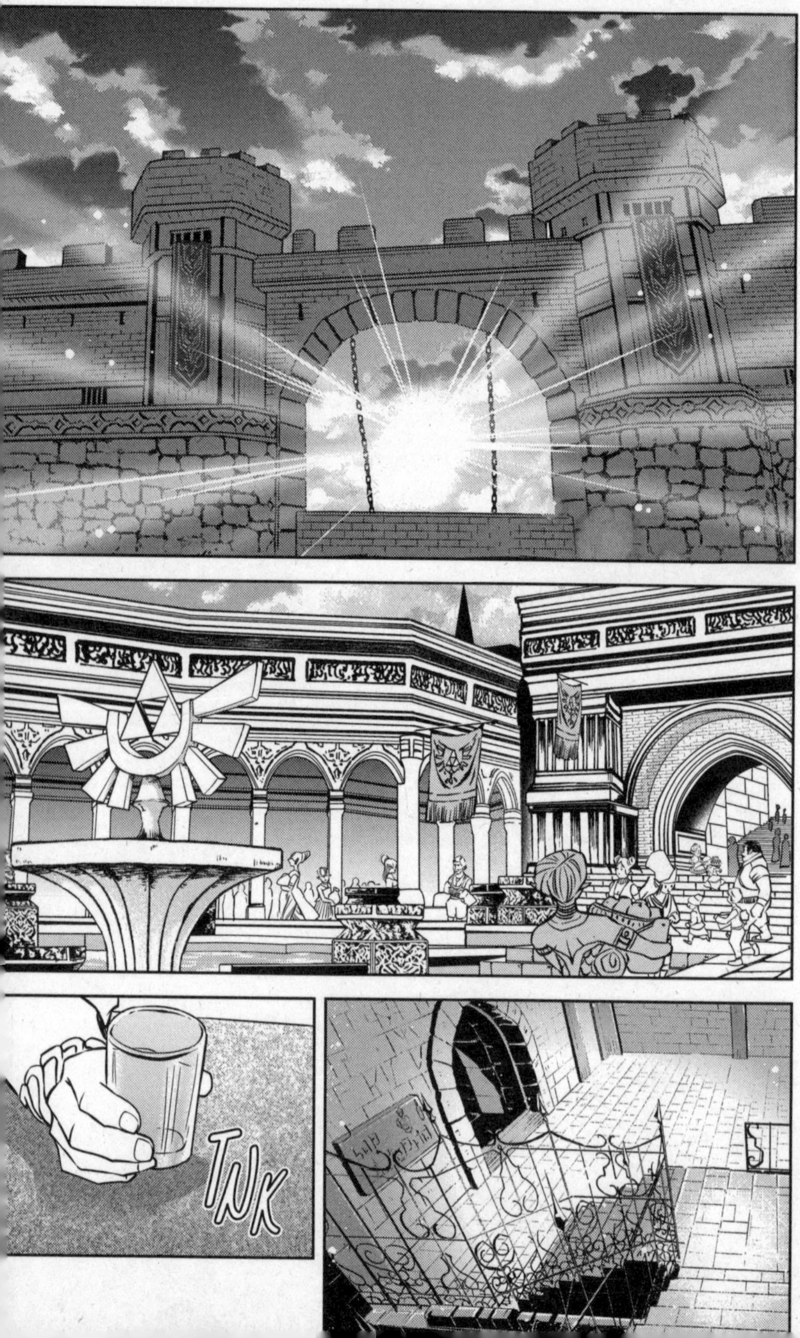
TNK

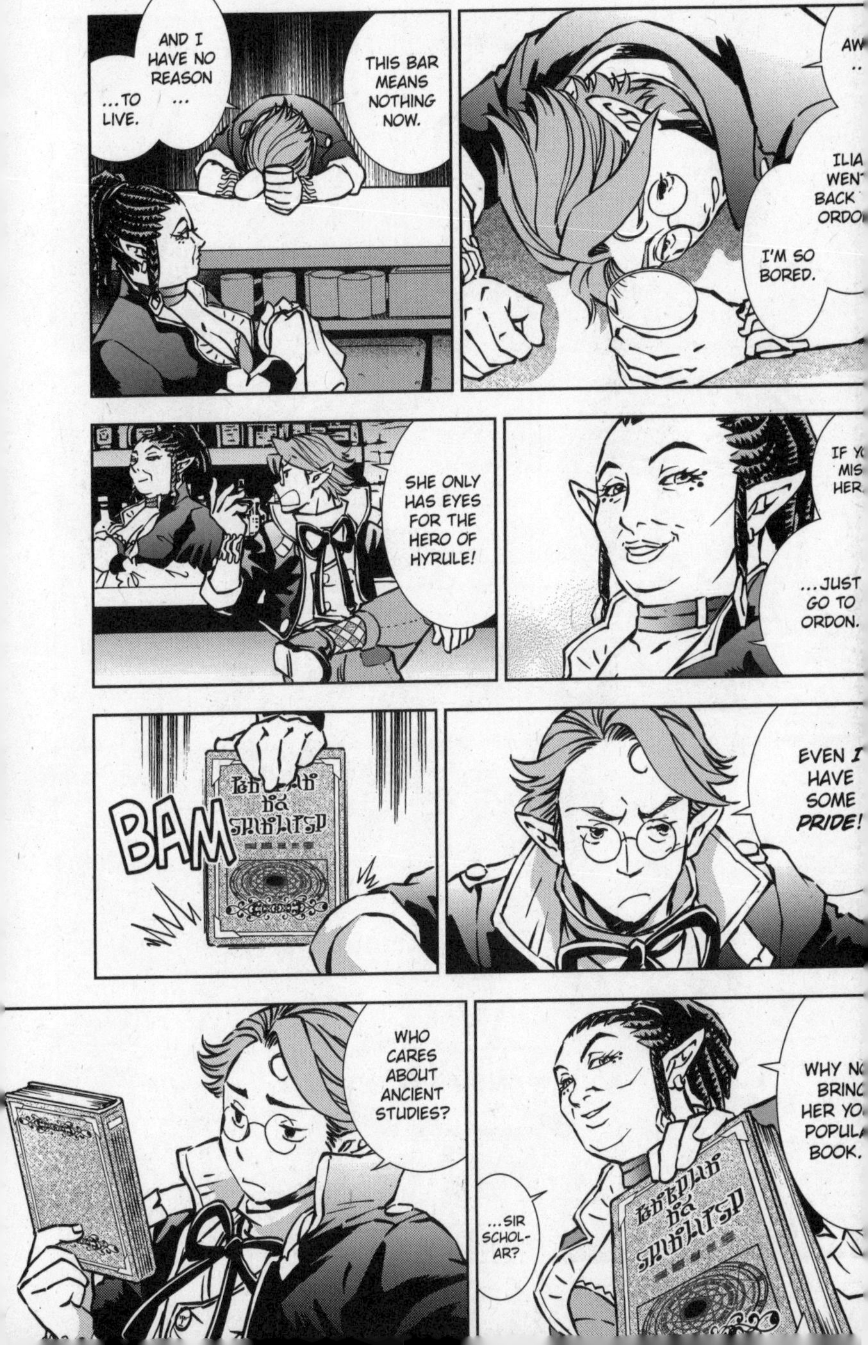
AW
ILIA WENT BACK ORDO
I'M SO BORED.
THIS BAR MEANS NOTHING NOW.
AND I HAVE NO REASON ...
...TO LIVE.
IF YO MIS HER.
...JUST GO TO ORDON.
SHE ONLY HAS EYES FOR THE HERO OF HYRULE!
EVEN *I* HAVE SOME *PRIDE!*
BAM
WHY NO BRIN HER YO POPUL BOOK.
...SIR SCHOL-AR?
WHO CARES ABOUT ANCIENT STUDIES?

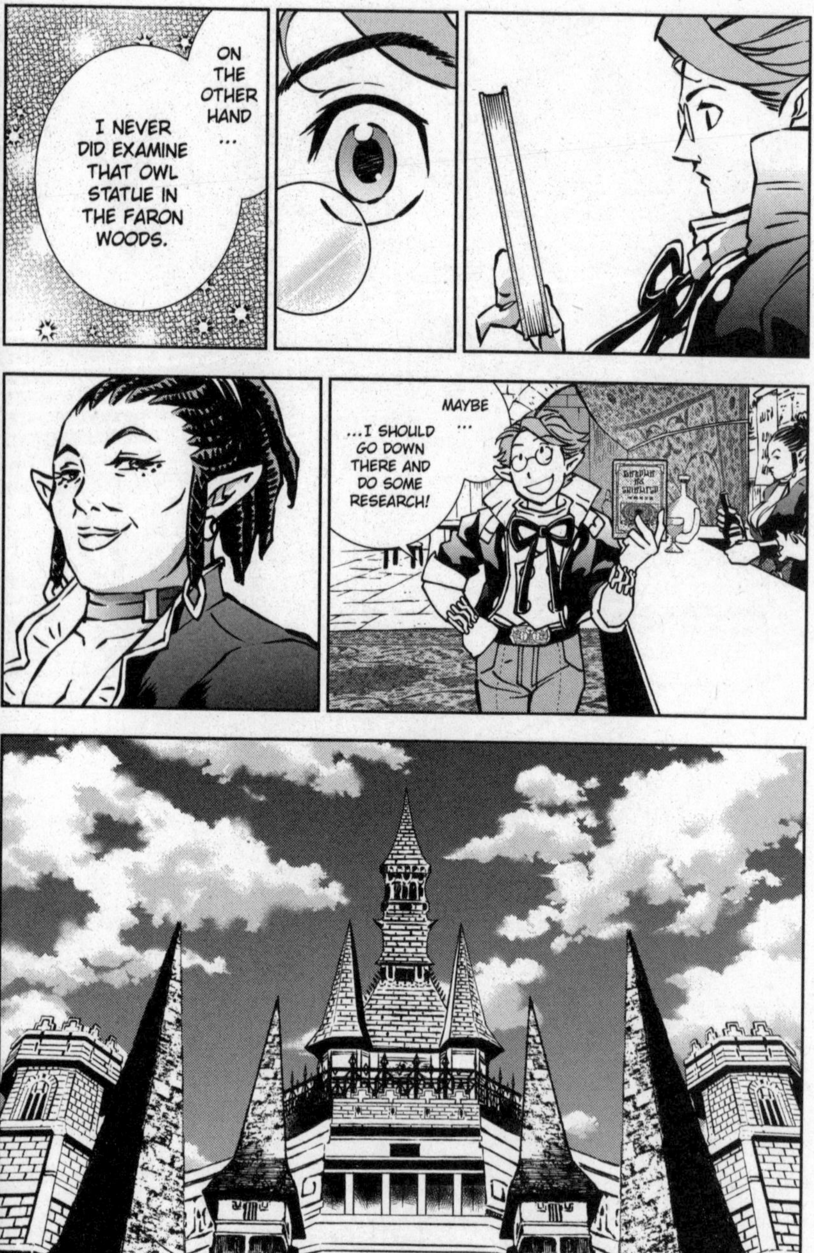
ON THE OTHER HAND ...
I NEVER DID EXAMINE THAT OWL STATUE IN THE FARON WOODS.
MAYBE ...
...I SHOULD GO DOWN THERE AND DO SOME RESEARCH!

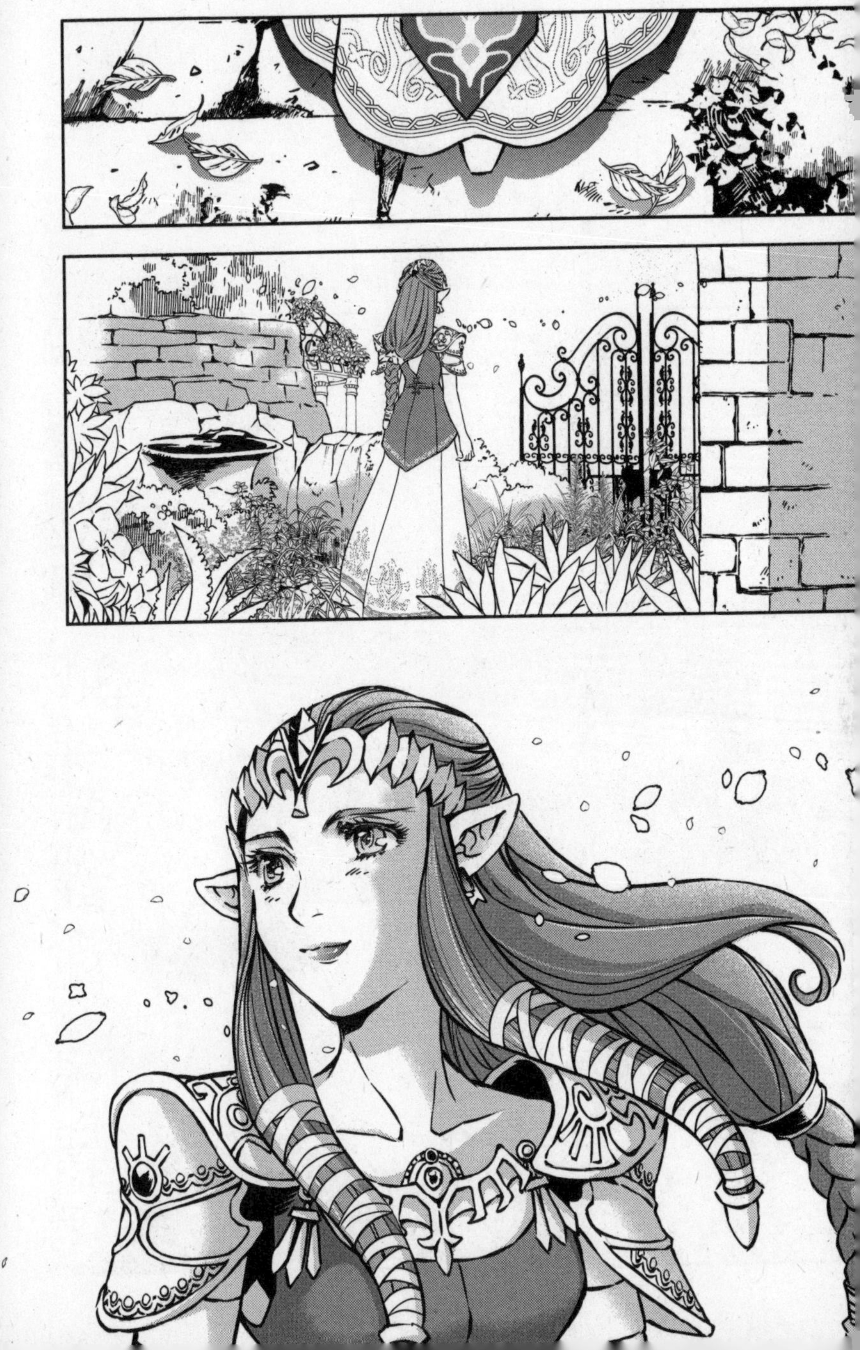

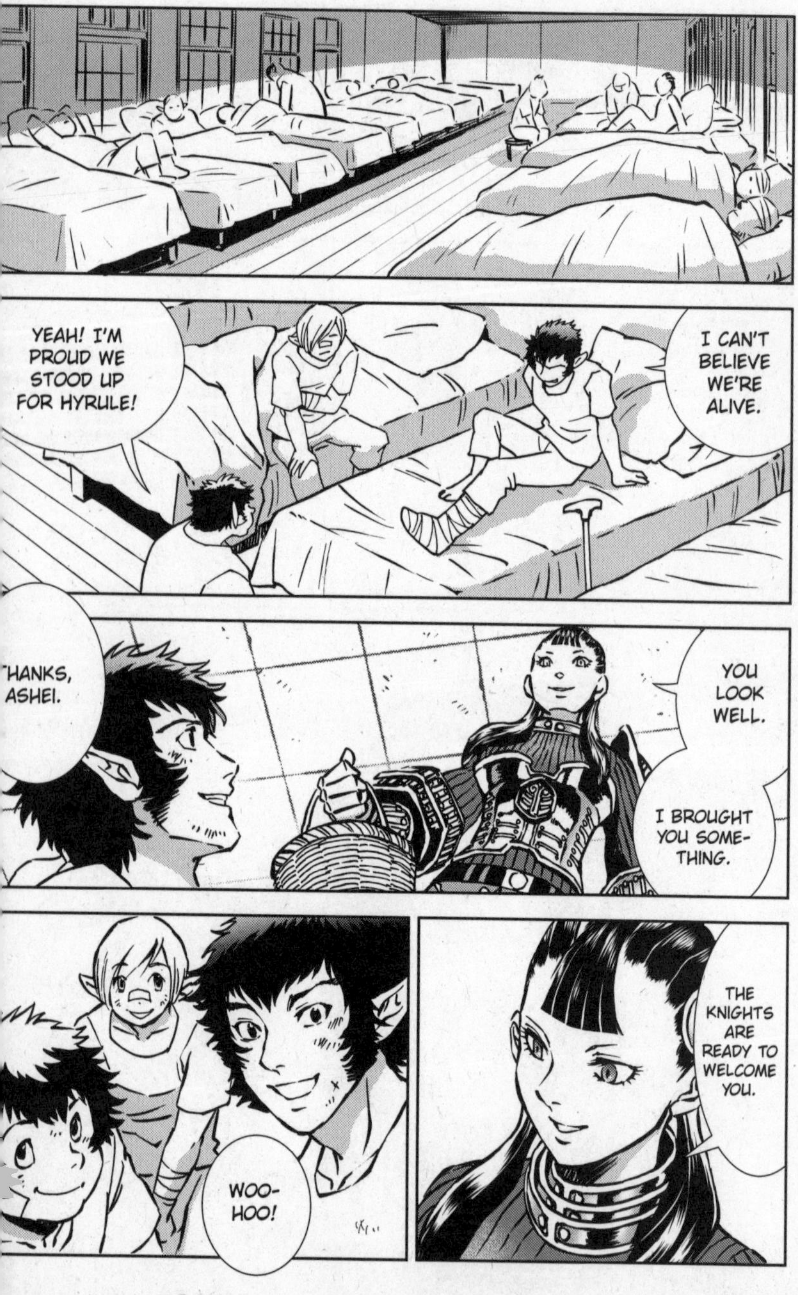
I CAN'T BELIEVE WE'RE ALIVE.
YEAH! I'M PROUD WE STOOD UP FOR HYRULE!
YOU LOOK WELL.
I BROUGHT YOU SOME-THING.
THANKS, ASHEI.
THE KNIGHTS ARE READY TO WELCOME YOU.
WOO-HOO!

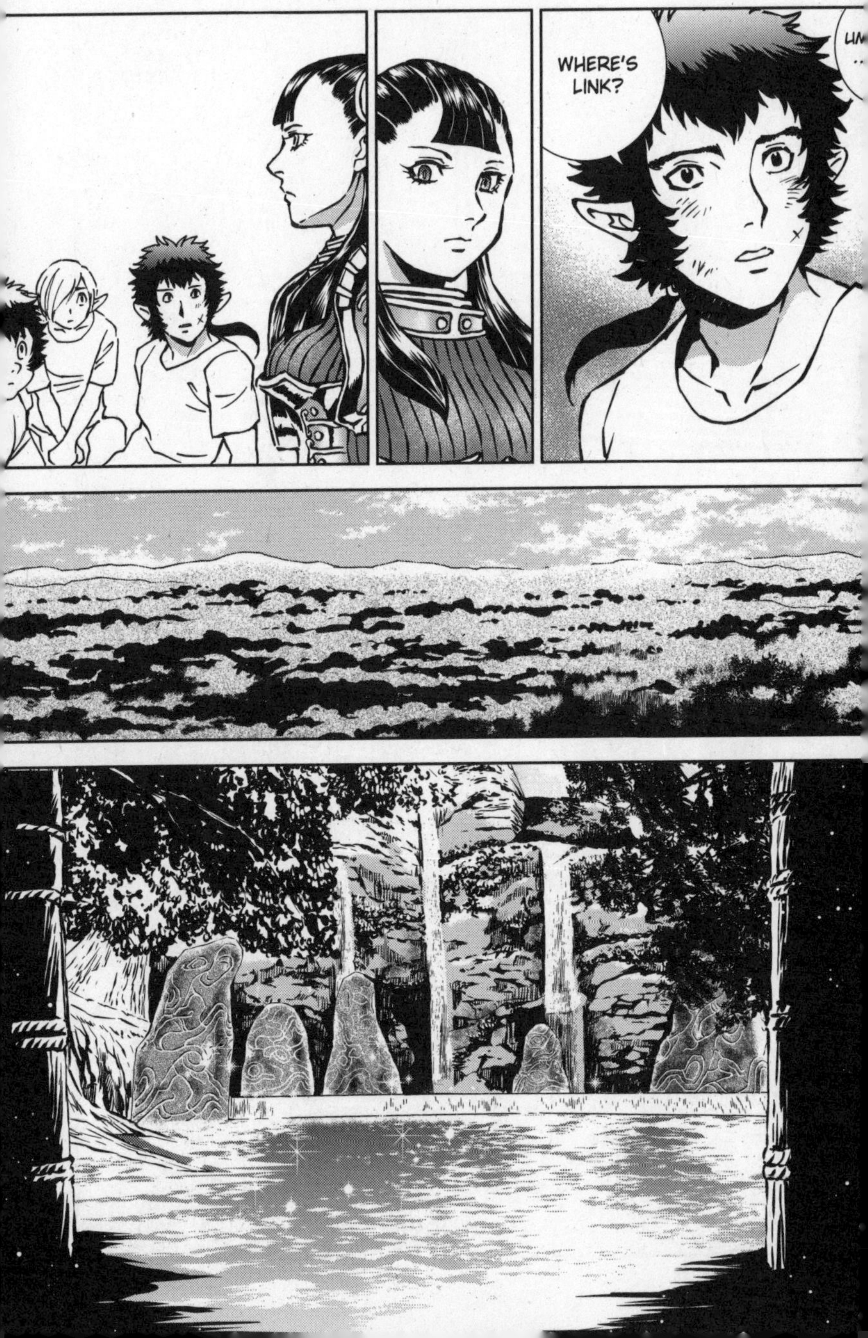
WHERE'S LINK?

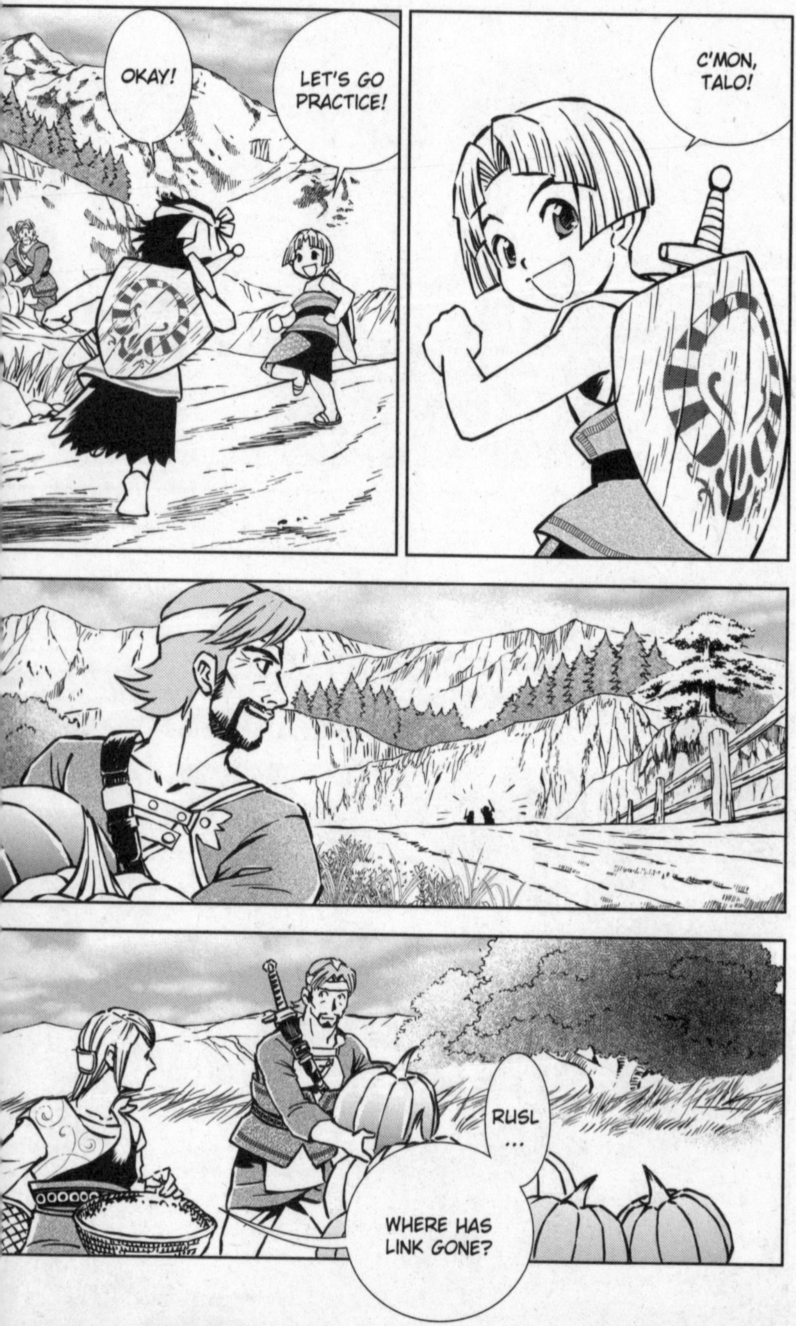
C'MON, TALO!
LET'S GO PRACTICE!
OKAY!
RUSL ...
WHERE HAS LINK GONE?

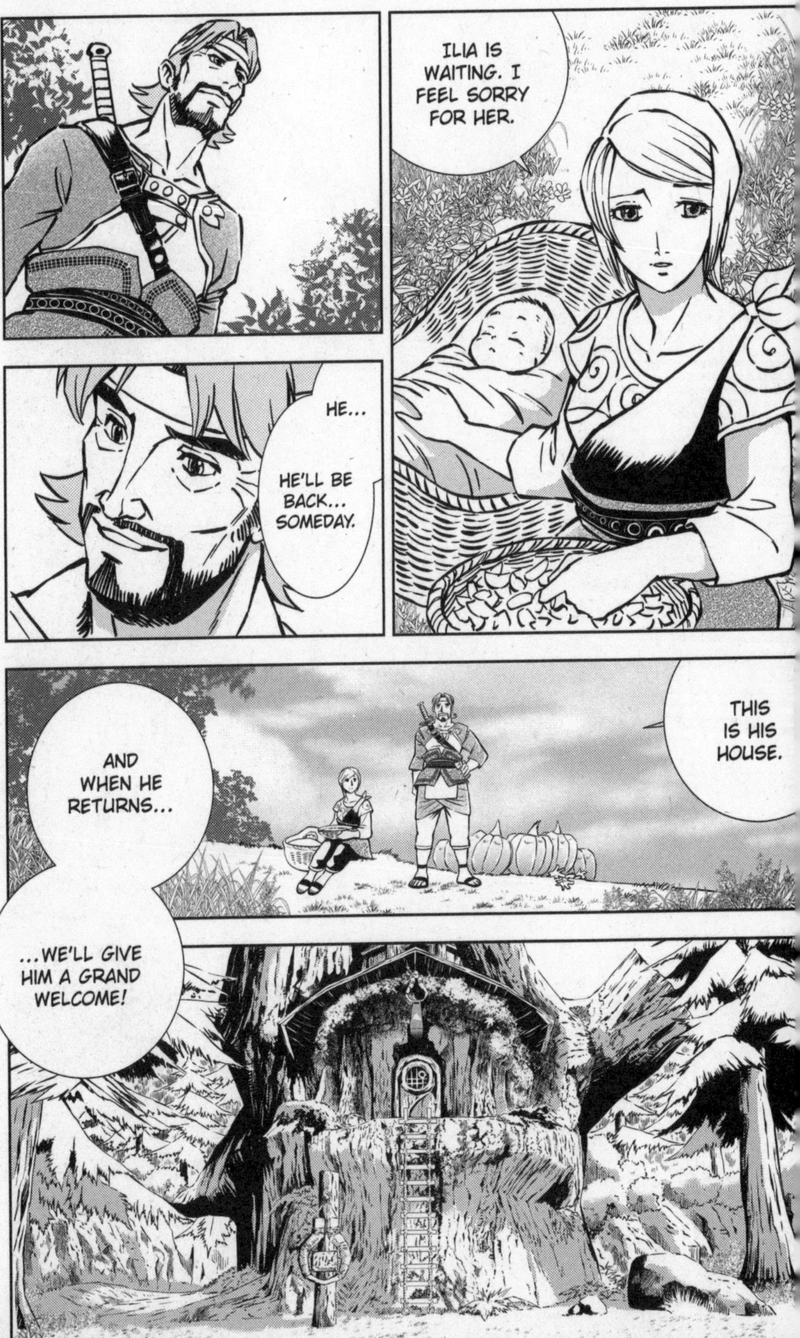
ILIA IS WAITING. I FEEL SORRY FOR HER.
HE...
HE'LL BE BACK... SOMEDAY.
THIS IS HIS HOUSE.
AND WHEN HE RETURNS...
...WE'LL GIVE HIM A GRAND WELCOME!

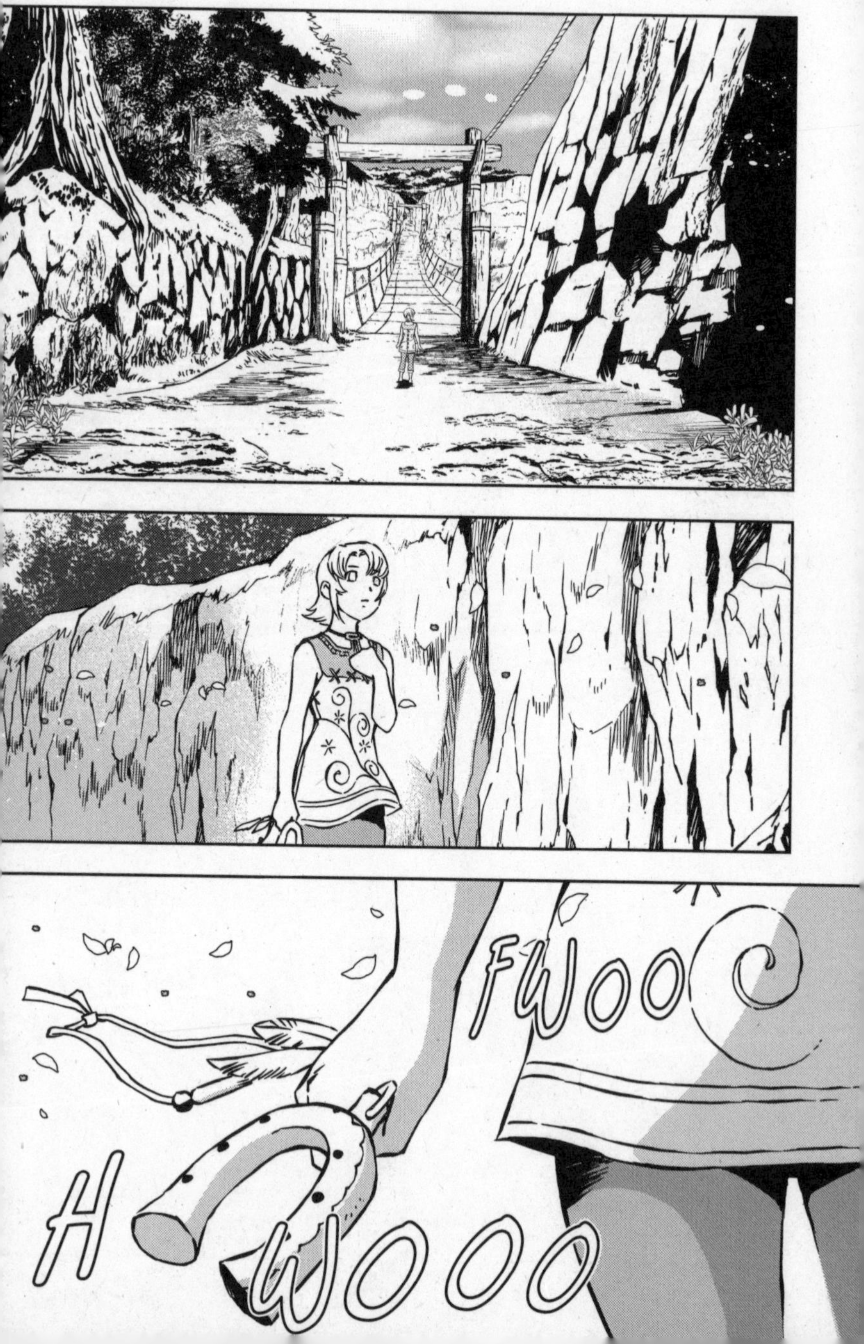
FWOO
HWOOO

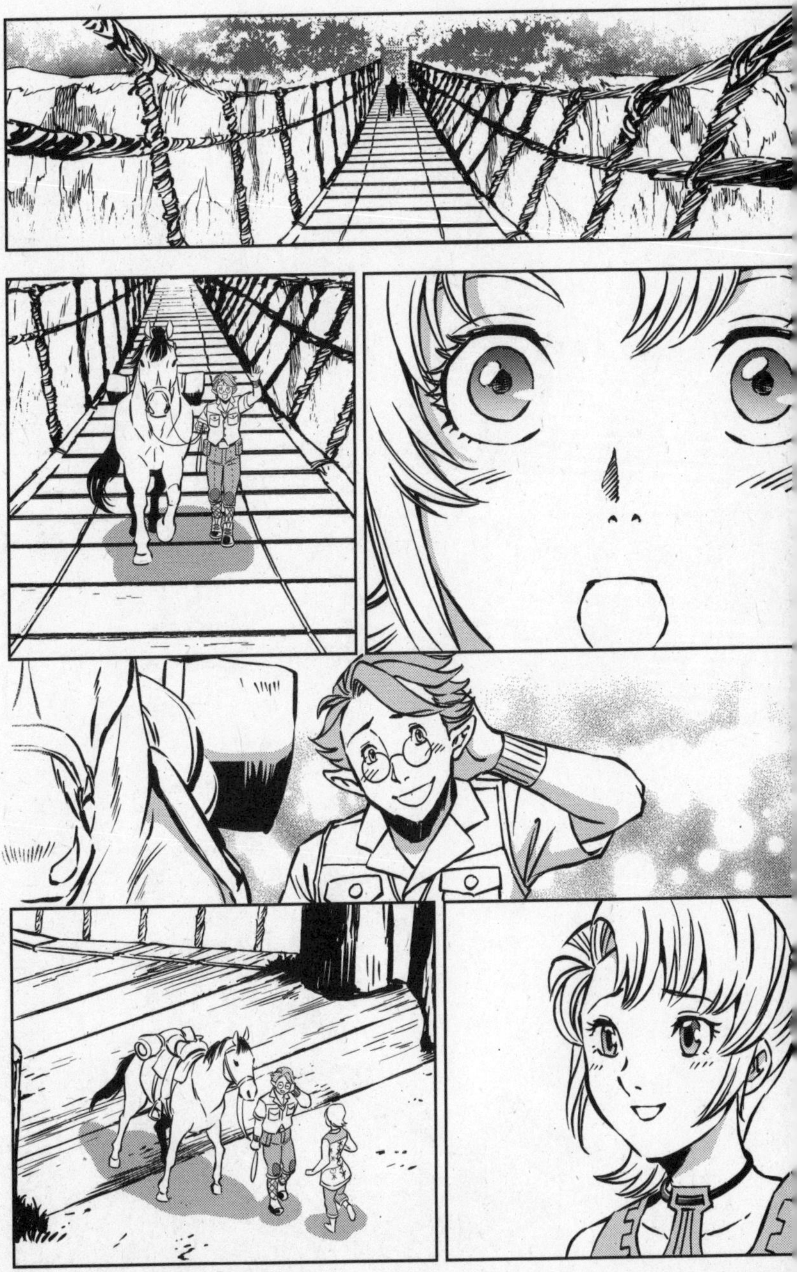

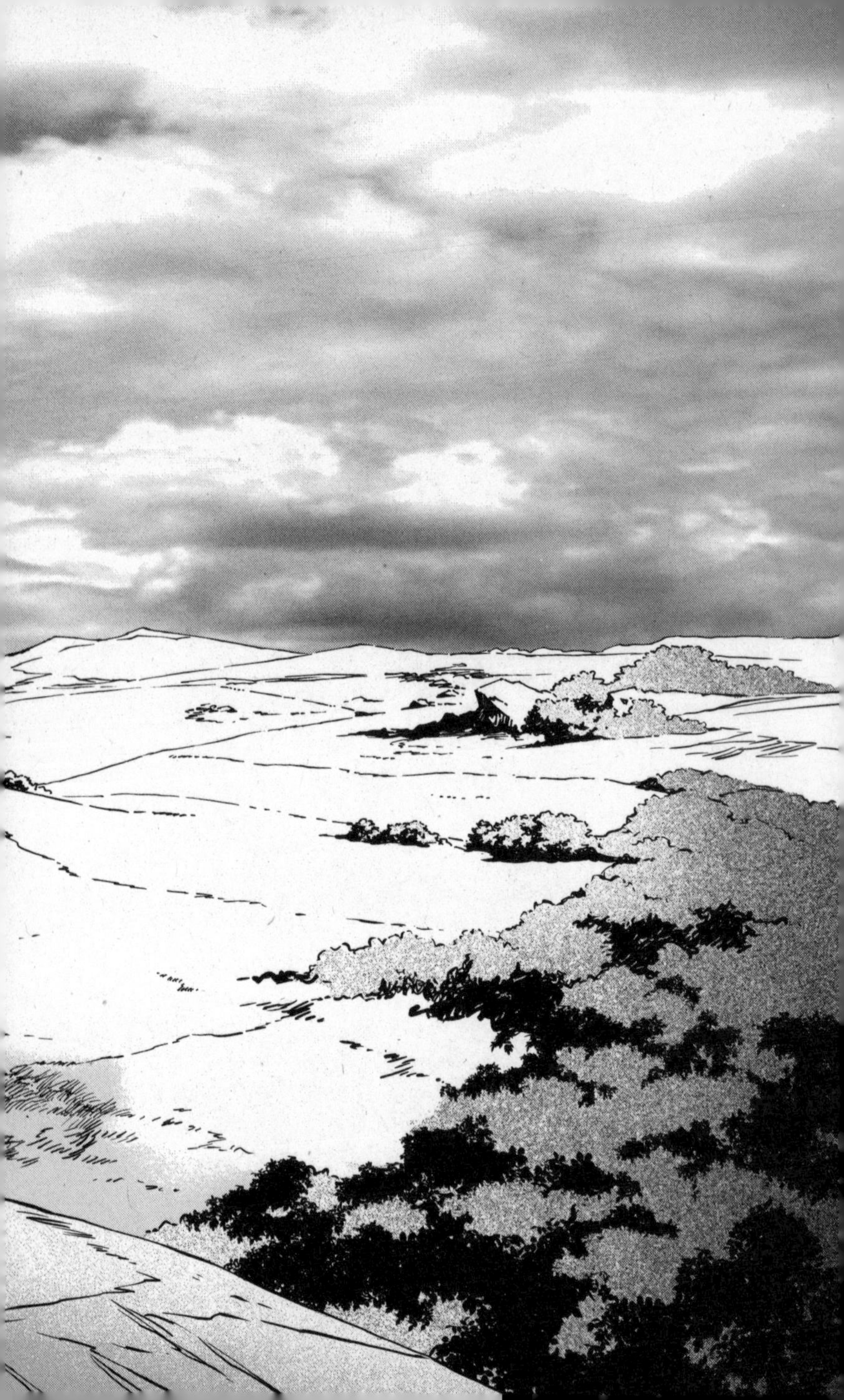

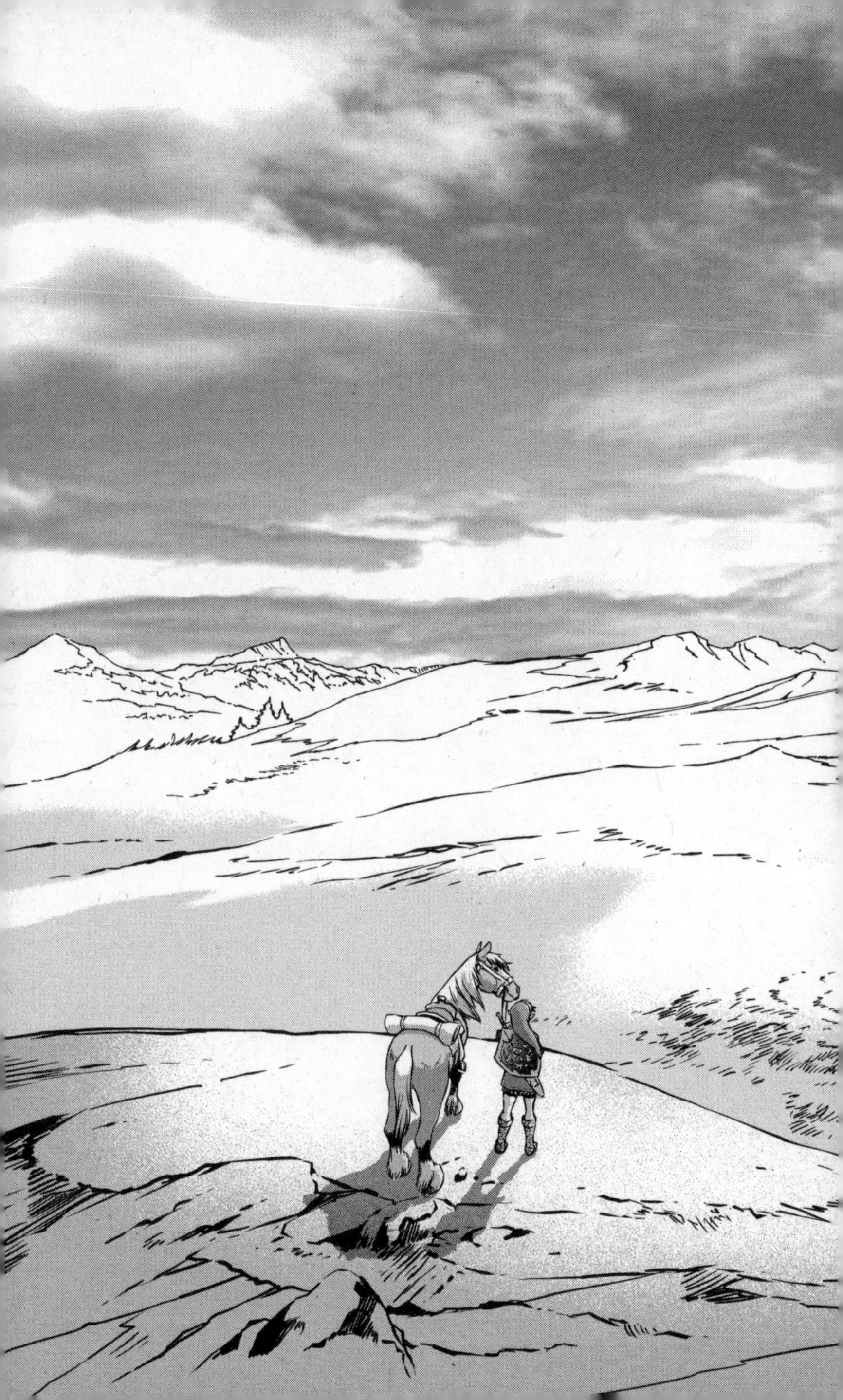

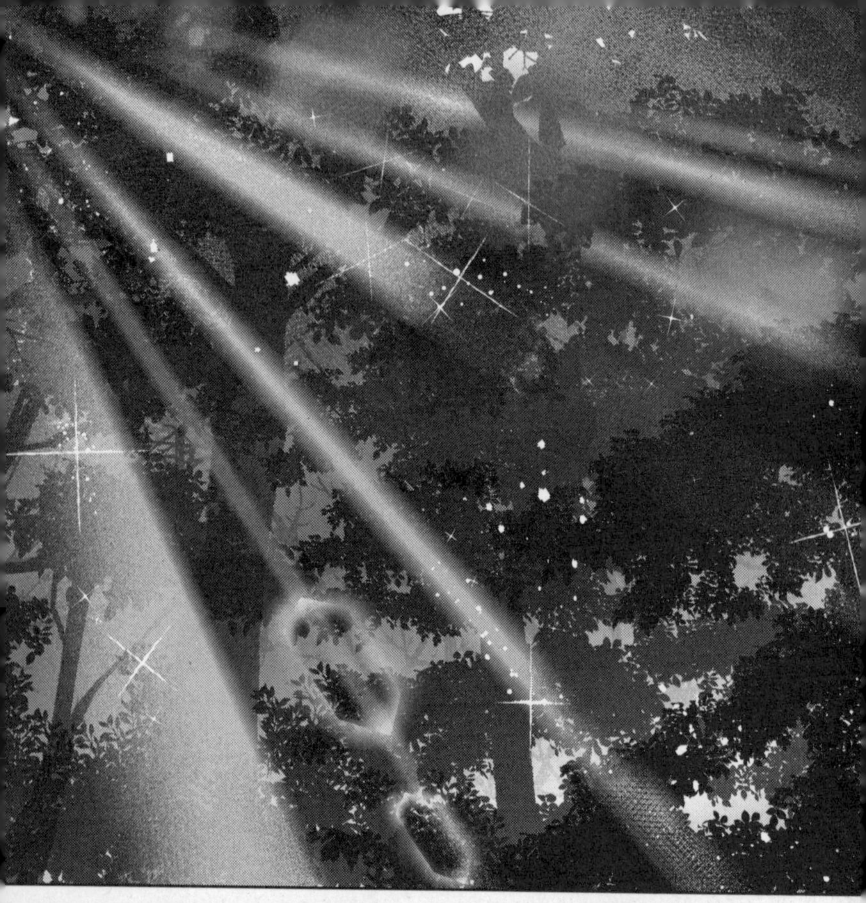
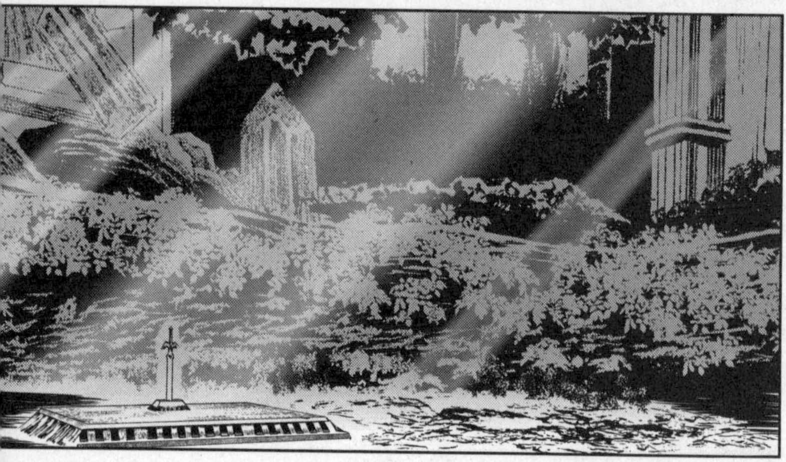

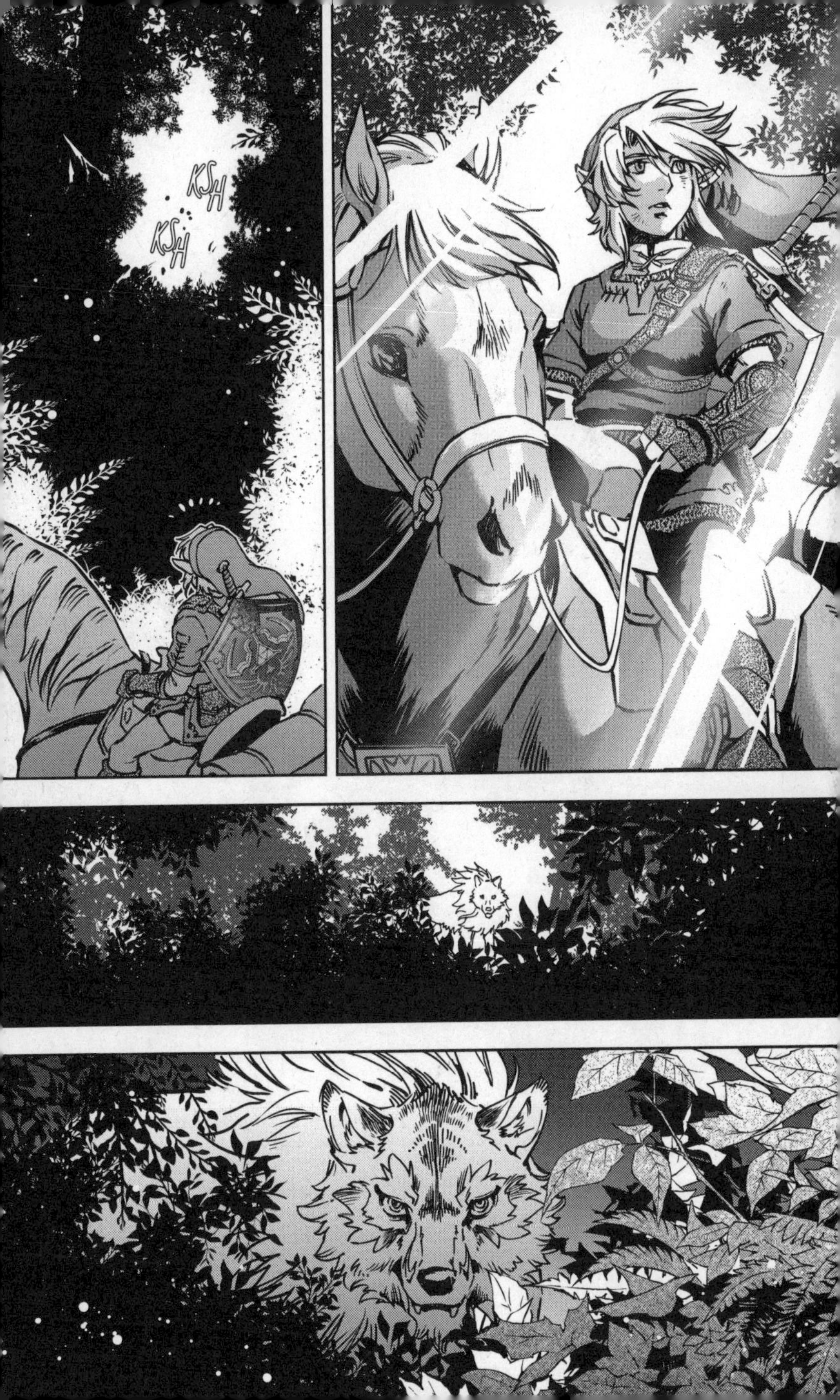
KSH
KSH

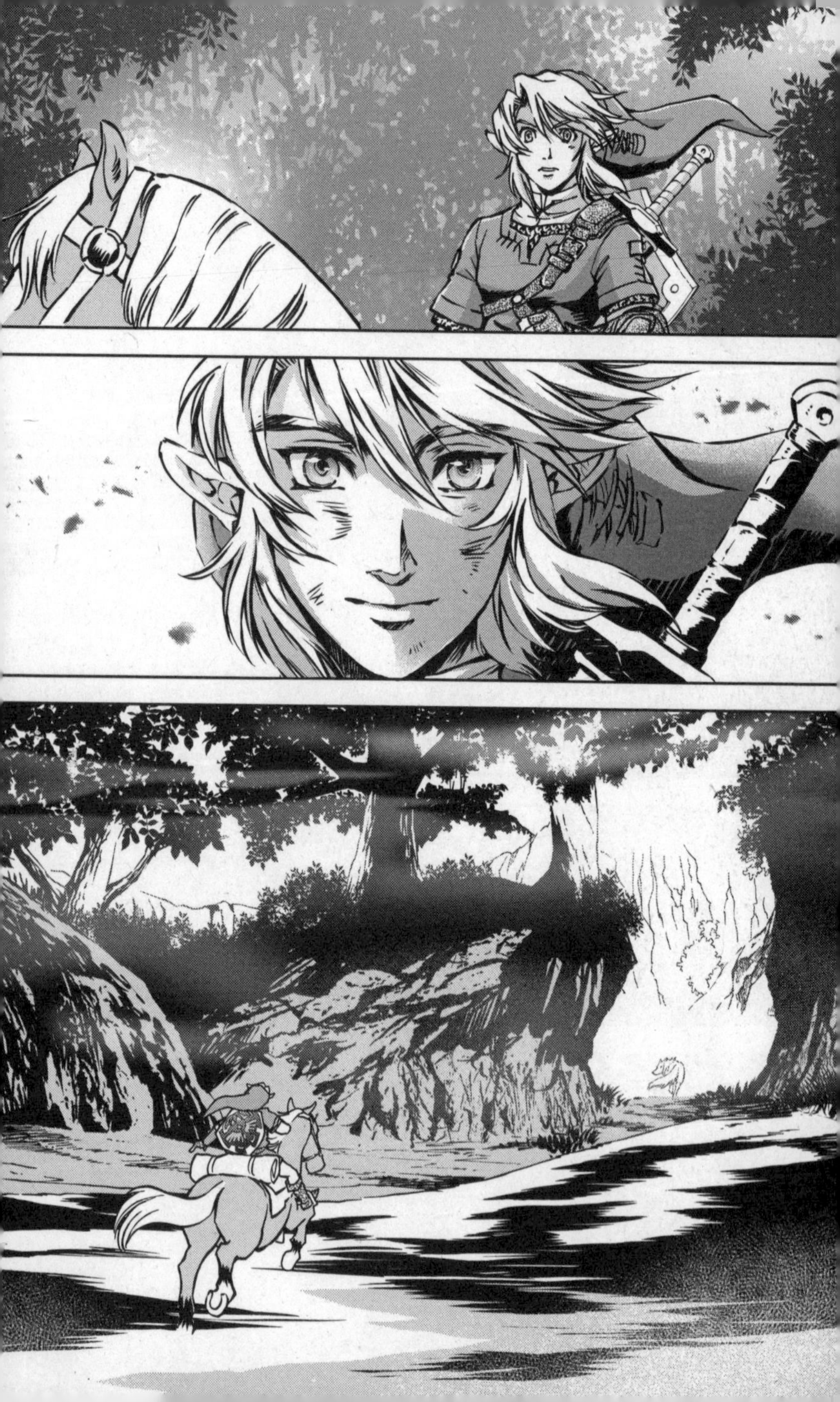

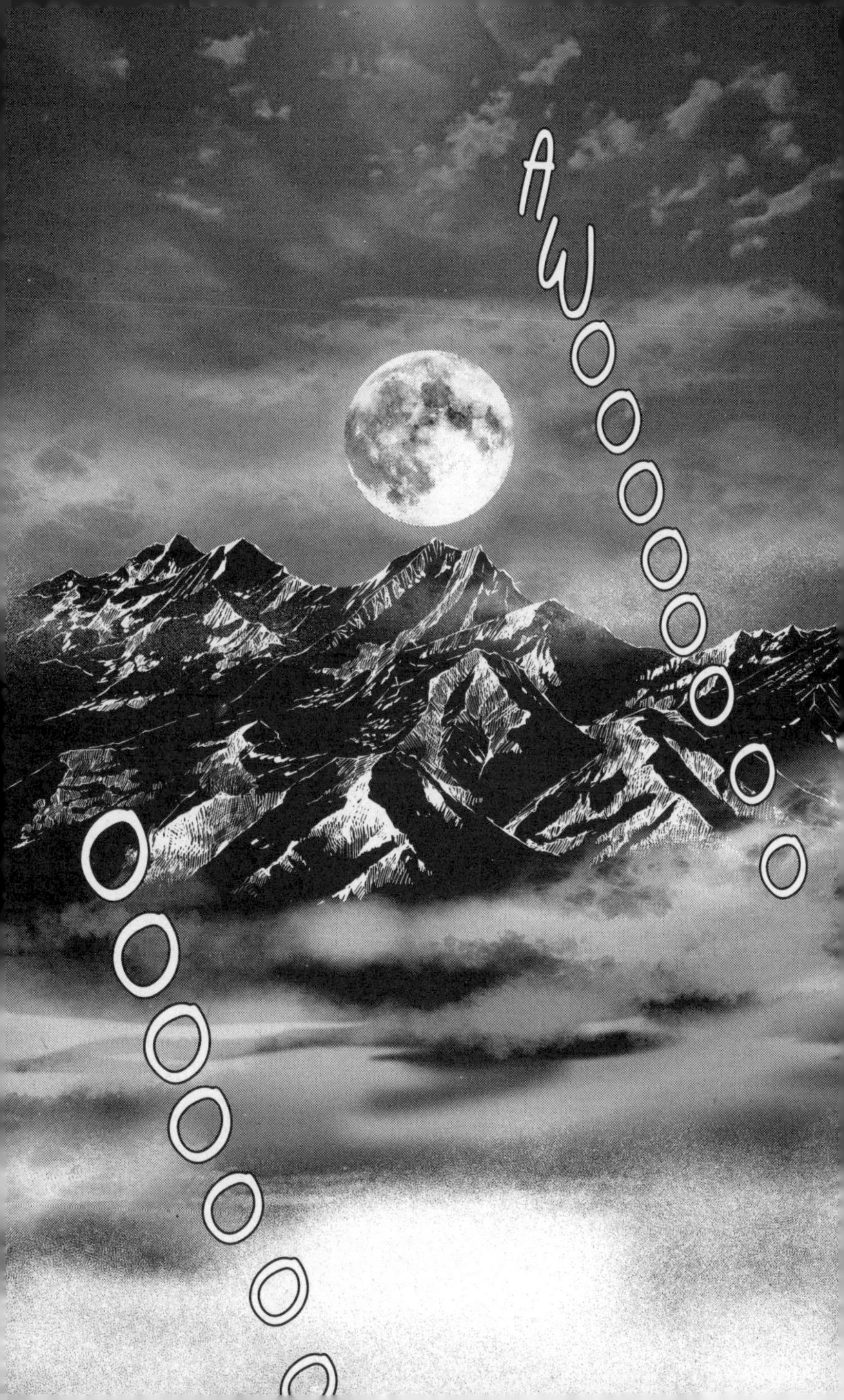
AWOOOOOOOO
OOOOOOO

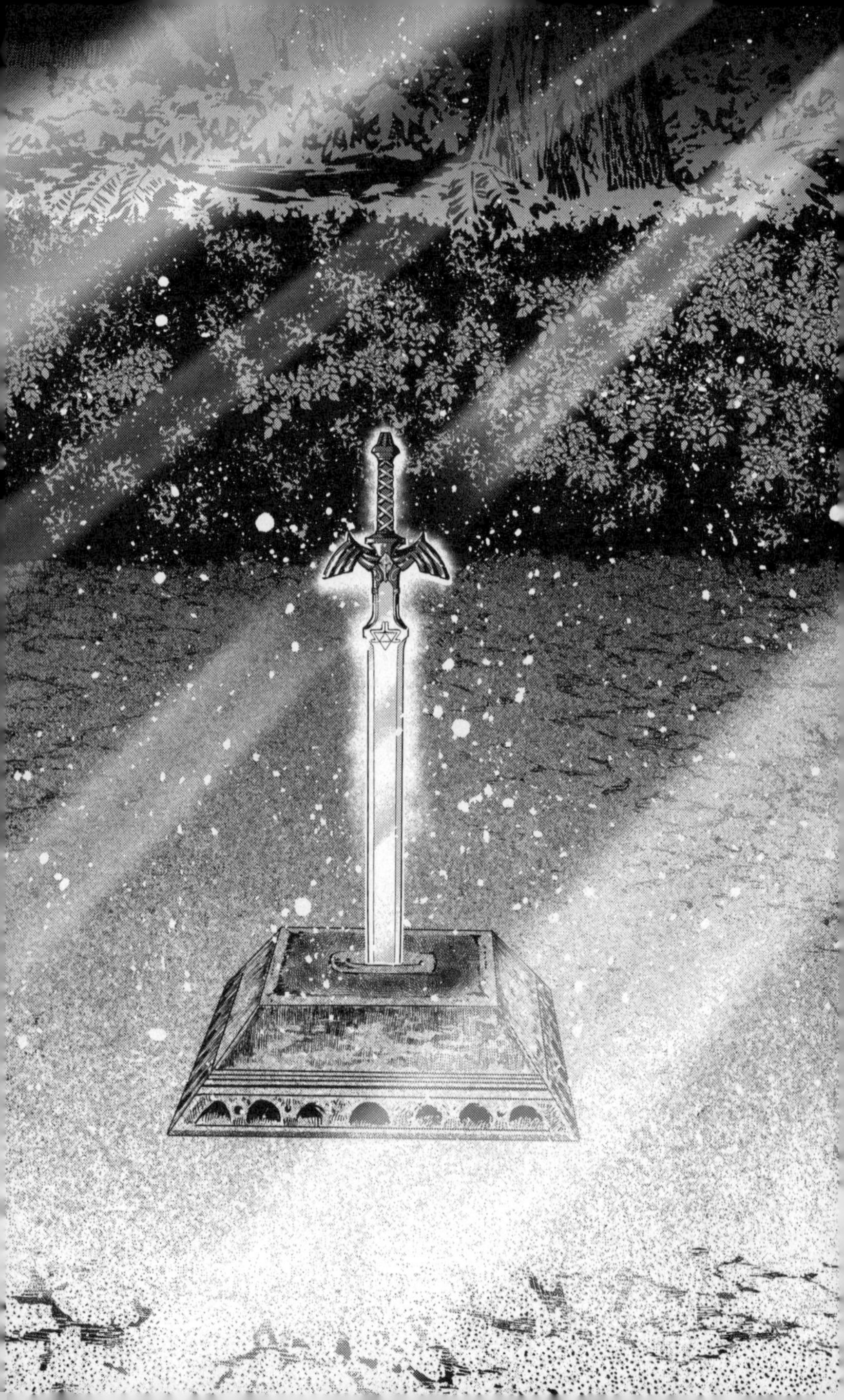

THE LEGEND OF ZELDA: TWILIGHT PRINCESS / THE END

AUTHOR'S NOTE

The decision to serialize *Twilight Princess*
was made in 2015. Then the series actually started
in February of 2016, so it's been exactly seven years.
This is the longest series we've ever worked on,
and our time on it has been intense and fulfilling.
We didn't know at the beginning that this was how the
final battle against Ganondorf would play out. Rather,
the answer developed naturally out of Link as he spent
years fighting his enemy. As he sets out on another
adventure, please imagine everything he might do next.
Thank you for reading along this whole time.

Akira Himekawa is the collaboration of two
women, A. Honda and S. Nagano. Together they
have created ten manga adventures featuring Link
and the popular video game world of *The Legend
of Zelda*™. Their most recent work, *The Legend of
Zelda*™: *Twilight Princess*, is serialized digitally
on Shogakukan's MangaONE app in Japan.

THE LEGEND OF ZELDA™

·TWILIGHT PRINCESS·

Volume 11—VIZ Media Edition

STORY AND ART BY

Akira Himekawa

DRAWING STAFF **Akiko Mori / Sakiho Tsutsui / Kanan**

TRANSLATION **John Werry**

ENGLISH ADAPTATION **Stan!**

TOUCH-UP ART & LETTERING **Evan Waldinger**

DESIGNER **Shawn Carrico**

EDITOR **Mike Montesa**

THE LEGEND OF ZELDA: TWILIGHT PRINCESS
TM & © 2023 Nintendo. All Rights Reserved.

ZELDA NO DENSETSU TWILIGHT PRINCESS Vol. 11
by Akira HIMEKAWA
© 2016 Akira HIMEKAWA
All rights reserved.
Original Japanese edition published by SHOGAKUKAN.
English translation rights in the United States of America,
Canada, the United Kingdom, Ireland, Australia and
New Zealand arranged with SHOGAKUKAN.

Original design by Kazutada YOKOYAMA

Printed in the U.S.A.

Published by VIZ Media, LLC
P.O. Box 77010
San Francisco, CA 94107

10 9 8 7 6 5 4 3 2 1
First printing, April 2023

VIZ MEDIA

viz.com